teach yourself®

bulgarian

ies

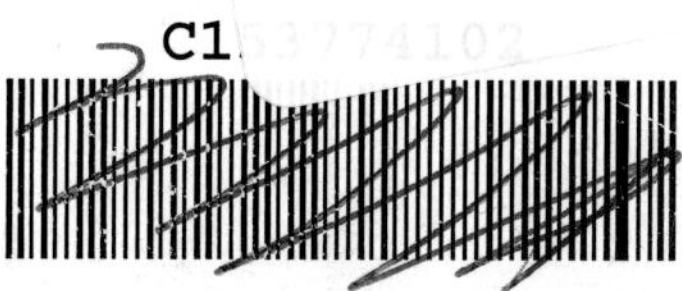

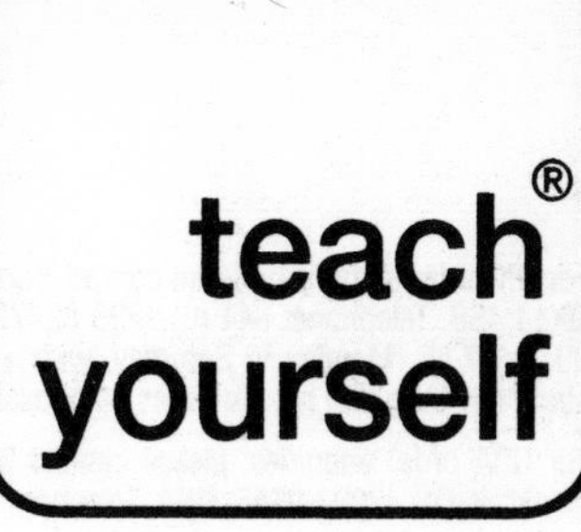

bulgarian

michael holman and
mira kovatcheva

Launched in 1938, the **teach yourself** series grew rapidly in response to the world's wartime needs. Loved and trusted by over 50 million readers, the series has continued to respond to society's changing interests and passions and now, 70 years on, includes over 500 titles, from Arabic and Beekeeping to Yoga and Zulu. What would you like to learn?

be where you want to be with **teach yourself**

For UK order enquiries: please contact Bookpoint Ltd, 130 Milton Park, Abingdon, Oxon, OX14 4SB. Telephone: +44 (0) 1235 827720. Fax: +44 (0) 1235 400454. Lines are open 09.00–17.00, Monday to Saturday, with a 24-hour message answering service. Details about our titles and how to order are available at www.teachyourself.co.uk

For USA order enquiries: please contact McGraw-Hill Customer Services, PO Box 545, Blacklick, OH 43004-0545, USA. Telephone: 1-800-722-4726. Fax: 1-614-755-5645.

For Canada order enquiries: please contact McGraw-Hill Ryerson Ltd, 300 Water St, Whitby, Ontario, L1N 9B6, Canada. Telephone: 905 430 5000. Fax: 905 430 5020.

Long renowned as the authoritative source for self-guided learning – with more than 50 million copies sold worldwide – the **teach yourself** series includes over 500 titles in the fields of languages, crafts, hobbies, business, computing and education.

British Library Cataloguing in Publication Data: a catalogue record for this title is available from the British Library.

Library of Congress Catalog Card Number: on file.

First published in UK 1993 by Hodder Education, part of Hachette UK, 338 Euston Road, London, NW1 3BH.

First published in US 1993 by The McGraw-Hill Companies, Inc.

This edition published 2009.

Typeset by Transet Limited, Coventry, England.
Printed in Great Britain for Hodder Education, part of Hachette UK, 338 Euston Road, London, NW1 3BH, by CPI Cox & Wyman Ltd, Reading, Berkshire, RG1 8EX.

Impression number 10 9 8 7 6 5 4 3 2 1
Year 2012 2011 2010 2009

contents

About the authors

Mira Kovatcheva was born in Sofia and studied English at Sofia University, where she is now Senior Lecturer in the Department of English Studies. Her field of research is English historical linguistics and languages in contact. She also has a special interest in the teaching of Bulgarian to native speakers of English. Between 1989 and 1992 she was on secondment to the universities of Leeds and Sheffield where she taught Bulgarian to English students.

Michael Holman is of mixed English and Russian parentage and was born in Kent, where he now lives. Between 1966 and 1999 he lived in Yorkshire, where he was latterly Professor of Russian and Slavonic Studies at the University of Leeds. He has taught Bulgarian, translated from Bulgarian into English and sought to promote Anglo-Bulgarian cultural interchange. He holds the 'Order of Stara Planina' (First Class) and is an honorary Doctor of Letters of Sofia University. His wife, Dorothea, without whom none of this would have been possible, was born in Sofia of mixed Bulgarian and Macedonian parentage.

Acknowledgements

It would be impossible to thank all our relatives and friends and also colleagues, past and present, who have helped us directly or indirectly with this book. We would, however, like to single out for special mention Christo Stamenov and Vladimir Filipov, both lecturers at Sofia University, who assisted us greatly in the latter stages of our work on the first edition. To everyone who has written to thank us for the book and to make suggestions for its improvement, we are grateful beyond measure. The responsibility for outstanding imperfections in this new edition, however, remains firmly with us.

introduction

Teach Yourself Bulgarian is a complete course for beginners in spoken and written Bulgarian. It has been designed for self-tuition, but may also be used for study with a teacher. It aims to teach you to understand and use the contemporary language in a variety of typical, everyday situations. Above all it is functional, enabling you to communicate and interact, using the language for positive, practical purposes. Although intended primarily for people with no knowledge of the language, you will also find it useful if you want to brush up or extend some previous knowledge.

The course is divided into 20 carefully graded and interlocking units. Each unit is devoted to a particular topic or situation and each successive unit builds naturally on material covered in previous units. In Unit 1, for example, you will learn how to introduce yourself, to use some simple greetings and to say 'please' and 'thank you'. In Unit 2 you will discover how to ask questions, and in Unit 3 you will learn how to answer questions saying where you come from, what you do for a job and indicating whether or not you are married. Unit 4 teaches you some numbers and how to use them when telling the time.

The first half of the book, up to the end of Unit 9, is a basic grammatical and thematic 'survival kit'. The emphasis here is on the present tense and on immediate situations you may well find yourself in on a visit to Bulgaria. Thus, Unit 5 enables you to describe your language knowledge – or lack of it! Unit 6 deals with wanting and asking for things and with changing money, Unit 7 with shopping, Unit 8 with eating out and Unit 9 with getting about and both asking for and giving assistance.

From Unit 10 on you progress to less immediate, but no less important matters. You will learn to ask about future events, inquiring about the weather, for example, or putting together a plan for the days ahead. You will also learn how to talk about things that happened in the past, how to make complaints and tell people what to do. And as your vocabulary and grammatical knowledge increase, you will be able to make more use of the tables and lists in the Appendix at the back of the book.

Each unit is divided into distinct but interlocking sections. An initial Dialogue is followed by a vocabulary with the new words and phrases and a few short questions in Bulgarian based on the Dialogue. Then (up to Unit 11) comes a short section (marked with **i**) of cultural comments and topical tips for first-time visitors to the country. This is followed by useful phrases relevant to the theme of the unit and worth learning by heart. Then come grammatical explanations which all proceed naturally from the new words and constructions used in the Dialogue. Finally there come the Exercises – lots of them, varied, practical, with all the answers in the back – so you can test yourself and see how you are doing. At the end of the Exercises there is always a second Dialogue, which takes you on a little further, incorporating material you will have already covered plus a few new words and phrases.

In the dialogues we have tried to concentrate on the activities of a limited number of characters, both English- and Bulgarian-speakers, whose paths cross in Bulgaria one year in May. First there is Michael Johnson, a man of entrepreneurial disposition from Chelmsford, UK. Mr Johnson is in Sofia for the first time and has wisely learnt some Bulgarian in preparation for his visit. He is on a two-week business trip, establishing contacts, especially with Boyan Antonov, director of a Sofia-based advertising agency. You will also meet members of Mr Antonov's staff: Nadya, his hard-working secretary, Nikolai Dimitrov, a junior colleague, and Milena Marinova, a photographer. (Particularly watch Nikolai and Milena...) Then there is a married couple from Manchester, Victoria and George Collins. Victoria is an interpreter and George is a teacher. They too are visiting Bulgaria, but not for the first time. Victoria speaks Bulgarian well. Nevena Petkova is the hotel receptionist. Nevena, too, is entrepreneurial! There are other characters as well taking part in a variety of situations and locations, from Sofia in the west to Plovdiv in the south and on to Varna and the Black Sea in the east. Good luck, and remember, *practice makes perfect* or, as the Bulgarians say, **óпитът прáви мáйстора**.

How best to use this book

Before starting Unit 1 you will need carefully to work through the sections on the alphabet and pronunciation. Look, too, at the section on pronunciation and spelling at the beginning of the Appendix. Despite the different script, you will soon find that there are many Bulgarian words you recognize, both in their written form and when you hear them on the recording which accompanies *Teach Yourself Bulgarian*.

Dialogues or other sections marked with ▶ are included on the recording. We strongly advise you to use it. As you listen to the native speakers and imitate their pronunciation, so your own pronunciation will improve. Keep the recording in the car and listen to it on your way to and from work. Repeat the words and phrases as often as possible so as to get your tongue round the foreign sounds. Before going on to a new unit, listen again to the dialogues recorded from the previous unit. The more you listen and the more you speak, the better you'll be!

Learning techniques obviously vary and you will probably need to experiment a little before adopting the procedure that suits you best. However, since each unit follows the same pattern, you might find the following procedure worth trying for a start.

Dialogue

Read the English introduction at the beginning of the opening *Dialogue*. This will establish the context for you.

If you have the recording, listen to the Dialogue and see how much you understand.

Now work through the Dialogue, reading aloud as you go. The vocabulary after the Dialogue gives you the meaning of all new words and key phrases in the order in which they occur. If, as you work through the book, you find this initial vocabulary doesn't list a word you cannot understand, turn to the Bulgarian–English vocabulary at the back of the book. All the words are listed there or in the Appendix. If you are searching for the Bulgarian equivalent of an English word, try looking in the English–Bulgarian vocabulary. This contains most of the words used in the different units.

Listen to the recording again, following the text of the Dialogue in the book.

Questions

Now read aloud the questions that follow the Dialogue and try and answer them individually as you go.

Notes

For a little light relief have a look at the *Notes*.

Grammar

Now study the *Grammar* section. In some units this section is longer than in others. Always, however, the grammatical explanations refer to material used in the Dialogue. The usage should, therefore, already be familiar to you. And since many of the examples used in the Grammar section are taken from the Dialogue, this should help further to consolidate your knowledge. The English translation is always given with words introduced for the first time in the Grammar section.

How do you say it?

Go over the *How do you say it?* section. Try to memorize as many of the words and phrases as possible.

Exercises

Once you feel you have a reasonable understanding of the material, test your knowledge by working through the *Exercises*. They have been designed not only to be useful and communicative, but also to test your mastery of the grammar. They are a vital part of the learning process, so try to do them all! The answers in the back of the book will give you an idea of how you are doing.

Do you understand?

After the exercises in each unit there is a second Dialogue. New words and phrases occurring in this Dialogue, and some from the exercises, are listed at the end of the unit, but try and see how much you understand without reference to the vocabulary, by reading the Dialogue aloud. You should work through this second Dialogue as you worked through the first one.

Finally, before proceeding to the next unit, listen again to all the recorded material of the unit you have just been working on. If you do not have the recording, read through the Dialogues aloud, making sure that you have understood everything.

Abbreviations

Abbreviations used in this book are: adj = adjective, f = feminine, m = masculine, lit. = literally, n = neuter, nn = noun, p. = page, pl = plural, sing = singular, vb = verb, T = true, F = false.

alphabet and pronunciation

Bulgarian is spoken by more than ten million people worldwide and is the official language of the Republic of Bulgaria. It is not a difficult language for English-speakers. In fact, of all the Slavonic languages, which include Russian, Ukrainian, Polish and Czech, its structure makes it one of the easiest for us to learn. True, the Cyrillic alphabet of 30 letters, which takes its name from the ninth century scholar and holy man St Cyril, may at first seem a bit of a barrier, but it is not difficult to master. The alphabet is very logical, extremely efficient and well adapted to rendering the sounds of Bulgarian. In the main, unlike English, the pronunciation is straightforward.

The letters can be conveniently divided into three manageable, easy-to-learn groups. They are:

1 letters that look the same in Bulgarian and English
2 letters that look different
3 letters that look the same, but are, in fact, pronounced very differently. These are the 'false friends' which, initially at least, cause the greatest difficulty.

Look at the alphabet table on pp. xiv–xv and see if you can decide which letters fall into which group.

Bulgarian has six simple vowels: **А**, **Е**, **И**, **О**, **У**, **Ъ** – one more than English – and two letters, **ю** and **я**, that really stand for a consonant plus a vowel – **й** + **у** and **й** + **а**, respectively.

The Bulgarian alphabet

Printed letters		Written letters	
capital	small*	capital	small
А	а	*А*	*а*
Б	б	*Б*	*б*
В	в (*в*)	*В*	*в*
Г	г (*г*)	*Г*	*г*
Д	д (*д*)	*Д*	*д*
Е	е	*Е*	*е*
Ж	ж	*Ж*	*ж*
З	з	*З*	*з*
И	и (*и*)	*И*	*и*
Й	й (*й*)	*Й*	*й*
К	к	*К*	*к*
Л	л (*л*)	*Л*	*л*
М	м	*М*	*м*
Н	н	*Н*	*н*
О	о	*О*	*о*
П	п (*п*)	*П*	*п*
Р	р	*Р*	*р*
С	с	*С*	*с*
Т	т (*т*)	*Т*	*т*
У	у	*У*	*у*
Ф	ф	*Ф*	*ф*
Х	х	*Х*	*х*
Ц	ц (*ц*)	*Ц*	*ц*
Ч	ч	*Ч*	*ч*
Ш	ш (*ш*)	*Ш*	*ш*
Щ	щ (*щ*)	*Щ*	*щ*
Ъ	ъ	*Ъ*	*ъ*
**	ь	**	*ь*
Ю	ю	*Ю*	*ю*
Я	я	*Я*	*я*

* The letters in brackets in the second column frequently replace their small printed counterparts in printed texts and public notices.

** The letter **ь** never comes at the beginning of a word, so it is not used as a capital.

Approximate English sound	Bulgarian example	English meaning
a as in 'art' (but shorter)	**А́на**	*Anna*
b as in 'book'	**бана́н**	*banana*
v as in 'vice'	**вода́**	*water*
g as in 'good'	**годи́на**	*year*
d as in 'dot'	**да́та**	*date*
e as in 'elephant'	**е́сен**	*autumn*
s as in 'pleasure'	**жена́**	*woman*
z as in 'zigzag'	**зи́ма**	*winter*
i as in 'inch'	**и́ме**	*name*
y as in 'yes'	**йо́га**	*yoga*
k as in 'king'	**как**	*how*
l as in 'label'	**легло́**	*bed*
m as in 'man'	**ма́лък**	*small*
n as in 'not'	**новина́**	*news*
o as in 'offer'	**о́коло**	*about*
p as in 'pet'	**па́пка**	*folder*
r as in 'rat'	**ресторáнт**	*restaurant*
s as in 'sister'	**сестрá**	*sister*
t as in 'tent'	**тóрта**	*cake*
oo as in 'foot'	**у́тре**	*tomorrow*
f as in 'fifteen'	**факс**	*fax*
h as in 'horrid'	**ху́бав**	*nice*
ts as in 'fits'	**цвéте**	*flower*
ch as in 'church'	**чадъ́р**	*umbrella*
sh as in 'ship'	**шáпка**	*hat*
sht as in 'fishtail'	**щáстие**	*happiness*
u as in 'curtain' (but shorter)	**ъ́гъл**	*corner*
y as in 'York'	**асансьóр**	*lift, elevator*
you as in 'youth' (but shorter)	**ю́ли**	*July*
ya as in 'yarn' (but shorter)	**я́года**	*strawberry*

Pronouncing Bulgarian

The English sounds you see in the table on p. xv are only very rough guides to correct Bulgarian pronunciation. Listening to native speakers and copying them is the best way to get things right, so try listening now to the pronunciation guide on the recording. To begin with you might find it helpful to put a ruler beneath the lines with the individual letters and words and move it down the page as you listen and repeat. Later you can just listen, trying to think of the shape of the individual letters as the words are read out.

Stress

You will notice that in each word of more than one syllable, for example **ю́ли** *July*, **годи́на** *year* and **ресторáнт** *restaurant*, we have put an accent above one of the vowels. We have also put an accent above the vowel in words of one syllable when they are stressed. We have done this to help your pronunciation. Although Bulgarians don't put in the accent when they write, when they speak they pronounce one syllable in every word more distinctly than the rest. (You probably noticed this as you listened to the recording.) This is the 'stressed' syllable. As you can see, the stress can fall on any syllable, just as in English. And as in English, if you stress the wrong syllable, the word will sound very odd, sometimes even incomprehensible. On the rare occasions when a word has two stresses, we have marked this too. So when you learn a new word, make sure you note which syllable is stressed.

You will find some additional notes on pronunciation right at the beginning of the Appendix, but for now it will be enough if you note the following points:

1 Unlike the vowels in English, the Bulgarian vowels don't differ in length. (They are all a little longer than the English short vowels and a little shorter than the English long vowels.)

2 The Bulgarian letter **p** is always rolled, 'r-r-r', as the Scots pronounce B**r**enda and B**r**uce.

3 The sound of the Bulgarian **х** is not found in standard English. It is very like the Scottish **ch** in lo**ch**, and is pronounced nearer the front of the mouth than the English letter **h**.

4 There is no equivalent English letter for **ъ**. We do almost have the sound, though, in a slightly longer version in the **u** in c**u**rtain and f**u**r, or in the letter **e**, when read quickly but clearly in the word th**e**, for example. (Read aloud the last part of this sentence from the word 'or', and you will get the **ъ** in 'the' about right.)

Writing Bulgarian

There are four things to note when writing Bulgarian:

- While there is very little difference between the capital and small letters in the printed script, the printed and the handwritten letters differ considerably. You will, however, come across longhand letters, more rounded in form, used in printed texts alongside their more angular printed counterparts. These are the letters in brackets on p. xiv. (You will find examples under 4 below and in the brochure extract on p. 147.)
- Compared with English, both in the printed and handwritten forms, Bulgarian has fewer letters that extend above and below the line. It is important to observe the relative height of the letters.
- When you write the letters **л**, **м** and **я** in longhand, you must make sure you begin the letters with a little hook:

  л *м* *я*

  This makes it impossible to join them to a preceding **о**.
- In general, Bulgarian avoids double consonants, even in foreign words. For example, Mr and Mrs Collins play a large part in this book, and their surname is written **Ко́линс**. Note too that it is written with a final **с**, not a **з**. More about this in the note on pronunciation in the Appendix! Now it's time for a little practice.

Trying out what you have learnt

To help you recognize the letters and to practise your pronunciation, here are some 'international' words, many of them names, and written out in their Bulgarian spelling. We have given both their printed and handwritten forms and have arranged the words in the three different groups mentioned earlier. You should have little difficulty in identifying their English equivalents. Check whether you've got them right by looking up the Key to the Introduction at the back of the book. You might also try writing out the words yourself. Watch the height of your letters!

1 Letters that look the same in Bulgarian and English (at least in their printed form, but see 4 below):

А	**А**ля́ска	*Аляска*	**а**дре́с	*адрес*
Е	**Е**сто́ния	*Естония*	**е**спре́со	*еспресо*

К	Кана́да	*Канада*	кре́дит	*кредит*
М	Мила́но	*Милано*	мину́та	*минута*
О	Ота́ва	*Отава*	омле́т	*омлет*
Т	Текса́с	*Тексас*	телефо́н	*телефон*

The handwritten forms of the Bulgarian letters **к** and **м** differ slightly from the English, while the Bulgarian handwritten **т** is completely different and confusingly resembles an English **m**.

2 Letters that look different:

Б	Берли́н	*Берлин*	бар	*бар*
Г	Гла́згоу	*Глазгоу*	гара́ж	*гараж*
Д	Дако́та	*Дакота*	во́дка	*водка*
Ж	Жене́ва	*Женева*	жу́ри	*жури*
З	Замбе́зи	*Замбези*	Аризо́на	*Аризона*
И	Истанбу́л	*Истанбул*	И́ндия	*Индия*
Й	Йорк	*Йорк*	Майо́рка	*Майорка*
Л	Ло́ндон	*Лондон*	Балка́н	*Балкан*
П	Пана́ма	*Панама*	поли́ция	*полиция*
Ф	Фра́нкфурт	*Франкфурт*	Со́фия	*София*
Ц	Цю́рих	*Цюрих*	Доне́цк	*Донецк*
Ч	Чад	*Чад*	Чъ́рчил	*Чърчил*
Ш	Ше́филд	*Шефилд*	шоу-би́знес	*шоу-бизнес*
Щ	Щу́тгарт	*Щутгарт*	Бу́дапеща	*Будапеща*
Ъ	Ъ́пдайк	*Ъпдайк*	Бълга́рия	*България*
Ь	шофьо́р	*шофьор*	синьо́ра	*синьора*
Ю	Ю́кон	*Юкон*	Лийдс юна́йтед	*Лийдс юнайтед*
Я	Я́лта	*Ялта*	я́нки	*янки*

3 Letters that look the same, but are pronounced differently ('false friends'):

В	**В**ие́на	*Виена*	**В**и́**в**иан	*Вивиан*
Н	**Н**ами́бия	*Намибия*	Ва́р**н**а	*Варна*
Р	**Р**и́чард	*Ричард*	Йо́**р**кшир	*Йоркшир*
С	**С**ина́тра	*Синатра*	А́м**с**тердам	*Амстердам*
У	**У**нга́рия	*Унгария*	Ли́въ**р**п**у**л	*Ливърпул*
Х	**Х**айд парк	*Хайд парк*	Са**х**а́ра	*Сахара*

Note that unlike the English letter **c** in **cat**, the Bulgarian letter **с** is always pronounced soft as in **Cincinnati** and like the English letter **s** in **S**inatra. It is, therefore, only partially a 'false friend'.

You will notice that the Bulgarian pronunciation of names and 'international' words differs slightly from the English. Sometimes, too, a different syllable is stressed, **телефо́н** and **паспо́рт**, for example. And do remember that Bulgarians say **Со́фия** (*Sófia*, not *Sophía*!)

And talking of 'international words', it has to be said that Cyrillic is increasingly under siege from the Latin script. Sometimes there is considerable uncertainty which script to use. This is particularly the case in business, commerce and communication technology. The Bulgarian mobile phone system, for example, is called GSM, email addresses can only be given in Latin script, and the word 'email' itself has only recently settled with **и́мейл** as an accepted Cyrillic equivalent. You will notice too that Latin script is frequently used alongside Cyrillic in brand and business names and in shop signs.

4 Here, side by side, are some words written using both the angular and the more rounded, longhand letters. All the words appear in the previous lists. See if you can recognize them:

адрéс/адрéс, еспрéсо/еспрéсо, телефóн/телефóн, кредит/кредит, Отáва/Отáва, гарáж/гарáж, минýта/минýта, Донéцк/Донéцк, шоу-бúзнес/шоу-бúзнес, Бýдапеща/Бýдапеща, Вúвиан/Вúвиан, Áмстердам/Áмстердам.

Saying *yes* and *no* – a vital word of warning

Another form of communication is non-verbal communication and it is very important in Bulgaria. In most European countries, you nod your head to say 'yes' and shake it to say 'no'. In Bulgaria, certainly among speakers less affected by contact with other languages, a shake of the head – actually more a rocking of the head from side to side – often accompanies *yes* (**да**), while a reverse nod – usually starting with a brisk, dismissive, upward movement of the head – accompanies *no* (**не**).

Whether you are buying an ice-cream, booking an excursion or doing a deal, listening carefully, interpreting the head movements correctly and making them correctly yourself will make all the difference to your negotiations! Have fun and start practising straightaway.

Exercises

Here are some reading exercises for you to practise what you have learnt so far about the alphabet.

1 Read the following place names matching the names in English with their Bulgarian equivalents. (In this exercise each English letter is replaced by a single Bulgarian letter.)

a	America	**i**	Ло́ндон
b	Amsterdam	**ii**	Саха́ра
c	Arizona	**iii**	Фра́нкфурт
d	Balkan	**iv**	Аме́рика
e	Berlin	**v**	Аризо́на
f	Frankfurt	**vi**	Пло́вдив
g	London	**vii**	Ри́ла
h	Plovdiv	**viii**	Во́лга
i	Rila	**ix**	Ва́рна
j	Sahara	**x**	Балка́н
k	Varna	**xi**	Берли́н
l	Volga	**xii**	А́мстердам

2 Do the same with this list. You might need to replace certain combinations of English letters by a single Bulgarian letter. (Remember that Bulgarian rarely uses double letters!)

a	Charing Cross	**i**	Вие́на
b	Chelmsford	**ii**	Ю́кон
c	Donetsk	**iii**	Че́лмсфорд
d	Shell	**iv**	Ню Йорк
e	Shetland	**v**	Ча́ринг крос
f	Stuttgart	**vi**	Ше́тланд
g	Vienna	**vii**	Доне́цк
h	Yalta	**viii**	Шел
i	New York	**ix**	Щу́тгарт
j	Yukon	**x**	Я́лта

3 Here, concentrate on the sound; read the Bulgarian and identify the English equivalent. Sometimes one English letter needs two letters in Bulgarian and vice-versa.

a	Ли́йдс	**i**	Woody Allen
b	Дже́нифър Ло́пец	**ii**	Beatles
c	Хе́лзинки	**iii**	Helsinki
d	Ли́върпул	**iv**	Oxford
e	Джеймс Бонд	**v**	Liverpool
f	Португа́лия	**vi**	James Bond
g	Че́лси	**vii**	Scotland
h	О́ксфорд	**viii**	Leeds

i	Би́йтълс	**ix**	Chelsea
j	Уди А́лън	**x**	France
k	Ко́рнуол	**xi**	Geneva
l	Гла́згоу	**xii**	Cambridge
m	Жене́ва	**xiii**	Cornwall
n	Шотла́ндия	**xiv**	Jennifer Lopez
o	Ке́ймбридж	**xv**	Glasgow
p	Фра́нция	**xvi**	Portugal

4 If you rang the following numbers, what service would you expect to answer? Read the Bulgarian words out loud!

201	БИ́ЗНЕС КЛУБ	205	БАР
202	РЕСТОРА́НТ	206	ТАКСИ́
203	РЕЦЕ́ПЦИЯ	207	ИНФОРМА́ЦИЯ
204	ФИ́ТНЕС ЦЕ́НТЪР	166	ПОЛИ́ЦИЯ

5 What are the names of (**a**) the pizzeria, (**b**) the restaurant, (**c**) the hotel and (**d**) the café on the following notices?

a ПИЦАРИ́Я „МИЛА́НО“ **c** ХОТЕ́Л „ШЕ́РАТОН“
b РЕСТОРА́НТ „МОСКВА́“ **d** КАФЕ́ „ОРИЕ́НТ“

6 When does your plane take off if you are flying to:

a Milan
b Geneva
c Frankfurt
d Paris
e Berlin
f Zurich
g Budapest?

Цю́рих ______	15.40
Бу́дапеща ____	16.10
Фра́нкфурт____	16.35
Жене́ва ______	17.05
Мила́но ______	17.25
Пари́ж ______	18.05
Берли́н ______	18.30

здраве́йте! как се ка́звате?

hello, what's your name?

In this unit you will learn:

- **how to say *hello***
- **how to give your name and nationality**
- **how to say *please* and *thank you***
- **how to say *yes* and *no* in answer to *is there?* and *are there?***

Michael Johnson, a businessman, arrives from London at his hotel in Sofia. When he enters the vestibule he is greeted by the doorman with the words **Заповя́дайте, мо́ля!** meaning, here: *Welcome, do come in, please.* (**Мо́ля** can also mean *I beg your pardon* and *Don't mention it.*)

You will often hear **заповя́дайте** and **мо́ля** in Bulgaria, used separately and together with a variety of meanings. They are always polite and welcoming words. Together with the two words for *thank you* – **Благодаря́** and **Мерси́** (*Merci* – as in the French!), and the word for *there isn't* **ня́ма** – they are what for you will probably be the five most important words in the Bulgarian language.

Dialogue 1

Michael goes up to the reception desk and is greeted by the receptionist, Nevena Petkova.

Неве́на Петко́ва	До́бър ден!
Ма́йкъл Джо́нсън	Здраве́йте! И́ма ли свобо́дна стая́?
Неве́на Петко́ва	(*Nodding.**) Не, ня́ма.
Ма́йкъл Джо́нсън	И́ма ли свобо́ден апартаме́нт?
Неве́на Петко́ва	(*Shaking her head.**) Да, и́ма. Тури́ст ли сте?
Ма́йкъл Джо́нсън	Не, не съм тури́ст. Бизнесме́н съм.
Неве́на Петко́ва	И́ме?
Ма́йкъл Джо́нсън	Мо́ля?
Неве́на Петко́ва	Как се ка́звате?
Ма́йкъл Джо́нсън	Ка́звам се Ма́йкъл Джо́нсън.
Неве́на Петко́ва	Англича́нин ли сте?
Ма́йкъл Джо́нсън	Да, англича́нин съм.
Неве́на Петко́ва	Паспо́рта, мо́ля.
Ма́йкъл Джо́нсън	Заповя́дайте!
Неве́на Петко́ва	Благодаря́!
Ма́йкъл Джо́нсън	Мо́ля!

*If this confuses you, look back to the vital word of warning on p. xx.

До́бър ден!	*Good morning/afternoon.*
Здраве́йте!	*Hello!*
И́ма ли свобо́дна стая́?	*Is there a room free?*
Не, ня́ма.	*No, there isn't.*
свобо́ден апартаме́нт	*a free apartment*
Да, и́ма.	*Yes, there is.*
Тури́ст ли сте?	*Are you a tourist?*

Не, не съм турист.	*No, I'm not a tourist.*
Бизнесмéн съм.	*I'm a businessman.*
йме	*name*
Мóля?	*(I beg your) Pardon?*
Как се кáзвате?	*What is your name?*
Кáзвам се...	*My name is...*
Англичáнин ли сте?	*Are you English?*
Да, англичáнин съм.	*Yes, I am (English).*
Паспóрта, мóля.	*Your (the) passport, please.*
Заповя́дайте!	*Here you are/There you go.*
Благодаря́!	*Thank you.*
Мóля!	*Not at all/Don't mention it/ My pleasure.*

1 Questions

Before answering these questions, listen to the recording again (if you have it), once without looking at the dialogue and once following the text as you listen. It would also be a good idea to read aloud the questions before you answer them.

You'll find all the answers in the Dialogue – except to **1c**! The answers are also in the Key at the back of the book.

- **a** Йма ли свобóден апартамéнт?
- **b** Йма ли свобóдна стáя?
- **c** Как се кáзвате? (Give your own name.)

2 True or false?

Write out correct versions of the false statements. Michael Johnson says:

- **a** Англичáнин съм.
- **b** Тури́ст съм.
- **c** Бизнесмéн съм.

Greetings

The most frequently heard greeting, and the one to use on formal occasions when addressing people you do not know, is **дóбър ден!** Literally translated it means *Good day*. You can say **дóбър ден!** at any time of the day except the early morning, when you should use **добрó ýтро!** *Good morning*, and the evening, when you say **дóбър вéчер!** *Good evening*.

Здраве́й! and **Здраве́йте!** are rather less formal and are used when you would say *Hello* or *Hi!* in English. Literally the words both mean *May you be healthy*. **Здраве́й!** is a singular form and **здраве́йте!** is a plural. You say **здраве́й!** to a friend or someone you know well. When greeting more than one person or someone you know less well you use **здраве́йте!** (Plural is always polite!) You might also use **здраве́йте!** (instead of the more official **до́бър ден!**) when addressing someone you know well but whom you still address with the polite, formal form. Both **здраве́й!** and **здраве́йте!** can be used at any time of the day, or night.

You will notice that the only difference between **здраве́й!** and **здраве́йте!** is the addition of the two letters **-те** to the greeting you use when meeting a friend. In fact, these two letters distinguish the plural (formal) from the singular (familiar) forms. They are found on the end of other 'polite', 'non-familiar' forms too. You will notice them, for example, on the end of the word **Заповя́дайте!** used by Michael Johnson when he gives Nevena Petkova his passport. (If Michael knew Nevena better, he would say **Заповя́дай!** without the letters **-те**.) You will also see them on the end of the words used by Nevena when she asks Michael his name: Как се ка́зва**те**? and inquires whether he is English: Англича́нин ли **сте?**

How do you say it?

- Asking somebody's name, and giving yours

Как се ка́звате?	*What is your name?*
Ка́звам се Ма́йкъл Джо́нсън.	*My name is Michael Johnson.*
Ка́звам се Неве́на Петко́ва.	*My name is Nevena Petkova.*

- Greeting people at different times of the day

Здраве́йте!	*Hello!* (polite or more than one person)
Здраве́й!	*Hello!* (informal, one person)
Добро́ у́тро!/До́бър ден!	*Good morning.*
До́бър ден!	*Good afternoon.*
До́бър ве́чер!	*Good evening.*

- Saying *please*, *thank you* and *(I beg your) pardon*?

Мо́ля!	*Please; don't mention it; not at all!*
Мо́ля?	*(I beg your) pardon?*
Благодаря́/Мерси́.	*Thank you.*

- Welcoming someone or extending an invitation

Заповя́дай!/Заповя́дайте!	*Won't you please...?; here you are; there you go!*

- Answering *yes* or *no* to *is there?* and *are there?*

Йма ли свобóдна стáя?	*Is there a room free?*
Да, и́ма.	*Yes, there is.*
Йма ли свобóден апартамéнт?	*Is there a free apartment?*
Не, ня́ма.	*No, there isn't.*

- Confirming your nationality

Англичáнин/англичáнка ли сте?	*Are you English?*
Да, англичáнин/англичáнка съм.	*Yes, I am English.*
Америкáнец/америкáнка ли сте?	*Are you American?*
Да, америкáнец/америкáнка съм.	*Yes, I am American.*
Канáдец/канáдка ли сте?	*Are you Canadian?*
Да, канáдец/канáдка съм.	*Yes, I am Canadian.*

Grammar

1 Things as *he*, *she* and *it*: gender

All words naming things, whether living or not, are referred to as *he*, *she* or *it* in Bulgarian. This means that all naming words, also called nouns, belong to one of three groups or genders: masculine, feminine or neuter. It is not difficult to recognize them:

masculine nouns usually end in a consonant or **-й**
feminine nouns usually end in **-а** or **-я**
neuter nouns usually end in **-о**, **-е** or sometimes **-и**
words of foreign origin ending in **-и**, **-у** and **-ю** are also neuter.

Masculine			
америкáнец	*an American man*	англичáнин	*an Englishman*
апартамéнт	*a flat*	българин	*a Bulgarian man*
ден	*a day*	музéй	*a museum*
мъж	*a man*	тури́ст	*a tourist*
Feminine			
америкáнка	*an American woman*	англичáнка	*an English woman*
българка	*a Bulgarian woman*	стáя	*a room*
женá	*a woman*		
Neuter			
кафé	*a coffee, a café*	морé	*a sea*
меню́	*a menu*	такси́	*a taxi*
писмó	*a letter*	ýтро	*a morning*

2 Adjectives

Describing words that tell you about a thing's qualities are called adjectives. Adjectives acquire similar endings to the nouns: consonants for masculine adjectives, **-a** for feminine ones and **-o** for neuter. You can see this in the expressions дóбъ**р** де**н**, свобóдн**а** стá**я**, добр**ó** ýтр**о**. This repetition of endings often seems to create semi-rhyming groups of words, especially in the feminine and the neuter. Here are some examples:

Masculine	**добър англичáнин**	*a good Englishman*	**свобóден ден**	*a free day*
Feminine	**добрá българка**	*a good Bulgarian woman*	**свобóдна стáя**	*a free room*
Neuter	**добрó ýтро**	*good morning*	**свобóдно мя́сто**	*a free place*

Many adjectives – like those in the box – have an 'extra' vowel (**ъ** or e) in their masculine form. This vowel is 'lost' in the feminine, neuter and plural forms. To help you, in this course we list all such adjectives with both the masculine and feminine forms.

3 Свобóден съм *I am free*

Also, an expression like *I am free* will change depending on whether a man or a woman is speaking. Michael Johnson will say of himself:

свобóде**н** съм. — *I am free.*

Whereas Nevena will say:

свобóдн**а** съм.

And you would say of them:

Невéна е свобóдн**а**. — *Nevena is free.*
Мáйкъл Джóнсън е свобóде**н**. — *Michael Johnson is free.*

A good-looking (but immodest) man might say of himself хýба**в** съм, while a good-looking (and equally immodest) woman would say of herself хýбав**а** съм. Хýбав represents the majority of other adjectives which do not lose a vowel.

4 Англичáнин ли сте? *Are you English?*

To ask questions which require answers *yes* or *no* you need to add **ли** immediately after the word, or group of words, to which your question is directed:

Англичáнин **ли** сте?	*Are you English?*
Да, англичáнин съм.	*Yes, I am English.*
Не, не съм англичáнин.	*No, I am not English.*
Турúст **ли** сте?	*Are you a tourist?*
Да, турúст съм.	*Yes, I am a tourist.*
Не, не съм турúст.	*No, I am not a tourist.*

By moving **ли** from one word to another you can shift the emphasis of your question. In English, you do this by changing your intonation.

Мáйкъл **в Сóфия ли** е?	*Is Michael **in Sofia**?*
Мáйкъл ли е в Сóфия?	*Is **Michael** in Sofia?*

5 Úма and ня́ма *There is and there is not*

The Bulgarian equivalent of both *there is* and *there are* is **úма**. The negative *there is not* and *there are not* is simply **ня́ма**:

Úма свобóдна стáя.	*There is a room free.*
Ня́ма свобóдна стáя.	*There isn't a room free.*
В Лóндон **úма** рекá.	*There is a river in London.*
В Сóфия **ня́ма** рекá.	*There isn't a river in Sofia.*

And if you want to ask a question you again add **ли**:

Úма **ли** свобóдна стáя?	*Is there a room free?*
Да, úма.	*Yes, there is.*
Úма **ли** рекá в Лóндон?	*Is there a river in London?*
Да, úма.	*Yes, there is.*

6 Не съм – saying *not*

The negative word in Bulgarian is **не**. It is normally placed immediately before the verb:

Не съм българин.	*I'm not a Bulgarian.*
Англичáнин съм.	*I'm an Englishman.*
Не съм българка.	*I'm not a Bulgarian.*
Англичáнка съм.	*I'm an English woman.*

Не is never stressed when followed immediately by a verb. Here **Не съм** is read as one word with emphasis on **съм**.

Exercises

1 Read the following 'international' words out loud in Bulgarian. This will help your pronunciation and build up your vocabulary.

a	агéнция	**i**	шóу	**q**	фи́рма
b	адрéс	**j**	мýзика	**r**	фýтбол
c	аспири́н	**k**	календáр	**s**	шофьóр
d	бáнка	**l**	проблéм	**t**	при́нтер
e	би́знес	**m**	сóда	**u**	óфис
f	би́ра	**n**	спорт	**v**	факс
g	вóдка	**o**	тóник	**w**	ви́део
h	компю́тър	**p**	тури́ст	**x**	ксéрокс

Which words are feminine and which are masculine or neuter?

2 How would you say *hello!* (**здравéй!** or **здравéйте!**) to:

- **a** a good friend?
- **b** your parents?
- **c** your boss?
- **d** a shop assistant?
- **e** a little boy?
- **f** a little girl?
- **g** a group of students?

3 How would you greet the hotel porter at the times shown on the pictures?

a (Добрó ýтро *or* дóбър ден?)

c (Добрó ýтро *or* дóбър ден?)

b (Добрó ýтро *or* дóбър ден?)

d (Дóбър ден *or* дóбър вéчер?)

4 Match the questions and answers. If you don't recognize a word, look it up in the Bulgarian–English vocabulary at the end of the book.

i	Америкáнка ли сте?	**a**	Не, не съм българин, англичáнин съм.
ii	Българка ли сте?	**b**	Да, англичáнка съм.
iii	Българин ли сте?	**c**	Да, англичáнин съм.
iv	Англичáнин ли сте?	**d**	Не, не съ́м америкáнец, англичáнин съм.
v	Америкáнец ли сте?	**e**	Не, не съ́м българка, англичáнка съм.
vi	Англичáнка ли сте?	**f**	Да, америкáнка съм.

5 Answer the following questions with yes or no (**Да, и́ма** or **Не, ня́ма**):

a И́ма ли кафé? Да, ________
b И́ма ли тóник? Да, ________
c И́ма ли сóда? Не, ________
d И́ма ли джин? (*gin*) Не, ________
e И́ма ли такси́? Да, ________
f И́ма ли би́ра? Не, ________

6 Repeat the dialogue, which inquires whether there is any mineral water, using the following:

a уи́ски *whisky*
b би́ра *beer*
c лимонáда *lemonade*
d чай *tea*

Сáндра И́ма ли минерáлна водá?
Николáй Да, заповя́дайте.
Сáндра Благодаря́!

7 Make your choice of drink following the model below:

Боя́н Джин или́ (*or*) вóдка?
Кен Джин, мóля.
Невéна Вóдка, мóля.

a **Боя́н** Уи́ски или́ джин?
Кен ________
Невéна ________

b **Боя́н** Би́ра или́ Кóка-Кóла?
Кен ________
Виктóрия ________
Виктóрия ________
Боя́н ________

c **Джон** Капучи́но или́ еспрéсо? (*espresso*)

d **Виктóрия** Кафé или́ чай?
Джон ________
Невéна ________

8 First read aloud and then say in English who is admiring what or whom. Remember that **ху́бав** can mean many things – *good-looking*, *nice*, *beautiful*, *lovely*. You could think up other words meaning *nice* which are appropriate to the object.

a	**Ма́йкъл Джо́нсън**	Ху́бав хоте́л!
b	**Неве́на**	Ху́бав мъж!
c	**Джу́ли**	Ху́баво море́!
d	**Са́ндра**	Ху́бава би́ра!
e	**Тре́йси**	Ху́баво и́ме!
f	**Кен**	Ху́бава бъ́лгарка!

Now, using **ху́бав**, **ху́бава** or **ху́баво**, express your own satisfaction with your room, your apartment or the lovely Bulgarian wine (бъ́лгарско ви́но):

g ——— ста́я!
h ——— апартаме́нт!
i ——— бъ́лгарско ви́но!

9 Michael Johnson has to sign the register at the hotel – in Bulgarian, of course – filling in his name and home address. Try writing out what he entered in Bulgarian longhand:

И́ме:	Майкъл Джонсън	*Michael Johnson*
Адре́с:	4, Маунт Драйв	*4, Mount Drive*
	Челмсфорд	*Chelmsford*
	Есекс	*Essex*
	Англия	*England*

He also needs to send his Sofia address to his wife, so she can try to address the envelope in Cyrillic. Have a go in longhand yourself! Notice how, in Bulgarian, the address is usually written back to front, following the actual route of the letter, moving from the country to the town, to the hotel and the apartment, and finally the addressee:

България	*Michael Johnson*
1000 София	*Apartment 8*
хотел „Родина“	*Rodina Hotel*
апартамент 8	*Sofia 1000*
Майкъл Джонсън	*Bulgaria*

Now write your own name and address in Cyrillic, placing the various components in the Bulgarian order. In actual fact, the Bulgarians are better at deciphering the English script than we are the Bulgarian, so you can get away with addressing your letters in English.

Do you understand?

Dialogue 2: В рестора́нта *In the restaurant*

Read the following conversation and answer the questions in English:

Ма́йкъл Джо́нсън	До́бър ве́чер!
Сервитьо́р	До́бър ве́чер! Заповя́дайте! Тук и́ма свобо́дно мя́сто.
Ма́йкъл Джо́нсън	Благодаря́! Ху́бав рестора́нт! И́ма ли му́зика тук?
Сервитьо́р	Не, ня́ма. Съжаля́вам.
Ма́йкъл Джо́нсън	Мно́го добре́! Мно́го ху́бав рестора́нт.
Сервитьо́р	Благодаря́! Тури́ст ли сте?
Ма́йкъл Джо́нсън	Не, бизнесме́н съм. Уиски, мо́ля.
Сервитьо́р	Со́да?
Ма́йкъл Джо́нсън	Не, мерси́. Минера́лна вода́, мо́ля.

сервитьо́р	*waiter*
тук	*here*
мя́сто	*seat; place*
ху́бав (ху́бава, ху́баво)	*nice, good-looking, lovely, beautiful*
съжаля́вам	*I'm sorry*
мно́го	*very*

Questions

Answer these questions in English.

1 What time of day is it?
2 Is there a place free?
3 Why does Michael Johnson like the restaurant?
4 Is Mr Johnson a tourist?
5 What does he order?

02

как сте? имате ли време?

how are you? do you have a moment?

In this unit you will learn:

- **how to ask simple questions using как?** ***how?*** **and кога́?** ***when?***
- **expressions with и́мам** ***have*** **and ня́мам** ***have not***
- **how to respond to какво́ е това́?** ***What is this?*** **and как сте?** ***How are you?***

Dialogue 1

Boyan Antonov, manager of an advertising agency in Sofia, calls in at the office to see Nadya, his secretary.

Антóнов Здравéй, Нáдя.
Нáдя Дóбър ден, господи́н Антóнов!
Антóнов Как си днес?
Нáдя Благодаря́, добрé съм. А Ви́е как сте?
Антóнов И аз съм добрé. Нéщо нóво?
Нáдя Ни́що.
Антóнов А каквó е товá?
Нáдя А, да. Товá е нóва брошýра от господи́н Джóнсън.
Антóнов Когá присти́га той?
Нáдя Днес. Самолéт от Лóндон и́ма в сéдем часá.
Антóнов Мнóго добрé. Тук ли са Николáй и Милéна?
Нáдя Тя е тук, но той днес не é на рáбота.
Антóнов Ни́що. Товá е всѝчко засегá.
Нáдя И́мате ли врéме за еднó кафé?
Антóнов Съжаля́вам, сегá ня́мам врéме. Днес и́мам мнóго рáбота.
Нáдя Дови́ждане, господи́н Антóнов! Прия́тна рáбота!
Антóнов Благодаря́, Нáдя! Дови́ждане и лек ден!

господи́н Антóнов	*Mr Antonov*
Как си днес?	*How are you today?* (familiar)
Благодаря́.	*Thank you.*
И аз съм добрé.	*I'm fine too.*
Добрé съм.	*I'm fine.*
А Ви́е как сте?	*And how are you?* (formal)
Нéщо нóво?	*Anything new?*
Ни́що.	*Nothing./Never mind.*
А каквó е товá?	*And what is this?*
Товá е нóва брошýра	*This is a new brochure*
от	*from*
Когá присти́га той?	*When is he arriving/ does he arrive?*
Самолéт от Лóндон и́ма	*There is a plane from London*

в сéдем часá.	*at seven o'clock*
мнóго добрé	*very good/fine*
Тук ли са Николáй и Милéна?	*Are Nikolai and Milena here?*
Тя е тук, но той	*She's here but he's not in*
днес не é на рáбота.	*(at work) today.*
Товá е вси́чко засегá.	*That's all for now.*
И́мате ли врéме за еднó кафé?	*Have you time for a coffee?*
сегá ня́мам врéме.	*I haven't time now.*
И́мам мнóго рáбота.	*I have a lot of work.*
Дови́ждане.	*Goodbye.*
Прия́тна рáбота!	*Have a good day (at work)!*
Лек ден!	*Have a nice day!*

1 Questions

Looking back to the dialogue, try to answer these questions instead of Nadya:

- **a** Здравéй, Нáдя. Как си днес? Добрé ли си?
- **b** И́ма ли нéшо нóво?
- **c** (*Picking up a brochure*) Каквó е товá?
- **d** Когá и́ма самолéт от Лóндон?
- **e** Днес ли присти́га господи́н Джóнсън?

2 True or false?

Write out correct versions of the false statements.

- **a** Нáдя не é добрé.
- **b** Товá е брошýра от господи́н Джóнсън.
- **c** Николáй не é тук.
- **d** Господи́н Антóнов и́ма врéме за кафé.
- **e** Господи́н Антóнов ня́ма мнóго рáбота.

i Mr, Mrs and Miss

The traditional Bulgarian equivalents of the English *Mr* and *Mrs* are **господи́н** (masculine) and **госпожá** (feminine). When written, **господи́н** is abbreviated to **г-н** and **госпожá** to **г-жá**. You address an unmarried woman as **госпóжица** (*Miss*).

When you address someone without using their surname, you use the words **господи́н**, **госпожá** and **госпóжица** in their special address forms: **господи́не, госпóжо** (note the stress change) and **госпóжице**. So you say:

Дóбър вéчер, **господи́не!**	*Good evening.* (to Mr)
Дови́ждане, **госпóжо!**	*Goodbye.* (to Mrs)
Здравéйте, **госпóжице!**	*Hello.* (to Miss)

When a surname is used, the special address form is obligatory with the Bulgarian word for *Miss*, so you say: **Здраве́йте, госпо́жице Петко́ва!** *Hello, Miss Petkova*. For *Mrs* you can either say **госпожа́** or **госпо́жо Бори́сова**, but for *Mr* with a surname the special form is never used, so you can only say: **До́бър ве́чер, господи́н Анто́нов!** *Good evening, Mr Antonov.*

Bulgarian does not yet have the equivalent of *Ms*.

Surnames

Masculine surnames usually end in **-ов** or **-ев**, while feminine surnames usually end in **-ова** or **-ева**. Thus Mr Antonov's wife is called **г-жа́ Анто́нова**, while Nevena Petkova's father is **г-н Петко́в**. The stress in feminine surnames is not necessarily on the **о** or **е** preceding the **в**. So, although you do say Петко́ва, for example, you have to say Анто́нова, Бори́сова, Кова́чева and Ста́нева.

How do you say it?

- Asking someone how they are and saying how you are

Как си? Как сте?	*How are you?*
Добре́ съм.	*I'm fine.*
И аз съм добре́.	*I'm fine too.*

- Asking *What is this?* and answering *This is...* or *This is not...*

Какво́ е това́?	*What is this?*
Това́ е календа́р.	*This is a calendar.*
Това́ не е́ писмо́.	*This is not a letter.*

- Asking *When?*

Кога́ присти́га г-н Джо́нсън?	*When does Mr Johnson arrive?*
Кога́ и́ма самоле́т от Ло́ндон?	*When is there a plane from London?*

- Saying *Goodbye*

Дови́ждане!	*Goodbye.*

- Expressing good wishes on parting

Прия́тен ден!/Лек ден!	*Have a good/nice day.*
Прия́тна ра́бота!	*Have a good day (at work).*
Прия́тна почи́вка!	*Have a good rest.*
Прия́тен уи́кенд!	*Have a nice weekend.*
Вси́чко ху́баво!/Вси́чко добро́!	*All the best.*

- Expressing regret

Съжаля́вам.	*I'm sorry.*

Grammar

1 Еди́н and English *a*

Normally, no equivalent of the English indefinite article *a* or *an* is necessary in Bulgarian. Compare:

Това́ е и́мейл.	*This is **an** email.*
Това́ е хоте́л.	*This is **an** hotel.*
Тук и́ма ресторáнт.	*There is **a** restaurant here.*
Аз съм англича́нин.	*I'm **an** Englishman.*

However, when the English *a* means *one*, *a certain* or *a single*, you need to use the Bulgarian word for *one* – **еди́н**. **Еди́н** is a counting word, a numeral. It is also an adjective and has different forms for the masculine, feminine and neuter.

Masculine	**еди́н** англича́нин	***one*** *Englishman*	**еди́н** и́мейл	***one*** *email*
Feminine	**една́** би́ра	***one*** *beer*	**една́** стáя	***one*** *room*
Neuter	**едно́** кафе́	***one*** *coffee*	**едно́** мя́сто	***one*** *place*
	едно́ писмо́	***one*** *letter*		

If you use the numeral on its own, you have to use the neuter form, as: стáя но́мер **едно́** *room number one*.

2 *I*, *you*, *he/she/it*, *we*, *you* and *they*

Bulgarian has almost the equivalents of the English words for these subject pronouns, but there are two small differences. First, the Bulgarian **аз** *I* is written with a small letter and, second, Bulgarian has two different words for *you*: **ти** for the singular, familiar form and **ви́е** for the plural. Moreover, when addressing just one person in the polite, formal mode, Bulgarians use the plural form and, when writing, spell it with a capital letter: **Ви́е**.

Singular		**Plural**	
аз	*I*	**ни́е**	*we*
ти	*you*	**ви́е/Ви́е**	*you*
той	*he*		
тя	*she*	**те**	*they*
то	*it*		

If you are using a verb, you can usually omit the subject pronouns, for the ending of the verb makes it clear who is involved. The only times you *must* use the subject pronouns are for emphasis or to avoid ambiguity:

Как си? Добрé съм.	*How are you? I'm fine.* (No emphasis here!)
А **Вúе** как сте?	*And how about **you**?* (Emphasis)
И **аз** съм добрé.	***I'm** fine too.* (Emphasis)

3 Съм *I am* and the verb *to be*

In Bulgarian, verbs, or action words, have no neutral or basic form corresponding to the English infinitive. There are, therefore, no equivalents of the English 'dictionary' forms *to be* or *to have*. Instead, in Bulgarian dictionaries, verbs are listed in the *I* form (1st person singular) *I am*, *I hav*e, etc.

Here are all the forms of **съм** in the present tense:

(аз)	**съм**	*I am*	**(нúе)**	**сме**	*we are*
(ти)	**си**	*you are*	**(вúе)**	**сте**	*you are*
(той)	**е**	*he is*			
(тя)	**е**	*she is*	**(те)**	**са***	*they are*
(то)	**е**	*it is*	*pronounced **(те съ)**		

You have already come across **е** in the question каквó **е** товá? and the answer товá **е** брошýра. Here are some more examples illustrating all forms of **съм**, including some negated forms:

Аз съм в Сóфия.	*I am in Sofia.*
Ти си тук.	*You are here.*
Джон не é в Лóндон.	*John is not in London.*
Нáдя е добрé.	*Nadya is well.*
Нúе сме добрé.	*We are well.*
Вúе сте тук.	*You are here.*
Те не cá тук.	*They are not here.*

The usage of the Bulgarian equivalent of *to be* differs from the English in two important ways:

(*a*) the negative marker **не** always comes before the verb. (Note that the usually unstressed forms of **съм** always carry the stress after **не**.)

(*b*) when the subject noun or pronoun (e.g. **Джон, аз**) is omitted, you cannot begin the sentence with any of the forms of **съм**. This means that the order of words changes so that the different forms of **съм** come second after some other introductory word or group of words.

Compare the above examples (where subject nouns/pronouns are used) with:

	В Сóфия съм.	*I am in Sofia.*
or	Не съ́м в Сóфия.	*I am not in Sofia.*
	Добрé е.	*(Nadya/she/he) is well.*
	Тук са.	*They are here.*

4 И́мам/ня́мам *I have* and *I have not*

One unusual feature of Bulgarian is that the negative of **и́мам** (*to have*) is not formed by placing **не** before the verb. Instead, a different verb is used: **ня́мам** (*not to have*). Otherwise, as you can see in this table and in the following examples, the two verbs have identical endings.

аз	**и́мам/ня́мам**	*I have/haven't*	**ни́е и́маме/ня́маме**	*we have/haven't*
ти	**и́маш/ня́маш**	*you have/haven't*	**ви́е и́мате/ня́мате**	*you have/haven't*
той	**и́ма/ня́ма**	*he has/hasn't*	**те и́мат/ня́мат**	*they have/haven't*
тя	**и́ма/ня́ма**	*she has/hasn't*		

И́мам мно́го ра́бота днес. — *I have a lot of work today.*
И́маш писмо́ от Ло́ндон. — *You have a letter from London.*
Г-н Анто́нов ня́ма факс. — *Mr Antonov does not have a fax.*
На́дя ня́ма мно́го ра́бота. — *Nadya does not have much work.*
Ни́е ня́маме вре́ме за кафе́. — *We don't have time for coffee.*
Ви́е и́мате ли вре́ме за кафе́? — *Do you have time for coffee?*
Те и́мат мно́го ра́бота днес. — *They have a lot of work today.*

The verbs **присти́гам** *to arrive*, **съжаля́вам** *to be sorry* and **ка́звам се** *to be called* also follow the pattern of **и́мам**:

Г-н Джо́нсън присти́га в се́дем часа́. — *Mr Johnson arrives at seven o'clock.*
Съжаля́ва**ме**, но ня́ма**ме** вре́ме. — *We are sorry, but we have no time.*
Как се ка́зва**ш**? — *What is your name?*

In Bulgarian, there are three basic verb patterns. This one is called the **a**-pattern, because all the endings are preceded by **a**. (You'll find out more in Unit 4.)

5 Asking questions

как?	*how?*	**Как са те?**	*How are they?*
какво́?	*what?*	**Какво́ е това́?**	*What is this?*
кога́?	*when?*	**Кога́ присти́гаш?**	*When do you arrive?*
къде́?	*where?*	**Къде́ е той?**	*Where is he?*

6 Counting to ten

0	ну́ла		
1	едно́	6	шест
2	две	7	се́дем
3	три	8	о́сем
4	че́тири	9	де́вет
5	пет	10	де́сет

7 И *and*, *also* and *too*

The little word **и** can have all these meanings in Bulgarian. Normally it is used to join two or more similar things and simply means *and*, as in:

Никола́й **и** Миле́на са на ра́бота. — *Nikolai* ***and*** *Milena are at work.*

Sometimes though, you'll find it used for emphasis to mean *also* and *too*:

И аз съм добре́. — *I'm fine* ***too.***

The word **a** can also mean *and*, but only when there is an element of contrast implied:

Той е добре́. А Ви́е как сте? — *He is fine. And* (*But*) *how about you?*

Тя е тук. А те са в Ло́ндон. — *She is here. And* (*But*) *they are in London.*

Exercises

1 Replace the personal names with the correct subject pronoun: **той, тя** or **те**.

a Къде́ е госпожа́ Джо́нсън?
b Господи́н Анто́нов е добре́.
c Как е господи́н Джо́нсън?
d Къде́ са Марк и Виоле́та?
e Неве́на е в хоте́л „Роди́на“.
f Господи́н Анто́нов и́ма ра́бота.
g Тук ли са Никола́й и Миле́на?

2 Read the following dialogues out loud completing them according to the model:

Тури́ст Аз съм Пол Те́йлър.
Неве́на Мо́ля? Как се ка́звате?
Тури́ст Ка́звам се Пол Те́йлър.

Note that **мо́ля** here is used to mean *I beg your pardon*. (**тури́стка** = *tourist* (woman); **тури́сти** = *tourists*)

a	**Тури́стка**	Аз съм Джу́ли Дже́ймсън.
	Неве́на	Мо́ля? Как се ка́звате?
	Тури́стка	________
b	**Дете́** (*child*)	Аз съм То́ни.
	Неве́на	Мо́ля? Как се ка́зваш?
	Дете́	________
c	**Анто́нов**	Аз съм Боя́н Анто́нов.
	Неве́на	Мо́ля? Как се ка́звате?
	Анто́нов	________
d	**Тури́сти**	Ни́е сме господи́н и госпожа́ Ко́линс.
	Неве́на	Мо́ля? Как се ка́звате?
	Тури́сти	________

3 In the previous exercise you asked questions in the singular and plural, as well as in the plural of formal speech. Bearing in mind the distinction between familiar and formal forms, ask the following people their names:

a a little girl
b an elderly lady
c a young couple

4 You are staying in room number 7. Nevena has rung through from reception. Read the following dialogue and then answer instead of Mrs Collins giving your own name and room number:

Неве́на	Ви́е ли сте г-жа́ Джо́нсън?
г-жа́ Ко́линс	Не, аз съм г-жа́ Ко́линс.
Неве́на	Ви́е в ста́я де́сет ли сте?
г-жа́ Ко́линс	Не, аз съм в ста́я но́мер о́сем.

5 Look at the following signs at the stop (**спи́рка**) for the tram (**трамва́й**) and the trolleybus (**троле́й**):

Now read the words on the signs, changing the number (**но́мер**) for the tram to 2, 5, 6 and 8, and the trolleybus to 1, 4, 7 and 9.

6 Ask questions to which the following could be answers, using either **как?** or **какво́?** (Don't forget to change from **аз** to **ти** and **ни́е** to **ви́е!**)

Model: Това́ е автобу́с (*bus*). (Какво́ е това́?)
Аз съм добре́. (Как си ти?/Как сте Ви́е?)

a Това́ е такси́.
b Тя е добре́.
c Те са добре́.
d Това́ е музе́й (masculine).
e Добре́ съм.
f Това́ е троле́й (masculine).
g Ни́е сме добре́.
h Това́ е фи́тнес це́нтър (*fitness centre*).

7 To test your knowledge of the question words **къде́?** *where?* and **кога́?** *when?*, read out loud, matching the questions and answers:

i Къде́ е той?
ii Кога́ и́ма самоле́т от Ло́ндон?
iii Кога́ присти́га той?
iv Къде́ са те?
v Къде́ е Че́лмсфорд?

a Той присти́га в три часа́.
b Той е в Со́фия.
c Че́лмсфорд е в А́нглия.
d Самоле́т от Ло́ндон и́ма в се́дем часа́.
e Те са в Шотла́ндия (*Scotland*).

8 Using the model that follows, ask for the places **a–e** in Sofia. And reply each time saying it is *over there*.

Тури́ст	Това́ ли е хоте́л „Пли́ска"?	*Is this the Pliska Hotel?*
Бъ́лгарин	Не, хоте́л „Пли́ска" е там.	*No, the Pliska Hotel is over there.*

a рестора́нт „Криста́л"
b булева́рд Ле́вски (*Levski Boulevard*)
c Центра́лна по́ща (*the Central Post Office*)
d хоте́л „Хе́мус"
e у́лица Рако́вски (*Rakovski Street*)

9 Complete the answers with **и́мам** or **ня́мам**:

a И́мате ли резерва́ция (*reservation*), госпожа́ Ко́линс?
Не, ————.

b И́мате ли мно́го бага́ж (*baggage*), госпо́жо?
Да, ————.

c И́мате ли но́ва ка́рта (*map*), господи́н Джо́нсън?
Не, ————.

d И́мате ли биле́т, госпо́жице?
Да, ————.

e И́мате ли ка́мера (*camcorder*), господи́не?
Да, ————.

10 Mr Johnson wants to post a letter. He asks a passer-by: **Мо́ля, къде́ и́ма по́ща** (*post office*)? What would you say if you wanted to find:

ресторáнт
бáнка
телефо́н
по́ща
тоалéтна
фи́тнес цéнтър

a

ЕВРО
БАНК

b

e

c

d

ФИТНЕС
ЦЕНТЪР

f

11 Complete the answers, using the correct forms of **съм**:

a Ви́е англичáнин ли сте?
Да, аз ... англичáнин, а той ... шотлáндец (*Scot*).

b Ви́е англичáнка ли сте?
Да, аз ... англичáнка, а тя ... шотлáндка (*Scotswoman*).

c Ти американец ли си?
Да, аз ... америкáнец, а той ... бъ́лгарин.

d Ви́е от Мáнчестър ли сте?
Ни́е ... от Мáнчестър, а те ... от Лийдс.

e Ви́е от Ло́ндон ли сте?
Аз ... от Ло́ндон, а тя ... от Глáзгоу.

Do you understand?

Dialogue 2: На информа́цията
At the information desk

Read the conversation below and then answer the questions on p. 24. It is not essential that you understand every word, but you should find all the new words in the vocabulary also on p. 24.

Michael Johnson is asking the woman at the information desk the way to Vitosha Boulevard. Together they examine this map of Sofia.

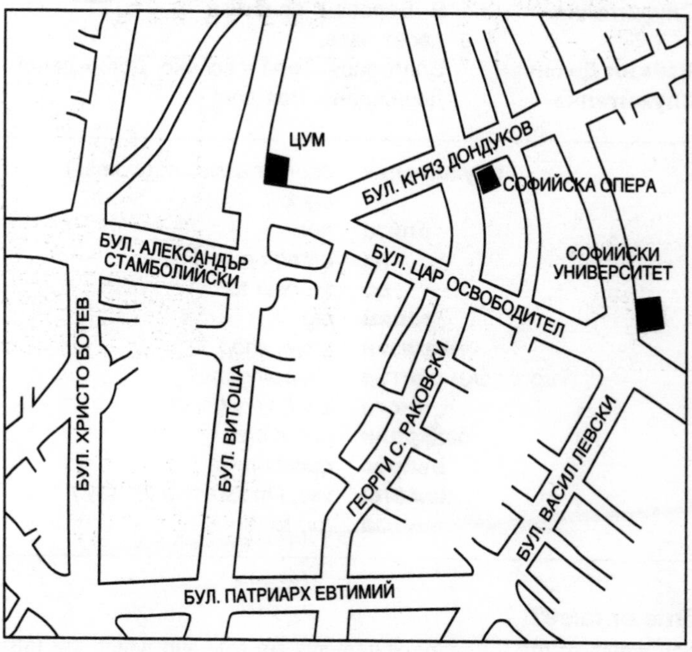

Ма́йкъл Джо́нсън До́бър ден! Мо́ля, къде́ е булева́рд Ви́тоша?

Служи́телка Булева́рд Ви́тоша не е́ бли́зо. И́мате ли ка́рта?

Ма́йкъл Джо́нсън Не, ня́мам.

Служи́телка Заповя́дайте, това́ е ка́рта на Со́фия. Булева́рд Ви́тоша е бли́зо до хоте́л „Ше́ратон".

Ма́йкъл Джо́нсън И́ма ли трамва́й до булева́рд Ви́тоша?

Служи́телка Да, трамва́й но́мер едно́ и трамва́й но́мер се́дем.

Ма́йкъл Джо́нсън	А какво́ е това́ тук?
Служи́телка	Това́ е голя́м търго́вски це́нтър с мно́го магази́ни. Ка́зва се ЦУМ.
Ма́йкъл Джо́нсън	Благодаря́ мно́го. И́мам о́ще еди́н въпро́с.
Служи́телка	Кaже́те!
Ма́йкъл Джо́нсън	Кога́ и́ма автобу́с за Бо́ровец?
Служи́телка	В о́сем часа́.
Ма́йкъл Джо́нсън	Кога́ присти́га той в Бо́ровец?
Служи́телка	В Бо́ровец присти́га в де́сет часа́.
Ма́йкъл Джо́нсън	Благодаря́. Това́ е вси́чко. Дови́ждане!
Служи́телка	Дови́ждане. Лек ден!

служи́телка	*counter assistant* (woman), *clerk*
бли́зо	*near*
на	*of; at; on*
до	*to; near to*
голя́м	*big*
магази́н	*store, shop*
търго́вски це́нтър	*shopping mall*
мно́го	*a lot, very* (*much*)
о́ще еди́н	*one more*
въпро́с	*question*
кaже́те!	*yes, I'm listening* (lit. *say!*)
за	*for; to*

True or false?

Say which of the following statements are true and which are false and rewrite the false ones:

1 Булева́рд Ви́тоша е бли́зо.
2 Г-н Джо́нсън и́ма ка́рта на Со́фия.
3 Хоте́л „Ше́ратон" е бли́зо до булева́рд Ви́тоша.
4 Ня́ма трамва́й до булева́рд Ви́тоша.
5 Г-н Джо́нсън и́ма о́ще еди́н въпро́с.
6 И́ма автобу́с за Бо́ровец в о́сем часа́.
7 Той (the word for *bus*, remember, is masculine!) присти́га в Бо́ровец в де́вет часа́.

какъ́в сте? каква́ сте?

who are you? what is your job?

In this unit you will learn:
- **how to ask people where they come from and what they do**
- **how to tell people where you come from and what you do**
- **how to give your nationality and marital status**

Dialogue 1

Nevena is now asking Mrs Collins, who has just arrived at the hotel and is wishing to register, some formal – and less formal – questions about herself and her family.

Нев́ена Откъде́ сте?
г-жа́ Ко́линс От Ма́нчестър.
Неве́на Така́, от А́нглия. Зна́чи сте англича́нка. А профе́сията Ви?
г-жа́ Ко́линс Превода́чка.
Неве́на Омъжена ли сте?
г-жа́ Ко́линс Да, омъжена съм.
Неве́на И́мате ли деца́?
г-жа́ Ко́линс Да, и́мам едно́ дете́.
Неве́на Мъжът Ви и дете́то Ви тук ли са?
г-жа́ Ко́линс Синът ми е в А́нглия, но мъжът ми е тук.
Неве́на Каква́ е профе́сията му?
г-жа́ Ко́линс Той е учи́тел.
Неве́на За първи път ли сте в Бълга́рия?
г-жа́ Ко́линс Не, не съм за първи път тук. Позна́вам страна́та ви добре́.
Неве́на Това́ е мно́го, интере́сно. А позна́вате ли Марк Де́йвис?
г-жа́ Ко́линс Не. Какъв е той?
Неве́на Журнали́ст. Той също позна́ва Бълга́рия мно́го добре́.
г-жа́ Ко́линс Англича́нин ли е?
Неве́на Не, америка́нец. Же́нен е за българка. Той и жена́ му Виоле́та са тук сега́.

Откъде́ сте?	*Where are you from?*
От Ма́нчестър.	*From Manchester.*
Така́, от А́нглия.	*Right, from England.*
Зна́чи сте англича́нка.	*So* (lit. *it means*) *you're English.*
А профе́сията Ви?	*And your profession/ occupation?*
превода́чка	*a translator/interpreter* (woman)
Омъжена ли сте?	*Are you married?* (asking a woman)
Да, омъжена съм.	*Yes, I am* (*married*).
И́мате ли деца́?	*Have you (any) children?*
Да, и́мам едно́ дете́.	*Yes, I have one child.*

Мъжъ́т Ви и детéто Ви тук ли са?	*Are your husband and your child here?*
Синъ́т ми е в А́нглия, но мъжъ́т ми е тук.	*My son is in England. but my husband is here.*
Каква́ е профе́сията му?	*What is his profession?*
Той е учи́тел.	*He's a teacher.*
За пъ́рви път ли сте в Бълга́рия?	*Are you in Bulgaria for the first time?*
Позна́вам страна́та ви добре́.	*I know your country well.*
Това́ е мно́го интере́сно.	*That's very interesting.*
А позна́вате ли Марк Де́йвис?	*And do you know Mark Davies?*
Какъ́в е той?	*What does he do for a job?*
журнали́ст	*journalist*
Той съ́що позна́ва Бълга́рия мно́го добре́.	*He also knows Bulgaria very well.*
Же́нен е за бъ́лгарка.	*He's married to a Bulgarian.*
Той и жена́ му Виоле́та са тук сега́.	*He and his wife Violeta are here now.*

1 Questions

- **a** Откъде́ е г-жа́ Ко́линс?
- **b** Каква́ профе́сия и́ма г-жа́ Ко́линс?
- **c** Омъ́жена ли е г-жа́ Ко́линс?
- **d** Тя и́ма ли деца́?
- **e** Какъ́в е г-н Ко́линс?
- **f** Добре́ ли позна́ва Бълга́рия г-жа́ Ко́линс?

2 True or false?

Say which of the following statements are true and which are false. Rewrite the false ones:

- **a** Госпожа́ Ко́линс е от Ли́вързпул.
- **b** Госпожа́ Ко́линс ня́ма деца́.
- **c** Господи́н Ко́линс е учи́тел.
- **d** Господи́н и госпожа́ Ко́линс и́мат еди́н син.
- **e** Госпожа́ Ко́линс е за пъ́рви път в Бълга́рия.
- **f** Госпожа́ Ко́линс не позна́ва Марк Де́йвис и жена́ му.

i *Married* or *single?* же́нен/неже́нен and омъ́жена/неомъ́жена

In Bulgarian there are two different words for *married*. When referring to a man who is married, you say **той е же́нен** (from **жена́** *wife*, *woman* – lit. *he is wifed*). If he is single you say **той не е́ же́нен**. When referring to a woman who is married, you say **тя е омъжена** (lit. *she is husbanded*). If she is single you say **тя не е́ омъжена**.

The words **же́нен** and **омъжена** are also used when filling in forms asking for your marital status. Here, however, if you are unmarried, you should join up the words (as in English!) and put either **неже́нен** if you are a man or **неомъжена** if you are a woman. If you are divorced you will enter **разве́ден** or **разве́дена** (lit. *separated*).

You will notice that the words have the appropriate feminine or masculine endings: **-а** for the woman and a consonant for the man. Thus, if you are a woman and are married, in official documents, for example, you will enter **омъжена**, and if you are a man and married **же́нен**. In everyday speech, however, you will find that a married woman will say of herself **же́нена съм**.

	For a man		For a woman
аз съм/не съ́м		аз съм/не съ́м	
ти си/не си́	**же́нен**	ти си/не си́	**омъжена**
той е/не е́		тя е/не е́	**(же́нена)**
Ви́е сте/не сте́		Ви́е сте/не сте́	

Remember that the **не** is not emphasized. As the stress marks show, the emphasis is placed on the forms of **съм**.

Still on the subject of masculine and feminine, you will notice that many naming words for women, especially for nationalities and professions, have **-ка** on the end. Often the **-ка** is simply added to the corresponding masculine noun:

студе́нт *student* (male) | студе́нт**ка** *student* (female)
учи́тел *teacher* (male) | учи́тел**ка** *teacher* (female)

Words ending in **-ец** or **-ин**, however, drop these letters before adding **-ка**:

българ**ин** *a Bulgarian* (male)	българ**ка** *a Bulgarian* (female)
америка́н**ец** *an American* (male)	америка́н**ка** *an American* (female)
кана́д**ец** *a Canadian* (male)	кана́д**ка** *a Canadian* (female)

How do you say it?

- Asking where someone is from and saying where you are from

Откъде́ си? От Ма́нчестър съм.	*Where are you from? I'm from Manchester.*
Откъде́ сте? Аз съм от Гла́згоу.	*Where are you from? I'm from Glasgow.*

- Asking someone what job they do (see also p. 45)

Каква́ профе́сия и́мате? / Каква́ е профе́сията Ви? or simply **Какъ́в сте? / Каква́ сте?**

- And answering

For a man

Аз съм учи́тел/Учи́тел съм.	*I'm a teacher.*
Аз съм ле́кар/Ле́кар съм.	*I'm a doctor.*
Аз съм превода́ч/Превода́ч съм.	*I'm a translator/interpreter.*
Аз съм сервитьо́р/Сервитьо́р съм.	*I'm a waiter.*

For a woman

Аз съм учи́телка/Учи́телка съм.	*I'm a teacher.*
Аз съм ле́карка/Ле́карка съм.	*I'm a doctor.*
Аз съм превода́чка/Превода́чка съм.	*I'm a translator/interpreter.*
Аз съм секрета́рка/Секрета́рка съм.	*I'm a secretary.*

- Saying whether you are married or not

For a man

Же́нен ли си/сте?	*Are you married?*
Да, же́нен съм.	*Yes, I am married.*
Не, не съ́м же́нен.	*No, I'm not married.*
Не, разве́ден съм.	*No, I'm divorced.*

For a woman

Омъ́жена ли си/сте?	*Are you married?*
Да, омъ́жена съм.	*Yes, I am married.*
Не, не съ́м омъ́жена.	*No, I am not married.*
Не, разве́дена съм.	*No, I'm divorced.*

• Referring to your family

With definite article:*		*Without definite article*:*	
дете́то ми	*my child*	**ба́ба ми**	*my grandmother*
мъжъ́т ми	*my husband*	**баща́ ми**	*my father*
синъ́т ми	*my son*	**брат ми**	*my brother*
		братовче́д(ка) ми	*my cousin*
		дъщеря́ ми	*my daughter*
		дя́до ми	*my grandfather*
		жена́ ми	*my wife*
		ма́йка ми	*my mother*
		сестра́ ми	*my sister*

*See Grammar sections 2 and 3 below.

Grammar

1 Какъ́в? каква́?

These are the masculine and feminine forms of the question word **какво́?** *what?* You already know **какво́** from **какво́ е това́?** *what is that?* where the neuter form is being used in a question. When you want to find out more about specific persons or things you have to use **какъ́в** for a masculine word, **каква́** for a feminine one and **какво́** for a neuter.

When you use **какъ́в** (or **каква́** or **какво́**) you are essentially asking what someone or something is like. However, depending on the situation, the simple question **Какъ́в е Ма́йкъл Джо́нсън?** may have at least three possible meanings:

What is Michael Johnson like?
What does Michael Johnson do for a job?
What is Michael Johnson's nationality?

Possible answers might be:

Той е висо́к и ху́бав.	*He is tall and handsome.*
Той е бизнесме́н.	*He is a businessman.*
Той е англича́нин.	*He is an Englishman.*

The context will tell you which is the most suitable.

2 -ът, -та, -то *the*

The difference between ***a** man* and ***the** man*, ***a** country* and ***the** country*, ***a** child* and ***the** child* is expressed in Bulgarian in the following way:

Masculine	мъж	becomes	мъж**ът**
Feminine	страна́	becomes	страна́**та**
Neuter	дете́	becomes	дете́**то**

From this you can see that the Bulgarian equivalent of the English definite article *the* is added to the end of the word. And, since all naming words in Bulgarian have either a masculine, feminine or neuter ending, there are also masculine (**-ът**), feminine (**-та**) and neuter (**-то**) forms of the definite article.

Most masculine naming words add -ът (pronounced -ъ, without the т)

Хоте́л**ът** е бли́зо.	*The hotel is nearby.*
Апартаме́нт**ът** е голя́м.	*The flat is big.*
Клу́б**ът** е до по́щата.	*The club is next to the post office.*

However, almost all nouns ending in **-тел** or **-ар** add **-ят**, and all masculine nouns ending in **-й** first drop the **-й** and then add **-ят**:

учи́**тел**	*teacher*	учи́тел**ят**	***the** teacher*
ле́**кар**	*doctor*	ле́кар**ят**	***the** doctor*
музе́**й**	*museum*	музе́**ят**	***the** museum*
трамва́**й**	*tram*	трамва́**ят**	***the** tram*
троле́**й**	*trolleybus*	троле́**ят**	***the** trolleybus*
ча**й**	*tea*	ча́**ят**	***the** tea*

Feminine naming words add -та

Стая́**та** е свобо́дна.	*The room is free.*
Ба́нка**та** и́ма нов телефо́н.	*The bank has a new telephone (number).*
Профе́сия**та** Ви е интере́сна.	*Your profession is interesting.*

Neuter naming words add -то

Дете́**то** е голя́мо.	*The child is big.*
Кафе́**то** е ху́баво.	*The coffee is nice.*
Свобо́дно ли е мя́сто**то**?	*Is the seat free?*

3 Ми and Ви (or ви) *My* and *your*

In the dialogue you met one of the ways of saying *my* and *your* in Bulgarian. These are short form possessive pronouns:

мъжъ́т **ми**	***my*** *husband*
мъжъ́т **Ви**	***your*** *husband* (polite)
дете́то **Ви**	***your*** *child* (polite)
синъ́т **ми**	***my*** *son*

You will notice that **ми**, the word for *my*, and **Ви** *your*, come after the naming word and that the naming word here has the definite article added.

It is very important to remember that, as an exception to the general rule, with most words for relatives the naming word has to be used without the definite article. You will find a list on p. 30.

You will learn other, longer and less conversational, ways of saying *my*, *your*, etc. in later units, but for the time being here is a full list of all the short form possessive pronouns used with the word **апартаме́нт** *flat*:

апартаме́нтът **ми**	***my*** *flat*	апартаме́нтът **ни**	***our*** *flat*
апартаме́нтът **ти**	***your*** *flat*	апартаме́нтът **ви/Ви**	***your*** *flat*
апартаме́нтът **му**	***his*** *flat*		
апартаме́нтът **ѝ**	***her*** *flat*	апартаме́нтът **им**	***their*** *flat*

Remember that **ѝ**, the little word for *her*, is *always* written with a grave accent so as to distinguish it from the word **и** meaning *and*. The stresses are indicated by an acute accent.

Exercises

1 Have another look at the dialogue, then rearrange the following words to form sentences:

- **a** едно́, и́мам, дете́
- **b** ли, омъ́жена, сте?
- **c** превода́чка, е, г-жа́ Ко́линс
- **d** профе́сията Ви, е, госпо́жо Ко́линс, каква́?
- **e** ли, за пъ́рви път, в Бълга́рия, е, г-жа́ Ко́линс?
- **f** г-жа́ Ко́линс, са, и, откъде́, г-н Ко́линс?
- **g** добре́, страна́та ви, позна́вам

2 Match these questions and answers (often the gender will be a useful clue):

i	От Ма́нчестър ли е г-жа́ Ко́линс?	**a**	От Ирла́ндия (*Ireland*) съм.
ii	Превода́ч ли е г-н Ко́линс?	**b**	Не. От Шотла́ндия (*Scotland*) съм.

iii Откъдé си?
iv От Ирлáндия ли сте?
v Какъ̀в сте?
vi Какви́ са Марк и Виолéта Дéйвис?
vii Ймате ли децá?
viii Откъдé е Николáй?

c Лéкар съм.
d Да, тя е от Мáнчестър.
e Той е от Вáрна.
f Не, той не é преводáч.
g Той е америкáнец, а тя е бъ̀лгарка.
h Да, и́мам две децá.

3 Complete the dialogues (**a**) to (**d**) below. Use **какъ̀в** or **каквá** to form the appropriate question and choose the correct gender form from the list of occupations and nationalities:

Model: Учи́телка ли сте?
Не, не съ̀м учи́телка.
Каквá сте?
Студéнтка съм. (*I'm a student.*)

Ирлáндец ли сте?
Не, не съ̀м ирлáндец.
Какъ̀в сте?
Шотлáндец съм.

преводáч	лéкар	америкáнец	шотлáндка
студéнт	учи́телка	ирлáндка	ирлáндец
секретáрка	шофьóр	англичáнка	шотлáндец

a Лéкарка ли сте?
Не, не ________
________ сте?
________ съм.

b Бъ̀лгарка ли сте?
Не, не ________
________ сте?
________ съм.

c Сервитьóр ли сте?
Не, не ________
________ сте?
________ съм.

d Англичáнин ли сте?
Не, не ________
________ сте?
________ съм.

4 Write out a short description of the following people, using the information given. Then go to the answer in the Key and read it out loud. This exercise will help you learn some words for the professions and also to practise using words for marital status.

Model: Г-н Кóлинс е учи́тел. Той е от Мáнчестър. Той е жéнен (or не é жéнен).

a Марк Де́йвис – журнали́ст – Са́нта Ба́рбара – же́нен
b Миле́на – фотогра́фка (*photographer*) – Со́фия – неомъ́жена
c А́ндрю – студе́нт – Гла́згоу – неже́нен
d г-жа́ Ко́линс – преводáчка – Ма́нчестър – омъ́жена
e На́дя – секрета́рка – Пло́вдив – неомъ́жена
f Ма́йкъл Джо́нсън – бизнесме́н – Че́лмсфорд – же́нен
g г-н Анто́нов – дире́ктор (*director*) – Бурга́с – же́нен
h Никола́й – програми́ст (*programmer*) – Ва́рна – неже́нен

Now give your own name, say what you do for a job and where you come from, and indicate your marital status.

5 Complete with the appropriate masculine or feminine definite forms (**-ът** or **-та**):

a Журнали́ст... е от Са́нта Ба́рбара.
b Фотогра́фка... е от Со́фия.
c Студе́нт... е от Гла́згоу.
d Преводáчка... е от Ма́нчестър.
e Секрета́рка... е от Пло́вдив.
f Бизнесме́н... е от Че́лмсфорд.
g Дире́ктор... е от Бурга́с.
h Програми́ст... е от Ва́рна.

6 To practise the use of the alternative (**-ят**) form of the masculine definite article, read and then answer the questions:

a Джеймс Ми́лър е ле́кар. Той е шотла́ндец.
Какъ́в е ле́карят?

b Джордж Ко́линс е учи́тел. Той е англича́нин.
Какъ́в е учи́телят?

c Ча́ят е ху́бав. Той е от А́нглия.
Какъ́в е ча́ят? Откъде́ е той?

7 Mr Antonov introduces his wife to Michael Johnson and says: Запозна́йте се – жена́ ми! *Meet my wife!* (lit. *Get to know one another – my wife*). What would you say when introducing the following people to a new Bulgarian acquaintance? (Beware of the vanishing definite article with the words for certain relatives!):

a your husband
b your son
c your daughter
d your brother
e your sister

8 Answer the questions below following this model:

Как се ка́зва мъжъ́т Ви/ти? Мъжъ́т ми се ка́зва Ива́н.
Как се ка́зва ма́йка Ви/ти? Ма́йка ми се ка́зва Еле́на.

a Как се ка́зва синъ́т Ви/ти? (А́ндрю)
b Как се ка́зва дете́то Ви/ти? (Ви́ктор)
c Как се ка́зва ма́йка Ви/ти? (Ири́на)
d Как се ка́зва жена́ Ви/ти? (Мари́я)
e Как се ка́зва дъщеря́ Ви/ти? (Си́лвия)
f Как се ка́зва баща́ ти? (Пол)

9 Mrs Collins has taught her husband some expressions to use in restaurants. He is in Bulgaria for the first time and likes his coffee, soup and tea hot. Read the model and then practise with him. Don't forget that **кафе́** (*coffee*), **су́па** (*soup*), **чай** (*tea*), etc. should be referred to as **то**, **тя** and **той** respectively!

Model: **Сервитьо́р** Кафе́то Ви, господи́не!
г-н Ко́линс Но то е студе́но! (*But it's cold!*)

a **Сервитьо́р** Су́пата Ви, господи́не!
г-н Ко́линс ________

b **Сервитьо́р** Ча́ят Ви, господи́не!
г-н Ко́линс ________

Nor does Mrs Collins like her beer, wine, water or gin warm (то́пъл, то́пла, то́пло). Complete and read out the following:

c **Сервитьо́р** Би́рата Ви, госпо́жо!
г-жа́ Ко́линс ________
d **Сервитьо́р** Ви́ното Ви, госпо́жо!
г-жа́ Ко́линс ________
e **Сервитьо́р** Вода́та Ви, госпо́жо!
г-жа́ Ко́линс ________
f **Сервитьо́р** Джи́нът Ви, госпо́жо!
г-жа́ Ко́линс ________

10 If asked to show your passport, your reply would be: Заповя́дайте, това́ е паспо́ртът ми. How would you reply if asked to show your visa (ви́за), your reservation (резерва́ция) or your ticket (биле́т)?

11 Look at the map of Bulgaria overleaf. Then complete and write out the sentences.

a Това́ е ____ на Бълга́рия.
b На и́зток гра́ницата (*the border*) е ____
c На се́вер гра́ницата е река́. Река́та се ка́зва ____
d На юг са ____ и ____
e Сто́лицата (*the capital*) на Бълга́рия е град (*town*) ____

Do you understand?

Dialogue 2: В асансьóра *In the lift*

Nikolai and Milena meet in the lift on their way to see Nadya, the secretary. They work for the same advertising agency, but they don't yet know one another.

Никола́й	Здраве́йте!
Миле́на	До́бър ден! Позна́ваме ли се?
Никола́й	Не. Да се запозна́ем! Ка́звам се Никола́й Димитро́в. А Ви́е как се ка́звате?
Миле́на	Аз се ка́звам Миле́на Мари́нова.
Никола́й	Прия́тно ми е! (*They go into the office.*) Е́то и На́дя, секрета́рката. Здраве́й, На́дя!
На́дя	Здраве́йте! Мо́ля, запове́дайте! Ви́е позна́вате ли се?
Никола́й	И да, и не. Миле́на, Ви́е каква́ сте?
Миле́на	Фотогра́фка съм.
На́дя	Миле́на е фотогра́фката на фи́рмата. Тя мно́го рабо́ти с компю́тър.
Никола́й	Разби́рам. Това́ е мно́го интере́сна профе́сия.
Миле́на	А Ви́е какъ́в сте?
Никола́й	Аз съм програми́ст.
На́дя	Никола́й е програми́стът на фи́рмата.
Миле́на	Съ́що интере́сна профе́сия.
На́дя	И́мате ли вре́ме за едно́ кафе́?
Миле́на	Да, разби́ра се.
Никола́й	Аз съ́що. За кафе́ ви́наги и́мам вре́ме!

да се запозна́ем!	*let's get acquainted!*
запозна́йте се...!	*meet...!*
прия́тно ми е!	*pleased to meet you!*
е́то	*here is*
фи́рма	*firm*
фотогра́фка	*photographer* (woman)
рабо́ти	*(she) works*
компю́тър	*computer*
разби́рам	*I understand*
разби́ра се	*of course*
интере́сен, интере́сна	*interesting*
програми́ст	*(computer) programmer*
съ́що	*too, also*
ви́наги	*always*
Гъ́рция	*Greece*
Македо́ния	*Macedonia*
Румъ́ния	*Romania*
Съ́рбия	*Serbia*
Ту́рция	*Turkey*
(на) за́пад	*(in/to) the west*
(на) и́зток	*(in/to) the east*
(на) се́вер	*(in/to) the north*
(на) юг	*(in/to) the south*
Ду́нав	*the Danube*
град	*town*
гра́ница	*border*
сто́лица	*capital*
то́пъл, то́пла	*warm, hot*
че́рен, че́рна	*black*

True or False?

Decide which of these statements are false and write out correct versions.

1 Никола́й и Миле́на не се́ позна́ват.
2 Миле́на е секрета́рката на фи́рмата.
3 Миле́на и́ма интере́сна профе́сия.
4 Никола́й е програми́ст.
5 Никола́й и Миле́на ня́мат вре́ме за кафе́.

04

ко́лко? в ко́лко часа́?

how much? how many? at what time?

In this unit you will learn:

- to ask about quantity
- to ask and tell the time
- to use some more numbers

Dialogue 1

The morning after Mr Johnson's arrival at the hotel, Nevena, the ever-obliging receptionist, stops him in the foyer.

Невéна	Дóбър ден, г-н Джóнсън! Ймате писмá днес.
г-н Джóнсън	Писмá? Кóлко писмá?
Невéна	Три – заповя́дайте! Йскате ли български вéстници?
г-н Джóнсън	Съжаля́вам, но не разби́рам добрé български.
Невéна	Ни́е и́маме вéстници и списáния и на англи́йски ези́к. Заповя́дайте!
г-н Джóнсън	Товá е чудéсно! Благодаря́! Лек ден!
Невéна	Извинéте, г-н Джóнсън, и́мате ли óще мáлко врéме?
г-н Джóнсън	(*hesitatingly*) Ймам срéща в цéнтъра…
Невéна	В кóлко часá е срéщата Ви?
г-н Джóнсън	Тóчно в дванáйсет.
Невéна	Знáчи и́мате óколо пет минýти.
г-н Джóнсън	Въпрóси ли и́мате?
Невéна	Сáмо еди́н въпрóс. За кóлко врéме сте в България?
г-н Джóнсън	За две сéдмици.
Невéна	Товá прáви четиринáйсет нóщи в хотéла, нали́?
г-н Джóнсън	Тóчно такá.
Невéна	Благодаря́.
г-н Джóнсън	Товá ли е всúчко!
Невéна	Да, да. Ня́мате врéме. Вéче е дванáйсет без двáйсет и пет.
г-н Джóнсън	Добрé. Дови́ждане!

Ймате писмá днес.	*You have some letters today.*
Кóлко писмá?	*How many letters?*
Йскате ли български вéстници?	*Do you want any Bulgarian newspapers?*
не разби́рам добрé български.	*I don't understand Bulgarian very well.*
Ни́е и́маме вéстници и списáния и на англи́йски ези́к.	*We have newspapers and magazines in English too.*
Товá е чудéсно!	*That's wonderful/ marvellous!*
Извинéте.	*Excuse me.*
óще мáлко	*a little more*
Ймам срéща в цéнтъра	*I have an appointment in the centre.*

В ко́лко часа́ е сре́щата Ви?	*At what time is your appointment?*
То́чно в двана́йсет	*At twelve precisely.*
Зна́чи и́мате о́коло пет мину́ти.	*So it means you have about five minutes.*
Въпро́си ли и́мате?	*Do you have any questions?*
Са́мо еди́н въпро́с.	*Just one question.*
За ко́лко вре́ме сте в Бълга́рия?	*How long are you in Bulgaria for?*
За две се́дмици.	*For two weeks.*
Това́ пра́ви четирина́йсет но́щи в хоте́ла, нали́?	*That makes fourteen nights in the hotel, doesn't it?*
То́чно така́.	*Exactly so.*
Ве́че е двана́йсет без два́йсет и пет.	*It's already twenty-five to twelve.*

1 Questions

- **a** Ко́лко писма́ и́ма за г-н Джо́нсън?
- **b** Добре́ ли разби́ра бъ́лгарски г-н Джо́нсън?
- **c** В ко́лко часа́ и́ма сре́ща той? (Don't forget to repeat **в** in the answer.)
- **d** Къде́ е сре́щата на г-н Джо́нсън?
- **e** Ко́лко вре́ме и́ма г-н Джо́нсън?
- **f** За ко́лко вре́ме е той в Бълга́рия? (Repeat **за** in the answer.)

2 True or false?

Write out correct versions of the false statements.

- **a** За г-н Джо́нсън и́ма три писма́.
- **b** Г-н Джо́нсън не и́ска бъ́лгарски ве́стници.
- **c** В хоте́ла ня́ма англи́йски ве́стници и списа́ния.
- **d** Неве́на и́ма мно́го въпро́си.
- **e** Г-н Джо́нсън е в Бълга́рия за една́ се́дмица.
- **f** Часъ́т е едина́йсет без два́йсет и пет.

i Morning, noon and night

The Bulgarians have no real equivalent for *a.m.* and *p.m.* To avoid misunderstanding, especially when referring to opening times of shops or to bus or train times, they use the 24-hour clock. Alternatively, in situations not involving travel, immediately after giving the time they insert the word **сутринта́** *in the morning*, **следо́бед** *in the afternoon*, **вечерта́** *in the evening* and **през нощта́** *at night*. So, if your plane arrives at 9.30 p.m. you will say: **самоле́тът присти́га в два́йсет и еди́н часа́ и три́йсет мину́ти**, but if you are merely getting together with a friend in the evening, you will arrange to meet **в де́вет и полови́на вечерта́**.

Interestingly, where in English we would say *at one* (or *two*) *in the morning*, the Bulgarians say **в едѝн** (or **два**) **часá през нощтá**. For us the night would seem to end at midnight, while for the Bulgarians it goes on at least until two in the morning!

One further important thing to note is that the Bulgarian word **óбед** or **обя̀д** means *lunch* or *lunchtime* as well as *noon* or *midday*. Punctuality is not a national trait, nor is noon such a precise time for Bulgarians. It is rather the general period between midday and two. So, if someone invites you for lunch (**на óбед**) at midday (**по óбед**), make sure you also agree on a precise time, or you could be in for a long wait for your meal!

How do you say it?

- Asking *How many?* and *How much?*

Кóлко писмá ѝмате?	*How many letters do you have?*
Кóлко врéме ѝмате?	*How much time do you have?*

- Asking *At what time?* and *For how long?*

В кóлко часá?	*At what time?*
За кóлко врéме сте в Бългáрия?	*How long are you in Bulgaria for?*

- Asking, and saying, what the time is

Кóлко е часъ̀т?	*What is the time?*
Часъ̀т е тóчно дванáйсет.	*It is exactly twelve o'clock.*

- Begging someone's pardon

Извинéте! or **Извиня̀вайте!**	*Excuse me!/I beg your pardon.*

- Seeking agreement or confirmation using **налѝ**?

Вѝе сте в Сóфия за четиринáйсет дни, налѝ?	*You are in Sofia for fourteen days, aren't you?*
Г-н Джóнсън е в Сóфия за 14 дни, налѝ?	*Mr Johnson is in Sofia for 14 days, isn't he?*

- Agreeing and approving

Тóчно такá!	*That's right!/Exactly so!/ Precisely!*
Такá е.	*That is so.*
Товá е чудéсно!	*That's wonderful!*

- Indicating the time of day

сутринтá	*in the morning*
следóбед	*in the afternoon*
вечертá	*in the evening*
през нощтá	*at night*

Grammar

1 Ко́лко? *How many? How much?*

Ко́лко is the question word for quantity:

Ко́лко писма́ и́ма за г-н Джо́нсън?	*How many letters are there for Mr Johnson?*
Ко́лко вре́ме и́ма той?	*How much time has he got?*
За **ко́лко** дни е г-н Джо́нсън в Бълга́рия?	*How many days is Mr Johnson in Bulgaria for?*

When **ко́лко** refers to quantity, it is used to express both *how many?* (with naming words for concrete or countable things) and *how much?* (with abstract or uncountable things).

You also use **ко́лко** when asking questions about the time, such as *what's the time?* or *at what time?*

Ко́лко е часъ́т?	*What's the time?*
В ко́лко часа́ е самоле́тът за Ло́ндон?	*What time is the plane for London?*
До ко́лко часа́ рабо́ти о́фисът?	*Until what time is the office open?* (lit. *is working*)

мно́го	*many, much, a lot of*
ма́лко	*few, a few, a little, not many, not much*

Мно́го is also used as the equivalent of the English *very* or *very much*:

Г-жа́ Ко́линс разби́ра бъ́лгарски **мно́го добре́**.	*Mrs Collins understands Bulgarian very well.*
Хоте́лът е **мно́го ху́бав**.	*The hotel is very beautiful/nice.*
Благодаря́ **мно́го**.	*Thank you very much.*
Извиня́вайте **мно́го!**	*I am very sorry!*

2 Plural of nouns

The most common (but not the only) plural ending is **-и**. It occurs with both masculine and feminine nouns.

Masculine nouns

The plural ending **-и** is attached to masculine words in a number of ways:

a by simply adding **-и** to the singular:

автобу́с	автобу́с**и**	*buses*

ресторáнт	ресторáнт**и**	*restaurants*
билéт	билéт**и**	*tickets*
лéкар	лéкар**и**	*doctors*
тури́ст	тури́ст**и**	*tourists*
óфис	óфис**и**	*offices*

Note that all these masculine nouns, as well as the following ones, have more than one syllable! Most masculine nouns of only one syllable form their plurals differently. You will learn them in Unit 7.

b by adding **-и** and also changing the final consonant of the singular. One of the most frequent changes is **-к** to **-ц**:

вéстни**к**	вéстни**ци**	*newspapers*
ези́**к**	ези́**ци**	*languages, tongues*
климати́**к**	климати́**ци**	*air conditioners*
часóвни**к**	часóвни**ци**	*watches, clocks*

c by adding **-и** and also dropping the vowel that comes before the final consonant of the singular. Certain combinations of vowel and consonant, such as **-ец** or **-ър**, favour this method, but there is no simple rule.

америкáн**ец**	америкáн**ци**	*Americans*	**-ец** (**е** is dropped)
чужден**é**ц	чужден**ци́**	*foreigners*	
шотлáнд**ец**	шотлáнд**ци**	*Scots*	
компю́т**ър**	компю́т**ри**	*computers*	**-ър** (**ъ** is dropped)
ли́т**ър**	ли́т**ри**	*litres*	
мéт**ър**	мéт**ри**	*metres*	
ден	**дни**	*days*	(**е** is dropped)

d by substituting **-и** for the singular ending in **-й**.

музé**й**	музé**и**	*museums*
трамвá**й**	трамвá**и**	*trams*
тролé**й**	тролé**и**	*trolleybuses*

Feminine nouns

The plural of feminine nouns is always **-и**, which replaces the singular ending **-а** or **-я**:

сéдмиц**а**	сéдмиц**и**	*weeks*
англичáнк**а**	англичáнк**и**	*English women*
фóнокáрт**а**	фóнокáрт**и**	*(pay) phone cards*
резервáци**я**	резервáци**и**	*reservations*
дъщер**я́**	дъщер**и́**	*daughters*
стá**я**	стá**и**	*rooms*

The few feminine nouns which end in a consonant form their plural by adding **-и** to the singular. You have already come across **нощ**,

ве́чер and **су́трин**:

една́ нощ	мно́го но́щ**и**	*many nights*
една́ ве́чер	мно́го ве́чер**и**	*many evenings*
една́ су́трин	мно́го су́трин**и**	*many mornings*

Neuter nouns

The most common plural endings for neuter nouns are **-а** and **-я**. The choice is determined by the endings in the singular.

a nouns in **-о** replace the final **-о** by **-а**:

писм**о́**	писм**а́**	*letters*
семе́йств**о**	семе́йств**а**	*families*

Note that the stress sometimes moves to the final syllable:

ви́но	**вина́**	*wines*

b nouns in **-ие** replace the final **-е** by **-я**:

списа́н**ие**	списа́н**ия**	*magazines*
съобще́н**ие**	съобще́н**ия**	*messages*

(More neuter plurals in Unit 8!)

3 Разби́рам *I understand* and и́скам *I want* (a-pattern verbs)

As with **и́мам** and **присти́гам**, the endings of these verbs contain the vowel **-а-**. We can refer to them as **а**-pattern verbs. They are also known as verbs of Conjugation 3. This is the most regular and the most common pattern, and also the easiest to learn:

аз	разби́р**ам**	*I understand*	ни́е разби́р**аме**	*we understand*
ти	разби́р**аш**	*you understand*	ви́е разби́р**ате**	*you understand*
той / тя / то	разби́р**а**	*he, she, it understands*	те разби́р**ат**	*they understand*

4 Пра́вя *I make*, *I do* and рабо́тя *I work* (и-pattern verbs)

аз	пра́в**я**/ рабо́т**я**	*I make/do, work*	ни́е пра́в**им**/ рабо́т**им**	*we make/do, work*
ти	пра́в**иш**/ рабо́т**иш**	*you make/do, work*	ви́е пра́в**ите**/ рабо́т**ите**	*you make/do, work*
той / тя / то	пра́в**и**/ рабо́т**и**	*he, she, it makes/ does, works*	те пра́в**ят**/ рабо́т**ят**	*they make/do, work*

As you can see, **пра́вя** and **рабо́тя** have **-и-** in all their endings except the forms for *I* and *they*. Verbs like **пра́вя** and **рабо́тя** belong to the **и**-pattern and are known as verbs of Conjugation 2.

Пра́вя can mean both *I make* and *I do*. Here, too, Bulgarian conveniently has one word with a number of different meanings in English. Compare:

Две и две пра́ви чѐтири.	*Two and two makes four.*
Какво́ пра́виш?	*What are you doing?*

Какво́ рабо́тиш? or **какво́ рабо́тите?** is another way to ask *What's your job?* (see p. 29) And, among friends, **какво́ пра́виш?** (you'll hear **кво пра́иш?**) is commonly used to ask *How are you?*

5 -а and -я: the short definite article

In Unit 3, you were introduced to the Bulgarian equivalent of the English definite article *the*. You learnt to add the endings **-ът** or **-ят** to masculine nouns. These forms, known as the full forms, are, however, only used when the noun is the subject in the sentence, determining the ending of the verb, as in the sentence: хоте́л**ът** е мно́го ху́бав *the hotel is very nice*:

Masculine nouns are also used with a short form of the definite article. This happens when the noun is not the subject in the sentence. The most obvious position is after prepositions. For example, if you want to say you are *in* the hotel, хоте́лът becomes хоте́ла: Аз съм **в** хоте́ла.

The short forms of the definite article (with masculine nouns only, remember) are **-а** or **-я**. This makes them look *and* sound like feminines, while the long forms only sound like feminines – so listen carefully and keep your wits about you! Compare:

	Це́нтър**ът** на Со́фия е краси́в.	*The centre of Sofia is beautiful.*
and	И́мам сре́ща в це́нтъ**ра**.	*I have a meeting in the centre.*
	Музе́**ят** е на у́лица Ива́н Ва́зов.	*The museum is on Ivan Vazov Street.*
and	И́ма мно́го тури́сти в музе́**я**.	*There are a lot of tourists in the museum.*

You will now understand why we wrote **В рестора́нта** as the heading of the second dialogue in Unit 1. And you will appreciate the difference, when written, between Ко́лко е час**ъ́т**? and **В** ко́лко час**а́**? (although час**а́** and час**ъ́т** are both pronounced час**ъ́!**).

street sign in Sofia

улица
ИВАН ВАЗОВ 21А→37

6 A note on pronunciation

Although in written Bulgarian a distinction is still made between the short and the long form, when speaking it is normal to ignore the final **т** of the full form and to pronounce the endings as if they were the short form. So, what you will hear for **трамвáят** and **трамвáя** will be **трамвáйъ**, for **учи́телят** and **учи́теля** you will hear **учи́телйъ** and for **хотéлът** and **хотéла, хотéлъ.**

Only in formal speech, in news bulletins on the radio or television, for example, or when people feel they need to be 'ultra-correct' in their speech, will you hear the long form articulated in full with the final **-т** pronounced. As you listen to the different speakers on the recording, see if you can detect any difference. (For further pronunciation changes in everyday speech, look again at the Appendix.)

7 Numerals 11 to 100

11 единáйсет	14 четиринáйсет	17 седемнáйсет
12 дванáйсет	15 петнáйсет	18 осемнáйсет
13 тринáйсет	16 шестнáйсет	19 деветнáйсет

The numbers from 11 to 19 are formed by the addition of **-нáйсет**, (the equivalent of the English *-teen*), to the numbers from 1 to 9. For 11 you add **-нáйсет** to the masculine **еди́н** and for 12 you add **-нáйсет** to **два** not to **две**.

20 двáйсет (двáдесет)	25 двáйсет и пет
21 двáйсет и еднó/еди́н/еднá	26 двáйсет и шест
22 двáйсет и две/два	27 двáйсет и сéдем
23 двáйсет и три	28 двáйсет и óсем
24 двáйсет и чéтири	29 двáйсет и дéвет

From 20 upwards the numerals are formed on the principle of *twenty and one*, *twenty and two*, etc. with the word for *and* **и** being inserted between **двáйсет**, **три́йсет**, **четúрисет**, etc. and **еднó**, **две**, **три**, etc. There are alternative more formal spellings and pronunciations – given in brackets – for some numbers. Be careful to distinguish between **дванáйсет** (12) and **двáйсет** (20) – all the teens are longer!

30 три́йсет (три́десет)	70 седемдесéт
40 чети́рисет (чети́ридесет)	80 осемдесéт
50 петдесéт	90 деветдесéт
60 шейсéт (шестдесéт)	100 сто

Remember that **едно́** has different forms for the three genders. Also that **две** has an alternative form **два**, as in **два часа́** *two o'clock*. (More about this in Unit 8.)

8 Telling the time

Ко́лко е часъ́т?	*What is the time?*
Часъ́т е...	*The time is...*

When telling the time in Bulgarian you begin with the hours and move on to the minutes. For times up to the half hour you give the hour first and add the minutes using the word **и**. As in English, the words for *hours* and *minutes* can be omitted:

Ко́лко е часъ́т?

Единáйсет часá **и** дéсет минýти. (*The time is*) *ten past eleven.*

or

(Часъ́т е) единáйсет **и** дéсет.

Ко́лко е часъ́т?

Дéвет часá **и** двáйсет и пет минýти. (*The time is*) *twenty-five past nine.*

or

(Часъ́т е) дéвет **и** двáйсет **и** пет.

For times after the half hour you give the number of the next hour first and take away the minutes from the next hour using the word **без** (*without* or *less*):

Ко́лко е часъ́т?
(Часъ́т е) сéдем **без** дéсет. (*The time is ten to seven.*)

Ко́лко е часъ́т?
(Часъ́т е) три без пет. (*The time is five to three.*)

Bulgarian has alternative forms for half past and the quarters:

Óсем **и полови́на**
or ósем **и три́йсет**

Half past eight
or *eight thirty.*

Пет **без чéтвърт**
or пет **без петна́йсет**

A quarter to five
or *four forty-five.*

Шест **и чéтвърт**
or шест **и петна́йсет**

A quarter past six
or *six fifteen*

9 Нали́? *Isn't it so?*

In conversational Bulgarian you will often hear the word **нали́** tagged on the end of statements making them into questions seeking confirmation. In English there is no proper one-word equivalent for **нали́** and you have to repeat the verb to achieve the same effect. Bulgarians learning English have great difficulty with our different forms, but as you will see from the following examples, **нали́** is very easy for us to use.

Хотéлът е мно́го ху́бав, **нали́**?	*The hotel is very nice,* ***isn't it****?*
Ви́е не сте́ бъ́лгарка, **нали́?**	*You are not Bulgarian,* ***are you****?*
Й́мате са́мо еди́н въпро́с, **нали́**?	*You do only have one question,* ***don't you****?*
Той не и́ска бъ́лгарски вéстници, **нали́**?	*He doesn't want Bulgarian newspapers,* ***does he****?*

Exercises

1 Make full sentences using the information on the bus departures and arrivals board below. Best use the 24-hour clock!

РАЗПИСА́НИЕ *(Timetable)*

За *(to)*	Замина́ва *(departs)*	Присти́га *(arrives)*
Мальо́вица	6.35	9.15
Ба́нкя	10.10	10.45
Са́моков	11.20	13.30
Бо́ровец	13.50	17.25

Model: Автобу́сът за ____ замина́ва в ____ часа́ и ____ мину́ти и присти́га в ____ часа́ и ____ мину́ти.

Now use the short version of the times omitting **часа́** and **мину́ти**.

2 Looking at the timetable above, answer the following questions, (the actual time is given in brackets):

Model: (Часъ́т е де́сет без пет.) След ко́лко мину́ти замина́ва автобу́сът за Ба́нкя? *In how many minutes does the bus leave for Bankya?*

- Автобу́сът за Ба́нкя замина́ва след петна́йсет мину́ти.

a (Часъ́т е едина́йсет и петна́йсет.) След ко́лко мину́ти замина́ва автобу́сът за Са́моков?
b (Часъ́т е еди́н и полови́на.) След ко́лко мину́ти замина́ва автобу́сът за Бо́ровец?
c (Часъ́т е шест и два́йсет и пет.) След ко́лко мину́ти замина́ва автобу́сът за Мальо́вица?

3 Answer these questions reading out the times on the clocks.

a В ко́лко часа́ замина́ва автобу́сът за Пло́вдив?

b Кога́ присти́га самоле́тът от Ло́ндон?

c Кога́ и́ма самоле́т за Ва́рна?

d Кога́ замина́ваш за Со́фия?

e В ко́лко часа́ е сре́щата на г-н Джо́нсън?

4 Answer the questions below presuming that:

a you are staying in Bulgaria for 12/15/20 days
b you are staying in the hotel for 3/13 nights
c you are staying in Varna for one/two weeks

i За ко́лко дни сте в Бълга́рия?
ii За ко́лко но́щи сте в хоте́ла?
iii За ко́лко се́дмици сте във Ва́рна? (When **в** is used before words beginning with the letters **в** or **ф** it is extended to **във**.)

5 Read the notices below:

ЦЕНТРА́ЛНА ПО́ЩА
Рабо́тно вре́ме
(*opening hours*) от (*from*)
7 до (*to*) 20.30 часа́

АПТЕ́КА (*Pharmacy*)
Рабо́тно вре́ме
от 9 до 21 часа́

РЕСТОРА́НТ
Рабо́тно вре́ме
от 18 до 23 часа́

ПОДА́РЪЦИ (*gifts*)
су́трин от 8 до 12 часа́
следо́бед от 16 до 20 часа́

СЛАДКА́РНИЦА
(*patisserie, café*)
су́трин от 10 до 13 часа́
следо́бед от 14 до 19 часа́

A more natural way to read the notices would be to use **рабо́ти** and a 12-hour clock, for example:

Магази́нът за пода́ръци рабо́ти от о́сем часа́ сутринта́ до двана́йсет часа́ на о́бед и от че́тири часа́ следо́бед до о́сем часа́ вечерта́.

Now complete the sentences as if answering the question **До ко́лко часа́ рабо́ти...?** using the 12-hour clock:

a По́щата ____ от 7 часа́ сутринта́ до 8.30 часа́ ____.
b Апте́ката рабо́ти от 9 ____ ____ до 9 ____ ____.
c Рестора́нтът рабо́ти ____ 6 ____ 11 часа́ ____.
d ____ рабо́ти ____ 10 часа́ ____ до еди́н часа́ на о́бед и от 2 часа́ ____ до 7 часа́ ____.

6 To practise using **ко́лко**, ask questions to which the following could be answers. Concentrate on the numbers involved and don't forget to repeat the prepositions.

a В хоте́ла и́ма две америка́нки.
b Г-н Джо́нсън е в Бълга́рия за две се́дмици.
c Брат ми присти́га след че́тири дни.

d Г-н и г-жá Кóлинс са в Сóфия от три дни.
e Автобу́сът заминáва в дéсет часá.
f Днес и́маш три съобщéния и две кáртички (*postcards*).
g Г-н Джóнсън и́ма две децá.

7 Do you take sugar (**зáхар**) and milk (**мля́ко**)? Read and then answer the questions:

Секретáрката Нáдя пи́е (*is drinking*) кафé с Николáй и Милéна. Нáдя пи́е кафéто с мáлко зáхар. Николáй и́ска кафé с мнóго зáхар, а Милéна и́ска кафé без зáхар. Те оби́чат (*like*) кафéто с мáлко мля́ко.

a Каквó прáви Нáдя?
b С кóлко зáхар пи́е кафéто Нáдя?
c С кóлко зáхар пи́е кафéто Николáй?
d Каквó кафé и́ска Милéна?
e Как оби́чат те кафéто – с мнóго или́ с мáлко мля́ко?
f Как оби́чате кафéто Ви́е?

Expressions to use

със зáхар *with sugar* (when **с** is used before a word beginning with **с** or **з** it is extended to **със** – remember what happened to **в** before **в** and **ф**?)

без зáхар, с мнóго зáхар, с мáлко зáхар, с мнóго мáлко зáхар *(with very little sugar)*

8 Continuing the milk and sugar theme, this exercise will help you practise different ways of saying the same thing. The short dialogues on the left below present situations identical to those on the right. Complete the right-hand column using the model. Don't forget to use the short definite form with **чай**.

Тури́стка	Чáят е със зáхар, нали́?	В чáя и́ма зáхар, нали́?
Сервитьóрка	Да, с мáлко зáхар.	Да, и́ма мáлко зáхар.
Тури́стка	Кафéто е със зáхар, нали́?	**a** ________
Сервитьóрка	Да, с мáлко зáхар.	________
Тури́стка	Кафéто е с мля́ко, нали́?	**b** ________
Сервитьóрка	Да, с мáлко мля́ко.	________
Тури́стка	Чáят е с мля́ко, нали́?	**c** ________
Сервитьóрка	Да, с мáлко мля́ко.	________

9 You can also use **нали́** in negative questions. Try it here, adapting the statements with **без**. Notice that the answer can be with **не** or **да**.

Тури́стка	Ча́ят е без мля́ко, нали́?	**В ча́я ня́ма мля́ко, нали́?**
Сервитьо́рка	Да, без мля́ко е.	**Не, ня́ма/ Да, ня́ма.**
Тури́стка	Кафе́то е без мля́ко, нали́?	**a** ________
Сервитьо́рка	Да, без мля́ко е.	________
Тури́стка	Кафе́то е без за́хар, нали́?	**b** ________
Сервитьо́рка	Да, без за́хар е.	________
Тури́стка	Ча́ят е без за́хар, нали́?	**c** ________
Сервитьо́рка	Да, без за́хар е.	________

10 Use the words in brackets in the plural:

a Г-н и г-жа́ Ко́линс и́скат ста́я с две ______ (легло́ *bed*).
b Г-н и г-жа́ Ко́линс са ______ (чуждене́ц).
c ______ ли са г-н и г-жа́ Ко́линс? (америка́нец).
d Ма́йкъл Джо́нсън не и́ска бъ́лгарски ______ (ве́стник).
e Никола́й и́ма мно́го ______ (въпро́с).
f Ма́йкъл Джо́нсън разби́ра мно́го ______ (ези́к).
g В ЦУМ и́ма мно́го ______ (продава́чка *shop assistant* f).
h На булева́рд Ви́тоша и́ма спи́рка на ______ но́мер 1, 7 и 9 (трамва́й).
i В сладка́рницата и́ма мно́го ______ (чужденка́ *foreigner* f).

11 Finally, to practise using the full and short definite article, answer the following questions, using the words in brackets with the preposition **до**:

a Къде́ е о́фисът? (ресторa̍нт)
b Къде́ е ресторa̍нтът? (о́фис)
c Къде́ е магази́нът? (теа́тър *theatre*)
d Къде́ е те́атърът? (магази́н)
e Къде́ е музе́ят? (парк *park*)
f Къде́ е па́ркът? (музе́й)

Do you understand?

Dialogue 2: В о́фиса *In the office*

Mr Antonov has some good news for Nikolai.

г-н Анто́нов Никола́й, запове́дай в о́фиса.

Никола́й	Благодаря́.
г-н Анто́нов	И́мам ху́бава новина́. Замина́ваш за А́нглия.
Никола́й	Но аз не разби́рам англи́йски!
г-н Анто́нов	О, програми́ст без англи́йски не мо́же.
Никола́й	Така́ е, зна́я...
г-н Анто́нов	Ни́що. Във фи́рмата и́ма еди́н англича́нин, ко́йто разби́ра ма́лко бъ́лгарски.
Никола́й	Мно́го интере́сно! В кой град е фи́рмата?
г-н Анто́нов	В Че́лмсфорд.
Никола́й	Не зна́я къде́ е Че́лмсфорд.
г-н Анто́нов	Че́лмсфорд е ма́лък град бли́зо до Ло́ндон.
Никола́й	Нов прое́кт ли и́маме с фи́рмата?
г-н Анто́нов	Да, рабо́тим с англи́йски специали́сти.
Никола́й	Чуде́сно! Кога́ замина́вам?
г-н Анто́нов	След три се́дмици.
Никола́й	За ко́лко дни?
г-н Анто́нов	За два́йсет дни. Ху́бава новина́, нали́?
Никола́й	Разби́ра се. Благодаря́ мно́го!

запове́дай в о́фиса!	*come into the office*
новина́	*(piece of) news*
замина́вам, -ваш	*to leave/depart*
англи́йски	*English (language)*
програми́ст без англи́йски не мо́же	*a programmer can't do without English*
ни́що	*no matter, never mind*
зна́я, -а́еш	*to know*
кой град	*which town*
ма́лък, ма́лка	*small, little*
нов прое́кт	*a new project*
специали́ст	*specialist*

True or false?

Write out correct versions of the false statements.

1 Никола́й замина́ва за Шотла́ндия.
2 Той разби́ра англи́йски добре́.
3 Еди́н англича́нин от фи́рмата разби́ра вси́чко на бъ́лгарски.
4 Фи́рмата е в Че́стърфийлд.
5 Фи́рмата е в ма́лък град бли́зо до Ло́ндон.
6 Никола́й не зна́е къде́ е Че́лмсфорд.
7 Прое́ктът с фи́рмата не е́ нов.
8 Той замина́ва след де́сет дни.

In this unit you will learn:

- **how to ask people if they speak your language**
- **how to ask people what languages they speak**
- **how to say what languages you know**

Dialogue 1

Although you do not need a third person to introduce you to someone in Bulgaria, Nevena's natural Bulgarian curiosity enables the English hotel guests to get to know one another.

Невéна	Г-н Джóнсън, знáете ли, че в хотéла ѝма и дрýги англичáни?
г-н Джóнсън	Нѝщо чýдно. Англичáни ѝма в мнóго странѝ по светá.
Невéна	Но не мнóго англичáни говóрят бъ́лгарски! Вѝе говóрите бъ́лгарски добрé, но г-жá Кóлинс говóри пó-добрé.
г-н Джóнсън	Кой говóри пó-добрé?
Невéна	Г-жá Кóлинс.
г-н Джóнсън	Но коя́ е г-жá Кóлинс? Не зная́ коя́ е тя.
Невéна	Говóря за англичáнката, коя́то живéе в стáя нóмер дéсет.
г-н Джóнсън	А Вѝе говóрите ли англѝйски, Невéна?
Невéна	За съжалéние, не. Но говóря ня́колко дрýги езѝка.
г-н Джóнсън	Каквѝ езѝци знáете?
Невéна	Фрéнски, рýски и испáнски. Фрéнски е езѝкът, кóйто знáя нáй-добрé.
г-н Джóнсън	Мнóго бъ́лгари говóрят чýжди езѝци.
Невéна	Товá е вя́рно. А, éто г-н и г-жá Кóлинс! (*Calls out to them.*) Г-н Кóлинс, г-жá Кóлинс, извинéте за минýта!
г-жá Кóлинс	Разбѝра се, госпóжице. Здравéйте!
Невéна	Мóля, запознáйте се. Товá е господѝн Джóнсън, англѝйски бизнесмéн, кóйто живéе в Чéлмсфорд.
г-жá Кóлинс	Мнóго ми е прия́тно!
г-н Кóлинс	(*Echoing Mrs Collins in Bulgarian.*) Прия́тно ми е!
Невéна	(*Aside.*) Кóлко интерéсно! Англичáни, кóито говóрят бъ́лгарски!

дрýги англичáни	*other English people*
Нѝщо чýдно.	*(That's) hardly surprising.*
по светá	*in the world*
Но не мнóго англичáни говóрят бъ́лгарски.	*But not many English people speak Bulgarian.*
Вѝе говóрите бъ́лгарски добрé, но г-жá Кóлинс говóри пó-добрé.	*You speak Bulgarian well, but Mrs Collins speaks better.*

Кой гово́ри по́-добре́?	*Who speaks better?*
Но коя́ е г-жа́ Ко́линс?	*But who is Mrs Collins?*
Не зна́я.	*I don't know.*
Гово́ря за англича́нката, коя́то живе́е в ста́я но́мер де́сет.	*I'm speaking about the English woman who is staying in room number ten.*
А Ви́е гово́рите ли англи́йски?	*And do you speak English?*
за съжале́ние	*unfortunately*
Но гово́ря ня́колко дру́ги ези́ка.	*But I speak several other languages.*
Какви́ ези́ци зна́ете?	*What languages do you know?*
фре́нски	*French*
ру́ски	*Russian*
испа́нски	*Spanish*
Фре́нски е ези́кът, ко́йто зна́я на́й-добре́.	*French is the language I know best.*
Мно́го бъ́лгари гово́рят чу́жди ези́ци.	*A lot of Bulgarians speak foreign languages.*
Това́ е вя́рно.	*That's true.*
извине́те за мину́та	*excuse me, just a minute*
англи́йски бизнесме́н, ко́йто живе́е в Че́лмсфорд	*an English businessman who lives in Chelmsford*
Ко́лко интере́сно!	*How interesting!*
Англича́ни, ко́йто гово́рят бъ́лгарски!	*English people who speak Bulgarian!*

1 Questions

a Къде́ и́ма англича́ни?
b Какъ́в чужд ези́к гово́ри г-жа́ Ко́линс мно́го добре́?
c Коя́ е г-жа́ Ко́линс?
d Ко́лко ези́ка гово́ри Неве́на?
e Какви́ ези́ци зна́е Неве́на?
f Къде́ живе́е г-н Джо́нсън?

2 True or false?

Write out correct versions of the false statements.

a Мно́го англича́ни гово́рят бъ́лгарски.
b Г-жа́ Ко́линс е америка́нката, коя́то живе́е в ста́я но́мер де́сет.
c Г-жа́ Ко́линс гово́ри бъ́лгарски мно́го добре́.
d Неве́на не зна́е англи́йски.
e Тя гово́ри ру́ски на́й-добре́.
f Ма́лко бъ́лгари гово́рят чу́жди ези́ци.

Does anyone speak English?

You should already be able to cope using your Bulgarian in a number of different situations. However, you will be reassured to know that English is now quite widely spoken in Bulgaria, especially by the younger generation in the larger towns. You will usually find English-speakers on the reception desks of big hotels, in money-changing bureaux, in tourist and airline offices and also in the more prestigious places for eating out. When speaking English, they will most probably shake their head for **не** and nod for **да** (see p. xx). With shop-assistants, taxi drivers and policemen, however, although you might still venture a timid **говóрите ли английски?** you would probably do best to resort to your Bulgarian straightaway.

Big or small? When to use capital letters

Bulgarian uses far fewer capital letters than English. The names of nationalities and the national languages all begin with small letters. You will therefore find, for example, **америкáнец, америкáнка (америкáнски)**; **англичáнин, англичáнка (английски)**; **испáнец, испáнка (испáнски** – *Spanish*); **италиáнец, италиáнка (италиáнски** – *Italian*); **нéмец, немкúня (нéмски** – *German*), and **францýзин, французóйка (фрéнски** – *French*).

Names of places begin with capital letters, but when the place name consists of more than one word, the second often begins with a small letter: **Злáтни пя́съци** (*Golden Sands*), **Слъ́нчев бряг** (*Sunny Beach*) and **Чéрно морé** (*the Black Sea*).

Adjectives formed from the names of places also begin with small letters: Лóндон: **лóндонски**, Сóфия: **софийски**, Вáрна: **вáрненски**.

Giving your phone number

In Bulgarian, as in English, there is no single pattern for writing or reading out the individual digits in phone numbers. Some speakers group the digits in pairs, others in threes, depending on the amount of digits in the number. However, the need for ever-increasing strings of numbers, coupled with the widespread use of mobile phones (**мобúлен телефóн** or **GSM** – the last written using English letters and pronounced **джиесéм**), means that the simplest way to give your phone number is by reading out the individual digits, one by one.

When you answer the phone, it's best to follow the Bulgarian practice and, without giving your name, say '**Áло?**' or '**Да, мóля?**' or just

'Да?' and wait for the person making the call to open the conversation.

When making a call yourself, be prepared to respond to an answerphone (**телефóнен секретáр** or just **секретáр** for short). The standard message goes something like this: **'Тук е телефóнният секретáр на...** [the name of the person]. **Мóля, оставéте съобщéние след сигнáла.'** ('*This is the answerphone of... Please leave your message after the beep.*')

ФОТО
СТУДИО ИНДЕР
БЛ.111 ВХ.Б ЕТ.2
ТЕЛ. 847 89 47

Abbreviations used in this sign are: БЛ. = блок (*block*), ВХ. = вход (*entrance*), ЕТ. = етáж (*floor*) and ТЕЛ. = телефóн (*telephone*).

How do you say it?

- Asking whether a person speaks a foreign language

Говóрите ли английски?	*Do you speak English?*
Знáете ли фрéнски?	*Do you speak (know) French?*
Какъ̀в (чужд) ези́к говóрите/знáете?	*What (foreign) language do you speak/know?*
Какви́ (чу́жди) ези́ци говóрите?	*What (foreign) languages do you speak?*

- Answering whether, and how well, you speak a language

Говóря добрé фрéнски.	*I speak French well.*
Разби́рам испáнски, но не говóря добрé.	*I understand Spanish but I don't speak (it) well.*
Знáя мáлко ру́ски.	*I know a little Russian.*
Не разби́рам бъ̀лгарски.	*I don't understand Bulgarian.*
Говóря фрéнски нáй-добрé.	*I speak French best.*

- Responding to what you hear

Товá е вя́рно.	*That's true.*
Ни́що чу́дно.	*(That's) hardly surprising.*

- Expressing interest, agreement or regret

Кóлко интерéсно!	*How interesting!*
разби́ра се	*of course/naturally*
за съжалéние	*unfortunately/sadly*

Grammar

1 Some plurals

Nationalities and masculine nouns ending in -(н)ин

This is one of the endings that form names of nationalities or inhabitants of a place. The plural of such names is once again **-и**, but it is not added to the singular. Instead, the **-н** of the singular is dropped:

англичáнин	*Englishman*	англичáни	*Englishmen*
българин	*Bulgarian*	българи	*Bulgarians*
грáжданин	*citizen*	грáждани	*citizens*
лондончáнин	*Londoner*	лондончáни	*Londoners*

Plural of adjectives and other defining words

In the plural, no matter what the gender of the noun they describe, all adjectives in Bulgarian end in **-и**. Compare:

чужд ези́к	*a foreign language*	чу́жди ези́ци	*foreign languages*
чу́жда странá	*a foreign country*	чу́жди страни́	*foreign countries*
чу́ждо списáние	*a foreign magazine*	чу́жди списáния	*foreign magazines*

Similarly, you will find the **-и** ending in **какви́** (*what*), the plural form of **какъ́в, каквá, каквó**:

Какъ́в ези́к говóрите?	*What language do you speak?*
Какви́ ези́ци говóрите?	*What languages do you speak?*

Adjectives which end in **-ски** in the masculine singular remain the same in the plural:

англи́йски ве́стник	*an English newspaper*
америка́нски бизнесме́н	*an American businessman*
бъ́лгарски куро́рт	*a Bulgarian resort*
ру́ски гра́жданин	*a Russian citizen*
англи́йски ве́стници	*English newspapers*
америка́нски бизнесме́ни	*American businessmen*
бъ́лгарски куро́рти	*Bulgarian resorts/spas*
ру́ски гра́ждани	*Russian citizens*

2 Друг/дру́ги *Another/other*

друг, дру́га, дру́го	*another*
дру́ги	*other*
не́що дру́го	*something else*

3 Special masculine plural after numbers

In the dialogue you came across two plurals of **ези́к** *language*, one ending in **-и** and the other in **-а**:

Какви́ **ези́ци** зна́ете?	*What languages do you know?*
Зна́я ня́колко **ези́ка**.	*I know several languages.*

The first is the regular plural, (remember the change of **-к** to **-ц**!). The second is the plural form used after any number or after the word **ня́колко** *several*. This plural form only occurs in masculine nouns for things and always ends in **-а** or **-я**. If the noun refers to people, you use the regular plural: **ня́колко учи́тели** *several teachers*. Examples:

Нев́ена зна́е **три ези́ка**.	*Nevena knows three languages.*
Де́сет биле́та, мо́ля.	*Ten tickets, please.*
В Га́брово и́ма **ня́колко музе́я.**	*In Gabrovo there are several museums.*

You must also use this special numerical masculine plural in questions after **ко́лко** *how many*:

Ко́лко ези́ка зна́е Неве́на?	*How many languages does Nevena know?*
Ко́лко биле́та и́скате, мо́ля?	*How many tickets do you want, please?*
Ко́лко музе́я и́ма в Га́брово?	*How many museums are there in Gabrovo?*

4 Говóря *I speak*

This is an **и**-pattern, Conjugation 2 verb:

аз	говóря	*I speak*	нúе	говóр**им**	*we speak*
ти	говóр**иш**	*you speak*	вúе	говóр**ите**	*you speak*
той / тя / то	говóр**и**	*he/she/it speaks*	те	говóрят	*they speak*

5 Знáя *I know*, игрáя *I play*, живéя *I live* (e-pattern verbs)

These verbs contain the vowel **-e-** in most of their present tense endings. They are examples of Conjugation 1, **e**-pattern verbs. Notice that once again the final vowel is the same in the *I* form and in the *they* form:

аз	знáя/игрáя/живéя	нúе	знá**ем**/игрá**ем**/живé**ем**
ти	знá**еш**/игрá**еш**/живé**еш**	вúе	знá**ете**/ игрá**ете**/живé**ете**
той / тя / то	знá**е**/ игрá**е**/живé**е**	те	знáят/игрáят/живéят

6 The present tense: patterns and meanings

To summarize, Bulgarian verbs have three patterns or conjugations:

Conjugation 1 verbs follow the **e**-pattern
Conjugation 2 verbs follow the **и**-pattern
Conjugation 3 verbs follow the **a**-pattern

The present tense in Bulgarian corresponds in meaning to two distinct tense forms in English. **Невéна говóри фрéнски** might mean, depending on the context, either *Nevena speaks French* or *Nevena is speaking French*. Similarly, **аз ýча бъ́лгарски** might mean either *I learn Bulgarian* or *I am learning Bulgarian*.

From now on in the vocabulary you will find all verbs given with the endings of both the *I* and the *you* forms (1st and 2nd singular). This will help you to identify the correct conjugation pattern. The endings of the *you* form will always be preceded by the letter to which the endings for the other forms need to be added:

Conjugation 1 живéя, -éеш; пúя, -úеш (*I drink*)
Conjugation 2 говóря, -риш; мúсля, -лиш (*I think*); ýча, -чиш (*I learn*)*
Conjugation 3 дáвам, -ваш (*I give*); запóчвам, -ваш; разбúрам, -раш
*After **ж**, **ч** and **ш** the **-я** in all the *I* and *they* forms appears as **-а**.

And pronunciation too...

The **-я, -ят** and **-а, -ат** endings of the *I* and *they* forms of Conjugation 1 and 2 verbs are pronounced **-йъ, -йът** and **-ъ, -ът**.

7 Кой? *Who?*

The question word for *who* in Bulgarian is **кой**. It stands in place of a noun and you use it to ask for the subject of a sentence no matter whether the subject is masculine, feminine, neuter or even plural.

Мáйкъл Джóнсън живéе в Чéлмсфорд.
Кой живéе в Чéлмсфорд? — ***Who** lives in Chelmsford?*
Г-жá Кóлинс говóри бъ́лгарски пó-добрé.
Кой говóри бъ́лгарски пó-добрé? — ***Who** speaks Bulgarian better?*
Мнóго бъ́лгари говóрят чýжди ези́ци.
Кой говóри чýжди ези́ци? — ***Who** speaks foreign languages?*

8 Кой? коя́? коé? and кои́? *Which?*

Кой also means *which* when used before a noun and then it has a different form for each of the three genders and for the plural:

Masculine
Кой? В кой град е фи́рмата? — *Which town is the firm in?*
Кой ези́к говóрите нáй-добрé? — *Which language do you speak best?*

Feminine
Коя́? В коя́ стáя сте? — *Which room are you in?*

Neuter
Коé? Коé списáние и́скате? — *Which magazine do you want?*

Plural
Кои́? Кои́ ези́ци знáете? — *Which languages do you know?*

When a feminine, neuter or plural noun (or pronoun) is mentioned in the question itself, the correct alternative form of **кой** has to be used, no matter whether it means *who* or *which*:

Коя́ е г-жá Кóлинс? — *Which one is Mrs Collins?*
Коé е товá детé? — *Who is that child?*
Кои́ са те? — *Who are they?* or *Which are they?*

9 Госпожáта, коя́то... *The woman who...*

In expressions like these, the words *who* and *which* relate to the last person or thing mentioned. They are called relative pronouns. In

Bulgarian, you have to concentrate not on the distinction between persons and things, but rather on whether the preceding noun is masculine, feminine, neuter or plural. In the singular, you have to use **кóйто** (кой+то) for masculine, **коя́то** (коя́+то) for feminine and **коéто** (коé+то) for neuter nouns. The plural form is **който** (кой+то). All the forms must be preceded by a comma:

Masculine
Товá е господи́нът, кóйто говóри български. — *This is the man who speaks Bulgarian.*

Feminine
Госпожáта, коя́то присти́га днес, ý чи български. — *The woman who arrives/is arriving today is learning Bulgarian.*

Neuter
Детéто, коéто говóри, е синъ́т на г-н Антóнов. — *The child who is speaking is Mr Antonov's son.*

Plural
Г-н и г-жá Кóлинс са англичáни, който живéят в Мáнчестър. — *Mr and Mrs Collins are English people living/ who live/in Manchester.*

Note that in English you can sometimes omit the words *who* and *which*. In Bulgarian the relative pronoun can *never* be omitted.

10 Аз знáя, че... *I know that...*

Че is the Bulgarian equivalent of *that*. It is used as the connecting word (conjunction) after certain verbs and, unlike *that*, can never be omitted. It must always be preceded by a comma:

Аз знáя, **че** Сóфия е стóлицата на България. — *I know (that) Sofia is the capital of Bulgaria.*
Знáете ли, **че** мнóго българи говóрят англи́йски? — *Do you know (that) many Bulgarians speak English?*

11 Comparison of doing *well*, *better* or *best of all*

In Bulgarian, when you want to compare the way in which something is done, you change the adverb, in this case **добрé** (*well*), by adding **пó-** and **нáй-** on the front. You add **пó-** when comparing the way in which two things are done and **нáй-** when you want to compare more than two. The **пó-** and **нáй-** are pronounced with an emphasis and in the book we will add a stress mark to remind you of this. Examples:

Г-н Джóнсън говóри български **добрé**, но г-жá Кóлинс говóри **пó-добрé**. — *Mr Johnson speaks Bulgarian* ***well****, but Mrs Collins speaks* ***better****.*
Невéна говóри ня́колко ези́ка, но знáе фрéнски **нáй-добрé**. — *Nevena speaks several languages, but knows French* ***best of all****.*

In the same way, the adverbs **бли́зо** *near* and **бързо** *quickly*, *fast* become:

пó-бли́зо	*nearer*	**нáй-бли́зо**	*nearest* (of all)
пó-бързо	*more quickly*	**нáй-бързо**	*quickest* (of all)

In Bulgarian, you use **от** in comparisons much as you use *than* in English:

Г-жá Кóлинс говóри български **пó-добрé от** г-н Джóнсън. — *Mrs Collins speaks Bulgarian* ***better than*** *Mr Johnson.*
Г-жá Кóлинс говóри **пó-бързо от** г-н Джóнсън. — *Mrs Collins speaks* ***more quickly than*** *Mr Johnson.*

Exercises

1 Turn the following sentences into questions requiring the answer 'yes' or 'no' by making the words in bold type the focus of your questions. Remember to put the verb immediately after the question word **ли**.

Model: Г-жá Кóлинс е **англичáнка. Англичáнка ли** е г-жá Кóлинс? Да.

- **a** В хотéла и́ма **мнóго англичáни**.
- **b** **Мнóго българи** говóрят английски.
- **c** Г-н Антóнов и Николáй са **българи**.
- **d** Във фи́рмата рабóтят **българи и англичáни**.
- **e** Г-н и г-жá Кóлинс са **англичáни**.

2 The following questions may be useful when you want to ask for something else, or something different, using the Bulgarian equivalent of *another* or *other*. Use **друг**, **дрýга**, **дрýго** or **дрýги** as appropriate:

- **a** Ймате ли _______ въпрóси?
- **b** Каквó _______ ви́но и́мате?
- **c** Къдé и́ма _______ бáнка?
- **d** Какви́ _______ ези́ци говóрите?

e Йма ли _______ банкомáт (*cashpoint, ATM*) до хотéла?
f Каквú _______ цигáри (*cigarettes*) úмате?
g Когá úма _______ автобýс за Мальóвица?
h Ймате ли _______ детé?
i Знáете ли къдé úма _______ аптéка?
j Ймате ли _______ свобóдни местá?

3 A tourist, map in hand, stops a passer-by and asks which of two places on the map is closer:

i Тук на кáртата úма два хотéла. Кой (хотéл) е пó-блúзо?

How would you ask about:

a ресторáнт
b град
c курóрт
d къмпинг (*campsite*)
e мотéл (*motel*)

When asking the same question about places which are feminine, remember, you have to use **кoя́**:

ii На кáртата úма две туристúчески агéнции. Коя́ (агéнция) е пó-блúзо?

How would you ask the same question about:

a аптéка
b бензиностáнция (*petrol station*)
c спúрка

4 Use **кой** or **коя́** as appropriate:

a ____ град е на́й-бли́зо до куро́рта Зла́тни пя́съци?
b ____ трамва́й е на́й-бли́зо до у́лица Рако́вски?
c ____ спи́рка е на́й-бли́зо до га́рата (*railway station*)?
d ____ магази́н е на́й-бли́зо до хоте́л „Ше́ратон"?
e ____ туристи́ческа аге́нция е на́й-бли́зо до спи́рката?
f ____ су́пермаркет (*supermarket*) е на́й-бли́зо до по́щата?

5 Ask questions with **ко́лко**, remembering to put the subject at the end of the question, as in the model: Г-н и г-жа́ Ко́линс и́скат два ча́я. Ко́лко ча́я и́скат г-н и г-жа́ Ко́линс?

a Неве́на гово́ри три чу́жди ези́ка.
b Те и́скат де́сет биле́та.
c Сервитьо́рът серви́ра (*serves*) три джи́на.
d Ма́йкъл Джо́нсън зна́е ня́колко чу́жди ези́ка.

6 In this exercise you need to change a word from the normal masculine plural form to the special numerical plural. (The two forms are often used very near to one another.)

Тури́ст Извине́те, и́ма ли магази́ни до га́рата?
Гра́жданин Да, до га́рата и́ма ня́колко магази́на.

Compose similar questions and answers to the above model using:

a хоте́л
b рестора́нт
c музе́й
d о́фис

7 Choose the correct combinations to make sentences:

(*a*)
Позна́вам
мъжа́, коéто живе́е в ста́я но́мер де́сет.
жена́та, ко́йто присти́га от Ло́ндон.
англича́ни, коя́то гово́ри ху́баво бъ́лгарски.
семе́йството, които живе́ят в Бълга́рия.

(*b*)
Позна́ваш ли
бъ́лгарина, коя́то е омъ́жена за англича́нин?
англича́ни, които не пи́ят уиски?
шотла́ндци, ко́йто замина́ва за А́нглия?
бъ́лгарката, които са же́нени за бъ́лгарки?

8 This exercise draws your attention to the fact that what looks like the same masculine form may have two distinct meanings. For instance, **хоте́ла** can be either *the hotel*, in the non-subject form, or, when used after numerals, *hotels*.

Compare: Товá е хотéлът.
with: Éто хотéла. *Here's the hotel.*
Éто два хотéла. *Here are two hotels.*

Using the examples as a model, practise pointing to one or two of the following:

a трамвáй **c** автобýс **e** компю́тър
b тролéй **d** къмпинг **f** банкомáт

You will see from the example that after **éто** you need to add the short definite article to the noun.

9 Michael Johnson writes down his home address and shows it to Nevena saying: **Éто адрéса ми.**

What would you say while showing or pointing to the following?

a your ticket
b your passport
c your husband
d your son
e your luggage (**багáж**)

10 This exercise will help you practise checking whether, when your correspondent answers the phone with '**Áло?**' or '**Да, мóля?**', you have got the right number. Read the short dialogue **На телефóна** (*On the telephone*) out loud:

Извинéте, 947 54 26 ли е? (дéвет, чéтири, сéдем, пет, чéтири, две, шест)
Да, кажéте! (*Yes, can I help you?*)

Now repeat, using the following numbers: 0888 32 18 91; 0898 15 67 32; 789 02 66.

Do you understand?

Dialogue 2: Ýча английски *I'm studying English*

Milena goes into the office and sees Nikolai who seems busy at the computer.

Милéна Здравéй, Николáй. Каквó прáвиш?
Николáй Ýча английски по ѝнтернет. Ти знáеш ли английски?
Милéна Да, но не мнóго добрé. Мѝсля, че е мнóго трýден езѝк.
Николáй И аз такá мѝсля. Ѝмам нýжда от учѝтел. Познáваш ли учѝтели по английски?
Милéна О да, познáвам някολко учѝтели, който живéят блѝзо.

Николáй	Чудéсно. Ѝмам нýжда и от учéбници по английски.
Милéна	Аз ѝмам два учéбника и някoлко компáктдиска. Ѝмам същo фѝлми без прéвод на дѝвидѝ.
Николáй	Мнóго добрé, но ѝмам мнóго мáлко врéме.
Милéна	Не сé оплáквай! Вéче сме в Еврóпа, налѝ? Сегá децá на чéтири-пéт годѝни ýчат чужд езѝк.
Николáй	Мѝсля, че вéче съм стар за чýжди езѝци.
Милéна	На кóлко годѝни си?
Николáй	На двáйсет и шест.
Милéна	Е да, вярно, мнóго си стар...

трýден, трýдна	*difficult*
такá	*so, likewise*
ѝмам нýжда от	*I need*
учéбник, -ици	*textbook*
компáктдиск	*CD*
прéвод	*translation*
филм	*film*
дѝвидѝ	*DVD*
Не сé оплáквай	*Don't complain*
Еврóпа	*Europe*
стар	*old*
на кóлко годѝни си?	*how old are you?*

True or false?

Write out correct versions of the false statements.

1. Николáй ýчи фрéнски.
2. Николáй ѝма нýжда от учѝтел.
3. Милéна не познáва учѝтели по английски.
4. Милéна ѝма три учéбника по английски.
5. Николáй няма нýжда от учéбници.
6. Николáй мѝсли, че е вéче стар за чýжди езѝци.
7. Николáй е на трѝйсет и шест годѝни.

и́скате ли да...?

would you like to...?

In this unit you will learn:

- **how to say *would you like to...?* and *may I...?***
- **how to answer to *would you like to...?* and *may I...?***
- **how to say you *must* or *have to* do something**

Dialogue 1

Michael Johnson is keeping his appointment with Boyan Antonov at the advertising agency.

г-н Джо́нсън (*Knocking on the office door and going in.*) Мо́же ли? До́бър ден! Ка́звам се Ма́йкъл Джо́нсън.

На́дя О, г-н Джо́нсън, добре́ дошли́! Мо́ля, запове́дайте.

г-н Джо́нсън Благодаря́. Тук ли е г-н Анто́нов? Аз и́мам сре́ща с не́го.

На́дя Да, разби́ра се. Г-н Анто́нов Ви ча́ка.

г-н Джо́нсън (*At the door into the director's office.*) Мо́же ли?

г-н Анто́нов Запове́дайте, г-н Джо́нсън. Седне́те! Ра́двам се да се запозна́я с Вас.

г-н Джо́нсън Аз също.

г-н Анто́нов Как се чу́вствате в Со́фия? Надя́вам се, че сте дово́лен от хоте́ла.

г-н Джо́нсън Да, всичко е наре́д.

г-н Анто́нов И́скате ли да обя́дваме за́едно?

г-н Джо́нсън Разби́ра се, ня́мам ни́що проти́в. Мо́же ли първо да оти́дем в ба́нката? Тря́бва да обменя́ пари́.

г-н Анто́нов Ня́ма пробле́ми. Ба́нката не е́ дале́че, а рестора́нтът е до не́я.

г-н Джо́нсън Извиня́вайте, г-н Анто́нов, мо́же ли да гово́рите по́-ба́вно?

г-н Анто́нов Мо́же, разби́ра се. Ра́двам се, че ня́маме ну́жда от преводá́ч. Ми́сля, че Ви́е гово́рите български мно́го добре́.

г-н Джо́нсън Но аз и́скам да разби́рам български о́ще по́-добре́! И́скам да гово́ря по́-добре́ от г-жа́ Ко́линс.

Мо́же ли?	*May I (come in)?*
О, г-н Джо́нсън, добре́ дошли́!	*Oh, Mr Johnson, welcome!*
Мо́ля, запове́дайте.	*Please, do come in.*
Г-н Анто́нов Ви ча́ка.	*Mr Antonov is expecting you.*
Седне́те!	*Do sit down!*
Ра́двам се да се запозна́я с Вас.	*Pleased to/meet you/make your acquaintance.*
Аз също.	*So am I/Me too.*
Как се чу́вствате в Со́фия?	*How are you feeling in Sofia?*
Надя́вам се, че сте дово́лен от хоте́ла.	*I hope you are happy with the hotel.*
Да, всичко е наре́д.	*Yes, everything is fine.*

И́скате ли да обя́дваме за́едно?	*Would you like to have lunch together?*
Разби́ра се, ня́мам ни́що проти́в.	*Certainly, why not?*
Мо́же ли първо да оти́дем в ба́нката?	*Could we (possibly) go to the bank first?*
Тря́бва да обменя́ пари́.	*I have to change some money.*
Ня́ма пробле́ми.	*No problem.*
Ба́нката не е́ дале́че, а рестора́нтът е до не́я.	*The bank is not far and the restaurant is next to it.*
мо́же ли да гово́рите по́-ба́вно?	*could you (please) speak more slowly?*
Мо́же, разби́ра се.	*I can, of course.*
Ра́двам се, че ня́маме ну́жда от прево́да́ч.	*I am glad we do not need an interpreter.*
Но аз и́скам да разби́рам български о́ще по́-добре́!	*But I want to understand Bulgarian even better.*

1 Questions

- **a** Кой и́ма сре́ща с г-н Анто́нов?
- **b** Кой ча́ка г-н Джо́нсън?
- **c** И́ма ли г-н Джо́нсън пробле́ми в Со́фия?
- **d** Къде́ и́ска да оти́де първо г-н Джо́нсън?
- **e** Кой тря́бва да обмени́ пари́?
- **f** Как тря́бва да гово́ри г-н Анто́нов?

2 True or false?

- **a** Г-н Джо́нсън не е́ дово́лен от хоте́ла.
- **b** Г-н Анто́нов и́ска да обя́два за́едно с г-н Джо́нсън.
- **c** Ба́нката и рестора́нтът са дале́че от о́фиса.
- **d** Г-н Джо́нсън тря́бва да гово́ри по́-ба́вно.
- **e** Г-н Анто́нов и г-н Джо́нсън и́мат ну́жда от превода́ч.
- **f** Г-н Джо́нсън и́ска да разби́ра български по́-добре́.

i Responding to words of welcome

Мо́ля, you will remember, is the set response to **благодаря́**. The Bulgarians also have set formal responses to the traditional words of welcome **Добре́ дошъ́л!**, **Добре́ дошла́!** and **Добре́ дошли́!** These responses are **Добре́ зава́рил!**, **Добре́ зава́рила!** and **Добре́ зава́рили!** (lit. *Well met!*). Once again, notice, you use differing forms for the masculine, feminine and plural. Both the words of welcome, and the responses, which are often immediately preceded or followed by **благодаря́**, are used particularly when someone has arrived safely after a long journey. If you cannot manage the full responses, nowadays **благодаря́** will also suffice.

Knocking and entering

In the Dialogue at the beginning of this unit you will have noticed Mr Johnson knocked at the door to Nadya's office and immediately went in. In the English-speaking world, this would have been considered rude. Being in Bulgaria, however, he was right not to wait, for it is normal, especially in offices, to knock and enter immediately. When knocking and entering you would do well simultaneously to give out a **Мо́же ли?** in the hope that, if you are a stranger, someone will eventually respond, inviting you to state your business with a **Да, мо́ля?** or a **кажѐте**! *Can I help you?* (lit. *Say!*).

Changing money

Sooner or later (probably sooner rather than later), you will need to change some money. This is not difficult in Bulgaria, certainly not in the bigger towns and the main tourist resorts. You will find all manner of agencies, from the larger hotels and banks to numerous small 'change' bureaux, all keen to take your **валу́та** (*currency*) banknotes in exchange for the local Bulgarian *lev*. The 'change' bureaux are indicated by notices such as **ОБМЕ́ННО БЮРО́**, **ОБМЯ́НА НА ВАЛУ́ТА** or simply **CHANGE**. Travellers' cheques can only be exchanged in banks. All the banks and agencies should present you with a certificate of exchange, which you should check carefully before you leave against the sum paid out to you.

ОБМЕННО БЮРО

ВСИЧКИ СВЕТОВНИ ВАЛУТИ И МОНЕТИ
ALL WORLD CURRENCIES AND COINS

ВАЛУТА	БАНКНОТИ	
	КУПУВА	ПРОДАВА
EUR	1,94	1,95
USD	1,23	1,25
GBP	2,44	2,49
CHF	1,22	1,23
CYP	3,34	3,38
JPY	1,19	1,22
CAD	1,21	1,23
AUD	1,16	1,19

Before changing any money, make sure you know the exchange rates. These can differ considerably from dealer to dealer, but are clearly displayed. The boards list, from left to right, the currency to be exchanged, then the rate at which the bureau buys and sells for levs. Commission is not usually charged, but, like everything else, it's worth checking!

How do you say it?

- Saying *Welcome!*

To a man:	**Добре́ дошъ́л!**
To a woman:	**Добре́ дошла́!**
To more than one person (and polite):	**Добре́ дошли́!**

- Attracting attention

Мо́же ли?	*May I? Excuse me, but...*

- Requesting politely

Мо́же ли да говоря с Вас?	*May I have a word with you?*
Мо́же ли да оти́дем в ба́нката?	*Could we (possibly) go to the bank?*
Мо́же ли да гово́рите по́-ба́вно?	*Could you (please) speak more slowly?*

- Asking *May I..?/Can I..?* and responding to the same request

Мо́же ли да обменя́ пари́ тук?	*Can I change (some) money here?*
Да, мо́же.	*Yes, you can.*
Не, не мо́же.	*No, you can't.*

- Saying *I'm pleased to/that..., I'm glad...*

Ра́двам се да се запозна́я с Вас.	*Pleased to meet you.*
Ра́двам се, че вси́чко е наре́д.	*I'm pleased/glad everything is all right.*

- Expressing satisfaction with the state of affairs

Вси́чко е наре́д.	*Everything is fine.*
Ня́ма пробле́м(и).	*No problem(s).*

- Agreeing with a proposal

Ня́мам ни́що проти́в.	*Why not?/I don't mind if I do.*

- Saying *I need/don't need*

Ймам ну́жда от учи́тел.	*I need a teacher.*
Ня́мам ну́жда от превода́ч.	*I don't need an interpreter.*

Grammar

1 Йскам да *I want to*

Verbs like **йскам** *I want* and **трябва** *I must* need another verb to complete their meaning. When two (or more) verbs are combined in Bulgarian the second verb is introduced by **да**. (Do not confuse it with **да** meaning *yes*!) The **да** form of the Bulgarian verb corresponds to the English infinitive with or without *to*. An essential difference from English, however, is that the **да** form has personal endings just like a main verb.

The personal endings of the main verb and the **да** form may agree or be different, depending on the meaning:

(*a*) When the two verbs share the same subject, both agree with that subject. The following examples go through all the persons:

Йскам да **говóря** български пó-добрé.	*I want to speak Bulgarian better.*
Йскаш ли да **ýчиш** английски?	*Do you want to study English?*
Милéна **иска** да **отиде** в Áнглия.	*Milena wants to go to England.*
Ние **искаме** да **обменим** парú.	*We want to change some money.*
Йскате ли да **отидете** в бáнката?	*Do you want to go to the bank?*
Милéна и Николáй **искат** да **пият** кафé.	*Milena and Nikolai want to drink coffee.*

(*b*) When the two verbs have different subjects, each agrees with its own subject (although the subject word may be omitted!). In the dialogue Mr Antonov asks:

Йск**ате** ли да обяд**ваме** зáедно?

This literally means *Do* ***you*** *want that* ***we*** *have lunch together?* Now compare the two – with the same subject and with different subjects:

Иск**ам** да обяд**вам** с тях.	*I want to have lunch with them.*
Те иск**ат** да обяд**вам** с тях.	*They want me to have lunch with them.*
Той иск**а** да обяд**ва** с тях.	*He wants to have lunch with them.*
Той иск**а** да обяд**ваш** с тях.	*He wants you to have lunch with them.*

So, to make sure you clearly express who wants to do what with whom you have to choose the endings of the **да** form very carefully. One letter can make all the difference between who gets a meal and who doesn't!

2 Тря́бва да... *Must* or *have to...*

You use **тря́бва да** + verb for both *must* and *have to*. As with **мо́же ли да...?** below, **тря́бва да**... itself stays the same for all persons. The verb that follows changes to fit the subject, which is not always expressed. Again, therefore, you have to be very careful to listen for the ending of the verb to work out the correct meaning:

(аз)	тря́бва да оти́д**а** в Пло́вдив.	*I have to go to Plovdiv.*
(ти)	тря́бва да оти́д**еш** в по́щата.	***You** must go to the post office.*
Миле́на	тря́бва да се запозна́**е** с г-н Джо́нсън.	***Milena** must get to know Mr Johnson.*
(ни́е)	тря́бва да оти́д**ем** в ба́нката.	***We** have to go to the bank.*
(ви́е, Ви́е)	тря́бва да обмени́**те** пари́.	***You** must change some money.*
(те)	тря́бва да оти́д**ат** в о́фиса.	***They** have to go to the office.*

3 Мо́же ли...? *May I...? Could you...?*

Мо́же ли...? is a commonly used phrase which never changes its form. It is used to attract attention, to ask whether something is possible or permitted, or to make a polite request. (**Мо́же** is, in fact, the *it* form of the verb meaning *can* or *be able*.)

Мо́же ли on its own

Мо́же ли is used on its own to attract attention or to ask *Is it all right?* (for me to do this, that or the other), or *Could you?* (do this, that or the other for me). For instance, you say **Мо́же ли?** on its own:

(*a*) at the door when you want permission to go in
(*b*) when people are in your way and you want to get past
(*c*) when you need to interrupt someone

In a restaurant you use **мо́же ли** on its own just to attract the waiter's attention, or you may add another word to make your meaning clear:

Мо́же ли меню́то?	*Could you bring (pass etc.) the menu?*

Similarly, at table, if you want someone to pass something, the milk, for example, you would say:

Мо́же ли мля́кото?	*Could you pass (bring etc.) the milk?*

Мо́же ли да...? *May I...?*

This is used to ask if something is possible or permitted. **Мо́же ли да** + main verb is used to formulate full questions. When the main verb involves the speaker (*I* or *we*), **Мо́же ли да...?** can be used to ask for permission, in which case the answer will be **Мо́же,** or **Да, мо́же** and, if you are unlucky, **Не мо́же**, or **Не, не мо́же**.

Мо́же ли да говоря́ с г-н Анто́нов?	*Can I speak to Mr Antonov?*
Не, сега́ не мо́же.	*No, it isn't possible now.*
Мо́же ли да оти́дем в ба́нката?	*Could we (possibly) go to the bank?*
Мо́же, разби́ра се.	*We could, of course.*
Мо́же ли да се́днем до вас?	*Can we sit next to you?*
Разби́ра се, заповя́дайте!	*Certainly, go ahead!*

Мо́же ли да гово́рите по́-ба́вно? *Could you please speak more slowly?*

When the main verb is addressed to someone else, in the 2nd person singular or plural, **Мо́же ли да...?** is used to make a polite request:

Мо́же ли да гово́риш по́-ба́вно?	*Would you please speak more slowly?*
Мо́же ли да се оба́дите по́-късно?	*Could you please ring/ call later?*

4 A bit more about verbs

Note that some verbs can only be used in the present tense when preceded by a **да**. You will learn more about these verbs in Unit 12, but from now on when listed in the vocabulary they will all be preceded by **(да)**.

5 И́мам сре́ща с не́го *I've a meeting with him*

As in English, personal pronouns have different forms when they are not used as subjects, for instance after prepositions. Compare: *I have a meeting **with him*** (**аз и́мам сре́ща с не́го**), and ***he** has a meeting **with me*** (**той и́ма сре́ща с ме́не**). Both subject and non-subject (full) forms are given in the table side by side for comparison:

И́скате ли да обя́двате с ме́не?	*Would you like to have lunch with me?*
Г-н Джо́нсън и́ма сре́ща с не́го.	*Mr Johnson has a meeting with him.*
Това́ е ба́нката, а рестора́нтът е до не́я.	*That is the bank and the restaurant is next to it.*

Йма три писмá за Вас.	*There are three letters for you.*
Нáдя пúе кафé с тях.	*Nadya is drinking coffee with them.*

Subject forms		**Non-subject (full) forms**	
Singular	аз	с мéне	*with me*
	ти	от тéбе	*from you*
	той	с нéго	*with him*
	тя	от нéя	*from her*
	то	до нéго	*next to it*
Plural	нúе	до нас	*near us*
	вúе (Вúе)	с вас (Вас)	*with you*
	те	от тях	*from them*

NB You'll find more on non-subject forms in Units 7 and 11.

6 Getting to know one another

Verbs that are accompanied by the 'satellite' word **се** are known as reflexive verbs. One of the uses of a reflexive verb is to express the meaning *each other* or *one another*.

Sometimes the same verb can be used with and without **се** with different meanings. Compare the non-reflexive *without* **се**:

Невéна úска да запознáе г-н Джóнсън със семéйство Кóлинс.	*Nevena wants to introduce Mr Johnson to the Collins family.*
Г-н Джóнсън разбúра бѣлгарски.	*Mr Johnson understands Bulgarian.*

Now the same verbs used *with* **се**:

Николáй и Милéна úскат да се запознáят.	*Nikolai and Milena want to meet (one another).*
Г-н Антóнов и г-н Джóнсън се разбúрат без преводáч.	*Mr Antonov and Mr Johnson understand one another without an interpreter.*

A number of reflexive verbs, usually denoting feelings or emotions, never appear without **се**: **надя́вам се** *I hope*, **рáдвам се** *I am glad*. (There's more about reflexives in Unit 20.)

7 Where to place 'се'

Strict rules govern the position of **се**. Most importantly, it can never be the very first word in a sentence. Like a satellite it remains close to its verb, but:

(**a**) it comes before the verb if there are other words in first position such as pronouns, adverbs, question words or even little words like **да** in a **да** form or the negative **не**

(**b**) it follows the verb if the verb is the first word in the sentence:

Before the verb	**After the verb**
Той се надя́ва, че г-н Джо́нсън е дово́лен. *He hopes Mr Johnson is pleased.*	Надя́вам се, че сте дово́лен. *I hope you are pleased.*
Как се чу́вствате? *How do you feel?* Не се́ чу́вствам добре́. *I don't feel well.*	Чу́вствам се добре́. *I feel well.*

(The Appendix has a table to help you with word order.)

Exercises

1 Form short dialogues following the model:

- Имате ли резерва́ция?
– Не. Тря́бва ли да и́мам резерва́ция?
- Да, тря́бва.

Use **паро́ла** (*password*), **кре́дитна ка́рта** (*credit card*), **пи́нкод** (*PIN code*) instead of **резерва́ция**.

2 Using the model: Искате ли да оти́дем на рестора́нт? ask someone to go:

a to the opera
b to a concert
c to a café
d to a disco (**дискоте́ка**)
e to the theatre
f on an excursion (**екску́рзия**)
g skiing (**на ски**)
h to the beach (**плаж**)

Logo of the National Palace of Culture in Sofia, Национа́лен Дворе́ц на Култу́рата (НДК, pronounced 'еН-Де-Ка́')

3 You fear you have misheard an important telephone message. On the basis of the following questions and answers, see if you can write out the original message in just one sentence.

Кой тря́бва да оти́де в А́нглия? – Никола́й.
В кой град тря́бва да оти́де Никола́й? – в Че́лмсфорд.

Кога́ тря́бва да оти́де Никола́й в Че́лмсфорд? – След три се́дмици.

4 Which of the **мо́же ли?** questions might you use in the following situations. In some of them, a variety of questions may be appropriate.

i at the information desk	**a** Мо́же ли?
ii looking for a place in a restaurant	**b** Мо́же ли да гово́ря с Миле́на?
iii in a crowded bus	**c** Мо́же ли това́?
iv at table	**d** Мо́же ли да се́дна до Вас?
v pointing at something in a shop	**e** Мо́же ли да обменя́ пари́ тук?
vi asking for Milena on the phone	**f** Мо́же ли солта́? (*the salt*)
vii at the bank	**g** Мо́же ли една́ ка́рта на Со́фия?
viii entering a room	
ix attracting the attention of a waiter	

5 By using pronouns instead of the names and the nouns in the next two exercises you will be able to practise using the non-subject forms.

a Позна́ваш ли Неве́на? И́мам писмо́ от ____ .
b Позна́ваш ли Марк? И́мам сре́ща с ____ .
c Позна́ваш ли г-н и г-жа́ Ко́линс? И́ма биле́ти за ____ .

6 You are giving directions using a well-known place as a reference point. Complete with the appropriate personal pronoun:

a Зна́ете къде́ е ба́рът (*bar*), нали́? Кафе́то е до ____.
b Зна́ете къде́ е кафе́то, нали́? Дискоте́ката е до ____.
c Зна́ете къде́ е дискоте́ката, нали́? Бюро́ „Информа́ция“ е до ____.
d Зна́ете къде́ е бюро́ „Информа́ция“, нали́? По́щата е до ____.
e Зна́ете къде́ е по́щата, нали́? Музе́ят е до ____ .
f Зна́ете къде́ е музе́ят, нали́? Магази́нът е до ____ .

7 Introduce yourself, using тря́бва да и́ма (*there should be*), and ask for the things listed below.

Model: Ка́звам се ____ . Тря́бва да и́ма **ста́я** за ме́не.

биле́ти / писма́ / пока́на / ве́стници / ма́са (*table*)

8 Read the following text and make it into a conversation between Nikolai, Mr Antonov and Nadya. It will help you practise using verbs in the *I* form.

Никола́й и́ска да гово́ри с г-н Анто́нов. Г-н Анто́нов съжаля́ва, но сега́ ня́ма вре́ме за не́го. Той и́ма сре́ща с г-н Джо́нсън. На́дя пи́та (*asks*) и́ма ли г-н Анто́нов ну́жда от не́я. Г-н Анто́нов ми́сли, че те ня́мат ну́жда от преводач. Той пи́та На́дя мо́же ли да напра́ви (*make*) кафе́ за тях. На́дя ня́ма ни́що проти́в.

9 This exercise will help you ask for things you might need. Prefacing your answer by Ймам ну́жда от, use the words listed below to reply to the question: От какво́ и́мате ну́жда?

a ютия́

b чадъ́р

c коли́чка

d такси́

e носа́ч

f пари́

10 Now for a few useful reflexives. Complete the following sentences without forgetting to alter the position of **се**. Here is a model to guide you:

Ра́двам се да се запозна́я с Вас! – И аз **се ра́двам**.

a Надя́вам се да оти́да във Ва́рна. – И аз ______
b Ра́двам се, че замина́ваш за А́нглия. – И аз ______
c Чу́вствам се добре́. – И аз ______

Do you understand?

Dialogue 2: Зае́та ли си? *Are you busy?*

(*The telephone rings.*)

Nadya asks a client to ring back later, and the office staff arrange to meet up after work.

На́дя Да, мо́ля?
Клие́нт А́ло, мо́же ли да гово́ря с дире́ктора г-н Анто́нов?
На́дя Съжаля́вам, г-н Анто́нов е зае́т в моме́нта. Мо́же ли да се оба́дите пак?
Клие́нт Кога́ да се оба́дя?
На́дя По́-къ́сно следо́бед, мо́ля.
Клие́нт Благодаря́. Дочу́ване.
Никола́й Дире́кторът с г-н Джо́нсън ли е?
На́дя Да, ти тря́бва да се запозна́еш с не́го.
Никола́й По́-късно. Сега́ г-н Джо́нсън и г-н Анто́нов са зае́ти.
На́дя Вя́рно, те гово́рят за прое́кта в моме́нта.
Никола́й Миле́на, ти зае́та ли си днес след ра́бота? И́скаш ли да оти́дем на те́нис?
Миле́на Добра́ иде́я. Мо́же ли и брат ми да игра́е с нас?
На́дя Су́пер! Да оти́дем зае́дно на те́нис! Брат ти мо́же да игра́е с ме́не, а Никола́й – с те́бе.
Миле́на Добре́, но пъ́рво тря́бва да гово́ря с брат ми.

клие́нт	*client, customer*
а́ло	*hello* (on the phone)
зае́т	*busy; occupied*
в моме́нта	*at the moment*
(да) се оба́дя, -диш	*to call, to ring*
пак	*again*
по́-къ́сно	*later*
дочу́ване	*goodbye* (on the phone)
те́нис	*tennis*
иде́я	*idea*

Questions

1 Кой и́ска да гово́ри с дире́ктора?
2 Свобо́ден ли е г-н Анто́нов?
3 Кога́ тря́бва да се оба́ди клие́нтът?
4 Къде́ и́ска да оти́де Никола́й след ра́бота?
5 И́ска ли На́дя да оти́де с Никола́й и Миле́на?

07 кóлко стрýва...?

how much is...?

In this chapter you will learn:

- **how to point out and ask for things**
- **how to ask *how much does it cost?***
- **how to shop at Bulgarian open-air fruit markets**

Dialogue 1

After consulting Nevena for advice, Mr and Mrs Collins go to the market to buy fresh fruit and vegetables.

г-жа́ Ко́линс Неве́на, покаже́те ни, мо́ля, откъде́ да ку́пим плодове́ и зеленчу́ци.

Неве́на За съжале́ние магази́нът за плодове́ и зеленчу́ци не е́ бли́зо. На́й-добре́ е да оти́дете на паза́ра. Плодове́те и зеленчу́ците там не са́ е́втини, но са на́й-пре́сни.

г-жа́ Ко́линс Бли́зо ли е паза́рът?

Неве́на Да, да, не е́ дале́че.

At the market, Mrs Collins is so carried away she speaks to her husband in Bulgarian and Mr Collins shows he is learning fast!

г-жа́ Ко́линс Виж, Джордж, та́зи жена́ прода́ва ху́бави зеленчу́ци. Да ку́пим дома́ти от не́я.

г-н Ко́линс Зеленчу́ци? Дома́ти? А-ха́...

Продава́чка Заповя́дайте, мо́ля! Вземе́те си!

г-н Ко́линс Какви́ са те́зи зеленчу́ци?

Продава́чка Това́ са ти́score тиквички, господи́не. Да Ви дам ли?

г-н Ко́линс Не, благодаря́. Жена́ ми не оби́ча ти́score тиквички.

Продава́чка Мно́го ми́ло! В Бълга́рия не са́ мно́го мъже́те, които пазару́ват.

г-н Ко́линс Мо́ля? Не разби́рам.

г-жа́ Ко́линс Паза́р – пазару́вам. Жена́та и́ска да ка́же, че мъже́те в Бълга́рия не оби́чат да пазару́ват.

г-н Ко́линс О, аз ня́мам ни́що проти́в да *пазару́вам*! Да́йте ми, мо́ля, еди́н килогра́м дома́ти. Жена́ ми оби́ча дома́ти.

г-жа́ Ко́линс Ко́лко стру́ват дома́тите?

Продава́чка Три ле́ва.

г-жа́ Ко́линс А пъпешите?

Продава́чка Два и петдесе́т за килогра́м.

г-жа́ Ко́линс Дайте ми то́зи пъпеш, ако́ оби́чате.

Продава́чка Гото́во – пъпешът е два килогра́ма и полови́на. И́скате ли о́ще еди́н плик за пъпеша?

г-жа́ Ко́линс Да благодаря́. Джордж, какви́ дру́ги плодове́ и́скаш?

Продава́чка И́маме ху́бави я́бълки, пра́скови и гро́зде.

г-жа́ Ко́линс Да́йте ни еди́н килогра́м от те́зи я́бълки и полови́н килогра́м бя́ло гро́зде.

Продава́чка Всичко двана́йсет ле́ва и осемдесе́т стоти́нки.

г-жа́ Ко́линс	Джордж, плати́, ако́ обичаш. (*Popping a grape into her mouth.*) Ммм, гро́здето е мно́го сла́дко. Джордж, купи́ о́ще полови́н киле́.
г-н Ко́линс	Добре́, добре́. О́ще и́ма мъже́, които пазару́ват с удово́лствие. Мно́го ми́ло!

Покаже́те ни, мо́ля откъде́ да ку́пим плодове́ и зеленчу́ци.	*Please show us where to buy fruit and vegetables from.*
На́й-добре́ е да оти́дете на паза́ра.	*You'd do best to go to the market.*
магази́нът за плодове́ и зеленчу́цин	*greengrocer's (shop)*
е́втин	*cheap*
на́й-пре́сни	*freshest*
Виж, Джордж, та́зи жена́ прода́ва ху́бави зеленчу́ци.	*Look, George, this woman is selling nice vegetables.*
Да ку́пим дома́ти от не́я.	*Let's buy (some) tomatoes from her.*
Вземе́те си!	*Help yourselves!*
те́зи	*these*
ти́score	*courgettes/zucchinis*
Да Ви дам ли?	*Shall I give you some?*
Жена́ ми не оби́ча ти́score.	*My wife doesn't like courgettes.*
мно́го ми́ло!	*very sweet/kind!*
Не са́ мно́го мъже́те, които пазару́ват!	*There aren't many men who do the shopping.*
Жена́та и́ска да ка́же, че мъже́те в Бълга́рия не оби́чат да пазару́ват.	*What the woman means is that men in Bulgaria don't like shopping.*
О, аз ня́мам ни́що проти́в да *пазару́вам*.	*Oh, I don't mind shopping.*
Да́йте ми, мо́ля, еди́н килогра́м дома́ти.	*Please give me one kilogram of tomatoes.*
Ко́лко стру́ват дома́тите?	*How much are the tomatoes?*
три ле́ва	*three levs*
А пъпешите?	*And the melons?*
два и петдесе́т за килогра́м	*two fifty a kilogram*
Дайте ми то́зи пъпеш, ако́ оби́чате.	*Give me this melon if you please.*
Гото́во!	*There you go* (lit. *ready*)!
Пъпешът е два килогра́ма и полови́на.	*The melon is* $2^1/_2$ *kilograms.*
о́ще еди́н плик	*another plastic bag*

какви́ дру́ги плодове́ и́скаш?	*what other fruit would you like?*
И́маме ху́бави я́бълки, пра́скови и гро́зде.	*We have apples, peaches and grapes.*
еди́н килогра́м от те́зи я́бълки	*a/one kilogram of these apples*
полови́н килогра́м	*half a kilogram of*
бя́ло гро́зде	*white grapes*
плати́, ако́ оби́чаш	*pay, (if you) please*
Гро́здето е мно́го сла́дко.	*The grapes are very sweet.*
Купи́ о́ще полови́н кило́.	*Buy me another half kilo.*
О́ще и́ма мъже́, който пазару́ват с удово́лствие.	*There still are men who gladly do the shopping.*

1 Questions

- **a** Къде́ е на́й-добре́ да оти́дат г-н и г-жа́ Ко́линс?
- **b** Какви́ са плодове́те и зеленчу́ците на паза́ра?
- **c** Какво́ не оби́ча г-жа́ Ко́линс?
- **d** Ко́лко килогра́ма дома́ти и́ска г-н Ко́линс?
- **e** Какви́ дру́ги плодове́ прода́ва жена́та?
- **f** Ко́лко стру́ва вси́чко?

2 True or false?

- **a** Г-н и г-жа́ Ко́линс и́скат Неве́на да им пока́же магази́н за чай и кафе́.
- **b** Г-н Ко́линс и́ска да ку́пи ти́квички.
- **c** Г-н Ко́линс е еди́н от те́зи мъже́, който оби́чат да пазару́ват.
- **d** Г-жа́ Ко́линс и́ска да взе́ме еди́н пъ́пеш.
- **e** Г-жа́ Ко́линс и́ска едно́ кило́ пра́скови.
- **f** Гро́здето е мно́го сла́дко и г-жа́ Ко́линс и́ска да ку́пи о́ще.

i More about money

Since the early 1880s, shortly after the liberation of Bulgaria from the Ottoman Empire, the basic Bulgarian currency unit has been the **лев** (*lev*, lit. *lion*, after the rampant lion that is the official emblem of free Bulgaria). The sub-unit (one hundred to every lev) is the **стоти́нка** (*stotinka*, from **сто** meaning *hundred*).

In English, the plural of 'lev' should rightly be 'levs'. The temptation, however, is to say 'leva' or 'levas', influenced by the masculine counting form **два ле́ва, три ле́ва** etc., which is far more frequently heard than the straight singular **лев**. Similarly, the plural of 'stotinka' in English should be 'stotinkas', but you will most likely be tempted to say 'stotinki', influenced by the Bulgarian feminine plural **стоти́нки**.

The Bulgarian for 'one dollar' – whether US or Canadian – is **еди́н до́лар**, so you say **сто до́лара** (only one **л** remember!) The pound sterling has a feminine and masculine form: **една́ англи́йска ли́ра** or **еди́н брита́нски па́унд**, so 'one hundred pounds' would be either **сто англи́йски ли́ри** or **сто брита́нски па́унда**. The euro is neuter and has no plural: **едно́ е́вро, сто е́вро** etc.

The Bulgarian national coat of arms: *UNION MAKES STRENGTH*

In everyday conversation, you will often hear **ле́вче** or **едно́ ле́вче** used instead of **еди́н лев**. This is the affectionate, diminutive form. There are coins for 1, 2, 5, 10, 20 and 50 stotinkas, and also for one lev(che). Notes come in denominations of 2, 5, 10, 20, 50 and 100 levs.

Buying fruit

The best place to buy fruit is at one of the many open-air markets. Here you will find a variety of largely seasonal fruit and vegetables being offered for sale by individual stallholders, all eager that you should leave your money with them. It is normal practice almost everywhere for you to select your own fruit. Sometimes the stall-holder will even offer you something to taste.

Fruit and vegetables are sold by the kilogram, and even cucumbers and melons are usually sold by weight. When buying quantities less than a kilogram, the weight is usually calculated in grams or fractions of a kilogram. So if you want half a kilogram of tomatoes you say **Полови́н килогра́м дома́ти, мо́ля**. And if you want 300 grams of feta cheese, say, you say **три́ста гра́ма си́рене, мо́ля**.

Bulgaria is a Mediterranean-type country and a 'bridge to the East', but you will not be expected to haggle over the prices of fruit and vegetables. Although not always marked up, the prices you will be given when you ask **Ко́лко стру́ва?** (or **Ко́лко стру́ват?**) will be firm. As with waiters, the arithmetic of stallholders can be unreliable, and overcharging is not unknown. So do tot up the various items yourself, preferably in Bulgarian and out loud!

In Bulgaria, courgettes (or zucchinis if you prefer) are more like small marrows. They are light in colour and larger than the ones we are used to.

How do you say it?

- Asking someone to give you/show you something

Да́йте ми, мо́ля, де́сет биле́та за метро́то!	*Please give me ten tickets for the metro.*
Покаже́те ми, мо́ля, това́ списа́ние!	*Please show me this magazine.*

- Asking how much something costs

Ко́лко стру́ва пъ̀пешът?	*How much is the melon?*
Ко́лко стру́ват я́бълките?	*How much do the apples cost?*

- Making suggestions

Да оти́дем на пааза́ра!	*Let's go to the market.*
Да ку́пим дома́ти от та́зи жена́!	*Let's buy some tomatoes from this woman.*

- Giving advice

На́й-добре́ е да оти́дете на пааза́ра!	*You'd do best to go to the market.*

- Expressing your likes and dislikes

Оби́чам гро́зде.	*I like grapes.*
Оби́чам да пазару́вам.	*I like shopping.*
Не оби́чам пра́скови.	*I don't like peaches.*
Не оби́чам да у́ча.	*I don't like studying.*

Grammar

1 More masculine plurals

Masculine nouns of one syllable have a plural ending all of their own. If they end in a consonant they add **-ове** to the singular. If they end in **-й** they add **-еве**. Some nouns keep the stress on the first syllable, while in others the stress jumps either to the middle or to the final syllable:

клуб	– клу́б**ове**	*clubs*				
ключ	– клю́ч**ове**	*keys*	плод	–	плод**ове́**	*fruit*
плик	– пли́к**ове**	*envelopes*	брой	–	бро́**еве**	*numbers; copies*
сок	– со́к**ове**	*juices*				
нож	– нож**о́ве**	*knives*				
град	– град**ове́**	*towns*				

Note that це́нтър (*centre*), although more than one syllable, has the plural це́нтр**ове**.

Only very few masculine nouns of one syllable form their plurals differently. Two common examples are:

брат – бра́тя *brothers* мъж – мъже́ *men/husbands*

2 Using *the* with plural nouns: adding -те and -та

The Bulgarian equivalent of *the* is added to the end of the word, as we saw earlier:

Singular		with *the*	
пъпеш	*a melon*	пъпеш**ът**	*the melon*
Plural		with *the*	
пъпеши	*melons*	пъпеши**те**	*the melons*

There are two alternative plural forms of *the*: **-те** and **-та**. Which you need depends entirely on the final letters of the plural form. Gender plays no part whatsoever. Once again, however, you will notice an element of rhyme or vowel harmony.

(*a*) **-те** is added to plurals in **-и** or **-е**:

зеленчу́к: зеленчу́**ци**	–	зеленчу́ц**ите**	*the vegetables*
плод: плодов**е́**	–	плодов**е́те**	*the fruit*
пра́скова: пра́ско**ви**	–	пра́ско**вите**	*the peaches*
я́бълка: я́бълк**и**	–	я́бълк**ите**	*the apples*

(*b*) **-та** is added to plurals in **-а** and **-я**:

ви́но: вин**а́**	–	вин**а́та**	*the wines* (note the stress change!)
се́ло: сел**а́**	–	сел**а́та**	*the villages* (stress change here too!)
дете́: дец**а́**	–	дец**а́та**	*the children*

писмó: писмá – писмáта *the letters*
брат: брáтя – брáтята *the brothers*

(There are more neuter plurals in Unit 8.)

3 Telling people what to do

Дáйте ми, мóля! *Please give me.*
Вземéте си, мóля! *Please help yourself.* (lit. *take to yourself*)
Покажéте ми, мóля! *Please show me.*

These are all commands or requests in the polite plural. You have already come across a number of similar forms (all ending in **-те**) **заповя́дайте! здравéйте!** and **кажéте!** These forms are known as imperatives. There is a singular imperative, for situations when you would need to use the singular **ти** form, and a plural imperative, for situations when you would use **Вúе** or **вúе**.

The endings of the imperative are either **-й** (**-йте**) or **-ú** (**-éте**).

(*a*) In **а**-pattern verbs and verbs with an *I* form ending in two vowels you replace the present tense endings of the *I* form with **-й** or **-йте**:

Present tense	**Imperative singular**	**Imperative plural**	
паркúрам (*I park*)	не паркúр**ай!**	не паркúр**айте!**	*don't park!*
рáдвам се	рáдв**ай** се!	рáдв**айте** се!	*be happy!*
игрáя	игрá**й**!	игрá**йте**!	*play!*
пúя	пú**й**!	пú**йте**!	*drink!*

(*b*) In most **е**- and **и**-pattern verbs the ending of the *I* form of the present tense is replaced by **-ú** in the singular and **-éте** in the plural:

Present tense	**Imperative singular**	**Imperative plural**	
(да) покáжа	покаж**ú**!	покаж**éте!**	*show!*
(да) сéдна	седн**ú**!	седн**éте**!	*sit down!*
(да) кýпя	куп**ú**!	куп**éте**!	*buy!*
(да) платя́	плат**ú**!	плат**éте**!	*pay!*

Note that in these verbs the stress is on the final syllable in the singular and on the penultimate syllable in the plural.

Some common irregular imperatives:

Present		Singular	Plural	
(да)	ви́дя	виж!	ви́жте!	*look!*
(да)	дам	дай!	да́йте!	*give!*
(да)	ям	яж!	я́жте!	*eat!*
(да)	до́йда	ела́!	ела́те!	*come!*

4 (Да) дам *I give*

This verb follows the **e**-pattern, but the *I* form is irregular. In the present tense **дам** only occurs after **да**. The examples below are therefore accompanied by **тря́бва**:

аз	тря́бва да дам	*I must give*	ни́е тря́бва да даде́м	*we must give*
ти	тря́бва да даде́ш	*you must give*	ви́е тря́бва да даде́те	*you must give*
той / тя / то	тря́бва да даде́	*he, she, it must give*	те тря́бва да дада́т	*they must give*

5 Да́йте ми! покаже́те ми! *Give me, show me*

When using verbs like *give* and *show* you usually need to mention both what you give or show (the direct object), and the person to whom the thing is given or shown (the indirect object).

Да́йте **ми**, мо́ля, еди́н килогра́м гро́зде!	*Please give* ***me*** *a kilogram of grapes.*
Покаже́те **ми**, мо́ля, та́зи ка́ртичка!	*Please show* ***me*** *this postcard.*
Купи́ **ми** я́бълки, мо́ля.	*Buy me (some) apples, please.*

In English, you often need two words (a preposition like *to* or *for* and a naming word or a pronoun like *me*) to express the indirect object: *Give it* ***to me*** or *Buy some* ***for me***. Bulgarian, however, usually manages without a preposition. Happily, the forms of the most common indirect object pronouns (the so-called 'short forms') are the same as those used to express possession (see Unit 3). Here is a list of those short indirect object pronouns with the subject forms in brackets:

(аз)	**ми**	*to me*	(ни́е)	**ни**	*to us*
(ти)	**ти**	*to you*	(ви́е)	**ви**	*to you*
(той)	**му**	*to him*			
(тя)	**й**	*to her*	(те)	**им**	*to them*
(то)	**му**	*to it*			

6 Where to put the indirect object pronoun

Like the reflexive pronoun **се**, the short indirect object pronoun usually comes immediately before the verb:

Йскам да **ти** пока́жа Со́фия.	*I want to show **you** Sofia.*
Мо́же ли да **ни** пока́жете пaза́ра?	*Could you show **us** the market?*

(Watch the stress of **пока́жете**. This is the *you* form, *not* the imperative!)

If the verb is the first word in the sentence, the pronoun comes immediately after the verb:

Покаже́те **ни** меню́то, мо́ля.	*Please show us the menu.*
Да́йте **ми** меню́то, мо́ля.	*Please give me the menu.*

7 Да *Let's!* and *shall we?*

Да can be used with the *we* form to express the English *let's!* or *shall we?*:

Да оти́дем на пaза́ра!	*Let's go to the market!*
Да ку́пим пъ́пеша!	*Let's buy the melon!*
Да плати́м!	*Let's pay!*

If we add **ли** and turn these examples into questions, the affirmative answer will involve two different usages of **да**:

Да оти́дем ли на пaза́ра?	*Shall we go to the market?*
Да, да оти́дем!	*Yes, let's!*
Да ку́пим ли пъ́пеш?	*Shall we buy a melon?*
Да, да ку́пим!	*Yes, let's!*

8 То́зи, та́зи, това́ and те́зи: *this, these*

In situations where in English you use *this* or *these* – when pointing to or referring to something or someone nearby – in Bulgarian you have to select one of four slightly different forms:

Masculine	**то́зи** голя́м магази́н	*this large shop*
Feminine	**та́зи** ста́ра жена́	*this old woman*
Neuter	**това́** ху́баво дете́	*this beautiful child*
Plural	**те́зи** мла́ди мъже́	*these young men*

9 Е́втин, по́-е́втин *Cheap, cheaper*

To say that something is cheaper, bigger or more beautiful, for example (i.e. to make the comparative form of the adjective), all you do is place **по́-** on the front, as you did with the adverbs in Unit 5. The adjectives, however, have to be changed according to gender, depending on what noun they go with. So you say:

То́зи пъпеш е е́втин/ **по́**-е́втин.	*This melon is cheap/cheaper.*
Та́зи ка́ртичка е ху́бава/ **по́**-ху́бава.	*This card is beautiful/ more beautiful.*
Това́ ви́но е сла́дко/ **по́**-сла́дко.	*This wine is sweet/sweeter.*
Те́зи кра́ставици са е́втини/ **по́**-е́втини.	*These cucumbers are cheap/ cheaper.*

As with the adverbs, the **по́-** is emphasized and we will again add a stress mark to remind you of this.

If you want to compare one thing (or person) with another, you use **от** in place of the English *than*, just as you did with the adverbs:

Я́бълките са по́-е́втини **от** пра́сковите.	*The apples are cheaper than the peaches.*
Неве́на е по́-ху́бава **от** На́дя.	*Nevena is more beautiful than Nadya.*

When there is a preposition before the noun, you have to use **отко́лкото** instead of **от**:

В Бълга́рия зеленчу́ците са по́-евти́ни **отко́лкото в** А́нглия.	*In Bulgaria the vegetables are cheaper than in England.*
На паза́ра плодове́те са по́-пре́сни **отко́лкото в** магази́ните.	*At the market the fruit is fresher than in the shops.*

Exercises

1 Select from the regular and numerical plural forms in the box (all masculines!) to complete these sentences:

плйка, плйкове	
бана́на, бана́ни (*banana*)	
пъпеша, пъпеши	
но́жа, ножо́ве	
гра́да, градове́	

a Йимате ли ____ .
b Неве́на и́ска да ку́пи два ____ .
c Два ____, мо́ля.
d Оби́чаш ли ____?
e Да ви дам ли два ____?
f Г-жа́ Ко́линс оби́ча ____ .
g Мо́ля, да́йте ни ____!
h Е́то тук и́ма ня́колко ____ .
i Г-н Джо́нсън и́ска да оти́де в ня́колко бъ́лгарски ____ .
j Ру́се и Тъ́рново са ____ в Бълга́рия.

2 Public notices are often instructions, sometimes given in the singular, sometimes in the plural. You would do well to note – and observe! – the following common instructions:

Which of the notices would you expect to find:

Бутни́! *Push.* **Дръпни́!** *Pull.* **Не пи́пай!** *Don't touch!*
Плате́те на ка́сата! *Pay at the cash desk.*
Пазе́те чистота́! *No litter* (lit. *Observe cleanliness*).
Не газе́те трева́та! *Keep off the grass!* (lit. *Don't trample down the grass*)

a in a shop or bank
b in a park
c on doors into a shop
d near live electricity cables

3 Ask the appropriate questions using the phrases given below and choosing between **павилио́н** (*kiosk*), **по́ща, апте́ка** and **ба́нка**.

Model: Мо́же ли да ми ка́жете къде́ и́ма павилио́н? Тря́бва да ку́пя биле́ти.

a Тря́бва да ку́пя пли́кове (*envelopes*) и ма́рки (*stamps*).
b Тря́бва да обменя́ пари́.
c Тря́бва да ку́пя аспири́н.
d Тря́бва да ку́пя ве́стници.

4 Imagine you are in a pharmacy/drugstore. Ask for the items listed below using Мо́же ли да ми пока́жете and either:

a то́зи, **b** та́зи, **c** това́ or **d** те́зи

ка́рта	ча́ша (*glass/cup*)
чадъ́р	писа́ния
крем (*cream*)	кре́мове
списа́ние	ча́ши
ножо́ве	лека́рство (*medicine*)

5 You've now moved to the open-air market. Ask for the items below using the model: Ко́лко стру́ват дома́тите? Да́йте ми едно́ кило́ дома́ти:

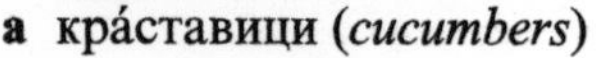

a кра́ставици (*cucumbers*) **b** ти́score тиквички

c я́бълки **d** пра́скови

6 Give affirmative answers to these questions following the model: Да ку́пим ли крем? Да, да ку́пим!

a Да оти́дем ли на Ви́тоша?
b Да оти́дем ли на те́нис?
c Да плати́м ли сега́?
d Да се оба́дим ли на Никола́й?

7 To practise saying what you do and do not like doing, and also to make sure you have not forgotten how to use the construction with **да**, answer the following questions:

a Оби́чате ли да пъту́вате (*travel*)?
Да, мно́го оби́чам ______.
b Оби́чаш ли да игра́еш (*play*) на компю́тър?
Не, не оби́чам ______.
c Оби́чате ли да пазару́вате? Не, не оби́чам ______.
d Оби́чате ли да ка́рате ски (*to go skiing*)?
Да, мно́го оби́чам ______.
e Оби́чаш ли да чете́ш?
Да, мно́го оби́чам ______.

8 First read aloud these polite (plural) forms of a number of common instructions. Then use their familiar, singular forms, as if you were talking to a child or a good friend:

a Купе́те мля́ко, мо́ля! **d** Ви́жте, мо́ля!
b Ела́те, мо́ля! **e** Каже́те, мо́ля!
c Седне́те, мо́ля! **f** Да́йте, мо́ля!

9 Try rearranging the words below to make proper sentences:

a ли, да дам, Ви, солта́...?
b пока́жете, ста́ята, мо́же ли, да, ни...?
c ни, да́йте, мо́ля, ключа́!
d това́, покаже́те, списа́ние, ми, мо́ля...!
e да, мо́же ли, пъпеш, ми, даде́те, то́зи...?

10 Practise some comparisons by making complete sentences out of the words below. With the exception of (**d**) you have to use the definite forms throughout.

Model: Пъпеш/бана́н/голя́м
Пъпешът е по́-голя́м от бана́на.

a Я́бълки/пра́скови/е́втини
b Дома́ти/ти́квички/пре́сни
c Пъпеш/гро́зде/сла́дък
d На́дя/Неве́на/зае́та
e Кра́ставици/ти́квички/голе́ми

Do you understand?

Dialogue 2: Пода́ръци *Presents*

Nevena is on her way to a birthday party. She stops off in a flower shop and finds everything she needs.

Неве́на Еди́н буке́т ро́зи, мо́ля.
Продава́чка Ето буке́тите. Кой да Ви дам?
Неве́на Този, голе́мият, е мно́го краси́в. Ко́лко стру́ва?
Продава́чка Осемна́йсет ле́ва.
Неве́на Хм, покаже́те ми по́-е́втини буке́ти, мо́ля.
Продава́чка Е́то, ви́жте, лале́тата са по́-е́втини. То́зи буке́т е са́мо шест ле́ва.
Неве́на Су́пер. И́скам да ку́пя и не́що за пода́рък.
Продава́чка И́маме краси́ви ва́зи. Да Ви пока́жа ли?
Неве́на Да, та́зи ма́лка ва́за е мно́го симпати́чна. И една́ ка́ртичка, мо́ля.
Продава́чка От кой?
Неве́на Не́що от Со́фия.

Продава́чка Е́то, ви́жте – с Наро́дния теа́тър, с Парламе́нта, с Университе́та...
Неве́на Та́зи с Наро́дния теа́тър, мо́ля.
Продава́чка Да Ви дам ли плик за пода́ръка?
Неве́на Какви́ пли́кове и́мате?
Продава́чка Ма́лки пли́кчета от осемдесе́т стоти́нки и по́-голе́ми пли́кове от лев и петдесе́т.
Неве́на Да́йте ми два пли́ка от лев и петдесе́т. Ко́лко тря́бва да Ви дам всѝчко?
Продава́чка Това́ пра́ви осемна́йсет и петдесе́т.

буке́т	*bunch, bouquet*
ро́за	*rose*
краси́в	*beautiful*
лале́	*tulip*
ва́за	*vase*
симпати́чен, -чна	*nice*
Наро́дният теа́тър	*The National Theatre*
Парламе́нт	*Parliament*
(да) пока́жа, -жеш	*to show*
плик	*(gift-)bag; envelope*
пли́кче	*small (plastic) bag*
ма́рка	*(postage) stamp*

Questions

1 Ко́лко стру́ва голе́мият буке́т ро́зи?
2 Кой цветя́ са по́-е́втини?
3 Какво́ о́ще и́ска да ку́пи Неве́на?
4 Какви́ пли́кове и́ма в магази́на?
5 Ко́лко тря́бва да плати́ Неве́на?

The Ivan Vazov National Theatre

08 какво предлагате?

what is your suggestion?

In this unit you will learn:

- **how to order a meal in a restaurant**
- **how to say what Bulgarian dishes you prefer**
- **how to suggest dishes to someone else**

Dialogue 1

Mr Antonov and Mr Johnson are about to order a meal.

г-н Анто́нов	Какво́ да поръ́чаме?
г-н Джо́нсън	Мо́же ли да ви́дя меню́то?
г-н Анто́нов	Заповя́дайте! (*Opening the menu and pointing.*) Е́то, това́ са су́пите и сала́тите. Това́ са бъ́лгарските специалите́ти.
г-н Джо́нсън	Какво́ ми предла́гате да взе́ма?
г-н Анто́нов	Шо́пската сала́та е типи́чно бъ́лгарска. Тя е с дома́ти, кра́ставици и си́рене.
г-н Джо́нсън	Добре́, една́ шо́пска сала́та за ме́не.
г-н Анто́нов	И́скате ли тарато́р?
г-н Джо́нсън	Какво́ е тарато́р?
г-н Анто́нов	Това́ е су́па от ки́село мля́ко и кра́ставици. Серви́ра се студе́на. Мно́го е вку́сна.
г-н Джо́нсън	Не, благодаря́. Предпочи́там то́пла су́па. (*Reading and pointing.*) Е́то та́зи – пи́лешка су́па.
г-н Анто́нов	Тога́ва Ви предла́гам да взе́мете то́зи бъ́лгарски специалите́т – пъ́лнени чу́шки.
г-н Джо́нсън	Добре́, да взе́мем пъ́лнени чу́шки.
г-н Анто́нов	(*To the waitress.*) Мо́же ли...?
Сервитьо́рка	Заповя́дайте, мо́ля.
г-н Анто́нов	Две шо́пски сала́ти, една́ пи́лешка су́па, еди́н тарато́р и два пъ́ти пъ́лнени чу́шки.
Сервитьо́рка	Ко́лко хляб?
г-н Анто́нов	Че́тири бе́ли хле́бчета, мо́ля.
Сервитьо́рка	Не́що за пи́ене?
г-н Анто́нов	А, да. Да взе́мем ли бути́лка ви́но, г-н Джо́нсън?
г-н Джо́нсън	Не, благодаря́. Аз оби́чам бъ́лгарските вина́, но на о́бед не пи́я алкохо́л. И́мате ли натура́лни пло́дови со́кове?
Сервитьо́рка	Не, за съжале́ние. Са́мо гази́рани напи́тки.
г-н Джо́нсън	За ме́не една́ гази́рана вода́, ако́ оби́чате.
Сервитьо́рка	А за Вас, господи́не? Бя́лото ви́но е мно́го ху́баво.
г-н Анто́нов	Добре́, тога́ва за ме́не ча́ша бя́ло ви́но, мо́ля.
Сервитьо́рка	Не́що дру́го?
г-н Анто́нов	Не, благодаря́.

Какво́ да поръ̀чаме?	*What shall we order?*
Мо́же ли да ви́дя менюто?	*Can I see the menu?*
Е́то, това́ са су́пите и сала́тите.	*Look, here are the soups and the salads.*
Това́ са българските специалите́ти.	*These are the Bulgarian specialities.*
Какво́ ми предга́гате да взе́ма?	*What do you suggest I take?*
Шо́пската сала́та е типи́чно българска.	*The 'shopska' salad is typically Bulgarian.*
си́рене	*feta cheese*
тарато́р	*tarator* (Bulgarian cold summer soup)
Това́ е су́па от ки́село мля́ко и кра́ставици.	*It is a soup made of yoghurt and cucumbers.*
Серви́ра се студе́на.	*It is served cold.*
Мно́го е вку́сна.	*It is delicious.*
Предпочи́там то́пла су́па.	*I prefer a hot soup.*
Е́то та́зи – пи́лешка су́па.	*This one here – chicken soup.*
Тога́ва Ви предла́гам да взе́мете то́зи български специалите́т.	*Then I suggest you take this Bulgarian speciality.*
пълнени чу́шки	*stuffed peppers*
два пъти	*twice*
Ко́лко хляб?	*How much bread?*
че́тири бе́ли хле́бчета	*four white bread rolls*
Не́що за пиене?	*Anything to drink?*
Да взе́мем ли бути́лка ви́но?	*Shall we take a bottle of wine?*
На о́бед не пи́я алкохо́л.	*I don't drink alcohol at lunchtime.*
Имате ли натура́лни пло́дови со́кове?	*Have you any natural fruit juices?*
гази́рани напи́тки	*fizzy drinks*
ако́ оби́чате	*if you please*
Бя́лото ви́но е мно́го ху́баво.	*The white wine is very good.*
Тога́ва за ме́не ча́ша бя́ло ви́но.	*A glass of white wine for me, then.*
Не́що дру́го?	*Anything else?*

1 Questions

- **a** Какво́ и́ска да ви́ди г-н Джо́нсън?
- **b** Какво́ предла́га г-н Анто́нов на г-н Джо́нсън?
- **c** Какво́ е тарато́р?
- **d** Какво́ предпочи́та г-н Джо́нсън?
- **e** Какво́ и́ска г-н Джо́нсън за пи́ене?
- **f** Кой и́ска да поръ́ча ча́ша ви́но?

2 True or false?

- **a** Шо́пската сала́та е с ки́село мля́ко и кра́ставици.
- **b** Тарато́рът се серви́ра студе́н.
- **c** Пъ́лнените чу́шки са бъ́лгарски специалите́т.
- **d** Г-н Анто́нов и г-н Джо́нсън не и́скат хляб.
- **e** Г-н Джо́нсън и́ска не́що за пи́ене, но не алкохо́л.
- **f** На о́бед г-н Анто́нов пи́е са́мо лимона́да.

i Food and eating out

Bulgarians enjoy eating out. They go as much for the company as for the food, which is often served warm rather than hot. They eat lots of bread – not just with their soup course – and spend a long time over their meals, especially in the evenings. The more popular, smaller restaurants often get very busy, noisy and full of cigarette smoke, so go early. And if the weather is good, try and find a table outside. For the more popular establishments, it's best to make a reservation (**резерва́ция**). If you want to try and escape from the cigarette smoke, ask for a **ма́са за непуша́чи** (*a table for non-smokers*). If you like the smoke, ask for a **ма́са за пуша́чи.** Service can be slow, so allow plenty of time for your meal and enjoy the company and the atmosphere!

If you go out in a group, you may be asked on entering **Ко́лко ду́ши сте?** *How many (people) are you?* and **Имате ли резерва́ция?** *Do you have a reservation?*

All restaurants serve alcohol – at any time of the day or night. Most have tables set aside for non-smokers, but the smokers do not always observe the instructions. Specifically vegetarian restaurants are few and far between, but you can usually make up a very decent vegetarian meal from the standard dishes on offer. When ordering your meal, remember that the courses, often beginning with fresh salads as a starter, are served in strict sequence. Subsequent courses will not be brought until everyone at your table has finished their starter. So if you want a starter as your main course or a salad with your main course, you need to tell the waiter.

Restaurants in tourist areas usually have menus in more than one language. In hotels with restaurants (**хоте́л-рестора́нт**) the restaurants are generally open to non-residents, unless they have been pre-booked for a closed function. They offer a wide choice of dishes, many of them 'international'. Some of these restaurants are quite formal, with waiters in black ties.

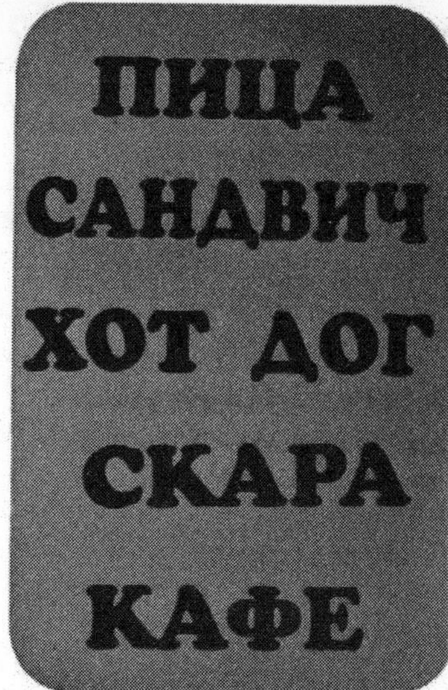

In the larger towns there are plenty of eating places to choose from, and a wide variety of traditional restaurants. Most of the well-known Western food chains are represented. There are innumerable Italian restaurants, both large and small, serving traditional pizza and pasta dishes. If you are wanting a Chinese restaurant, look for **Кита́йски рестора́нт**.

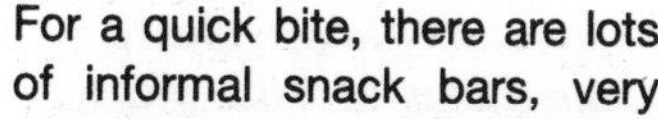

For a quick bite, there are lots of informal snack bars, very functional, self-service establishments, often with limited seating. Pop in for a sandwich, maybe toasted, a Bulgarian **ба́ничка** (*pasty*), a cup of coffee or a **ко́ла** – usually Coca-Cola or Pepsi. Many of these establishments have foreign names, usually English. There are also many small eating places offering dishes such as grilled chicken to take away (**пи́ле на грил за вкъщи**). Some sell Middle Eastern food and have appropriate Middle Eastern names.

Grilled meat dishes are served in most establishments and are rightly very popular. Look for the word **ска́ра** (*grill*) in the menu. If you want something traditional, tasty and inexpensive, go for freshly grilled meatballs (**кюфте́та**) – the really hot ones are called **нерво́зни** – or delicious, spicy grilled sausages (**кеба́пчета**). Order any number – of either or both – and eat with plenty of bread and **лю́теница**, a piquant red sauce made of tomatoes, red peppers and finely chopped onions. Wash down with beer or red wine. Delicious!

There are many small street bars – look for **Бар** or **Кафе́** – with tables out on the pavement in the summer. Here you can find soft drinks, a variety of alcoholic drinks, coffee, hot chocolate, tea etc. Although traditionally in Bulgaria you only drank tea (without milk) when you were unwell, you can find all kinds of tea, including tea made from a variety of different herbs. Remember, though, that if you do want a traditional 'cuppa', **че́рен чай** (*black tea*), you will probably be presented with a cup or, more likely, a glass of hot water, some sugar and a tea bag. You will be expected to brew up yourself at the table. And if you want milk, you will have to ask for it!

How do you say it?

- Asking *What do you suggest* or *offer?* and suggesting or offering something yourself

Каквó ми предлáгаш? *What do you suggest (for me)?*
Предлáгам да порѝчаш тáзи сýпа. *I suggest you order this soup.*
Предлáгаме товá вѝно. *We suggest this wine.*

- Asking for someone's preference and expressing your own

Вѝе каквó предпочѝтате? *What do you prefer?*
Предпочѝтам тóпла сýпа. *I prefer hot soup.*

- Saying *once*, *twice*, etc.

едѝн път *once* (lit. *one time*)
два пъ̀ти *twice*
три пъ̀ти *three times*
чѐтири пъ̀ти, etc. *four times*

- Asking for something to eat or drink

Нéщо за я̀дене, мóля! *Something to eat, please.*
Нéщо за пѝене, мóля! *Something to drink, please.*

- Saying *please* in a more formal way

акó обѝчате *if you please*

- Saying a *glass of..., a cup of..., a bottle of...*

чáша вѝно *a glass of wine*
чáша кафé *a cup of coffee*
бутѝлка вѝно *a bottle of wine*

Grammar

1 *The* with adjectives

When an adjective is added to a noun used with the definite article, the definite article moves from the noun to the adjective:

Feminine	салáт**ата** *the salad*	becomes	шóпск**ата** салáта *the 'shopska' salad*
Neuter	вѝн**ото** *the wine*	becomes	червéн**ото** вѝно *the red wine*
Plural	сýпи**те** *the soups*	becomes	тóпли**те** сýпи *the hot soups*

If you use more than one adjective, you only put the definite article on the end of the first adjective:

специалите́тите *the specialities*	becomes	ху́бавите български специалите́ти *the lovely Bulgarian specialities*

As you can see, the definite article added to adjectives is the same as the definite article added to nouns of the same gender. Only with masculine nouns is there any change. (You will learn about this in Unit 9.)

2 More neuter plurals

Many neuter nouns ending in **-(ч)е** form their plural by adding **-та**:

едно́ хле́бче	че́тири хле́бчета	*four bread rolls*
едно́ кафе́	три кафе́та	*three coffees*
едно́ парче́	две парче́та	*two pieces*
едно́ пли́кче	мно́го пли́кчета	*many small (plastic) bags*

Some words adopted from other languages, words like **интервю́**, **меню́**, **такси́** and **у́иски**, which are considered neuter nouns, also take this plural ending:

мно́го интервю́та	*many interviews*
ня́колко меню́та	*several menus*
мно́го такси́та	*many taxis*
ня́колко у́искита	*several whiskies*

Be careful not to confuse these plurals with singular feminine nouns used with the definite article – they both end in **-та**!

When neuter plurals like **меню́та** and **парче́та** are used with the definite article, they end in a double **-тата**, and the resulting 'rhyme' creates the distinctive Bulgarian 'machine-gun' effect:

хле́бче**тата**	*the bread rolls*	меню́**тата**	*the menus*
кафе́**тата**	*the coffees*	такси́**тата**	*the taxis*
парче́**тата**	*the pieces*	у́иски**тата**	*the whiskies*

3 Два and две: two times two

You have already briefly come across these two forms of the numeral for two in Unit 4. **Два**, as in **два часа́**, remember, goes with masculine nouns denoting things and animals (but not persons). **Две** goes with neuter and feminine nouns.

Masculine		**Feminine**	**Neuter**
два тарато́ра	but	две сала́ти	две парче́та
два со́ка		две ма́рки	две писма́
два пли́ка		две ча́ши	две такси́та
два килогра́ма		две ста́и	две места́

4 Два́ма *two* and три́ма *three*: persons

You have to use special forms of certain numerals with masculine nouns for people. These forms exist for the numerals from *two* to *six*, but you will probably only come across **два́ма** *two* and **три́ма** *three*. These numerals are used with the normal plural of the noun, not with the special counting form:

два́ма англича́ни и три́ма америка́нци	*two Englishmen and three Americans*
два́ма студе́нти и три́ма учи́тели	*two students and three teachers*

два́ма ду́ши *two people* (lit. *two souls*)

5 Бя́ло and бе́ли, я and е: fickle vowels

Depending on stress and the vowels that occur in the following syllable, you will find that the vowels **я** and **е** may alternate. Happily, the rules governing these alternations are well-defined. The changes are confusing, though, and you would do well to learn the rules, perhaps putting a slip of paper between these pages, so you can find them easily.

я́ is used either	(*a*)	if it is stressed and the vowel in the following syllable is **а**, **о**, **у** or **ъ**;
or	(*b*)	if it is stressed and occurs in the final syllable.
е is used either	(*a*)	if it is stressed and the vowels **е** or **и** occur in the following syllable;
or	(*b*)	if it is unstressed.

So you will find:

бял, бя́ла, бя́ло *white*	but	**бе́ли**
мя́сто *place*	but	**места́** (note the stress change!)
свят *world*	but	по **света́** *around the world*

6 Плод, пло́дов сок *Fruit, fruit juice*

By adding **-ов** (**-ова**, **-ово**, **-ови**) to a noun you can often form an adjective with the meaning *made of...* If the noun is feminine or neuter, you first have to remove the final vowel:

плод:	пло́д**ов** сок	*fruit juice*
	пло́д**ова** то́рта	*fruit gateau*
	пло́д**ово** мля́ко	*fruit-flavoured milk*
	пло́д**ови** то́рти	*fruit gateaux* or *pieces of fruit gateau*
гро́зде:	гро́зд**ова** раки́я	*grape brandy*
сли́ва:	сли́в**ова** раки́я	*plum brandy*
портока́л:	портока́л**ов** сок	*orange juice*
я́бълка:	я́бълк**ов** сок	*apple juice*

Exercises

1 The Bulgarian verbs for *order* **(да) поръ́чам** and *prefer* **предпочи́там** sound very much alike. Practise them using the following words in place of the words in bold:

Model: Сервитьо́рката предла́га **бя́ло ви́но**, но аз предпочи́там **черве́но**. Да поръ́чаме **черве́но ви́но!**

- **a** пи́лзенска (*Pilsner*) би́ра, бъ́лгарска би́ра
- **b** гро́здова раки́я, сли́вова раки́я
- **c** пи́лешка су́па, зеленчу́кова (*vegetable*) су́па

2 In a restaurant, which of the Bulgarian words for *order*, *offer* and *prefer* would you use to complete these sentences?

- **a** Какво́ су́па ____ -ате?
- **b** Г-н Анто́нов и́ска да ____ -а бути́лка ви́но.
- **c** Кое́ ви́но ____ -ате, черве́ното или́ бя́лото?
- **d** Г-н Анто́нов ____ -а пъ́лнените чу́шки.
- **e** Да ____ -ме то́зи бъ́лгарски специалите́т!
- **f** Г-н Джо́нсън ____ -а пло́дов сок, а не ви́но.
- **g** И́скате ли да ____ -ате шо́пска сала́та?

3 Here are the ingredients for tarator soup:

ки́село мля́ко
една́ кра́ставица
че́сън (*garlic*)
сол
о́лио (*vegetable oil*)
о́рехи (*walnuts*)

Now answer the question: Какво́ и́ма в тарато́ра?

4 Read the following list of drinks and cakes out loud:

не́с(кафе) = *instant* (*coffee*)
кафе́ еспре́со = *espresso*
че́рен чай
ме́нтов чай
би́лков чай
пло́дова то́рта
шокола́дова (*chocolate*) то́рта
о́рехова то́рта
портока́лов сок
гро́здов сок
я́бълков сок
сок от я́годи (*strawberries*)

Now, using **и́ма**, say what is on offer in the way of:

a coffee
b tea
c cakes
d fruit juices

Words you might need to know are: **би́лка** *herb*, **ме́нта** *peppermint* and **о́рех** *walnut*.

5 So as to fix in your mind the correct use of the different Bulgarian words for *two*, use **два**, **две** or **два́ма** as appropriate. Here you can again see the special plural form of masculine nouns used after numbers – but not after **два́ма** and **три́ма**.

a Да́йте ми ____ парче́та пи́ца (*pizza*) и ____ о́рехови то́рти.
b Да поръ́чаме ____ гро́здови со́ка и ____ сала́ти.
c Там и́ма ____ свобо́дни места́.

- **d** ____ деца́ игра́ят те́нис. (Remember the singular of деца́ is дете́.)
- **e** Да ку́пим ____ пли́ка и ____ ма́рки.
- **f** Да́йте ни ____ лимо́нови сладоле́да (*lemon ice-creams*), мо́ля.
- **g** В ста́ята и́ма ____ бъ́лгарски студе́нти.
- **h** Йскаш ли да поръ́чаме ____ тарато́ра?
- **i** В хоте́ла и́ма ____ англича́нки.
- **j** Ни́е сме са́мо ____ ду́ши. *(There are only two of us.)*
- **k** Ймаме ну́жда от ____ ча́ши.
- **l** До га́рата и́ма ____ магази́на.

6 Choose a soup and another item from the list below and order:

- **a** just for yourself
- **b** another combination for yourself and a companion
- **c** a third combination for your family of four

Меню́
зеленчу́кова су́па
вегетариа́нска (*vegetarian*) су́па
омле́т (*omelette*) със си́рене
пи́ца с кашкава́л (*yellow cheese*)
омле́т с шу́нка (*ham*)
кюфте́та (*meatballs*)

7 You go into a snack bar with a group of friends. Complete the dialogue below, acting as the customer:

Продава́чка	За вас, мо́ля? (*What would it be for you?*)
Клие́нт	(Ask what sandwiches they have.)
Продава́чка	Ймаме са́ндвичи с шу́нка и с кашкава́л.
Клие́нт	(Ask for two sandwiches with ham and one with cheese.)
Продава́чка	Дру́го? (*Anything else?*)
Клие́нт	(Ask for one orange juice, two cokes and three coffees.)

8 Now you want two sausages, two bread rolls and two meatballs. Ask how much they are in two ways, with and without the numeral.

i **a** Ко́лко стру́ват две ____? (кеба́пчета, кеба́пчетата)

b Ко́лко стру́ват ____?

ii a Ко́лко стру́ват две ____? (хле́бчета, хле́бчетата)
b Ко́лко стру́ват ____?
iii a Ко́лко стру́ват две ____? (кюфте́та, кюфте́тата)
b Ко́лко стру́ват ____?

9 Using the model Предла́гам да поръ́чаме черве́ното ви́но, suggest to your dining companion in a Bulgarian restaurant that you should order.

a	бя́ло ви́но	**d**	шокола́дова то́рта
b	сли́вова раки́я	**e**	бъ́лгарски специалите́ти
c	вегетариа́нска су́па	**f**	пи́лзенска би́ра

10 Your dining partner praises the food – all except the chicken soup and the Bulgarian yoghurt. You agree. Using the words in brackets, follow the model to give your reaction in more precise terms.

Your partner Сала́тата е мно́го вку́сна!
You Да, шо́пската сала́та е мно́го вку́сна!

This will help you remember that the definite article moves from the noun to the defining word!

a	Су́пата е мно́го вку́сна!	(вегетериа́нска)
b	Чу́шките са мно́го вку́сни!	(пъ́лнени)
c	Гро́здето е мно́го вку́сно!	(бя́ло)
d	Су́пата не е́ мно́го вку́сна!	(пи́лешка)
e	Я́бълките са мно́го вку́сни!	(черве́ни)
f	То́ртата е мно́го вку́сна!	(пло́дова)
g	Хле́бчетата са мно́го вку́сни!	(бе́ли)
h	Мля́кото не е́ мно́го вку́сно!	(бъ́лгарско, ки́село)

Do you understand?

Dialogue 2: В кафе́то *At the café*

Nadya and Milena meet in front of the office early one morning.

На́дя Здраве́й, Миле́на. О́ще е ра́но за ра́бота. Да оти́дем в кафе́то.
Миле́на Не е́ ли затво́рено?
На́дя Ко́лко е часъ́т?
Миле́на О́сем и полови́на.
На́дя Тря́бва да е отво́рено ве́че.
(*Inside*.)
Сервитьо́р До́бро у́тро. Каже́те, мо́ля!
На́дя Какво́ и́ма за заку́ска?

Сервитьо̀р Са̀ндвичи, кѝфли, ба̀нички.
Милѐна Нѐщо сла̀дко?
Сервитьо̀р Ѝма кроаса̀ни, кекс, ѝма също пло̀дова то̀рта.
На̀дя За мѐне едѝн са̀ндвич и парчѐ то̀рта.
Милѐна За мѐне същото.
Сервитьо̀р Зна̀чи два са̀ндвича и две парчѐта то̀рта. Дру̀го?
На̀дя И две кафѐта.
Сервитьо̀р Нес илѝ еспрѐсо?
Милѐна Еспрѐсо, мо̀ля. Каквѝ напѝтки ѝма?
Сервитьо̀р Натура̀лни со̀кове, ко̀ла, газѝрана вода̀.
Милѐна Добрѐ, два я̀бълкови со̀ка, ако̀ обѝчате.
(*The waiter comes back with the order.*)
На̀дя Мо̀же ли да платѝм ведна̀га?
Сервитьо̀р Разбѝра се. Ѐто, това̀ е смѐтката.

ра̀но	*early*
сла̀дък, сла̀дка	*sweet*
затво̀рен	*closed*
отво̀рен	*open*
заку̀ска	*breakfast, snack*
кѝфла	*bun*
ба̀ничка	*cheese roll, pasty*
нѐщо сла̀дко	*something sweet*
кроаса̀н	*croissant*
кекс	*(sponge) cake*
са̀мо	*only*
(да) платя̀, -тѝш	*to pay*
ведна̀га	*immediately*
смѐтка	*bill*

Questions

1 Ко̀лко е часъ̀т?
2 Ра̀но ли е за ра̀бота?
3 Затво̀рено ли е кафѐто?
4 Какво̀ ѝма за заку̀ска?
5 Какво̀ ѝскат На̀дя и Милѐна за я̀дене?
6 Какво̀ ѝскат те за пѝене?

с какво́ мо́га да Ви помо́гна?

how can I help you?

In this unit you will learn:

- **how to ask for help**
- **how to offer assistance**
- **how to describe things and people**

Dialogue 1

Violeta and Mark Davies are preparing to leave their hotel.

Виоле́та А́ло, аз съм Виоле́та Де́йвис. Неве́на ли е?
Неве́на Каже́те, госпо́жо Де́йвис, с какво́ мо́га да Ви помо́гна?
Виоле́та Мо́ля, поръ́чайте едно́ такси́ за лети́щето.
Неве́на За ко́лко ча́са?
Виоле́та За де́сет и петна́йсет. Мо́ля също пи́колото да ни помо́гне с бага́жа.
Неве́на Разби́ра се, госпо́жо Де́йвис.
Виоле́та Благодаря́. Дочу́ване!

(Violeta is now in the hotel lobby.)

Пи́коло Бага́жът ви е ве́че във фоайе́то, но такси́то о́ще го ня́ма.
Виоле́та Благодаря́ ти, момче́.
Пи́коло Ня́ма защо́.
Виоле́та Хм, това́ не е́ са́мо на́шият бага́ж. Тук и́ма ку́фари и ча́нти на дру́ги го́сти на хоте́ла.
Пи́коло И те ча́кат такси́.
Виоле́та Е́то, това́ на́шето такси́ ли е?
Пи́коло Не, ми́сля, че дру́гото такси́ е за вас.
Виоле́та Мъжът ми о́ще го ня́ма. Мо́жете ли пак да ми помо́гнете с бага́жа?
Шофьо́р Да́йте, аз мо́га да Ви помо́гна. Покаже́те ми кой бага́ж е Ваш.
Виоле́та Благодаря́ мно́го. Че́рният ку́фар и си́нята ра́ница са на́ши. Но къде́ е ча́нтата на мъжа́ ми?
Шофьо́р Не мо́жете ли да я наме́рите? Как изгле́жда тя?
Виоле́та Голя́ма че́рна ча́нта.
Пи́коло Ви́жте зад о́нзи син ку́фар.
Виоле́та Ня́ма я...
Пи́коло Мно́го неприя́тно. Пи́тайте Неве́на.
Виоле́та А, е́то го Марк. Той но́си сво́ята ча́нта!
Пи́коло Зна́чи ня́ма пробле́м.
Виоле́та Да, всѝчко е наре́д. Марк, дай не́що на момче́то.
Пи́коло Благодаря́. Прия́тен път.

С какво́ мо́га да Ви помо́гна?	*How can I help you?*
лети́ще	*airport*
Мо́ля също пиколото да ни помогне с бага́жа.	*Let the bellboy also help us with the luggage, please.*

фоайе́	*foyer/lobby*
такси́то о́ще го ня́ма	*the taxi is still not here*
момче́	*boy, lad*
Ня́ма защо́.	*You're welcome/Don't mention it.*
на́шият бага́ж	*our luggage*
го́сти на хоте́ла	*residents at the hotel*
Мо́жете ли пак да ми помо́гнете с бага́жа?	*Could you help me with the luggage again?*
аз мо́га да Ви помо́гна	*I can help you*
Покаже́те ми кой бага́ж е Ваш.	*Show me which luggage is yours.*
Че́рният ку́фар и си́нята ра́ница са на́ши.	*The black suitcase and the blue rucksack are ours.*
ча́нта	*bag*
Не мо́жете ли да я наме́рите?	*Can't you find it?*
Как изгле́жда тя?	*What does it look like?*
Ви́жте зад о́нзи син ку́фар.	*Look behind that blue suitcase.*
Мно́го неприя́тно.	*Very unpleasant.*
Пи́тайте Неве́на.	*Ask Nevena.*
Той но́си сво́ята ча́нта.	*He's carrying his (own) bag.*
вси́чко е наре́д	*everything's fine*

1 Questions

a Какво́ и́ска да поръ́ча Виоле́та?
b С какво́ ще помо́гне пи́колото?
c Какви́ ку́фари и ча́нти и́ма във фоайе́то?
d Какво́ не мо́же да наме́ри Виоле́та?
e Какво́ но́си Марк?
f Как изгле́жда ча́нтата на Марк?

2 True or false?

a Виоле́та и́ска да поръ́ча такси́ за едина́йсет и полови́на.
b Мъжъ́т на Виоле́та о́ще го ня́ма във фоайе́то.
c Шофьо́рът предла́га да помо́гне с бага́жа.
d Си́ният ку́фар и че́рната ра́ница са на Марк и Виоле́та.
e Ча́нтата на Марк не е́ зад си́ния ку́фар.

i Getting about in town

For travel within the larger towns you will find well-developed networks of trams, buses, trolleybuses and minibuses. Movement is slow in the centre and – especially in the rush hours – not always a pleasant experience. And beware of pickpockets! Services are, however, frequent and still relatively cheap. The only underground in

Bulgaria is a single line in Sofia running from the Obelya district in the northwest into the centre of town. The line is being extended out to the huge housing estates to the southeast.

In Sofia there are no conductors on buses, trams or trolleybuses. Best buy your tickets in a block (**талóни**) of ten in advance – it's cheaper! Do this at one of the many small street kiosks with their minuscule, low-down windows through which, if you are lucky, you will just be able to see the assistant's hands and the tickets. The kiosks display signs **ГРÁДСКИ ТРАНСПÓРТ – БИЛÉТИ И KÁРТИ**, and the tickets are all one price for bus, tram and trolleybus.

You get on by any door. Once on, and in rush hours, you may have to push a bit, make sure you punch a ticket as soon as possible in one of the small machines fixed to the side of the vehicle. The driver will not want to see your ticket. Ticket inspectors will, though. Dressed in plain clothes, armed with passes and usually in groups, they make collective raids to deter ticket dodgers. To be caught without a punched ticket inevitably leads to altercation and most probably a fine. Most locals have season tickets.

If you want to move about more quickly, take a taxi or a minibus. There are plenty of both, but different taxi firms have differing tariffs, so check the charges. Taxis all have meters registering distance and time. Seat belts are fitted and should be worn, but the driver will probably suggest you ignore them or merely lay them across your lap. The minibuses (**маршрýтни таксúта**, or, more colloquially, **маршрýтки**) ply predetermined routes, but pick up and set down on request anywhere along the route. There is a single fixed fare for any distance. So, far cheaper than taxis, but more expensive than the normal tram ticket. Good for longer distances, bad for short.

ГРАДСКИ ТРАНСПОРТ
БИЛЕТИ и КАРТИ

How do you say it?

- Asking for and offering help

Мо́жете ли да ми помо́гнете?	*Can you help me?*
С какво́ мо́га да Ви помо́гна?	*How can I help you?*
Мо́га ли да Ви помо́гна с не́що?	*Can I help you with anything?*

- Saying that *something* or *somebody* is missing

(Къде́ е ча́нтата?)	
Ня́ма я./Ча́нтата я ня́ма.	*It's missing./ The bag is missing.*
(Къде́ е г-н Анто́нов?)	
Ня́ма го./Г-н Анто́нов го ня́ма.	*He's not in./ Mr Antonov is not in.*
(Там ли е г-жа́ Ко́линс?)	
Ня́ма я./Г-жа́ Ко́линс я ня́ма.	*She's not in./ Mrs Collins is not in.*

- Saying *one (of the...)*

Masculine	
Еди́ният ку́фар го ня́ма.	*One (of the) case(s) is missing.*
Feminine	
Една́та ча́нта е голя́ма.	*One (of the) bag(s) is large.*
Neuter	
Едно́то момче́ е тук.	*One (of the) boy(s) is here.*

- Responding to unpleasant news

Мно́го неприя́тно!	*Very unpleasant.*

- Responding to being thanked

Ня́ма защо́.	*You're welcome./ Don't mention it.*

Grammar

1 Мо́га да *I can, I am able to*

The Bulgarian verb expressing ability or a particular skill to do things is **мо́га** *I can/I am able to/I am in a position to*. **Мо́га** belongs to the **е**-pattern. The *he/she/it* form **мо́же** with its distinct usage will be familiar to you from Unit 6. In addition to the change of personal endings, there is a change of **г** to **ж** in all forms containing **е** in the ending:

Мóга requires a **да** form of the following main verb:

(аз)	**мóга**	(нúе)	**мóжем**
(ти)	**мóжеш**	(вúе)	**мóжете**
(той) (тя) (то)	**мóже**	(те)	**мóгат**

(Аз) мóга да кáрам ски. — *I know how to ski.*
(Ти) мóжеш да говóриш английски. — *You can speak English.*
Те не мóгат да намéрят багáжа. — *They cannot find the luggage.*

2 -ият and -ия: *the* with masculine adjectives

(a) To make a masculine adjective definite, you add **-ият** to the simple masculine form (or **-ия** if the phrase is not the subject in the sentence):

хýбав мъж *a handsome man* хýбав**ия(т)** мъж ***the** handsome man*
млад мъж *a young man* млáд**ия(т)** мъж ***the** young man*

(b) If the adjective ends in **-ски**, you only need to add **-ят** or **-я**:

англúйски – англúйски**я(т)** рéчник
бъ̀лгарски – бъ̀лгарски**я(т)** рéчник

(c) If the adjective loses **ъ** or **е** from its ending in the feminine, neuter and plural, then it does so in the definite form as well (see Appendix, p. 294):

добъ̀р (добрá, добрó, добрú)
добрúя(т) бъ̀лгарин *the kind Bulgarian*

чéрен (чéрна, чéрно, чéрни)
чéрния(т) чадъ̀р *the black umbrella*

(d) If there is **я** in the basic form, it will naturally be affected by the rules governing the change of **я** to **е** before **и** (see Unit 8):

бял – бéлия(т)
голя́м – голéмия(т)

(e) If you use more than one adjective, you only add **-ият** or **-ия** to the first adjective:

хýбав**ият** млад мъж — *the handsome young man*
голéм**ият** чéрен кýфар — *the large black case*

3 *My, your, his, her,* etc.

When you say **мъжъ́т ми** *my husband*, **ку́фарът Ви** *your suitcase* or **бага́жът им** *their luggage*, you are using a noun in the definite form followed by a short possessive pronoun (see Unit 3). It is also possible to express the same meaning, but with a different emphasis, by a full possessive adjective which comes before the noun and bears the definite article. Like all adjectives, the full possessive adjectives have different endings depending on whether they are used with masculine, feminine, neuter or plural words. Here are examples used with the Bulgarian for *my, you, our* and *their*:

ку́фарът ми/ти	becomes	мо́ят/тво́ят ку́фар	*my/your case*
ча́нтата ми/ти	becomes	мо́ята/тво́ята ча́нта	*my/your bag*
дете́то ми/ти	becomes	мо́ето/тво́ето дете́	*my/your child*
деца́та ми/ти	becomes	мо́ите/тво́ите деца́	*my/your children*
бага́жът ни/им	becomes	на́шият/те́хният бага́ж	*our/their luggage*
ста́ята ни/им	becomes	на́шата/тя́хната стая	*our/their room*
такси́то ни/им	becomes	на́шето/тя́хното такси́	*our/their taxi*
ра́ниците ни/им	becomes	на́шите/те́хните ра́ници	*our/their rucksacks*

(See p. 297 for a full list of possessive adjectival forms. Look at the list when you do the exercises.)

4 Бага́жът ми or мо́ят бага́ж?

Normally you can use the short possessive pronoun, as explained in Unit 3. However, for purposes of contrast, when the ownership is being emphasized, as in the sentence *this bag is* ***mine****, not yours*, for example, you must use the *full* possessive adjective with the definite article.

Мо́ите ку́фари са голе́ми.	***My*** *cases are big.*
Тво́ите са ма́лки.	***Yours*** *are small.*
Тво́ят син е в А́нглия.	***Your*** *son is in England.*
Мо́ят син е в Бълга́рия.	***My*** *son is in Bulgaria.*
Това́ не е́ мо́ят бага́ж.	*This is not* ***my*** *luggage.* (i.e. it belongs to someone else)
Това́ тво́ята ча́нта ли е?	*Is this* ***your*** *bag?* (i.e. not someone else's?)

5 Ча́нтата е мо́я *The bag is mine*

The possessive adjective can sometimes be used without the definite article to render the English independent possessives like *mine*, *yours*, *his*, *hers*, etc. Usually this happens when there is no word following the possessive word as in:

Тво́я ли е та́зи ча́нта?	*Is this bag yours?*
Да, ча́нтата е мо́я.	*Yes, the bag is mine.*
Твой ли е то́зи бага́ж?	*Is this luggage yours?*
Не, не е́ мой.	*No, it isn't mine.*
Тво́е ли е това́ дете́?	*Is this child yours?*
Да, мо́е е.	*Yes, it is mine.*
Тво́и ли са те́зи ку́фари?	*Are these suitcases yours?*
Да, мо́и са.	*Yes, they are mine.*

Here is a summary of the different ways you can express possession. Remember that the full possessive forms are used for stronger emphasis or contrast.

Та́зи ча́нта е на Марк.	*This bag is **Mark's**.*
Та́зи ча́нта е не́гова.	*This bag is **his**.*
Това́ е ча́нтата на Марк.	*This is **Mark's** bag.*
Това́ е не́говата ча́нта.	*This is **his** bag.*
Това́ е ча́нтата му.	*This is **his** bag.*

6 Свой, сво́я, сво́е and сво́и *Mark's own* or *someone else's?*

When in English you say *Mark is carrying his bag* or *they can't find their suitcases*, it is not clear whether Mark is carrying his own or somebody else's bag and whether they can't find their own or someone else's suitcases. In Bulgarian, to emphasize *own* and avoid this ambiguity, you use the special words listed in the heading, most frequently in their definite forms, as in the box below.

Here are the different definite forms:

Subject pronoun	Masculine	Feminine	Neuter	Plural
той/то/тя/те	сво́я(т)	сво́ята	сво́ето	сво́ите

These are adjectives, so no matter whether you want to say *his*, *her* or *their own*, the masculine, feminine, neuter and plural forms go with the gender and number of the word that follows.

Compare:

Марк но́си **сво́ята ча́нта**. *Mark is carrying **his (own) bag**.*

with

Шофьо́рът но́си не́говата ча́нта. *The driver is carrying his* (i.e. Mark's) *bag.*

and

Виолéта чáка **своя́ мъж.** — *Violeta is waiting for* ***her (own) husband.***

with

Невéна чáка нéйния мъж. — *Nevena is waiting for her* (i.e. Violeta's) *husband.*

also

Гóстите не мóгат да намéрят **свóите кýфари.** — *The residents can't find* ***their (own) suitcases.***

with

Момчéтата не мóгат да намéрят тéхните кýфари. — *The boys can't find their* (i.e. the residents') *suitcases.*

7 Ня́ма го *He isn't here*

With **ня́ма** you don't use **той**, **тя**, **то**, **те** but rather **го**, **я**, **го** and **ги** for the person(s) absent or the thing(s) missing. These are short object pronouns, the Bulgarian non-subject equivalents for *him*, *her*, *it*, *them*. (You will learn more about them in Unit 11.)

Къдé е багáжът? Ня́ма **го**.	*Where is the luggage? It's missing.*
Къдé е чáнтата? Ня́ма **я**.	*Where is the bag? It's missing.*
Къдé са кýфарите? Ня́ма **ги**.	*Where are the cases? They're missing.*

Oddly enough, you have to use the short object pronoun even if you also name the person or thing, so you get a repetition:

Чáнтата я ня́ма.	*The bag is missing.*
Момчéто го ня́ма.	*The boy is not here.*
Кýфарите ги ня́ма.	*The suitcases are missing.*
Багáжът им го ня́ма.	*Their luggage is missing.*

8 Помогнéте ми! *Give me a hand!*

The Bulgarian verb **(да) помóгна** is used more like the English phrase *to give help to* rather than just *to help*. So you need to use the indirect object pronouns as explained in Unit 7:

Мóжете ли да **ми** помóгнете? — *Can you help* ***me?*** (as if you were saying *Can you give help* ***to me?***)

Exercises

1 Look again at the Dialogue and then rearrange the words below to make sentences:

a Ви, мо́га, да, помо́гна, какво́, с..?
b от, и́мат, го́стите, Аме́рика, такси́, ну́жда, от.
c не, ча́нтата, Виоле́та, на сво́я мъж, да наме́ри, мо́же.
d бага́ж, не, това́, мо́ят, е́
e си́ня, на, ма́лката, е, ча́нта, Марк

2 Answer the following questions as appropriate to your own skills and abilities:

a Мо́жете ли да игра́ете те́нис?

b Мо́жеш ли да ка́раш ски?

c Мо́жете ли да плу́вате?

d Мо́жете ли да ка́рате кола́?

e Мо́жеш ли да игра́еш на ка́рти?

3 Read the following short dialogue:

You	Извинéте, мóжете ли да ми покáжете къдé е спи́рката на трамвáй нóмер четиринáйсет?
Passer-by	Съжаля́вам, не мóга. Аз съ́що съм тури́ст.

Now use the same pattern to ask to be shown the way to:

a the chemist's
b the underground/subway
c the Sheraton Hotel
d the stop for trolleybus No. 2
e the Central Railway Station

4 Match the questions with the answers on the right:

i	Кой пъпеш и́скате, голéмия или́ мáлкия?	**a**	Не, стáрият.
ii	Кой е Вáшият кýфар?	**b**	Англи́йския.
iii	Млáдият мъж ли е англичáнин?	**c**	Чéрния.
iv	Кой вéстник и́скате?	**d**	Си́ният.
v	Кой чадъ́р да Ви дам?	**e**	Мáлкия.

5 Repeat the dialogue below substituting the word in bold with different words from the box. Make sure you change the defining words (all underlined) according to gender.

Your friend	Твóята **чáнта** ли е товá?
You	Не, тáзи **чáнта** не é мóя. Мóята **чáнта** е пó-голя́ма.

кýфар	*suitcase*
портмонé	*purse, wallet*
чадъ́р	*umbrella*
пáпка	*folder*
моби́лен телефóн	*mobile phone*
моли́в	*pencil*
белéжник	*diary*
химикáлка	*ball-point pen*

6 Disaster has struck: you have lost your purse, your luggage, your umbrella, your diary, your folder and your money. Making up separate sentences for each item, tell a policeman that they are missing. You may find the words in Ex. **5**. useful. And don't forget that the word for *money* **пари́** is always plural!

7 Read the story below about a tourist who has lost his way in Sofia. First answer the questions to test your understanding, then turn the story into a dialogue between a tourist and a policeman.

Тури́ст пи́та еди́н полица́й (*policeman*) мо́же ли да му помо́гне. Тури́стът не мо́же да наме́ри сво́я хоте́л. Полица́ят пи́та как се ка́зва не́говият хоте́л. Тури́стът отгова́ря (*answers*), че не зна́е и́мето на хоте́ла. Той зна́е са́мо, че хоте́лът е бли́зо до спи́рката на троле́й но́мер едно́ и троле́й но́мер пет. Полица́ят пи́та зна́е ли господи́нът на коя́ у́лица е хоте́лът. Тури́стът отгова́ря, че не зна́е у́лицата, но зна́е, че хоте́лът е бли́зо до Университе́та. Полица́ят ка́зва, че и́ма два хоте́ла бли́зо до Университе́та. Еди́ният се ка́зва „Со́фия Ра́дисън“, дру́гият се ка́зва хоте́л „Бълга́рия“. Тури́стът сега́ ве́че зна́е и́мето на хоте́ла. Не́говият хоте́л се ка́зва „Со́фия Ра́дисън“. Той благодари́ на полица́я.

a Какво́ не мо́же да наме́ри тури́стът?
b Зна́е ли тури́стът и́мето на хоте́ла?
c Къде́ е хоте́лът?
d Ко́лко хоте́ла и́ма до Университе́та?
e Как се ка́зва не́говият хоте́л?

8 Complete the answers in the following dialogue using **го**, **я** or **ги** as appropriate:

На телефо́на:

a Извине́те, там ли е Неве́на?
Ня́ма ______ .

b Извине́те, там ли е г-н Джо́нсън?
Ня́ма ______ .

c Извине́те, там ли е дире́кторът?
Ня́ма ______ .

d Извине́те, там ли са Никола́й и Миле́на?
Ня́ма ______ .

e Извине́те, там ли е секрета́рката?
Ня́ма ______ .

f Извине́те, там ли е пи́колото?
Ня́ма ______ .

Do you understand?

Dialogue 2: Да се запознáем! *Let's get acquainted!*

Milena goes into a café and sees that there are two free seats at the table where Mr and Mrs Collins are having coffee.

Милéна	Извинéте, мóже ли да сéдна до вас?
г-жá Кóлинс	Разбúра се, заповя́дайте! Местáта са свобóдни.
Милéна	(*To the waitress.*) Еднó кафé и едúн сладолéд, мóля. (*To Mr and Mrs Collins.*) Днес е мнóго тóпло, налú?
г-жá Кóлинс	Да, найстина. Врéмето е хýбаво за турúсти.
Милéна	На почúвка ли сте в България?
г-жá Кóлинс	Да, úскаме да отúдем с мъжá ми на Злáтни пя́съци, но пъ́рво úмаме мáлко рáбота в Сóфия.
Милéна	Вúе говóрите мнóго добрé бъ́лгарски.
г-жá Кóлинс	Благодаря́, аз тря́бва да говóря добрé бъ́лгарски, защóто бъ́лгарският езúк е мóята профéсия.
Милéна	Разбúрам. Сúгурно сте преводáчка.
г-жá Кóлинс	Тóчно такá.
Милéна	Да се запознáем! Кáзвам се Милéна Марúнова.
г-жá Кóлинс	Прия́тно ми е, Виктóрия Кóлинс.
г-н Кóлинс	Аз съм Джордж Кóлинс.
Милéна	Вúе сúгурно сте англичáни.
г-жá Кóлинс	Да, англичáни сме.
Милéна	Едúн мой колéга заминáва скóро за Áнглия. И аз úскам да отúда ня́кой ден.
г-жá Кóлинс	Пожелáвам Ви скóро да мóжете да отúдете.
Милéна	Надя́вам се. Мóга ли да ви помóгна с нéщо, докатó сте в Сóфия?
г-жá Кóлинс	Мúсля, че мóжете. Тря́бва да отúдем в Централна пóща, а не знáем къдé е.

найстина	*indeed*
врéме	*weather*
на почúвка	*on holiday*
отговáрям, -ряш	*to answer*
защóто	*because*
сúгурно сте преводáчка	*you must be an interpreter*
пожелáвам ви да	*I wish you* (to do something)
докатó	*while*

True or false?

1 До г-н и г-жа́ Ко́линс ня́ма свобо́дни места́.
2 Вре́мето е мно́го то́пло.
3 Г-н и г-жа́ Ко́линс са на почи́вка в Бълга́рия.
4 Г-н и г-жа́ Ко́линс ня́мат ра́бота в Со́фия.
5 Г-жа́ Ко́линс гово́ри добре́ бъ̀лгарски, защо́то е преводачка.
6 Миле́на замина́ва ско́ро за А́нглия.
7 Г-н и г-жа́ Ко́линс зна́ят къде́ е Центра́лна по́ща.

какво́ ще бъ́де вре́мето?

what will the weather be?

In this unit you will learn:

- **how to discuss the weather**
- **how to offer your opinion**
- **how to talk about future events**

Dialogue 1

Nikolai and Nadya make plans for two outings and keep an eye on the weather.

Никола́й (*Nikolai rushes into the office.*) На́дя, здраве́й! Мо́жеш ли да ми помо́гнеш? Тря́бва да организи́рам екску́рзия до Ви́тоша за г-н Анто́нов и за на́шия гост от А́нглия.

На́дя По́-споко́йно, Никола́й! Говори́ по́-ба́вно. Защо́ бъ́рзаш то́лкова?

Никола́й Защо́то тря́бва да пору́чам такси́ и да запа́зя ма́са в ресторанта за у́тре.

На́дя Ня́ма пробле́ми. На́й-ва́жно е вре́мето да бъ́де ху́баво.

Никола́й Вя́рно. И́маш ли ве́стник с прогно́за за вре́мето?

На́дя Не, но мо́жем да чу́ем прогно́зата по ра́диото.

(*Some time later they are listening to the radio.*)

Ра́дио У́тре вре́мето ще бъ́де слъ́нчево, но ветрови́то. По висо́ките планини́ ще е о́блачно. Възмо́жно е да вали́. Температу́рите бъ́дат между́ осемна́йсет и два́йсет и два гра́дуса.

(*Later …*)

Никола́й Жа́лко, вре́мето на Ви́тоша ня́ма да е мно́го ху́баво. Си́гурно ще вали́ дъжд. И си́гурно г-н Джо́нсън не но́си марато́нки.

На́дя Ни́що, не е́ фата́лно. Предла́гам да оти́дете на юг – в Ме́лник. Там вре́мето си́гурно ще е ху́баво. На Ви́тоша мо́же да оти́дете в съ́бота.

Никола́й Добра́ иде́я, но какво́ ще е вре́мето в съ́бота?

На́дя Споре́д прогно́зата в кра́я на се́дмицата ня́ма да вали́ и ще бъ́де по́-то́пло.

Никола́й Ше́фът ще се съгласи́ ли с но́вия план?

На́дя Ще се съгласи́. Аз ще гово́ря с не́го. В Ме́лник е изключи́телно краси́во.

Никола́й Да, зна́я. На́дя, предла́гам и ти да до́йдеш. Съгла́сна ли си?

На́дя Съгла́сна съм. Ще до́йда с удово́лствие!

да организи́рам екску́рзия до Ви́тоша	*to organize an outing to Mount Vitosha*
По́-споко́йно!	*Take it easy!*
Защо́ бъ́рзаш то́лкова?	*What's the hurry?*

да поръ̀чам таксѝ и да запáзя мáса	*to order a taxi and reserve a table*
ýтре	*tomorrow*
Нáй-вáжно е врéмето да бъде хýбаво.	*The main thing is for the weather to be fine.*
прогнóза за врéмето	*weather forecast*
Мóжем да чýем прогнóзата по рáдиото.	*We can hear the forecast on the radio.*
Врéмето ще бъде слъ̀нчево.	*The weather will be sunny.*
ветровѝто	*windy*
По висóките планинѝ ще е óблачно.	*Over the high mountains it will be cloudy.*
Възмóжно е да валѝ.	*It is likely to rain.*
Температýрите ще бъдат междý осемнáйсет и двáйсет и два грáдуса.	*The temperatures will be between 18° and 22° Centigrade*
Жáлко.	*What a pity.*
Врéмето на Вѝтоша нямa да е мнóго хýбаво.	*The weather on Mount Vitosha isn't going to be very good.*
Сѝгурно ще валѝ дъжд.	*It will most probably rain.*
Сѝгурно г-н Джóнсън не нóси маратóнки.	*Mr Johnson surely doesn't have trainers with him.*
не é фатáлно	*it isn't fatal*
Предлáгам да отѝдете на юг.	*I suggest you go south.*
Там врéмето сѝгурно ще е хýбаво.	*The weather is sure to be good there.*
в съ̀бота	*on Saturday*
Каквó ще е врéмето?	*What is the weather going to be like?*
Спорéд прогнóзата в крáя на сéдмицата ня́ма да валѝ.	*According to the forecast at the weekend it isn't going to rain.*
Шéфът ще се съгласѝ ли с нóвия план?	*Will the boss agree to the new plan?*
Аз ще говóря с нéго.	*I'll speak to him.*
изключѝтелно красѝво	*exceptionally beautiful*
Предлáгам и ти да дóйдеш.	*I suggest you come too.*
Съглáсна ли си?	*Do you agree?*
Съглáсна съм!	*I agree!*
Ще дóйда с удовóлствие!	*I'd love to come!* (lit. *I'll come with pleasure!*)

1 Questions

- **a** Защó бъ́рза Николáй?
- **b** Как мóгат Николáй и Нáдя да разберáт (*find out*) прогнóзата?
- **c** Каквó ще бъ̀де врéмето ýтре по висóките планинѝ?
- **d** Каквó предлáга Нáдя?
- **e** Каквá е прогнóзата за крáя на сéдмицата?
- **f** Кой ще говóри с шéфа?

2 True or false?

- **a** Николáй трябва да организѝра екскýрзия до Вѝтоша за г-н Джóнсън и г-н Антóнов.
- **b** Той трябва да кýпи билéти за автобýс за ýтре.
- **c** Във вéстника ѝма прогнóза за врéмето, но Нáдя нямa вéстник.
- **d** Ýтре врéмето на Вѝтоша ще бъ̀де хýбаво.
- **e** Г-н Джóнсън сѝгурно нóси маратóнки.
- **f** Шéфът нямa да се съгласѝ да отѝде в Мéлник.

i Relying on the weather

Bulgaria has a continental climate – hot summers and cold winters. The extremes of temperatures are, however, tempered by the Black Sea in the east and the Aegean to the south. At the Black Sea resorts, even in the summer there is usually a slight breeze and the temperatures are bearable. In the winter, you will find the coldest weather to the north of the Balkan Mountains which stretch from the west to the east of the country. In the Thracian Plain to the south of the Balkan range, and in the valleys leading down towards Greece, the winters are milder.

In the spring and autumn the weather is less reliable. Particularly in March and April, and sometimes into May, you can expect a good deal of rain, so do take an umbrella. In the higher mountains, of course, rain at these times usually means snow, and snow in Bulgaria means skiing. In the Rila and Pirin Mountains to the south of Sofia and also on Mount Vitosha, which majestically rises to nearly 2,300 metres, just half an hour's drive from the centre of the capital city, you can often ski into May.

Getting out of town

Everywhere in Bulgaria there are mountains. Having access to the mountains is, of course, wonderful, but do go prepared for rapid changes of weather, especially in the spring and autumn. It can be sunny and warm in the valleys and snowing hard higher up.

The distances in Bulgaria are not great, and it is well worth hiring a car to get out of town. (Book well in advance!) There are some very good roads – as well as many very bad ones. Do remember though, Bulgarian driving patterns are rather like the climate, a mixture of continental and Mediterranean. Remember too that Bulgarian traffic police make on-the-spot fines (**гло́ба**) and are particularly hot on speeding and unauthorized overtaking.

The rail network is small and trains are slow, so, unless you hire a car, you may prefer the large selection of cross-country minibuses and long-distance coaches. It's safer to buy your tickets in advance, and do take your passport with you. In fact, it's best to take your passport wherever you go – just in case!

How do you say it?

- Asking *what will the weather be like?*

Какво́ ще е/бъде вре́мето? *What will the weather be?*

- Describing the weather

То́пло е.
It's warm.

Студе́но е.
It's cold.

Слъ̀нчево е.
It's sunny.

О́блачно е.
It's cloudy.

Ветрови́то е.
It's windy.

Вали́ дъжд.
It's raining.

Вали́ сняг.
It's snowing.

- Evaluating a situation

Ху́баво е/Не е́ ху́баво.	*It's fine/not good.*
Интере́сно е/Не е́ интере́сно.	*It's interesting/not interesting.*
Ва́жно е/Не е́ ва́жно.	*It's important/not important.*
Не е́ фата́лно.	*It's not fatal.*
Възмо́жно е.	*It's possible/likely.*

- Suggesting what to do.

Предла́гам да оти́дем на Ви́тоша.	*I suggest we go to Mount Vitosha.*
Предла́гам да оти́дете в Ме́лник.	*I suggest you go to Melnik.*

- Agreeing or disagreeing

For a man

Съгла́сен съм.	*I agree.*
Не съ́м съгла́сен.	*I disagree.*

For a woman

Съгла́сна съм.	*I agree.*
Не съ́м съгла́сна.	*I disagree.*

- Expressing regret

Жа́лко!	*What a pity!*

Grammar

1 Слъ́нчево е *It's sunny*

When describing the weather in Bulgarian you do not need an equivalent of the English *it*:

Слъ́нчево е.	*It is sunny.*
Я́сно е.	*It is clear.*

As you see, you use the neuter form of the corresponding adjective and put **е** after the 'weather' word. You follow the same pattern for sentences describing the situation in more general terms:

Тъ́мно е.	*It is dark.*
Ра́но е.	*It is early.*
Къ́сно е.	*It is late.*

You can also begin with the actual word for *weather*:

Вре́мето е мно́го ло́шо днес.	*The weather is very bad today.*
Вре́мето днес е я́сно.	*The weather is clear today.*

Very often weather sentences begin with a reference to where and when it is warm, cold, dark, etc. In such cases the verb **е** comes before the neuter adjective:

В Мéлник вúнаги е тóпло.	*In Melnik it is always warm.*
През зúмата е студéно.	*In winter it is cold.*
В стáята е тъмно.	*It is dark in the room.*

2 Валú (дъжд) *It's raining*

For descriptions of the weather involving precipitation Bulgarian uses the *it* form of an old verb meaning *fall*: **валú**. Depending on the context, **валú** can mean *it is raining* or *it is snowing*. To be more specific you add the word for *rain* or *snow*:

Валú **дъжд**.	*It is raining.*
Валú **сняг**.	*It is snowing.*

3 Чудéсно е, че... *It is wonderful that...*

Some evaluating expressions like *it is wonderful* or *it is important* are linked to further statements. If the linking word in English is *that*, in Bulgarian you use **че**:

Чудéсно е, **че** сте тук!	*It's wonderful (that)* you *are here.*
Жáлко е, **че** нúмаме врéме.	*It's a pity (that) we have no time.*

In English, you often omit *that*. In Bulgarian, you can *never* leave out **че**.

If the linking word is *to*, followed by a verb, you need a **да** form of the following verb:

Вáжно е **да пристúгнем** наврéме.	*It's important for us to get there on time.*
Приятно е **да пътýваш** с колá.	*It's pleasant to travel by car.*

Note that the verb **е** always comes second no matter what other word is used in first position:

Не **é** вярно, че...	*It is not true that...*
Мнóго **е** приятно да...	*It is very pleasant to...*

4 (Аз) Ще дóйда *I will come* (future tense)

It is very easy to refer to future events in Bulgarian. You merely insert **ще** in front of the verbal forms for the present tense. With **(да) дóйда**, therefore, you say:

(аз)	**ще** до́йда	*I'll come*	(ни́е)	**ще** до́йдем	*we'll come*
(ти)	**ще** до́йдеш	*you'll come*	(ви́е)	**ще** до́йдете	*you'll come*
(той) (тя) (то)	**ще** до́йде	*he/she/it will come*	(те)	**ще** до́йдат	*they'll come*

To say *I will not*, *you will not*, etc. instead of **ще** you insert **ня́ма** followed by **да**:

(аз)	**ня́ма да** до́йда	*I won't come*
(ти)	**ня́ма да** до́йдеш	*you won't come*
(той)	**ня́ма да** до́йде	*he won't come*
(ни́е)	**ня́ма да** до́йдем	*we won't come*
(ви́е)	**ня́ма да** до́йдете	*you won't come*
(те)	**ня́ма да** до́йдат	*they won't come*

5 Аз ще съм and аз ще бъда *I will be*

You have two verb forms to choose from to express *I will be* or *I am going to be*, etc. The form with **бъда**, etc. tends to be more formal:

(аз)	ще съм/ ще бъда	*I will be*	(ни́е)	ще сме/ ще бъдем	*we will be*
(ти)	ще си/ ще бъдеш	*you will be*	(ви́е)	ще сте/ ще бъдете	*you will be*
(той) (тя) (то)	ще е/ ще бъде	*he/he/it will be*	(те)	ще са/ ще бъдат	*they will be*

Аз ще съм/бъда в Пло́вдив у́тре.	*I will be in Plovdiv tomorrow.*
Той ще е/бъде на екску́рзия в съ́бота.	*He will be going on an excursion on Saturday.*

To say *I will not*, etc. you simply replace **ще** with **ня́ма да**:

Ня́ма да съм/бъда в Со́фия.	Ня́ма да сме/бъдем свобо́дни.
Ня́ма да си/бъдеш свобо́ден.	Ня́ма да сте/бъдете във фи́рмата.
Ня́ма да е/бъде на те́нис.	Ня́ма да са/бъдат в Пло́вдив.

6 In what manner?

A great number of words that tell us *how* or *in what manner* something is done (adverbs) can be formed from adjectives. In English, you often add **-ly** to adjectives to form adverbs. In Bulgarian, many adverbs look exactly like the neuter form of an adjective because they end in **-o**:

Adverbs

Той гово́ри мно́го бързо.	*He speaks very quickly.*
Тря́бва да гово́риш по́-споко́йно.	*You must speak more calmly.*

Adjectives

Такси́то е мно́го бързо.	*The taxi is very quick.*
Оби́чам споко́йно море́.	*I like a calm sea.*

Adverbs are also used to make adjectives more specific as in:

Вре́мето ще бъде **мно́го** ху́баво.	*The weather will be very nice.*
Ме́лник е **изключи́телно** краси́во градче́.	*Melnik is an exceptionally beautiful little town.*

7 На́й- for *biggest* and *best*

To say that something or someone is *the biggest* or *the best* or *the most beautiful*, (i.e. to make the superlative form of the adjective), you place **на́й-** on the front of the adjective, and, usually, the definite article on the end.

На́й-голе́ми**ят** пъпеш е тук.	*The biggest melon is here.*
Та́зи англича́нка е **на́й**-ху́бава**та**.	*This English woman is the most beautiful one.*
Това́ е **на́й**-сла́дко**то** ви́но.	*This is the sweetest wine.*
На́й-е́втини**те** кра́ставици са на паза́ра.	*The cheapest cucumbers are at the market.*

But, as in English, you can sometimes use the superlative without the definite article:

Вре́мето е **на́й**-то́пло в Ме́лник.	*The weather is hottest in Melnik.*

Exercises

1 To practise talking about the weather, first read the following short dialogue:

– Днес е слъ̀нчево, но ветрови́то. У́тре ще бъ̀де ли също слъ̀нчево и ветрови́то?
• Не, у́тре ня́ма да бъ̀де слъ̀нчево и ветрови́то.

Now complete these dialogues following the same pattern:

a Днес е о́блачно и мра́чно (*dull*). ___________________?
Не, _________________.
b Днес е мъгли́во (*foggy*). ___________________?
Не, _________________.
c Днес е то́пло и слъ̀нчево. ___________________?
Не, _________________.
d Днес е студе́но и вла́жно (*damp*). ___________________?
Не, _________________.
e Днес е дъждо́вно (*rainy*). ___________________?
Не, _________________.

2 Agree or disagree with the following comments, using the model:

– Интере́сно е.
• Наистина, мно́го е интере́сно. (*Indeed, it is very interesting*)
• Не съм съгла́сен/съгла́сна. Изо́бщо не е́ интере́сно. (*I don't agree. It isn't interesting at all.*)

a Горе́що е. (*It's hot.*)
b Къ̀сно е. (*It's late.*)
c Заба́вно е. (*It's amusing.*)
d Удо́бно е. (*It's convenient, comfortable.*)
e Възмо́жно е. (*It's possible.*)

3 Choose a good reason for the statements below from the list on the right:

i Г-н Джо́нсън ня́ма да оти́де на екску́рзия, ___
ii Ня́ма да оти́да на Ви́тоша, ___
iii Тря́бва да поръ̀чаме такси́, ___
iv В Бълга́рия и́ма мно́го тури́сти, ___
v Кита́йският (*Chinese*) рестора́нт е затво́рен, ___

a защо́то е къ̀сно и ня́ма трамва́и.
b защо́то е мно́го ра́но.
c защо́то ля́тото (*the summer*) е дъ̀лго и то́пло.
d защо́то ня́ма удо́бни обу́вки (*shoes*).
e защо́то ще вали́ дъжд.

4 You turn on the radio and hear the following weather forecast:

У́тре в ця́лата (*the whole*) страна́ ще бъ́де я́сно и горе́що. По Черномо́рието (*Black Sea Coast*) ще и́ма слаб (*light*) до уме́рен (*moderate*) и́зточен (*from the east*) вя́тър. Температу́рата на въ́здуха (*air*): между́ два́йсет и о́сем и три́йсет и два гра́дуса, а на мо́рската вода́ (*the sea water*) – о́коло два́йсет и три гра́дуса.

Now, using full sentences, try to answer the following questions.

a О́блачно ли ще бъ́де у́тре?
b Ще и́ма ли си́лен (*strong*) вя́тър по Черномо́рието?
c Ко́лко горе́що ще бъ́де?
d Каква́ ще бъ́де температу́рата на море́то?

5 Imagine you are Nikolai and complete this conversation:

Миле́на Ще до́йдеш ли днес с нас на те́нис, Никола́й?
Никола́й (*I won't come because I haven't got time.*)
Миле́на Жа́лко. Кога́ ще и́маш вре́ме?
Никола́й (*Tomorrow.*)
Миле́на Къде́ предла́гаш да оти́дем у́тре?
Никола́й (*I suggest we go on an outing. Do you agree?*)
Миле́на Какво́ ще бъ́де вре́мето?
Никола́й (*The weather will be sunny and warm.*)
Миле́на Добре́, съгла́сна съм. Но все пак (*all the same*) ще взе́ма я́ке (*jacket*).
Никола́й (*Good. I'll take my jacket too.*)

6 Use **бързо** *quickly*, **тру́дно** *with difficulty/not easily* or **по́-ти́хо** *more quietly* to complete these sentences:

a Г-н Анто́нов ще се съгласи́ ______.
b ______ ще наме́рим га́рата.
c Шшш! Говори́ ______!
d ______ ще наме́рим бага́жа.

Do you understand?

Dialogue 2: Ела́ с нас! *Come with us!*

Milena succumbs to gentle GSM* persuasion and agrees to go to Melnik.

Никола́й Здраве́й, Миле́на.
Миле́на Ти ли си, Никола́й? Защо́ не си́ на екску́рзия?

(*Bulgarian mobile phone, remember?)

Никола́й Вре́мето е ло́шо.
Миле́на Не изгле́жда ло́шо. Слъ̀нчево е.
Никола́й Да, но и́ма си́лен вя́тър и на Ви́тоша е студе́но?
Миле́на Вя́рно, там ви́наги е по́-студе́но.
Никола́й Да, защо́то е висо́ко. Затова́ и́скаме у́тре да оти́дем в Ме́лник.
Миле́на В Ме́лник е чуде́сно. Си́гурно ще бъ́де то́пло, защо́то е на юг.
Никола́й Но все пак ще взе́мем я́кета. И́скаш ли да до́йдеш и ти, Миле́на?
Миле́на Възмо́жно ли е?
Никола́й Разби́ра се, че е възмо́жно. Ела́ с нас! На́дя съ́що ще до́йде. Ще бъ́де по́-интере́сно с две ху́бави моми́чета*.
Миле́на Добре́, съгла́сна съм. Кога́ замина́вате?
Никола́й В се́дем и полови́на.
Миле́на Серио́зно? Но това́ е ужа́сно ра́но!
Никола́й Не, не, шегу́вам се, защо́то зна́я, че не оби́чаш да ста́ваш ра́но. Сре́щата ни е в де́вет и полови́на пред хоте́ла на г-н Джо́нсън.
Миле́на Добре́, ще до́йда.

[*Although моми́че means *girl*, the word itself is neuter!]

висо́ко	*high*
все пак	*all the same*
изгле́ждам, -даш	*to look, seem*
си́лен, си́лна	*strong*
затова́	*that is why*
я́ке	*jacket*
серио́зно?	*are you serious?*
ужа́сно	*terribly*
шегу́вам, -ваш се	*to joke*
ста́вам, -ваш	*to get up*
пред	*in front of*

True or false?

1 Никола́й не е́ на екску́рзия, защо́то вре́мето на Ви́тоша е ло́шо.
2 На Ви́тоша ви́наги е по́-то́пло.
3 Ме́лник е на и́зток.
4 Миле́на е съгла́сна да оти́де в Ме́лник.
5 Миле́на оби́ча да ста́ва ра́но.
6 Сре́щата на Никола́й с г-н Джо́нсън е пред хоте́ла му.

план за слéдващата сéдмица

a plan for the coming week

In this unit you will learn:

- **how to refer to the days of the week**
- **some time expressions**
- **how to give the date**
- **some more numbers**

Dialogue 1

Mr Johnson firms up plans for his second week in Bulgaria.

г-н Антóнов (*Looking at his diary*.) Мáйкъл, днес е четвъ́ртък, четиринáйсети май. Вéче е четвъ́ртият ден от Вáшия престóй. Остáват óще дéсет дни. Тря́бва да напрáвим план за слéдващата сéдмица.

г-н Джóнсън В понедéлник и́скам да оти́да в Бóровец, за да разглéдам хотéлите. Женá ми и синъ́т ми и́скат да дóйдат през зи́мата на ски в Бългáрия.

г-н Антóнов И́скате ли ня́кой да Ви придружи́?

г-н Джóнсън Не, благодаря́. Ще наéма колá и ще оти́да сам.

г-н Антóнов Добрé, кáкто предпочи́тате. Във втóрник преди́ óбед сме покáнени на излóжба на плакáти. След товá е запланýван óбед с дизáйнера, кóйто организи́ра излóжбата. Следóбед тря́бва да отговóрим на фи́рмата, от коя́то ще кýпим компю́три. И́мам еднá молбá към Вас – да ни дадéте съвéт за нáй-изгóдните цени́.

г-н Джóнсън Разби́ра се. Ще оти́дем ли в Плóвдив слéдващата сéдмица?

г-н Антóнов Да. Плóвдивският панаи́р запóчва на двáйсети май, в сря́да. Ще оти́дем на пъ́рвия ден, за да и́маме врéме да разглéдаме всичко.

г-н Джóнсън Когá ще бъ́дат прéговорите?

г-н Антóнов На втóрия и трéтия ден. Тря́бва да поръ́чаме ня́кои материáли и маши́ни за фи́рмата. Вáшата пóмощ е добрé дошлá.

г-н Джóнсън Разби́ра се, аз съм тук, за да помóгна на фи́рмата Ви.

г-н Антóнов За съжалéние, на двáйсет и втóри май тря́бва да се въ́рна в Сóфия. На тóзи ден тря́бва да посрéщна делегáцията, коя́то присти́га от Япóния. Николáй ще бъ́де с Вас до кpáя на сéдмицата.

г-н Джóнсън Тогáва, ще обясня́ на Николáй кои́ материáли са нáй-подходя́щи и кои́ са нáй-модéрните маши́ни.

г-н Антóнов Отли́чно, товá ще е изключи́телно полéзно за нас. Нáдя, обади́ се на Николáй. Пи́тай го свобóден ли е. Кажи́ му за прогрáмата на г-н Джóнсън. Обясни́ му защó и́маме нýжда от нéго слéдващия пéтък.

г-н Джóнсън Извинéте, Боя́не, когá ще се въ́рнем от Плóвдив?

г-н Антóнов А, да! С Николáй ще се вър́нете в събота, а в недéля сте у нас на гóсти.

г-н Джóнсън Благодаря́. Втóрата ми сéдмица в България изглéжда дóста интерéсна!

Днес е четвъртък, четиринáйсети май.	*Today is Thursday May 14.*
четвъртият ден от Вáшия престóй	*the fourth day of your stay*
Остáват óще дéсет дни.	*There are still ten days left.*
Тря́бва да напрáвим план за слéдващата сéдмица.	*We must do a plan for the coming week.*
в понедéлник...	*on Monday...*
за да разглéдам хотéлите	*(in order) to take a look at the hotels*
И́скате ли ня́кой да Ви придружи́?	*Would you like someone to accompany you?*
Ще наéма колá.	*I'll hire a car.*
кáкто	*as*
Във втóрник преди́ óбед сме покáнени на излóжба на плакáти.	*On Tuesday, before lunch we are invited to a poster exhibition.*
След товá е запланýван óбед	*After that a lunch has been planned*
с дизáйнера,	*with the designer*
кóйто организи́ра...	*who is organizing...*
И́мам едá молбá към Вас.	*I have a favour to ask of you.*
съвéт за нáй-изгóдните цени́	*advice concerning the most favourable prices*
Плóвдивският панаи́р запóчва на двáйсети май.	*The Plovdiv Trade Fair begins on May 20.*
в сря́да	*on Wednesday*
на пъ́рвия ден	*on the first day*
да разглéдаме всичко	*to look round everything*
Когá ще бъ́дат прéговорите?	*When will the talks be?*
на втóрия и трéтия ден	*on the second and third day*
ня́кои материáли и маши́ни	*certain materials and machines*
Вáшата пóмощ е добрé дошлá.	*Your help is welcome.*
за да	*(in order) to*
На двáйсет и втóри май тря́бва да се вър́на в Сóфия.	*On May 22 I must return to Sofia.*
На тóзи ден тря́бва да посрéщна делегáцията, кóято присти́га от Япóния.	*That day I must meet the delegation arriving from Japan.*

до края на седмицата	*until the end of the week*
Ще обясня на Николай кой материали са най-подходящи.	*I'll explain to Nikolai which materials are the most suitable.*
кой са най-модерните машини	*which are the most up-to-date machines*
отлично	*excellent*
полезно	*useful*
Питай го свободен ли е.	*Ask him whether he is free.*
Кажи му за програмата на г-н Джонсън.	*Tell him about Mr Johnson's programme/schedule.*
Обясни му защо имаме нужда от него следващия петък.	*Explain to him why we need him next Friday.*
В неделя сте у нас на гости.	*On Sunday you are guests at our place.*
доста	*pretty (very), quite*

1 Questions

- **a** За кога трябва да направят план г-н Антонов и г-н Джонсън?
- **b** Защо г-н Джонсън иска да отиде в Боровец?
- **c** Кога са поканени на изложба г-н Джонсън и г-н Антонов?
- **d** Защо ще отидат на панаира на първия ден?
- **e** Кога трябва да се върне в София г-н Антонов?

2 True or false?

- **a** Г-н Джонсън иска някой да го придружи до Боровец.
- **b** Панаирът в Пловдив започва на двайсети май.
- **c** Преговорите ще бъдат на първия и втория ден.
- **d** Г-н Антонов ще посрещне делегация, която пристига от Франция.
- **e** Майкъл Джонсън и Николай ще се върнат от Пловдив в събота.

i Of high days and holidays

Although Bulgaria is on the south-eastern fringe of Europe and, for nearly five centuries, was within the Ottoman Empire, the people share with us most of the traditional feast days in the Christian calendar. They belong, however, to the Eastern Orthodox branch of Christianity and occasionally there are differences of emphasis. They place less importance on Christmas (**Ко́леда**) and more on Easter (**Вели́кден**), for example, and sometimes the dates of Easter in Bulgaria and in Western Europe and America do not coincide.

The Bulgarian Orthodox service on the Saturday night before Easter Sunday is a very beautiful occasion with candles, rich vestments and wonderful singing.

The Bulgarians also have a number of special days in their calendar that are to do with nationality, their cultural identity and the political experiences of their recent past rather than with religion. March 3 (**тре́ти март**), for example, is Bulgaria's day of national liberation and is a public holiday. Bulgarians then celebrate the end of the Russo-Turkish War of 1877–8 and their liberation from the Ottoman Empire.

May 24 (**два́йсет и четвъ̀рти май**) is a very old holiday. It has a cultural significance for all the Slav peoples and has survived numerous changes of regime. It is dedicated to Saints Cyril and Methodius, the so-called 'Apostles of the Slavs' whom the Bulgarians regard very much as their own. This holiday, which is probably Bulgaria's most popular 'high day', celebrates the achievements of Bulgarian education and culture through the ages and has traditionally seen street parades, singing, dancing and other public festivities.

How do you say it?

- Giving the date

Днес е ше́сти ю́ни.	*Today is June 6.*

- Saying *on* with a date

на петна́йсети май	*on May 15*

- Saying *on* with days of the week

в понеде́лник	*on Monday*
във вто́рник	*on Tuesday*
в сря́да	*on Wednesday*
в четвъ̀ртък	*on Thursday*
в пе́тък	*on Friday*
в съ̀бота	*on Saturday*
в неде́ля	*on Sunday*

- Asking for advice/a favour

Мóля, дáйте ми съвéт.	*Please give me some advice.*
Какъв съвéт ще ми дадéте?	*What advice would you give me?*
Ймам еднá молбá към Вас.	*I have a favour to ask of you.*

- Stating your purpose

Ще отúдем рáно, за да úмаме врéме.	*We'll go early so as to have time.*
Обадú се на Николáй, за да го пúташ когá ще дóйде.	*Get in touch with/ Ring Nikolai (in order) to ask him when he'll be coming.*

- Inviting someone home

Елá(те) у нас на гóсти.	*Come to our place.*

Grammar

1 Първи, втóри, трéти *First, second, third*

The numerals indicating order (ordinals) are used as adjectives:

Masculine	**Feminine**	**Neuter**
първи *first*	първа	първо
втóри *second*	втóра	втóро
трéти *third*	трéта	трéто
четвърти *fourth*	четвърта	четвърто

From *fifth* on, you obtain the masculine forms by adding **-и** to the number. For feminine and neuter words you replace **-и** with **-а** or **-о** as above. Note the occasional shift of stress.

(пет)	пéти	*fifth*		единáйсети	*eleventh*
(шест)	шéсти	*sixth*		дванáйсети	*twelfth*
(сéдем)	сéдми	*seventh*	(with loss of **е**	тринáйсети	*thirteenth*
(óсем)	óсми	*eighth*	before **м**)	четиринáйсети	*fourteenth*
(дéвет)	девéти	*ninth*		петнáйсети	*fifteenth*
(дéсет)	десéти	*tenth*		шестнáйсети	*sixteenth*

Note that the **-нáйсети**, **-нáйсета**, **-нáйсето** endings are pronounced **-нáйсти**, **-нáйста** and **-нáйсто**.

For numbers consisting of more than one word you add **-и** (**-а**, **-о**) only to the last part of the number:

двáйсет и пъpв**и**	*twenty-first*
двáйсет и втóр**и**	*twenty-second*
двáйсет и трéт**и**	*twenty-third*

Like all other adjectives, the ordinal numerals also have definite forms:

втóрата сéдмица	*the second week*
четвъ̀ртият ден	*the fourth day*

(You will find a full list of all the numerals in the Appendix on p. 292.)

2 Пъpви януáри *January 1*

To give the date in Bulgarian you say **днес е** *today is* followed by the day and the masculine ordinal numeral (an adjective, remember!) in the indefinite form:

(днес е) втóрник, трéти февруáри	*(today is) Tuesday 3 February*

Here are some dates together with the names of all the months. Certain of the dates are particularly important in the Bulgarian calendar. The significance of some of them was explained in the information section:

пъpви	**януáри**	*1 January*	(1.I.)
óсми	**февруáри**	*8 February*	(8.II.)
трéти	**март**	*3 March*	(3.III.)
двáйсет и девéти	**апрúл**	*29 April*	(29.IV.)
двáйсет и четвъ̀рти	**май**	*24 May*	(24.V.)
втóри	**ю́ни**	*2 June*	(2.VI.)
сéдми	**ю́ли**	*7 July*	(7.VII.)
четиринáйсети	**áвгуст**	*14 August*	(14.VIII.)
шéсти	**септéмври**	*6 September*	(6.IX.)
трúйсети	**октóмври**	*30 October*	(30.X.)
десéти	**ноéмври**	*10 November*	(10.XI.)
двáйсет и пéти	**декéмври**	*25 December*	(25.XII.)

The names of the months are spelt with a small letter. When you write the number of the month in figures, you normally use Roman numerals, as in the brackets.

3 101 and above

101	сто и еднó	300	трúста
110	сто и дéсет	400	чéтиристотин
123	сто двáйсет и три	500	пéтстотин
200	двéста	600	шéстстотин

700	сéдемстотин	1 000	хиля́да
800	óсемстотин	2 000	две хи́ляди
900	дéветстотин	1 000 000	еди́н милиóн

(Note the change of stress in **хиля́да** and **две хи́ляди**!)

4 През две хи́ляди и óсма годи́на *In 2008*

For English *in* with the year you use the preposition **през**. The year is given in thousands (**хиля́да** *thousand* or **две хи́ляди** *two thousand*), followed by the hundreds and the tens. Only the last element of the number is an ordinal, the feminine form agreeing with **годи́на**:

Родéн съм **през хиля́да деветстóтин осемдесéт и втóра годи́на**.	*I was born in 1982.* (In Bulgarian you have to say *I **am** born.*)

Note that **и** comes before the final numeral (see Unit 4).

5 *When*: prepositions in time expressions

Here are some of the most common prepositions used with time expressions. Try to learn the expressions as whole phrases:

в сря́да	*on Wednesday*
до десéти ноéмври	*before/until November 10*
за две сéдмици	*for 2 weeks* (looking to the future)
от една́ сéдмица	*for a week** (looking to the past)
на óсми март	*on March 8*
от сря́да **до** пéтък	*from Wednesday till Friday*
преди́ óбед	*before lunch*
преди́ три дни	*three days ago*
през деня́	*during the day*
през есента́	*in autumn*
през нощта́	*at night*
през пролетта́	*in spring*
през (мéсец) януа́ри	*in January*
след една́ сéдмица	*a week later/in a week*

*Note that with expressions like от една́ сéдмица when they answer the question *How long have you been here for?* Bulgarian uses the present tense:

От кóлко врéме сте в Бълга́рия?	*How long have you been in Bulgaria for?*
В Бълга́рия съм **от** една́ сéдмица.	*I've been in Bulgaria for a week.*

6 Го and я *Him/it* and *her*

When they are not subjects, things and persons are most frequently substituted by the short object pronouns. Unlike English, these little words usually precede the verb and are normally unstressed:

Кой ще напра́ви план?	*Who is going to do a plan?*
Секретáрката ще **го** напрáви.	*The secretary will do it.*
Кой нóси чáнтата?	*Who is carrying the bag?*
Мъжъ̀т на Виолéта **я** нóси.	*Violeta's husband is carrying it.*

However, after **не** the short object pronouns are stressed, and if the verb comes first in the sentence, they follow it.

Не **мé** чáкай!	*Don't wait for me!*
Пи́тай **го** свобóден ли е.	*Ask him whether he's free.*
Придружéте **ме** до бáнката, мóля.	*Accompany me to the bank, please.*

Here are all the short object pronouns (corresponding subject forms in brackets). For a list of the full forms, see Unit 6 (non-subject forms after prepositions).

(аз)	**ме**	*me*	(ни́е)	**ни**	*us*
(ти)	**те**	*you*	(ви́е)	**ви/Ви**	*you*
(той)	**го**	*him/it*			
(тя)	**я**	*her/it*	(те)	**ги**	*them*
(то)	**го**	*it*			

(You'll find the short indirect object pronouns in Unit 7 and parallel lists in the Appendix.)

7 Ще обясня́ на Николáй *I'll explain to Nikolai*

In Unit 7, you learned what pronouns to use with verbs that require an indirect object – the person to whom or for whom something is done. If, however, you want to use the person's name or a noun, you need to introduce it by the preposition **на** (which in most cases corresponds to the English *to*). Here are examples with some of the most common verbs that require an indirect object in Bulgarian: (да) дам, (да) помóгна, (да) обясня́ and (да) кáжа:

Той ще дадé съвéт **на момчéто**.	*He will give the boy some advice.*
Невéна ще помóгне **на Марк и Виолéта**.	*Nevena will help (give help to) Mark and Violeta.*

Ма́йкъл Джо́нсън ще обясни́ сво́ите пла́нове **на Никола́й**.	*Michael Johnson will explain his plans to Nikolai.*
Никола́й ще ка́же **на Миле́на** за но́вия план.	*Nikolai will tell Milena about the new plan.*

8 Ще му обясня́ *I'll explain to him*

Compare the examples in the last section with their alternatives where the short indirect object pronouns replace **на** + noun and move to the left of the verb:

Той ще **му даде́** съве́т.	*He'll give him some advice.*
Неве́на ще **им помо́гне**.	*Nevena will help them.*
Ма́йкъл Джо́нсън ще **му обясни́** сво́ите пла́нове.	*Michael Johnson will explain his plans to him.*
Никола́й ще **ѝ ка́же** за но́вия план.	*Nikolai will tell her about the new plan.*

When **на** is used with the full non-subject pronoun as an alternative to the short pronoun to the left of the verb, this highlights a contrast. Compare:

Ще се оба́дя **на не́я** (не на не́го!).	*I'll ring her (not him).*

with Ще **ѝ** се оба́дя.

Ще помо́гна **и на те́бе** (не са́мо на тях!).	*I'll help you too (not just them).*

with Ще **ти** помо́гна.

9 Ни́е сме пока́нени *We are invited*

Some verbal forms can be used with the verb *to be* as in *we are* or *we have been **invited***. In such sentences you are not interested in who does the inviting but who is or has been invited. That is why they are called passive sentences. Such **-ed** forms of the verb are known as passive participles and are used as adjectives. In Bulgarian, you form the passive participle of most verbs by replacing the personal endings of the past form by **-ен**:

(да) пока́н**я** *to invite* becomes пока́н**ен** *invited*:
аз съм пока́нен — *I am invited*

This is the masculine form to which you can then add the feminine, neuter or plural endings: **тя е пока́нена, то е пока́нено, ни́е сме пока́нени**.

А-pattern verbs add **-ан**, so заплану́вам *to plan* becomes **заплану́ван (-а, -о, -и)** *planned*:

Конферéнцията **е запланýвана** за сéдми септéмври.	*The conference is planned for September 7.*

A small number of verbs add **-ян** or **-т**. You will find some of them among the participles listed in the Appendix.

Exercises

1 Read this notice found just inside the entrance to a department store:

ПÁРТЕР (*ground floor*):	подáръци и козмéтика (*cosmetics*)
I ЕТÁЖ (*floor*):	всѝчко за детéто
II ЕТÁЖ:	обýвки
III ЕТÁЖ:	телевѝзори (*televisions*), компю́три. мобѝлни телефóни
IV ЕТÁЖ:	килѝми (*carpets*)
V ЕТÁЖ:	ресторáнт, тоалéтна

Now answer Каквó ѝма:

a на пáртера?
b на пъ̀рвия етáж?
c на втóрия етáж?
d на трéтия етáж?
e на четвъ̀ртия етáж?
f на пéтия етáж?

2 Still looking at the notice, say on which floor they sell the indicated items. На кой етáж продáват:

a маратóнки?
b парфю́ми? (*perfumes*)
c компю́три
d шампоáни? (*shampoos*)

3 Try using some object pronouns by replacing the names and filling the spaces with the Bulgarian for *him, her,* etc.

Обадѝ се:

a на Марк и __ поканѝ у нас на гóсти.
b на Невéна и __ поканѝ у нас на гóсти.
c на Николáй и __ поканѝ у нас на гóсти.
d на г-н и г-жá Антóнови и __ поканѝ у нас на гóсти.

4 You are looking at your diary and making plans for the days ahead. Following the model, complete the sentences with the appropriate days of the week or time expressions:

Днес е понеде́лник. След три дни ще бъ́де четвъ́ртък. Ще ку́пя биле́т (for за) четвъ́ртък.

a Днес е четвъ́ртък. След два дни ще бъ́де ____ Ще запа́зя ма́са (for) ____ .

b Днес е неде́ля. След пет дни ще бъ́де ____ Ще оти́да на изло́жбата (on) ____ .

c Днес е вто́рник. У́тре ще бъ́де ____ Ще ку́пя биле́т (for tomorrow) ____.

5 Look carefully at this page from a brochure, then answer the questions below in Bulgarian. For the rounded, long-hand letters look back at p. xiv.

БЕЛГРАД

ЕДИН ПРИЯТЕН УИКЕНД

ДАТИ НА ЗАМИНАВАНЕ	ЦЕНА
април – 26	*193 лв.*
май – 31	*193 лв.*
август – 2	*193 лв.*
септември – 6	*193 лв.*
октомври – 11	*193 лв.*

1 ДЕН – Отпътуване в 6,00 ч. по маршрут София - Белград. Пристигане в Белград в ранния следобед. Настаняване. Кратка почивка. Панорамна обиколка на Белград с екскурзовод на български език. Свободно време. По предварителна заявка – вечеря в бохемския квартал «Скадарлия». Нощувка.

2 ДЕН – Закуска. Целодневна екскурзия до Нови Сад с екскурзовод на български език. Разглеждане на Старата Патриаршия и Катедралата; посещение на манастира Ново Хопово; разглеждане на средновековната крепост Петроварадин. Свободно време. Връщане в Белград. По желание – разходка с корабче по р.Дунав и р.Сава. Нощувка.

3 ДЕН – Закуска. Отпътуване за България. Пристигане в София в късния следобед.

ЦЕНАТА ВКЛЮЧВА

- транспорт с луксозен автобус*** (климатик, видеосистема, мини бар - безплатни топли напитки);
- 2 нощувки със закуски в хотел*** в центъра на Белград;
- панорамна обиколка на Белград с екскурзовод на български език;
- целодневна екскурзия до Нови Сад с екскурзовод на български език;
- застраховка.

ЦЕНАТА НЕ ВКЛЮЧВА

- вечеря в бохемския квартал «Скадарлия»;
- разходка с корабче по р.Дунав и р. Сава;
- входни такси и билети за музеи.

ОТСТЪПКИ

- ученици и студенти: 8 лв.;
- деца до 12 г., настанени в стаята на двамата си родители: 18 лв.;
- пенсионери: 8 лв.

a How does the agency describe the trip to Belgrade?
b What is the means of transport?
c Where will the participants be staying?
d Reckoning on two nights away, what will the return dates be for the different departures?
e What trips does the price include?
f What language will the guide use?
g Does the price include entrance tickets to museums?

6 Read the following page from Nadya's diary for the week ahead. This exercise will help you practise talking about future events:

Понедéлник	Да помóгна на Николáй с докумéнтите (*documents*).
Втóрник	Да кáжа на шéфа за дáтата (*the date*) на излóжбата. (Two different meanings of **на** here, notice!)
Сря́да	Да отговóря на писмóто на дизáйнера. (Here too!)
Четвъ́ртък	Да изпрáтя покáни (*send invitations*) на вси́чки, който рабóтят във фи́рмата.
Пéтък	Да се обáдя на колéгата в Плóвдив.
Съ́бота	Да кýпя подáрък на синá на Антóнови. (And here...)
Недéля	Да покáжа на Милéна нóвите плакáти.

Now answer Каквó ще прáви Нáдя?

a в понедéлник?
b във втóрник?
c в сря́да?
d в четвъ́ртък?
e в пéтък?
f в съ́бота?
g в недéля?

Now, instead of using the days of the week, use dates starting from Monday, May 18, to ask Nadya **Каквó ще прáвиш на...?**

Do you understand?

Dialogue 2: На добър път! *Have a good journey!*

Jim, a young American staying at the same hotel as the Collinses, changes his air ticket – with a little help from his friends.

Невéна Добрó ýтро, г-жá Кóлинс! Заминáвате ли вéче?

г-жá Кóлинс Да, отúваме във Вáрна. Предú да замúнем úмам една́ молба́. Акó някой ни търси, мóля, дáйте тóзи телефóн. Ще бъдем в хотéл „Одéса" до четвъ́рти юни.

Невéна Разбúра се, ще го напрáвя. На добър път и приятно изкáрване! (*She sees Jim obviously anxious to speak to Mrs Collins.*) Вúжте, тóзи америкáнец úска да Ви кáже нéщо.

г-жá Кóлинс (*After having exchanged a few words with Jim.*) Невéна, товá е Джим. Той úска да върне свóя билéт на áвиокомпáнията. Ня́ма да мóже да пътýва на двáйсет и втóри юли. Úска да отúде в Копривщица, за да вúди фолклóрния фестивáл.

Невéна Добрé. Ще се опúтам да помóгна и на нéго. Úмам приятелка в тáзи áвиокомпáния. Едúн момéнт, ще úскам съвéт от нéя. (*After speaking on the phone.*) Такá, всúчки éвтини билéти от двáйсет и втóри юли до дванáйсети áвгуст са продáдени. Úма билéти за тринáйсети áвгуст, сря́да.

г-жá Кóлинс Мóля, запазéте едúн билéт за тринáйсети áвгуст.

Невéна (*Finishes conversation and rings off.*) Кажéте на Джим, че мóже да отúде в агéнцията в понедéлник и да върне билéта на приятелката ми. Тя говóри английски.

г-жá Кóлинс Благодаря́ Ви за помощтá!

Джим Благодаря́, Невéна!

Невéна Ня́ма защó. Аз съм тук, за да помáгам на гóстите на хотéла.

(да) замúна, -неш	*to leave*
На добър път!	*Have a good/safe journey!*
Приятно изкáрване!	*Have a good time/pleasant stay!*

а́виокомпа́ния	*airline*
фолкло́рен фестива́л	*folk festival*
тъ́рся, -сиш	*to look/ask for*
(да) опи́там, -таш	*to try*
прода́вам, -ваш	*to sell*
прода́ден	*sold*
по́мощ (f)	*help*

True or false?

1 Ако́ ня́кой тъ́рси г-н и г-жа́ Ко́линс, Неве́на ще му даде́ те́хния телефо́н.
2 Г-н и г-жа́ Ко́линс ще бъ́дат във Ва́рна до четвъ́рти ю́ли.
3 Джим и́ска да въ́рне сво́я биле́т.
4 Джим мо́же да пъту́ва на два́йсет и вто́ри ю́ли.
5 Вси́чки е́втини биле́ти от два́йсет и вто́ри ю́ли до двана́йсети а́вгуст са прода́дени.
6 Джим тря́бва да оти́де в аге́нцията във вто́рник.

почáкай, не поръ́чвай óще!

wait, don't order yet!

In this unit you will learn:

- **how to use negative imperatives to tell people not to do things**
- **how to choose between two verbs describing the same situation**
- **how to talk about being on time**
- **how to select a table in a café or restaurant**

Dialogue 1

Nadya and Milena are looking for a table in a café.

Милéна Нáдя, елá! Тук ́има свобóдна мáса.
Нáдя Не обúчам да ся́дам до вратáта.
Милéна Хáйде да сéднем до прозóреца тогáва.
Нáдя Добрé, каквó ще поръ́чаме?
Милéна Не поръ́чвай óще. Николáй трябва да дóйде след мáлко. Да го почáкаме.
Нáдя Ня́мам нúщо протúв, но той вúнаги закъсня́ва.
Милéна Таќа ли? Надя́вам се, че днес ня́ма да закъснéе. Нóся му два английски учéбника.
Нáдя Той ня́ма да дóйде за учéбниците, а за да те вúди.
Милéна Каквó ́искаш да кáжеш?
Нáдя Не вúждаш ли, че те харéсва?
Милéна О, не знáя, мóже би... Все еднó, не обúчам да чáкам.
Нáдя Не сé оплáквай! (*Milena takes our her mobile.*) Каквó прáвиш?
Милéна Ще се обáдя на Николáй и ще го попúтам защó не ́идва.
Нáдя Недéй да се обáждаш! Почáкай óще мáлко. Сúгурна съм, че ще дóйде. А, éто го, ́идва.
Николáй Здравéйте, момúчета. Извинéте за закъснéнието. Отдáвна ли ме чáкате?
Нáдя Не, сáмо от две минýти.
Милéна (*Significantly.*) Кáкто кáзва Нáдя, ти вúнаги си тóчен...
Николáй Ха-ха! Нáдя ́има чýвство за хýмор.
Нáдя Хáйде, ня́ма ли да сéднеш?
Николáй Ще сéдна, разбúра се. Обúчам да ся́дам до хýбави момúчета!

Не обúчам да ся́дам до вратáта.	*I don't like sitting by the door.*
Хáйде да сéднем до прозóреца тогáва.	*Come on, let's sit by the window then.*
Не поръ́чвай óще.	*Don't order yet.*
Николáй трябва да дóйде след мáлко.	*Nikolai should be coming soon.*
Да го почáкаме.	*Let's wait for him.*
той вúнаги закъсня́ва	*he's always late*
днес ня́ма да закъснéе	*today he won't be late*

Нóся му два англи́йски учéбника.	*I'm bringing him two English textbooks.*
Той ня́ма да дóйде за учéбниците.	*He won't be coming for the textbooks.*
за да те ви́ди	*(in order) to see you*
Не ви́ждаш ли, че те харéсва?	*Can't you see he likes you?*
мóже би	*maybe*
все еднó	*all the same*
Ще се обáдя на Николáй.	*I'm going to phone Nikolai.*
ще го попи́там защó не и́два	*I'll ask him why he isn't coming*
Недéй да се обáждаш.	*Don't ring.*
Почáкай óще мáлко.	*Wait a bit longer.*
Си́гурна съм, че ще дóйде.	*I'm sure he'll come.*
Извинéте за закъснéнието.	*Sorry I'm late.*
Отдáвна ли ме чáкате?	*Have you been waiting long for me?*
Кáкто кáзва Нáдя, ти ви́наги си тóчен ...	*As Nadya says, you are always punctual ...*
Ха-ха!	*Ha-ha!*
чу́вство за ху́мор	*sense of humour*
ня́ма ли да сéднеш?	*won't you sit down?*
Ще сéдна.	*I will sit down.*

1 Questions

- **a** Каквó не оби́ча Нáдя?
- **b** Защó Милéна кáзва на Нáдя да не порѐчва óще?
- **c** Защó спорéд Нáдя ще дóйде Николáй?
- **d** Защó Милéна и́ска да се обáди на Николáй?
- **e** И́ма ли Милéна моби́лен телефóн (GSM)?
- **f** Къдé оби́ча да ся́да Николáй?

2 True or false?

- **a** Николáй трябва да дóйде след половин час.
- **b** Нáдя кáзва, че Николáй вúнаги е тóчен.
- **c** Николáй харéсва Милéна.
- **d** Милéна няма нúщо протúв да чáка.
- **e** Нáдя е сúгурна, че Николáй ще дóйде.

How do you say it?

- Saying *Don't* (do something)

Не сé оплáквай! Не сé оплáквайте! *Don't complain.*
Недéй да поръчваш!
Недéйте да поръчвайте! } *Don't order.*

- Saying *Come on!* and *Come on, let's…!*

Хáйде!	*Come on!*
Хáйде да сéднем!	*Come on, let's sit down!*

- Asking someone to wait

Почáкай/почáкайте мáлко!	*Wait a minute.*

- Excusing yourself for being late

Извинéте за закъснéнието.	*Forgive me for being late.*
Извинявайте за закъснéнието.	*I am sorry for the delay.*

- Asking someone to be more explicit

Каквó úскаш да кáжеш?	*What do you mean?*

- Saying *Maybe*

Мóже би ще дóйда.	*Maybe/Perhaps I'll come.*

Grammar

1 Verb twinning

If you look carefully at the dialogue you will notice that it contains a number of verbs which differ slightly in Bulgarian, but which are translated in a similar way in English. Here, with a couple added, is a list of these 'twinned' verbs in alphabetical order with the significant differences highlighted:

A	B	
ви́**жд**ам	(да) ви́**д**я	*to see*
закъсня́**ва**м	(да) закъс**не́**я	*to be late*
и́д**ва**м	(да) до́йда	*to come*
ка́з**ва**м	(да) ка́**ж**а	*to say*
оба́**жд**ам се	(да) се оба́**д**я	*to ring, call*
пом**а́га**м	(да) пом**о́гна**	*to help*
поръ́ч**ва**м	(да) поръ́чам	*to order*
пра́вя	(да) **на**пра́вя	*to do, make*
прод**а́ва**м	(да) прод**а́**м	*to sell*
ся́дам	(да) се́д**на**	*to sit*
харе́с**ва**м	(да) харе́сам	*to like*
ча́кам	(да) **по**ча́кам	*to wait*

In Bulgarian, an action can be seen from two different points of view, or *aspects*: either as incomplete and still going on (column A), or as momentary and complete (column B). We refer to verbs in column A as imperfective and those in column B as perfective verbs. In fact, you can think of most Bulgarian verbs as having a 'twin' with which it forms an 'aspectual pair', and when you come across a new verb you should try and learn it together with its twin.

In the English–Bulgarian vocabulary we have, where appropriate, given both verbs.

Formally, the verbs in a pair may differ in one of four main ways:

(**a**) Imperfective verbs (A) often have the suffix **-ва-**, as in закъсня́**ва**м, ка́з**ва**м and поръ́ч**ва**м.
(**b**) Perfective verbs (B) often have the suffix **-на-**, as in се́д**на**, запо́ч**на** and ста́**на** (*to get up*).
(**c**) Perfective verbs frequently have extra letters (a prefix) added on the front as in **на**пра́вя, **по**пи́там and **по**ча́кам.
(**d**) There may be some other internal alternation of letters, often a change of vowel or consonant, as in разб**и́**рам – (да) разб**е**ра́, затв**а́**рям – (да) затв**о́**ря (*to close*), оти́**ва**м – (да) оти́да (*to go*), оба́ждам се – (да) се оба́дя *(to ring, call*) and разгле́**жд**ам – (да) разгле́**д**ам *(to take a look at, inspect*).

Some verbs such as **обя́двам**, **организи́рам**, **парки́рам** and **пъту́вам** have the same form for both imperfective and perfective. They are identical twins!

Occasionally, two very different verbs form an imperfective/perfective pair, **и́двам** and **(да) до́йда**, for example. In Dialogue 1, remember, you came across Е́то го, **и́два** and Никола́й тря́бва да **до́йде** след ма́лко.

2 Imperfective and perfective: which to use when

Which of a pair with the present tense?

In the present tense you always use an imperfective verb because the action is still going on:

Каквó прáвиш?	*What are you doing?*
Каквó кáзва той?	*What is he saying?*
Вѝждаш ли табéлката?	*Can you see the notice?*

You also use an imperfective verb when making generalizations:

Г-н Джóнсън обѝча хýбаво вѝно.	*Mr Johnson loves good wine.*
Николáй вѝнаги закъснява.	*Nikolai is always late.*

You normally cannot use perfective verbs to describe actions in the present tense. The only exception is when you envisage a completed action that is not really taking place yet – it is still potential. This happens:

(a) when you say that you *want to*, *have to* or *can* do something using verbs like **ѝскам (да), трябва (да), мóже (да)**:

Ѝскам **да порѐчам** салáта.	*I want to order a salad.*
Трябва **да отѝда** в бáнката.	*I have to go to the bank.*
Мóже ли **да сéдна** до Вас?	*May I sit next to you?*

(b) after words such as **когáто** (*when*) and **акó** (*if*) indicating that an action will only take place if certain conditions are fulfilled, as in **когáто дóйде** (*when he comes*) and **акó дóйде** (*if he comes*).

(c) after **за да** (*in order to*) or just **да** on its own, when there is a sense of purpose or a need to 'get something done'. Here again there is an emphasis on the completion of an action:

Той ѝдва, за да те вѝди.	*He is coming (in order) to see you.*
Ще се обáдя да го попѝтам.	*I'll ring to ask him.*

Which of a pair with the future tense?

You will usually need to use the perfective twin when talking about future events:

Ще сéдна до прозóреца.	*I'll take a seat by the window.*
Ýтре **няма да закъснéя**.	*Tomorrow I won't be late.*
Ще напрáвя кáкто ми кáзвате.	*I'll do what you tell me.*
Ще Ви донесá менюто.	*I'll bring you the menu.*

In all these examples you are concerned with one specific occasion and concentrating on getting something done.

Sometimes, however, when you are not concerned with one specific occasion or not concentrating on getting something done, you use the imperfective twin:

(a) Вúнаги **ще стáвам** рáно. *I'll always get up early.*
(b) **Ще чáкам** до 11 часá. *I'll wait until 11 o'clock.*

Here you are referring either **(*a*)** to something you are going to do regularly in the future, or **(*b*)** to something that is going to go on for some time.

3 With да and without

The verbs that have been listed with **(да)** are all perfective verbs. They were listed in this way so as to indicate that perfective verbs cannot be used without a 'prop' such as **да** (or **когáто** or **акó**) in the present tense.

You should note, however, that **да** is not used exclusively with perfective verbs. In generalizations when there is no concentration on the need to complete an action or achieve a result, it can also be used with imperfectives. Thus you can say **обúчам да помáгам** *I like to help* and **не обúчам да ся́дам до прозóреца** *I don't like sitting by the window*. In both cases you are making generalizations.

4 Do and don't

If you look back at Unit 7 where – among other things – you learnt how to give instructions, you will see that almost all the verbs were used in their perfective forms: **вземéте си!**, **дáйте ми!**, **платú!** etc. In fact, you almost always use the perfective twin in positive instructions, when you are telling someone to do something specific on a particular occasion:

Седнéте до прозóреца! *Sit by the window.*
Затворú вратáта! *Close the door.*
Направú кафé! *Make some coffee.*
Обадú се! *(Do) ring/call!*

Contrariwise, you use the imperfective twin in negative instructions, when you want to stop someone from doing something, no matter whether it is on a specific occasion or as a general rule:

Не ся́дайте до прозóреца! *Don't sit by the window.*
Не затвáряйте вратáта! *Don't close the door.*
Не правú кафé! *Don't make any coffee.*
Не сé обáждай! *Don't ring/call!*

Almost the only time you use the imperfective twin in positive instructions is when you issue a general prohibition valid not just on one particular occasion. You will find the following notice on doors, for example:

Затвáряйте вратáта!	*Close the door.* (i.e. always)

You will also find that Bulgarians use the imperfective **Извиня́вайте мнóго!** in preference to the perfective **Извинéте!** for *Excuse me!* when they want to be especially polite or insistent.

5 Недéй(те) да *Don't*!

Instead of using **не** with the special command (imperative) forms of the verb, you can tell someone not to do something by using **недéй да** or **недéйте да**:

Недéй да спи́раш тук! **Недéйте да** спи́рате тук!	*Don't stop here.*
Недéй да закъсня́ваш! **Недéйте да** закъсня́вате!	*Don't be late.*

You can see that this is followed by the normal present tense endings of the *you* form of the verb, in the singular or plural as the occasion demands. The verb must be in the imperfective, remember, because it is a negative command. You will also have noticed that in Bulgarian, imperative forms are usually followed by an exclamation mark, thereby emphasizing the urgency of the situation.

(Don't forget that there is a list of imperatives in the Appendix and that positive command forms are explained in Unit 7.)

6 Оби́чам and харéсвам *To love* and *to like*

Both **оби́чам** and **харéсвам** may be translated as *I like*:

Оби́чам класи́ческа му́зика.	*I like/love classical music.*
Харéсвам тáзи му́зика.	*I like/love this music.*
Оби́чам сладолéд.	*I like/love ice-cream.* (i.e. all ice-cream)
Харéсвам тóзи сладолéд.	*I like/love this ice-cream.*

As you can see from these examples, however, **харéсвам** is normally used with individual, specified things, while **оби́чам** is used for more general statements. But when you use **оби́чам** with people it always means *I love*:

Оби́чам товá моми́че.	*I love that girl.*
Обичам те!	*I love you!*

When **харéсвам** is used with people it simply means *I like*, nothing more exciting, alas!

Do remember, though, that when you want to say you like doing something, you have to use **обѝчам да**, as in **обѝчам** (or more likely **не обѝчам**) **да чáкам** *I like/don't like waiting*.

Exercises

1 In the short dialogue below you will find the 'twin' verbs for *to leave*: **остáвям (а-/я**-pattern and imperfective) and **(да) остáвя (и**-pattern and perfective). First work out which is which and note how they are used.

В теáтъра

Николáй Акó ѝскаш, оставѝ чáнтата на гардерóба (*cloakroom*).

Милéна Нѝма да я остáвя.

Николáй Защó?

Милéна Виж табéлката: Не остáвяйте цéнности на гардерóба! (*Valuables left at your own risk*, lit. *Don't leave valuables in the cloakroom*)

Николáй В такъв слýчай (*in that case*), недéй да я остáвяш. Оставѝ сáмо чадъ̀ра.

Now complete the following sentences with the appropriate verb for *to leave*:

a ________ тáзи тéжка (*heavy*) чáнта вкъщи (*at home*)!
b Сѝгурно ще валѝ. Нѝма да ________ чадъ̀ра вкъщи.
c Недéй да ________ вратáта отвóрена.

2 Here are some common Bulgarian notices with their English equivalents:

a

ОПАСНО
ЗА
ЖИВОТА

DANGER OF DEATH!

b

НЕ Е ВХОД

NO ENTRY

c

ПАЗЕТЕ ЧИСТОТА!

NO LITTER!

d

СНИМАНЕТО ЗАБРАНЕНО

NO PHOTOGRAPHY!

e

СЛУЖЕБЕН ПАРКИНГ

OFFICIAL PARKING

f

ПУШЕНЕТО ЗАБРАНЕНО

NO SMOKING!

Now see if you can match the notices with these negative imperatives which have been translated literally:

i Не влѝзайте!	*Don't go in.*
ii Не пѝпай!	*Don't touch.*
iii Не паркѝрай!	*Don't park.*
iv Не пушéте!	*Don't smoke.*
v Не хвъ̀рляйте отпáдъци!	*Don't throw litter.*
vi Не правéте снѝмки!	*Don't take pictures.*

3 Try to memorize these time words which usually go with imperfective verbs:

вѝнаги	*always*	**обикновéно**	*usually*
чéсто	*often*	**ря́дко**	*rarely*

Now look for them in the following sentences which you should complete choosing the imperfective verb and the right personal ending. (For once the perfective verbs have been given without **да**!)

a Г-н Кóлинс чéсто (помáгам/помóгна) на свóята женá.
b Нѝе вѝнаги (стáвам/стáна) (*to get up*) рáно.
c Обикновéно Нáдя (ѝдвам/дóйда) на рáбота в óсем и половѝна.
d Мáйкъл Джóнсън ря́дко (поръ́чвам/поръ́чам) вѝно за обя́д.

4 Here Nevena is talking to another receptionist and enviously watching a very smart lady enter the restaurant. Nevena is describing what she sees using imperfective verbs. Try to complete her story choosing the correct form of the perfective verb after **и́скам да**..., **хáйде да**..., **за да**... and **ще, мóга да**. (Use the English–Bulgarian vocabulary to track down the twins.)

Невéна Виж, и́два еднá мнóго краси́ва женá. И́скам да (*I, see*) и́ма ли срéща. Ще (*you, come*) ли с мéне? Éто, и́два еди́н хýбав мъж. Те вли́зат в ресторáнта. Хáйде да (*we, go in*) и ни́е. Те ся́дат на мáсата до прозóреца и изби́рат нéщо за пи́ене. И́скам да (*we, sit*) на тáзи мáса и ни́е да (*we, choose*) нéщо. Мóжеш ли да ги (*you, see*)? Аз ги ви́ждам – поръ́чват джин. Хáйде да (*we, order*) и ниé два джи́на. Сегá мъжъ́т се обáжда по джи́есéма. А тя каквó прáви? Виж, и тя и́ска да (*she, make a call*), но джи́есéмът ѝ не рабóти. Ще (*she, take a picture*) сни́мка на ресторáнта. И́скам да (*I, go*) пó-бли́зо, за да (*I, hear*) на какъ́в ези́к говóрят. Почáкай ме мáлко... Краси́вата женá е америкáнка! Óще ýтре ще (*I begin*) да ýча англи́йски!

5 Read the passage below, following Nadya's thoughts when she fails to make a meeting with Milena.

Милéна **ще дóйде**, **ще ви́ди**, че не съм там и **ще влéзе** в сладкáрницата. **Ще ви́ди** свобóдна мáса и **ще сéдне**. **Ще изберé** (*choose*) нéщо за закýска и веднáга **ще поръ́ча**. Сервитьóрката **ще донесé** кафé и сáндвич сáмо за нéя. **Ня́ма да ме почáка** дори́ (*even*) пет минýти! **Ще плати́**, **ще стáне** (*get up*) и **ще оти́де** в ЦУМ – без мéне!

Now imagine you are observing Milena and, beginning with **Éто**, recount what you see, turning all the verbs into the present. You will need to replace each perfective verb with its imperfective twin.

6 **Оби́чам** or **харéсвам?** Choose one of the verbs to complete the sentences.

- **a** Невéна ______ да говóри с чужденци́.
- **b** Николáй ______ Милéна.
- **c** Г-н Кóлинс ______ да игрáе голф (*golf*).
- **d** Нáдя ______ тáзи излóжба.
- **e** Г-жá Кóлинс ______ кафé без зáхар.

f Вúе сúгурно ще ______ тóзи град. (Use the perfective: **(да) харéсам)**
g Те ______ бъ́лгарските специалитéти.
h Не ______ да чáкам.
i Мáйкъл Джóнсън ______ бъ́лгарско вúно.
j Милéна ще ______ тóзи нов прúнтер. (Again you need **(да) харéсам)**
k Николáй не ______ тóзи учéбник.

Do you understand?

Dialogue 2: Вниманúе! *Danger! Watch Out!*

Michael Johnson has a hard time on his own in out-of-season Borovets.

Полицáй Мóля, не паркúрайте тук. Опáсно е. Вúжте табéлката.

г-н Джóнсън Вúждам я, но не я̀ разбúрам. Аз съм чужденéц. Каквó знáчи „Вниманúе! Пáдащи предмéти"?

Полицáй Товá знáчи, че хотéлът е в ремóнт и понякóга пáдат тéжки предмéти. Мóже нéщо да пáдне върхý колáта Ви.

г-н Джóнсън Такá ли? Къдé мóже да паркúрам? Тъ́рся ресторáнт, но не вúждам пáркинг наóколо.

Полицáй Пáркингът е зад хотéла. Ще вúдите табéлката. В кой ресторáнт отúвате?

г-н Джóнсън Не знáя. Кажéте ми кой ресторáнт е нáй-добъ́р.

Полицáй Предлáгам Ви да отúдете в мáлкия ресторáнт до лúфта. Сегá ня́ма мнóго турúсти и мúсля, че ня́ма да чáкате дъ́лго.

г-н Джóнсън Благодаря̀ за съвéта. Ще напрáвя кáкто ми кáзвате.

(*Later, in the small restaurant by the ski lift, Mr Johnson is about to take a seat at a corner table.*)

Сервитьóрка Извиня́вайте мнóго, господúне, но не ся́дайте на тáзи мáса, акó обúчате. Мáсата в ъ́гъла е запáзена.

г-н Джóнсън Съжаля́вам, грéшката е мóя. Сегá вúждам табéлката. Изглéжда днес прáвя всúчко не кáкто тря́бва.

Сервитьóрка Заповя́дайте, седнéте до прозóреца. Товá е мáса за непушáчи. И́ма чудéсен и́зглед към планинáта. Сегá ще Ви донесá менюто. Ще дóйда за поръ́чката след катó изберéте.

г-н Джóнсън Мóля, недéйте да бъ́рзате. Аз изби́рам мнóго бáвно, защóто не разби́рам всúчко.

Сервитьóрка Тогáва и́двам веднáга. Ще Ви помóгна да изберéте.

г-н Джóнсън Благодаря́ мнóго. Запóчвам да харéсвам Бóровец.

опáсно	*dangerous*
вниmáние!	*danger! watch out! attention!*
пáдащи предмéти	*falling objects*
поня́кога	*sometimes*
пáдам, -даш	*to fall*
тéжък, тéжка	*heavy*
(да) пáдна, -неш	*to fall*
такá ли?	*really? is that so?*
пáркинг	*car park, parking lot*
наóколо	*nearby*
зад	*behind*
лифт	*ski/chairlift*
ъ́гъл	*corner*
запáзен	*reserved*
непушáч	*non-smoker*
и́зглед	*view*
(да) донесá, -сéш	*to bring*
поръ́чка	*order*
изби́рам, -раш	*to choose*
(да) изберá, -рéш	*to choose*
вли́зам, -заш	*to enter*
вход	*entrance*
живóт	*life*
забранéно	*forbidden, not allowed*
отпáдък, -ъци	*litter, rubbish*
пу́ша, -шиш	*to smoke*
пу́шене	*smoking*
служéбен, -бна	*official, for staff only*
хвъ́рлям, -ляш	*to throw*
чистотá	*cleanliness*

Questions

1 Защó г-н Джóнсън не тря́бва да паркúра до табéлката?
2 Къдé е пáркингът?
3 Защó полицáят предлáга мáлкия ресторáнт?
4 Защó не мóже г-н Джóнсън да сéдне на мáсата в ъ́гъла?
5 Как г-н Джóнсън кáзва на сервитьóрката да не бъ́рза?
6 Защó сервитьóрката ще помóгне на г-н Джóнсън да изберé нéщо за я́дене?

как да сти́гнем до хоте́л „Оде́са“?

how can we get to the Odessa hotel?

In this unit you will learn:

- **how to ask the way**
- **how to give and understand directions**
- **how to talk about events in the past**

Dialogue 1

Mr and Mrs Collins have just arrived in Varna. Mr Collins stops the car so Mrs Collins can ask a policeman the way.

г-жá Кóлинс Извинéте, мóжете ли да ни кáжете как да сти́гнем до хотéл „Одéса“?

Полицáй Хотéл „Одéса“ е бли́зо до цéнтъра. Кáрайте напрáво и ще сти́гнете до еди́н площáд. На нéго и́ма цъ́рква. Ще зави́ете налявo и ще кáрате до пъ́рвия светофáр. На светофáра зави́йте надя́сно. Ще пресечéте еди́н булевáрд и ще сти́гнете до вхóда на еди́н парк. Товá е Мóрската гради́на. Хотéл „Одéса“ е вдя́сно, срещý Мóрската гради́на.

г-жá Кóлинс Благодаря́ мнóго.

Полицáй Ня́ма защó. Акó загýбите пъ́тя попи́тайте пак.

(*Mr and Mrs Collins do lose their way and it is rather late when they eventually arrive at the hotel.*)

г-жá Кóлинс Дóбър вéчер. И́маме запáзена стáя в тóзи хотéл.

Администрáторка Дóбър вéчер. И́мето, мóля?

г-жá Кóлинс Джордж и Виктóрия Кóлинс.

Администрáторка Да, и́ма стáя за вас. Добрé дошли́! Не ви́ очáквахме тóлкова къ́сно. И́махте ли проблéми по пъ́тя?

г-жá Кóлинс Не, пътýването бéше прия́тно. Проблéмите запóчнаха, когáто присти́гнахме във Вáрна, защóто ня́махме кáрта на градá.

Администрáторка Когá присти́гнахте?

г-жá Кóлинс Присти́гнахме преди́ óколо два чáса, към сéдем часá. Бéше óще свéтло.

Администрáторка Не попи́тахте ли за пъ́тя?

г-жá Кóлинс Да, попи́тахме еди́н полицáй. Кáрахме напрáво, но не сти́гнахме до площáда с цъ́рквата. Ýлицата бéше в ремóнт и и́маше отклонéние. На слéдващата ýлица зави́хме наля́во и загýбихме пъ́тя.

Администрáторка Защó не попи́тахте пак?

г-жá Кóлинс В товá врéме запóчна да вали́ и ня́маше хóра по ýлиците. Ня́маше когó да попи́таме.

Администра́торка	Как наме́рихте пъ́тя?
г-жа́ Ко́линс	Еди́н шофьо́р на такси́ ни помо́гна.
Администра́торка	Си́гурно сте уморе́ни и гла́дни. Рестора́нтът е о́ще отво́рен.
г-жа́ Ко́линс	О, да. Уми́раме за ча́ша чай.
Администра́торка	Заповя́дайте, рестора́нтът е на па́ртера вля́во.
г-жа́ Ко́линс	Благодаря́ мно́го. Къде́ мо́жем да оста́вим бага́жа?
Администра́торка	Пи́колото ще напра́ви това́. Ста́ята ви е на четвъ́ртия ета́ж, коридо́рът вдя́сно. Прия́тна почи́вка! Ле́ка нощ!

The city crest of Varna

администра́торка	*receptionist*
как да сти́гнем до	*how we can get to*
ка́райте напра́во	*drive straight ahead*
ще сти́гнете до еди́н площа́д	*you'll get to a square*
цъ́рква	*church*
ще зави́ете наля́во	*you (will) turn left*
светофа́р	*traffic lights*
надя́сно	*to the right*
ще пресече́те	*you (will) cross*
Мо́рската гради́на	*The Marine Park*
вдя́сно	*on the right*
ако́ загу́бите пъ́тя...	*if you lose the way...*
И́махте ли пробле́ми по пъ́тя?	*Did you have any problems on the way?*
пъту́ването бе́ше прия́тно	*the journey was pleasant*
Пробле́мите запо́чнаха, кога́то присти́гнахме във Ва́рна.	*The problems started when we arrived in Varna.*

ня́махме	*we didn't have*
преди́ о́коло два ча́са	*about two hours ago*
към се́дем часа́	*at about 7 o'clock*
бе́ше о́ще све́тло	*it was still light*
Не попи́тахте ли за пътя?	*Didn't you ask the way?*
попи́тахме еди́н полица́й	*we asked a policeman*
ка́рахме напра́во	*we drove straight ahead*
не сти́гнахме до площа́да с църквата	*we didn't get to the square with the church*
у́лицата бе́ше в ремо́нт	*the road was under repair*
и́маше отклоне́ние	*there was a diversion*
зави́хме наля́во	*we turned left*
загу́бихме пътя	*we lost the way*
запо́чна да вали́	*it started raining*
ня́маше хо́ра по у́лиците	*there weren't any people out in the streets*
Как наме́рихте пътя?	*How did you find the way?*
Еди́н шофьо́р на такси́ ни помо́гна.	*A taxi driver helped us.*
Си́гурно сте уморе́ни и гла́дни.	*You must be tired and hungry.*
Уми́раме за ча́ша чай.	*We are dying for a cup of tea.*
вля́во	*on the left*
Ле́ка нощ!	*Good night!*

1 Questions

Imagine you are Mrs Collins: see if you can answer the questions she and her husband are asked on arrival at the hotel.

- **a** Към ко́лко часа́ присти́гнахте?
- **b** Как бе́ше пъту́ването ви?
- **c** Защо́ и́махте пробле́ми?
- **d** Кога́ запо́чнаха пробле́мите ви?
- **e** Тъмно ли бе́ше, кога́то присти́гнахте?
- **f** Защо́ не сти́гнахте до площа́да с църквата?

2 True or false?

- **a** Г-н и г-жа́ Ко́линс ще зави́ят наля́во и ще сти́гнат до една́ църква.
- **b** Хоте́л „Оде́са“ е вля́во, зад Мо́рската гради́на.
- **c** Г-н и г-жа́ Ко́линс присти́гнаха във Ва́рна към шест и полови́на.

d Еди́н шофьо́р на такси́ им помо́гна.
e Ресторáнтът е в коридóра вдя́сно.

How do you say it?

- Asking the way

Как да сти́гна до гáрата?	*How do I get to the station?*
В коя́ посóка е пóщата?	*In which direction is the post office?*
Мóжете ли да ми покáжете пътя за...?	*Can you show me the way to...?*

- Giving directions

Кáрайте напрáво./Вървéте напрáво.	*Drive straight on./Go straight on.*
Зави́йте наля́во.	*Turn **to** the left.*
Зави́йте надя́сно.	*Turn **to** the right.*
Върнéте се обрáтно.	*Go back.*

- Saying ***On** the left/**on** the right*

Трéтата вратá вля́во.	*The third door **on** the left.*
Коридóрът вдя́сно.	*The corridor **on** the right.*
Фоайéто е вдя́сно/вля́во от асансьóра.	*The foyer is **on** the right/**on** the left of the lift.*

- Giving approximate times

Присти́гнахме преди́ óколо полови́н час.	*We arrived about half an hour ago.*
Сти́гнахме Вáрна за óколо шест чáса.	*We reached Varna in about six hours.*
Пóщата е на óколо пет мину́ти.	*The post office is about five minutes away.*
Запóчна да вали́ към три часá.	*It started to rain towards three o'clock.*
Николáй ще дóйде към единáйсет часá.	*Nikolai will come towards eleven o'clock.*

- Saying *I am tired* and *Good night*

Уморéн съм/уморéна съм.	*I am tired.*
Уморéни сме.	*We are tired.*
Лéка нощ!	*Good night!*

Grammar

1 Past tense

Verbs describing past events also have special endings. In the following sentences, which take you from the *I* form to the *they* form, these endings (**-х**, -, -, **-хме**, **-хте**, **-ха**) and the preceding vowel have been highlighted. You will see that in the *you* (familiar) and *he/she/it* forms there is no special ending added to the vowel.

Ку́п**их** но́ва програ́ма за компю́търа.	*I bought a new computer program.*
Ти пи́т**а** ли къде́ е площа́дът?	*Did you ask where the square is?*
Тя помо́гн**а** на г-жа́ Ко́линс.	*She helped Mrs Collins.*
Присти́гн**ахме** във Ва́рна към се́дем часа́.	*We arrived in Varna about 7 o'clock.*
Сти́гн**ахте** ли до площа́да?	*Did you get to the square?*
Деца́та игр**а́ха** до къ́сно.	*The children played until late.*

The endings are the same for all three verb patterns, but they are added to a variety of vowels and this makes forming the past tense in Bulgarian a little tricky. You will, however, be able to take things gradually, learning in this and the following units which vowels go with which groups of verbs. To make things easier we will move from the regular to the less regular forms.

(a) Verbs that add past endings to **-а-**

With all **а**-pattern verbs (Conjugation 3) like **пи́там**, **ка́рам** *to drive*, (да) **разгле́дам** *to look at* you replace the **-м** of the *I* form with the special past endings. So пи́та-**м*** becomes:

(аз)	пи́т**ах**	*I asked*	(ни́е)	пи́т**ахме**	*we asked*
(ти)	пи́т**а**	*you asked*	(ви́е)	пи́т**ахте**	*you asked*
(той) / (тя) / (то)	пи́т**а**	*he/she/it asked*	(те)	пи́т**аха**	*they asked*

You will notice that there is no difference between the past той **пи́та** and the present той **пи́та**. You therefore have to rely on the context to tell you whether it means *he asked*, *he asks* or *he is asking*.

You form the past tense of some **е**-pattern verbs in the same way: **(да) сти́гна**, **(да) присти́гна**, **(да) запо́чна**, **(да) помо́гна**, for example. You can recognize this group by the presence of **-на** in the dictionary form.

*(да) **попи́там** is the 'twin' perfective verb of **пи́там**.

Сти́г**нах** до хоте́ла.	*I reached the hotel.*
Вче́ра Никола́й запо́ч**на** да у́чи англи́йски.	*Yesterday Nikolai began to study English.*
Помо́г**нахме** на америка́неца.	*We helped the American.*
Присти́г**наха** къ́сно във Ва́рна.	*They arrived late in Varna.*

(b) Verbs adding past endings to **-и-**
Most **и**-pattern verbs (Conjugation 2) have the vowel **-и-** before the past endings: **(да) загу́бя** *to lose*, **(да) ку́пя**, **(да) наме́ря**, **(да) напра́вя** as well as **пра́вя**, **рабо́тя**, **тъ́рся**, etc.

(аз)	ку́п**их**	*I bought*	(ни́е)	ку́п**ихме**	*we bought*
(ти)	ку́п**и**	*you bought*	(ви́е)	ку́п**ихте**	*you bought*
(той) (тя) (то)	ку́п**и**	*he/she/it bought*	(те)	ку́п**иха**	*they bought*

Тъ́рсих г-н Анто́нов, но не го **наме́рих**.	*I looked for Mr Antonov but didn't find him.*
На́дя **напра́ви** кафе́ за вси́чки.	*Nadya made coffee for everyone.*
Какво́ **загу́бихте**?	*What did you lose?*

(c) For the past tense forms of **е**-pattern verbs in **-и́я** and **-а́я** like **(да) зави́я** *to turn*, **пи́я** *to drink*, **игра́я** *to play* you simply replace the **-я** of the first person *I* form by the appropriate past endings. The resulting forms look just like the ones in **(*a*)** and **(*b*)** above:

Та́зи су́трин **пих** мля́ко.	*This morning I drank some milk.*
Кола́та **зави́** надя́сно.	*The car turned to the right.*
Деца́та **игра́ха** до къ́сно.	*The children played until late.*

2 И́мах *I had* and ня́мах *I didn't have*

When describing past situations, both **и́мам** and **ня́мам** have different past endings in the *you* (familiar) and *he/she/it* forms:

(аз)	и́мах/ня́мах	*I had/ didn't have*	(ни́е)	и́махме/ня́махме	*we had/ didn't have*
(ти)	и́ма**ше**/ня́ма**ше**	*you had/ didn't have*	(ви́е)	и́махте/ня́махте	*you had/ didn't have*
(той) (тя) (то)	и́ма**ше**/ня́ма**ше**	*he she it had/ didn't have*	(те)	и́маха/ня́маха	*they had/ didn't have*

(You will find out more about these past forms in Unit 17.)

3 Аз бях *I was*

(аз)	**бях**	*I was*	(ние)	**бяхме**	*we were*
(ти)	**беше**	*you were*	(вие)	**бяхте**	*you were*
(той) (тя) (то)	**беше**	*he/she/it was*	(те)	**бяха**	*they were*

4 When and how to use the past forms

The verb endings for the past are used when you want to describe an action that was fully completed in the past. You can use them either with the perfective or with the imperfective twin, but they tend to be used more with the perfective. There are other ways of describing past actions and you will learn about them in later units.

When describing past actions using two and more verbs linked by **да**, you should remember that only the first (main) verb needs the past endings. The verb(s) after **да** remain in the present tense:

Запóчна **да валú**.	*It started to rain.*
Едúн полицáй ни помóгна **да намéрим** пътя.	*A policeman helped us find the way.*
В Лóндон úмах възмóжност **да вúдя** катедрáлата „Светú Пáвел“.	*In London, I had a chance to see St Paul's.*

5 Кой or когó *Who* or *whom*

Когó *whom* is a form of **кой** *who* and you should use it in the non-subject position:

Subject position			**Non-subject position**	
Кой по пúта?	*Who asked?*	but	**Когó** попúтахте?	*Whom did you ask?*
Кой помóгна?	*Who helped?*	but	**На когó** помóгнахте?	*Whom did you help?*
			Нямаше когó да пúтаме.	*There was nobody (whom) we could ask.*

6 Едúн/еднá/еднó: An alternative for *a* or *a certain*

Very often **едúн/еднá/еднó** (see Unit 2) doesn't mean *one* in a counting sense. Instead it can be an equivalent of the English *a* or *a certain* as in:

Ще сти́гнете до **еди́н** площа́д. *You'll come to **a** square.*
Еди́н шофьо́р на такси́ ни помо́гна. *A taxi driver helped us.*

You will also find the plural form **едни́** meaning *some* or *certain*:

Едни́ па́ркинги са по́-ма́лки, а дру́ги са по́-голе́ми. *Some/certain car parks are smaller and others are larger.*

7 (Да) пресека́ у́лицата *To cross the street*: к changes to ч

Verbs with a **-к-** immediately before the ending of the *I* and the *they* forms change the **-к-** to **-ч-** in all the other persons:

(аз)	ще пресе**ка́**	*I will cross*	(ни́е)	ще пресе**чѐм**	*we will cross*
(ти)	ще пресе**чѐш**	*you will cross*	(ви́е)	ще пресе**чѐте**	*you will cross*
(той) (тя) (то)	ще пресе**чѐ**	*he/she/it will cross*	(те)	ще пресе**ка́т**	*they will cross*

Exercises

1 Match the following questions and answers:

i На ко́лко мину́ти е га́рата?
ii Напра́во ли е къ̀мпинг „Оа́зис“?
iii Към ко́лко часа́ да до́йдем?
iv Кого́ тъ̀рсите?
v В та́зи посо́ка ли е цъ̀рквата „Света́ (*Saint*) Со́фия“?
vi Къде́ е отклоне́нието за магистра́лата (*motorway*)?

a Ела́те към се́дем часа́.
b За отклоне́нието зави́йте надя́сно на тре́тата у́лица.
c Тъ̀рся секрета́рката на фи́рмата.
d Не, Света́ Со́фия е в обра́тната (*opposite*) посо́ка.
e Га́рата е на о́коло де́сет мину́ти.
f Не, за къ̀мпинг „Оа́зис“ тря́бва да зави́ете наля́во.

2 To what questions might the following be answers? The important bits are highlighted!

a Запо́чна да вали́ **към 6 часа́**.
b Загу́бихме пъ̀тя, **защо́то бе́ше тъ̀мно**.

c Ба́нката е **вля́во от катедра́лата** (*the cathedral*).
d Пи́тахме **еди́н мъж** къде́ е магистра́лата.
e **Едно́ момче́** ни помо́гна да наме́рим пътя.
f **На тре́тата у́лица** зави́хме надя́сно.

3 This exercise will help you use some key verbs in the past tense. Complete the answers following the model.

Model: Йскате ли да Ви **обясня́** къде́ живе́е г-н Анто́нов?
Той ве́че ми **обясни́**.

a Йскате ли да **обя́дваме** за́едно?
Аз ве́че ______
b Да **ку́пя** ли биле́ти за „Травиа́та“?
На́дя ве́че ______
c Кога́ **ще зами́нат** г-н и г-жа́ Ко́линс?
Те ве́че ______
d Да **напра́вя** ли кафе́?
Неве́на ве́че ______
e Кога́ **ще запо́чне** конце́ртът?
Той ве́че ______
f Да **по пи́там** ли къде́ е магистра́лата?
Ни́е ве́че ______
g Да **поръ́чам** ли такси́?
Аз ве́че ______
h **Ще изпра́тиш** ли и́мейл в Че́лмсфорд?
Никола́й ве́че ______

4 A friendly policeman tells you how to get to the museum by car:

Върне́те се по съ́щата у́лица. Ще сти́гнете до еди́н булева́рд. Зави́йте надя́сно и ка́райте напра́во. Като́ сти́гнете до площа́да, парки́райте на па́ркинга и по пи́тайте пак (*again*). Музе́ят не е́ дале́че от площа́да.

You successfully follow his instructions. Now tell your friend how you got there. You will need to put the verbs into the past and change them to the *I* form.

5 Look at the map opposite and tell a stranger how to get from the museum to the chemist's.

6 You too need to get to the chemist's. Having checked the instructions you gave in Ex. **5** (in the Key!), say how you and your companion drove there.

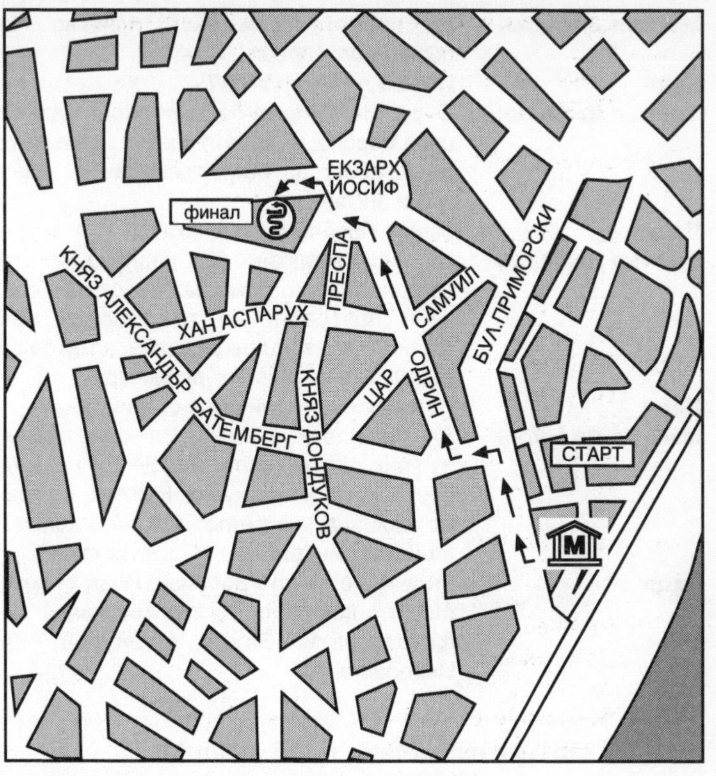

Do you understand?

Dialogue 2: В Пло́вдив *In Plovdiv*

Nadya is curious to hear about Mr Johnson's adventures in Bulgaria's second city.

На́дя	Дово́лен ли сте от престо́я в Пло́вдив?
Ма́йкъл Джо́нсън	Мно́го съм дово́лен. За ме́не бе́ше стра́шно интере́сно. Ня́мах предста́ва от бъ́лгарската исто́рия.
На́дя	И́махте ли вре́ме да разгле́дате ста́рия град?
Ма́йкъл Джо́нсън	Да, бях в на́й-интере́сните ста́ри къ́щи, разгле́дах Ри́мската стена́, ста́рия теа́тър и цъ́рквата „Свети́ Константи́н и Еле́на“.
На́дя	Ху́баво ли бе́ше вре́мето?

Мáйкъл Джóнсън	Да, врéмето бéше мнóго приятно. Не бéше мнóго горéщо.
Нáдя	Ѝмаше ли мнóго хóра?
Мáйкъл Джóнсън	О, да. На панаѝра бéше пълно с хóра от цяла Еврóпа. (*Tongue in cheek.*) Дáже ѝмах възмóжност да бъда преводáч на еднá грýпа англичáни.
Нáдя	Защó? Проблéми ли ѝмаха?
Мáйкъл Джóнсън	Не, нѝщо сериóзно. Бях наблѝзо, когáто те пристѝгнаха. Помóгнах им да намéрят своя преводáч. Те го търсиха във фоайéто вляво от рецéпцията, а той бéше във фоайéто вляво от асансьóра.
Нáдя	Напрáвихте ли снѝмки в стáрия град?
Мáйкъл Джóнсън	Да, напрáвих снѝмки. За съжалéние, загýбих фóтоапарáта си! Ще Ви покáжа кáртичките, който кýпих. Éто тук, вдясно от площáда, е хотéлът. А товá е къщата на Ламартѝн, вляво е Рѝмската стенá.
Нáдя	Рáдвам се, че сте довóлен. И ще бъдете óще пó-довóлен, когáто Ви кáжа, че фóтоапарáтът Ви не é загýбен – у Николáй е!

стрáшно интерéсно	*terribly interesting*
представа	*idea*
истóрия	*history*
Рѝмската стенá	*the Roman Wall*
дáже	*even*
възмóжност (f)	*opportunity, chance*
грýпа	*group*
наблѝзо	*nearby*
рецéпция	*reception*
фóтоапарáт	*camera*
къща	*house*
Ламартѝн	*Lamartine* (French poet)
загýбен	*lost*
у	*with*

Questions

To practise narration in the first person, imagine you have shared Michael Johnson's experience in Plovdiv and answer instead of him:

1. От каквó ня́махте представа, преди́ да оти́дете в Плóвдив?
2. Каквó разглéдахте в стáрия град?
3. Защó бéше приятно врéмето?
4. Каквá възмóжност и́махте, когáто присти́гна грýпа англичáни?
5. Къдé търсиха англичáните своя преводáч?
6. Защó ще покáжете на Нáдя кáртички, а не сни́мки?

Plovdiv Trade Fair logo

поздравя́вам те!

congratulations!

In this unit you will learn:

- **how to congratulate people on special occasions**
- **how to name items and places in the home**

Dialogue 1

It is Sunday, May 24, the day of Bulgarian letters and culture, traditionally associated with Saints Cyril and Methodius. Nikolai meets Michael Johnson to take him to Mr Antonov's house.

Ма́йкъл Никола́й, оти́ваме на го́сти, нали́? Какъв пода́рък се но́си на домаки́нята в Бълга́рия?

Никола́й Обикнове́но се но́сят цветя́ или́ бонбо́ни.

Ма́йкъл Ела́те да ку́пим цветя́ за г-жа́ Анто́нова. (*At the florist's.*) До́бър ден! Ви́ждам, че мно́го хо́ра купу́ват цветя́ днес.

Никола́й Да, защо́то е пра́зник.

Ма́йкъл Какъв пра́зник?

Никола́й Днес се празну́ва деня́т на бъ́лгарската култу́ра.

Ма́йкъл Тря́бва да ми разка́жеш по́вече. Те́зи ро́зи ми харе́сват. Ще ку́пя буке́т ро́зи.

(*At the Antonovs' Zlatka Antonova opens the door helped by Sashko, their 7-year-old son.*)

Зла́тка Добре́ дошли́! Заповя́дайте. Какви́ краси́ви цветя́!

Са́шко А за ме́не и́ма ли не́що?

Зла́тка Са́шко!

Ма́йкъл Мо́же би и́ма не́що и за те́бе, но първо ми кажи́ какво́ се ка́зва, кога́то и́скаш да поздрави́ш ня́кого.

Са́шко Мо́жеш да ми ка́жеш „Чести́т рожде́н ден!"

Зла́тка Са́шко, но днес не е́ тво́ят рожде́н ден!

Са́шко Да, но на рожде́н ден се получа́ват пода́ръци.

(*After some conferring with Nikolai, Michael gives Sashko a bar of chocolate and a set of coloured pencils.*)

Ма́йкъл Чести́т пра́зник! Заповя́дай – еди́н шокола́д и кути́я моли́ви. Ти си учени́к, нали́? Поздравя́вам те по слу́чай пра́зника на Свети́те бра́тя Ки́рил и Мето́дий!

Са́шко Благодаря́ мно́го. И аз те поздравя́вам, че ми доне́се шокола́д. И моли́вите ми харе́сват.

Зла́тка Са́шко, мно́го гово́риш. Иди́ и донеси́ ва́зата от спа́лнята. Внима́вай да не я счу́пиш!

Боя́н Зла́тке, покани́ го́стите в хо́ла.

Ма́йкъл Ко́лко краси́во е нареде́на ма́сата! Са́шко, ти ли я нареди́?

Зла́тка	Да, той нареди́ ви́лиците, ножо́вете и салфе́тките. Той оби́ча да пома́га.
Са́шко	Ма́мо, доне́сох ва́зата. Мо́же ли да донеса́ и ви́ното за го́стите?
Зла́тка	Не, баща́ ти ще го донесе́. Боя́не, мо́ля те донеси́ ви́ното от ку́хнята.

(*Boyan returns with the wine and pours it out.*)

Боя́н	Гото́во! Да запо́чваме! Наздра́ве! Чести́т пра́зник!
Ма́йкъл	Чести́т пра́зник! Наздра́ве!
Зла́тка	Заповя́дайте, докато́ е то́пла ба́ницата. Надя́вам се, че ще ви харе́са.

оти́ваме на го́сти	*we are going visiting*
Какъв пода́рък се но́си на домаки́нята?	*What kind of present does one take to the lady of the house?*
Обикнове́но се но́сят цветя́ или бонбо́ни.	*Usually one takes flowers or chocolates.*
мно́го хо́ра купу́ват цветя́	*a lot of people are buying flowers*
пра́зник	*a special day, festival, holiday*
Днес се празну́ва деня́т на ...	*Today we are celebrating the day of...*
Тря́бва да ми разка́жеш по́вече	*you must tell me more*
какво́ се ка́зва кога́то и́скаш да поздрави́ш ня́кого	*what one says when you want to congratulate someone*
Чести́т рожде́н ден!	*Happy birthday!*
На рожде́н ден се получа́ват пода́ръци.	*On one's birthday one gets presents.*
Чести́т пра́зник!	*Congratulations!*
кути́я моли́ви	*a box of pencils*
Поздравя́вам те по слу́чай пра́зника на Свети́те бра́тя Ки́рил и Ме́тодий!	*I congratulate you on the occasion of the festival of the Saints, brothers Cyril and Methodius!*
че ми доне́се шокола́д	*that you brought me a bar of chocolate.*
Иди́ и донеси́ ва́зата.	*Go and bring the vase.*
спа́лня	*bedroom*
Внима́вай да не я счу́пиш!	*Watch you don't break it!*
нареде́н	*arranged*

Покани́ го́стите в хо́ла.	*Ask our guests into the living-room.*
Той нареди́ ви́лиците, ножо́вете и салфе́тките.	*He arranged the forks, knives and serviettes.*
Той оби́ча да пома́га.	*He likes to help.*
Доне́сох ва́зата.	*I've brought the vase.*
ку́хня	*kitchen*
Гото́во!	*Ready!*
Да запо́чваме!	*Let's begin!*
Наздра́ве!	*Cheers!/Your good health!*
докато́ е то́пла ба́ницата	*while the banitsa cheese pasty is still warm*
ще ви харе́са	*you will like it*

1 Questions

- **a** Какво́ се но́си на домаки́нята, кога́то се хо́ди на го́сти в Бълга́рия?
- **b** Какво́ се празну́ва днес?
- **c** Защо́ Ма́йкъл Джо́нсън не мо́же да ка́же на Са́шко „Чести́т рожде́н ден“?
- **d** За какво́ благодари́ Са́шко на Ма́йкъл Джо́нсън?
- **e** Кога́ се получа́ват пода́ръци?
- **f** Откъде́ ще донесе́ ви́ното Боя́н Анто́нов?

2 True or false?

- **a** Ни́кой (*nobody*) не купу́ва цветя́ днес.
- **b** Ма́йкъл купу́ва буке́т ро́зи, защо́то ро́зите му харе́сват.
- **c** На Са́шко му харе́сват моли́вите.
- **d** Зла́тка ще пока́ни го́стите в ку́хнята.
- **e** Са́шко не оби́ча да пома́га.
- **f** Зла́тка се надя́ва, че ба́ницата ще им харе́са.

How do you say it?

- Offering general congratulations on any festive occasion

Чести́то!/Чести́т пра́зник!	*Congratulations!*

- Congratulating someone on an achievement

Поздравя́вам те/Ви с успе́ха!	*Congratulations on your success!*
Поздравле́ния!	*Congratulations!*

- Offering good wishes on specific occasions

Поздравя́вам те/ Ви с рожде́ния ден!	*Many happy returns of the day!*
Чести́т рожде́н ден!	*Happy birthday!*
Ве́села/Чести́та Ко́леда!	*Merry/Happy Christmas!*
Чести́та Но́ва Годи́на! (ЧНГ*)	*Happy New Year!*

*This abbreviation is mainly found on New Year cards.

За мно́го годи́ни!	*Many happy returns!* (lit. *for many more years.* Also used on other festive occasions such as New Year.)
Жела́я ти/Ви здра́ве и щa̓стие!	*I wish you health and happiness!*

- Wishing someone *Good health* (on drinking!)

Наздра́ве!	*Cheers!*

- Giving a warning

Внима́вай(те)!	*Watch out!*
Внима́вай да не па́днеш!	*Mind you don't fall.*

- Saying *on the occasion of...*

По слу́чай тре́ти март...	*On the occasion of the March 3 holiday...*

Grammar

1 Какво́ се пра́ви? *What do people do?*

There are two ways to generalize. You can either use the *you* singular form as in English, but leaving out **ти**:

Кога́то и́скаш да поздрави́ш ня́кого, кажи́ „Чести́то!".	*When you want to congratulate someone, say 'Congratulations!'.*

Or, with most verbs, you can put **се** in front of the *it* form making the verb reflexive:

Какво́ **се пра́ви** на Ко́леда в Бълга́рия?	*What do people do* (*is done*) *for Christmas in Bulgaria?*
Какво́ **се ка́зва** на Ко́леда?	*What do people say* (*is said*) *at Christmas?*
Какво́ **се но́си** на домаки́нята, кога́то **се хо́ди** на го́сти?	*What does one take* (*is taken*) *to the lady of the house when one goes visiting?*
Как **се ка́зва** „Happy birthday" на бъ̀лгарски?	*How does one say 'Happy birthday'* (*is 'Happy birthday' said*) *in Bulgarian?*

Note that although there is no separate word for *one* in Bulgarian, this form with **се** is, in fact, the Bulgarian equivalent. And remember too, that **какво́** is a singular word and is followed by a singular verb.

As you can see from the alternative translation given above in brackets, and also from the little homily Ези́кът се у́чи, кога́то се гово́ри *Language is learned when it is spoken*, there is more of an emphasis here on what is done and not so much on the person who does it. (Look back too to the True or false? section in Unit 8 and you will find the sentence: **Тарато́рът се серви́ра студе́н** *The tarator soup is served cold.*)

The **се** may also be used with the *they* form of certain verbs, again when you want to emphasize what is done and not the person who does it.

Обикнове́но **се но́сят** цветя́ или́ бонбо́ни.	*Usually people take flowers or chocolates (flowers or chocolates are taken).*
На рожде́н ден **се получа́ват** пода́ръци.	*On one's birthday one receives presents (presents are received).*

(This is another way of expressing the passive which you came across in Unit 11 and about which you can discover more in the Appendix.)

You will find this generalizing form used widely in public notices and instructions:

Тук не се́ пу́ши!	*No smoking here.*
Тук се прода́ват биле́ти.	*Tickets sold here.*
Тук не се́ парки́ра.	*No parking here.*

Most of these constructions with **се** have no subject: they are impersonal constructions.

тук се продават билети за ГРАДСКИЯ ТРАНСПОРТ

2 Another way of saying *I like*

In Unit 12 you learnt the verbs **оби́чам** and **харе́свам/(да) харе́сам**. You can use **харе́свам** and **(да) харе́сам** in a slightly different way, focusing not so much on your liking – or disliking – something, but rather on the effect something – or someone – has on you. So, instead of saying you like something, you are, in effect, saying it 'appeals' to you. You can therefore say:

Either Аз харе́свам те́зи ро́зи or Те́зи ро́зи ми харе́сват (*I like these roses*).

Either Ма́йкъл Джо́нсън харе́са ро́зите or Ро́зите харе́саха на Ма́йкъл Джо́нсън (*Michael Johnson liked the roses*).

Either Той харе́са ро́зите or Ро́зите му харе́саха (*He liked the roses*).

In fact, the more usual form is the second one with the indirect object pronouns (cf. Unit 7) as in:

Надя́вам се, че ба́ницата ще ви харе́са.	*I hope you will like the banitsa.*
Ба́ницата харе́са на го́стите.	*The guests liked the banitsa.*
Ба́ницата им харе́са.	*They liked the banitsa.*

You will notice that when you use a person's name or a noun (instead of a pronoun) you have to use **на**.

3 Present and past forms of *to bring/carry, take, to buy*, and *to see*

When you want to say that something is happening at the moment or happens often, you need to use the imperfective verb. So, in the following examples, you can see the imperfective verbs **но́ся**, **купу́вам** and **ви́ждам** used in the present:

Миле́на **но́си** два учё́бника на Никола́й.	*Milena is taking two textbooks to Nikolai.*

Мно́го хо́ра **купу́ват** цветя́ днес.	*A lot of people are buying flowers today.*
Ма́йкъл Джо́нсън не **ви́жда** табе́лката.	*Michael Johnson does not see the notice.*

To say the same things in the past, you need to choose the perfective equivalents of the verbs **(да) донеса́**, **(да) ку́пя** and **(да) ви́дя**:

Миле́на **доне́се** два учéбника на Никола́й.	*Milena took two textbooks to Nikolai.*
Мно́го хо́ра **ку́пиха** цветя́ днес.	*A lot of people bought flowers today.*
Ма́йкъл Джо́нсън не **видя́** табе́лката.	*Michael Johnson did not see the notice.*

хо́ра *(people)* is the plural of **чове́к** *(person)*.

4 Some more about past endings

(a) Verbs adding past endings to -я́-

These are **е**-pattern verbs in **-е́я** (**пе́я** *to sing*, **живе́я** *to live*):

живя́х	*I lived/used to live*	живя́хме	*we lived, used to live*
живя́	*you lived*	живя́хте	*you lived*
живя́	*he/she/ it lived*	живя́ха	*they lived*

A small group of **и**-pattern verbs also belong here, especially ones with stress on the final syllable like **вървя́** *to walk* and **стоя́** *to stay/stand*. Although not with final stress, **(да) ви́дя** adds the past ending to **-я́-**:

видя́х	*I saw*	видя́хме	*we saw*
видя́	*you saw*	видя́хте	*you saw*
видя́	*he/she/it saw*	видя́ха	*they saw*

(b) Past tense of (да) до́йда *to come*, (да) донеса́ *to bring/carry/take*

Verbs of the **е**-pattern with **д, з, к, с** or **т** before their present endings have **-о-** in front of all their past endings, except in the 2nd and 3rd singular:

(аз)	дойд**о́х**	доне́с**ох**	(ни́е)	дойд**о́хме**	доне́с**охме**
(ти)	дойд**е́**	доне́се	(ви́е)	дойд**о́хте**	доне́с**охте**
(той) (тя) (то)	дойд**е́**	доне́се	(те)	дойд**о́ха**	доне́с**оха**

Note the different stress in the past. Other similar verbs you already know are: **(да) оти́да** *to go* and **(да) пресека́** *to cross*. Remember the change from **к** to **ч** (Unit 13)!

5 Хо́дя and оти́вам *To go*

Usually you use the same verb to say that something is happening at the moment or happens often. **Хо́дя** and **оти́вам**, however, are special. You can only use **хо́дя** when you go somewhere often, while **оти́вам** can only be used when you are going somewhere from here, now, this very moment:

Все́ки ден хо́дя на ра́бота.	*Every day I go to work.*
Вся́ко ля́то хо́дя на море́.	*Every summer I go to the seaside.*
Вся́ка неде́ля хо́дя на ць́рква.	*Every Sunday I go to church.*

And the answer to: Къде́ оти́ваш? *Where are you going?* is

Оти́вам на ра́бота.	*I am going to work.* (Now!)
Оти́вам на море́.	*I am going to the seaside.* (Now!)
Оти́вам на ць́рква.	*I am going to church.* (Now!)

Only **оти́вам** has a perfective counterpart:

Тря́бва веднáга да **оти́да** на ра́бота.	*I have to go to work immediately.*

6 Къде́ and ня́къде *Where* and *somewhere*

All question words can be made into indefinite words by adding **ня́-**:

как	*how*	**ня́**как	*somehow*
какъ́в	*what sort of*	**ня́**какъв	*some sort of*
кога́	*when*	**ня́**кога	*sometime*
ко́лко	*how many*	**ня́**колко	*some, a few, several*
къде́	*where*	**ня́**къде	*somewhere*

Ня́кой *somebody* or *someone* is formed in a similar way. It has the non-subject form **ня́кого**.

7 Зла́тка and Зла́тке: a special address form for names

You may just remember from way back in Unit 2, when addressing someone using their name or title, you often need to use special forms of address, as in:

господи́не! госпо́жо! госпо́жице!

Some names of people have similar special forms, usually involving the change or addition of a single letter:

Masculine names ending in consonants add **-е**:

(Боя́н) Боя́не! (Ива́н) Ива́не!

Most feminine names don't have a special form, but certain names ending in **-ка** change to **-ке**:

(Зла́тка) Зла́тке! (Ра́дка) Ра́дке!

Exercises

1 Using the model: Поздравя́вам Ви с рожде́ния ден. Части́то!, congratulate a Bulgarian on:

a getting a new job
b moving to a new flat (use **апартаме́нт**)
c getting married (use **сва́тба** *wedding*)
d some special achievement (use **успе́х** *success*)
e a festive occasion (use **пра́зник**)
f a good choice (use **добъ́р и́збор**)

Don't forget to use definite nouns!

2 Read the sentences below and then alter them, following the model: Полу́чихме пока́на за конце́рт/Пока́нени сме на конце́рт (*We have received an invitation for a concert/We've been invited to a concert*). Note the different use of **за** and **на**.

This exercise will help you practise using the right gender of the passive participles and the right form of **съм**.

a Миле́на полу́чи пока́на за о́пера.
b Полу́чих пока́на за сва́тба.
c Ма́йкъл Джо́нсън полу́чи пока́на за изло́жба.
d Те полу́чиха пока́на за па́рти (*party*).
e Полу́чихте ли пока́на за кокте́йла (*the cocktail party*)?

3 Ask questions about the words in bold using the question words **къде́, какво́** and **кога́**.

a Валу́та се обме́ня **на ка́са 14**.
b **Цига́ри и алкохо́л** на малоле́тни (*juveniles, young people*) не се́ прода́ват.
c Резерва́ции се пра́вят **все́ки ден от 9 до 11 часа́**.

d С то́зи трамва́й се оти́ва **до поли́цията**.
e Оттýк (*from here*) се ви́жда **хоте́л „Роди́на“**.
f Оттýк се ви́ждат **ЦУМ и хоте́л „Ше́ратон“**.

Тук се продава
sim карта
Prima!

4 Now for some irregular verbs! First read aloud this dialogue between two couples sightseeing in Sofia. Then change the dialogue to indicate that only you and a friend are talking. (The forms in bold will remind you which bits need altering.)

– **Видя́хте** ли катедра́лата „Свети́ Алекса́ндър Не́вски“?
• Да, **видя́хме** я.
– Харе́са ли **ви**?
• Мно́го **ни** харе́са.
– Разгле́да**хте** ли кри́птата (*the crypt*)?
• Да, разгле́да**хме** и не́я. Пред кри́птата се прода́ваха ико́ни. Кýпи**хме** една́ ма́лка ико́на (*icon*).
– Мо́же ли да я ви́д**им**?
• Разби́ра се. Е́то я. Харе́сва ли **ви**?
– **Ни́е** не разби́р**аме** от ико́ни, но та́зи **ни** харе́сва.

5 This exercise will help you practise saying *I like*. Give a full answer to the following short questions.

Model: Харе́сва ли ти шампа́нското (*champagne*)? Да, шампа́нското мно́го ми харе́сва.

a Харе́сва ли Ви то́зи компа́ктдиск (*CD*) с българска мýзика?

b Харе́сва ли Ви тарато́рът?
c Харе́сва ли Ви ба́ницата?
d Харе́сват ли ти те́зи цветя́?
e Харе́сва ли Ви бъ́лгарското ви́но?
f Харе́сват ли ти пъ́лнените чу́шки?
g Харе́сват ли Ви бонбо́ните?
h Харе́сва ли Ви шо́пската сала́та?

6 First read the following sentences out loud in which people are taking things somewhere. Then read the sentences again as if the various errands were completed yesterday.

Model: Аз но́ся те́жкия ку́фар. Вче́ра доне́сох те́жкия ку́фар.

a Ма́йкъл Джо́нсън и Никола́й но́сят ро́зи за Зла́тка Анто́нова.
b Миле́на но́си еди́н уче́бник за Никола́й.
c Ни́е но́сим брошу́ри от пана́йра в Пло́вдив.
d Но́сите ли пода́рък за сво́ите прия́тели?
e Ма́йкъл Джо́нсън но́си шокола́д за Са́шко.
f Г-н Анто́нов и синъ́т му но́сят две бути́лки ви́но от ку́хнята.

Do you understand?

Dialogue 2: Прия́телски съве́т *Friendly advice*

Michael Johnson consults an estate agent and then seeks advice from Boyan Antonov on a possible purchase.

Ма́йкъл До́бър ден. Дойдо́х при Вас за съве́т.
Бро́керка Ще се ра́двам да Ви помо́гна. Ви́е англича́нин ли сте?
Ма́йкъл Да, и́мам би́знес конта́кти с бъ́лгарска фи́рма. Че́сто пъту́вам до Бълга́рия. И́скам да зна́я как се купу́ва къ́ща тук.
Бро́керка Предпола́гам, че се интересу́вате от къ́ща в прови́нцията.
Ма́йкъл Да, да, извъ́н Со́фия.
Бро́керка Сега́ ще Ви пока́жа ня́колко къ́щи на на́шия сайт. Като́ избере́те къ́ща, добре́ е да оти́дете да я ви́дите с Ва́шия адвока́т.
Ма́йкъл Благодаря́. Ще до́йда пак при Вас.

(*A few days later.*)

Ма́йкъл Бо́яне, хо́дих да ви́дя ня́колко къщи в прови́нцията. Харе́сах една́ романти́чна къща бли́зо до Ба́нско.

Боя́н Не тря́бва да се купу́ва без съве́т от специали́ст. Мо́же къщата да е мно́го ста́ра. Жена́ Ви видя́ ли я?

Ма́йкъл Тя я видя́ са́мо на сни́мка. Е́то, доне́сох сни́мката да Ви пока́жа къщата.

Боя́н Симпати́чна къща, но и́ма ли гради́на?

Ма́йкъл Да, гради́ната също ми харе́са.

Боя́н Внимава́йте за шума́. Аз ку́пих една́ къща бли́зо до дискоте́ка, къде́то се чу́ва му́зика ця́ла нощ...

Ма́йкъл Мно́го неприя́тно. И това́ мя́сто не е́ мно́го ти́хо, кога́то и́ма пра́зник или́ сва́тба.

Боя́н Защо́?

Ма́йкъл Къщата е до еди́н манасти́р. Хо́дих там на пра́зника на Свети́ Ки́рил и Мето́дий. И́маше мно́го хо́ра и цветя́.

Боя́н Да, на то́зи пра́зник се но́сят цветя́ в църквите.

Ма́йкъл На нас ни харе́сва иде́ята да живе́ем до манасти́р. Така́ ще ви́дим как се празну́ва в Бълга́рия.

Боя́н Тога́ва, поздравле́ния за добри́я и́збор! Жела́я Ви щастли́ви дни и мно́го пра́зници в Бълга́рия!

бро́керка	*(real) estate agent* (woman)
конта́кт	*contact*
че́сто	*often*
предпола́гам, -гаш	*to suppose*
прови́нция	*the country* (outside the capital)
извън	*outside*
сайт	*(internet) site*
адвока́т	*lawyer, attorney*
романти́чен, -чна	*romantic*
манасти́р	*monastery*
щастли́в	*happy*

Questions

1 Какво́ и́ска да зна́е г-н Джо́нсън?
2 Какъ́в е съве́тът на бро́керката?
3 Къде́ е къщата, коя́то г-н Джо́нсън харе́сва?
4 Кога́ се но́сят цветя́ в църквата?
5 Какво́ пожела́ва Боя́н Анто́нов на г-н Джо́нсън?

бях на ле́кар

I went to see the doctor

In this unit you will learn:

- **how to talk about feeling ill and getting better**
- **how to describe feelings**

Dialogue 1

Nadya and Milena are coming to the end of their coffee break.

Нáдя Искаш ли óще кекс?
Милéна Не, благодаря́.
Нáдя Не тú ли харéса?
Милéна Мнóго ми харéса, но не мú се ядé.
Нáдя Ти вúнаги внимáваш каквó ядéш, грúжиш се за килогрáмите си. Пак ли си на диéта?
Милéна Не, не é товá. Не сé чýвствам добрé.
Нáдя Каквó ти е?
Милéна Лóшо ми е. От вчéра ме болú стомáхът.
Нáдя Защó не отúдеш на лéкар?
Милéна Бях на лéкар тáзи сýтрин. Страхýвах се, че úмам апендисúт. Слáва Бóгу, не é апендисúт. Лéкарят кáза, че сúгурно е ня́какъв лек грип.
Нáдя Отидú си вкъщи, акó не сú добрé.
Милéна Ня́ма нýжда, нúщо дрýго не мé болú. Ня́мам хрéма илú кáшлица. Кáкто ти кáзах, úмам бóлки в стомáха и непрекъснато ми се пúе водá.
Нáдя За стомáх пий мéнтов чай – мнóго помáга. Сегá ще ти напрáвя.
Милéна Недéй, ня́ма нýжда. Не мú се пúе чай след кафéто.
Нáдя Студéно ли ти е?
Милéна Не, не мú е студéно, ня́мам температýра. Не сé безпокóй, ще ми мúне.
Нáдя Да, щом ня́маш температýра, скóро ще ти мúне. Спóмням си, мúналата годúна по товá врéме úмах стрáшен грип с висóка температýра и сúлна кáшлица. Не можáх да се опрáвя цял мéсец. Тря́бваше да взúмам антибиóтик.
Милéна Аз не обúчам да взúмам антибиóтици.
Нáдя И аз не обúчам, но човéк тря́бва вúнаги да се грúжи за здрáвето си.
Милéна Прáва си.

Не тú ли харéса?	*Didn't you like it?*
Не мú се ядé.	*I don't feel like eating.*
Грúжиш се за килогрáмите си.	*You're worrying about your weight.* (lit. *kilograms*)
на диéта	*on a diet*
Не сé чýвствам добрé.	*I don't feel well.*
Каквó ти е?	*What is the matter with you?*

Лóшо ми е.	*I'm not well.*
От вчéра ме болѝ стомáхът.	*I've had stomachache since yesterday.*
на лéкар	*to the doctor's*
Страхýвах се, че ѝмам апендисѝт.	*I was afraid I had appendicitis.*
Слáва Бóгу!	*Thank heavens!*
нѝкакъв лек грип	*a kind of mild flu*
Отидѝ си вкъщи,	*Go home*
акó не сѝ добрé.	*if you are not (feeling) well.*
нѝщо дрýго не мé болѝ	*nothing else is hurting*
хрéма	*cold* (in the head)
кáшлица	*cough*
Ѝмам бóлки в стомáха.	*I have stomach pains.*
Непрекъснато ми се пѝе водá.	*I feel like drinking water all the time.*
Не мѝ се пѝе чай.	*I don't feel like drinking tea.*
Студéно ли ти е?	*Are you cold?*
Не сé безпокóй.	*Don't worry.*
Ще ми мѝне.	*It will pass./I'll be fine.*
щом нѝмаш температýра	*since you don't have a temperature*
скóро	*soon*
спóмням си	*I remember*
мѝналата годѝна по товá врéме	*last year at this time*
Не можáх да се опрáвя цял мéсец.	*It took me a whole month to get over it.*
Трѝбваше да взѝмам антибиóтик.	*I had to take an antibiotic.*
Човéк трѝбва вѝнаги да се грѝжи за здрáвето си.	*One always has to look after one's health.*

1 Questions

- **a** Защó Милéна не ѝска пóвече (*more*) кекс?
- **b** Каквó ѝ е?
- **c** Каквó ѝ се пѝе?
- **d** Когá ѝмаше Нáдя грип с висóка температýра?
- **e** За каквó трѝбва да се грѝжи човéк?

2 True or false?

- **a** Милéна не и́ска кекс, защóто се гри́жи за килогрáмите си.
- **b** Кéксът не ѝ харéса.
- **c** Милéна и́ма бóлки в стомáха от вчéра.
- **d** Тя и́ма хрéма и кáшлица.
- **e** Ми́налата годи́на Нáдя не можá да се оправи от грип цял мéсец.

How do you say it?

- Asking someone how they feel

Как се чу́встваш?/чу́вствате?	*How do you feel?*

- Asking someone what is the matter with them

Каквó ти/Ви е?	*What is the matter with you?*
Каквó те/Ви боли́?	*What is hurting?*

- Complaining of ill health

Не сé чу́вствам добрé.	*I don't feel well.*
Чу́вствам се зле.	*I feel unwell.*
Лóшо ми е.	*I'm not well.*
И́мам бóлки в стомáха.	*I have stomach pains.*

- Saying you'll get better

Ще ми ми́не.	*It'll pass.*
Ще се опрáвя.	*I'll get better.*

- Telling someone not to worry

Не сé безпокóй!	*Don't worry!*

- Saying that you do or don't feel like doing something

Пи́е ми се водá.	*I feel like a drink of water.*
Не ми́ се пи́е чай.	*I don't feel like tea.*
Ядé ми се нéщо слáдко.	*I feel like something sweet.*
Не ми́ се рабóти.	*I don't feel like working.*

Grammar

1 Каквó ти е? *What's the matter with you?*

To ask someone how they feel, physically or mentally, or what is the matter with them, you say **Каквó ти е?** or **Каквó Ви е?** You will notice that the indirect object pronouns (Unit 7) are used to refer to the person affected. Similarly, to tell someone how you feel, you describe your state (in the neuter!) e.g. студе́но *cold* and then refer to yourself using the indirect object pronoun **ми**:

Студе́но **ми** е.	*I am (feeling) cold.*

These expressions are related to the weather descriptions you came across in Unit 10. Here are some examples for all persons:

Ло́шо ми е.	*I'm not well./I'm sick/poorly.*
Горе́що ли ти/Ви е?	*Are you hot?*
Ло́шо ѝ е.	*She is sick/poorly/not well.*
Студе́но му е.	*He is (feeling) cold.*
Интере́сно ни е.	*It is interesting for us./ We find it interesting.*
Ску́чно им е.	*They are bored.*

In the negative, **не** is placed first, the word coming immediately after **не** is stressed, and the word expressing the feeling is placed after the verb:

Не ми́ е ло́шо.	*I'm not unwell/sick/poorly.*
Не ти́ ли е горе́що?	*Aren't you hot?*
Не му́ е студе́но.	*He is not (feeling) cold.*

You can also use the alternative ways to indicate the person affected (Unit 11):

на + name

На На́дя ѝ е ло́шо.	*Nadya is not feeling well.*

на + noun

На секрета́рката ѝ е ло́шо.	*The secretary is not feeling well.*

на + full pronoun

На не́я ѝ е ло́шо.	*She's not feeling well.*

You will have noticed that you still need to keep the indirect object pronoun. Here are some more examples:

На Никола́й/на не́го му е студе́но.	*Nikolai/He is cold.*
На го́стите/на тях им е ску́чно.	*The guests/They are bored.*

2 Боли́ ме *It hurts*

If you want to say that some particular part (or parts) of your body hurts (or hurt) you use **боли́** – or **боля́т** – with the short object pronoun **ме** (there's a full list in Unit 11):

Болú **ме** главáта	*My head hurts/*
(*or* Главáта **ме** болú).	*I have a headache.*
Болят **ме** очúте	*My eyes hurt.*
(*or* Очúте **ме** болят).	

It is as though you were saying *My head hurts me* or *My eyes hurt me*. And the doctor might ask you **Каквó Ви болú?** (or **Каквó те болú?** if he knows you well) *What is hurting you?*

Note that many parts of the body, especially those that come in pairs, have irregular plural forms:

зъб	–	зъби	*tooth*	–	*teeth*
колянo	–	коленá	*knee*	–	*knees*
крак	–	кракá	*foot/leg*	–	*feet/legs*
окó	–	очú	*eye*	–	*eyes*
ръкá	–	ръцé	*hand/arm*	–	*hands/arms*
ухó	–	ушú	*ear*	–	*ears*

In the following examples people, other than you, are in pain, and **ме** is replaced by the appropriate short object pronouns:

Болú ли те гъ́рлото?	*Does your throat hurt?*
Болú го ухóто.	*His ear hurts/He has earache.*
Болú я кракъ́т.	*Her leg hurts.*
Болят ли те ушúте?	*Are your ears hurting?*
Болят го ръцéте.	*His hands/arms hurt.*
Болят я зъ́бите.	*Her teeth hurt.*
Болят ги кракáта.	*Their feet hurt.*

3 Ядé ми се *I'm hungry*

Another very useful way of saying how you feel is to use the *it* form of the verb with **се** (cf. Unit 14). You merely insert the indirect object pronoun between the verb and **се**:

Ядé **ми** се.	*I'm hungry.*
Пúе **ми** се.	*I'm thirsty.*
Спи **ми** се.	*I'm sleepy.*

If you don't feel like doing something, put **не** first and the verb last:

Не **мú** се ядé.	*I'm not hungry.*
Не **мú** се пúе.	*I'm not thirsty.*
Не **мú** се спи.	*I'm not sleepy.*

This construction can be extended:

Ядé **ми** се сладолéд.	*I feel like an ice-cream.*
Пúе **ми** се водá.	*I feel like a drink of water.*

If you use a person's name you still have to use the pronoun:

На Сáшко не **мý** се спи.	*Sashko isn't sleepy.*
На Милéна не **й** се ядé сладолéд.	*Milena doesn't feel like an ice-cream.*

You can use this pattern with almost any verb to express your wish to do (or not do) something:

Хóди **ми** се на морé.	*I feel like going to the seaside.*
Не **мú** се хóди на рáбота.	*I don't feel like going to work.*
Не **мú** се рабóти.	*I don't feel like working.*

4 Some awkward past tense forms

Past tense of *to say/tell* кáзвам/да кáжа – кáзах

In the present tense you have to use the imperfective **кáзвам**, but in the past you change to the perfective **(да) кáжа**:

Чýваш ли каквó ти **кáзвам**?	***Do you hear*** *what* ***I'm telling*** *you?*
Чу ли каквó ти **кáзах**?	***Did you hear*** *what* ***I told*** *you?*

(Да) кáжа belongs to a small group of **е**-pattern verbs that change their last consonant from the present to the past, in this case **ж** to **з**. (For other changes and other examples see the Appendix, and also **мóга** with the change from **г** to **ж** below.) Compare the forms of **(да) кáжа**:

	Present		**Past**	
(трябва да)	кáжа	*I must say*	кáзах	*I said*
(трябва да)	кáжеш	*you must say*	кáза	*you said*
(трябва да)	кáже	*he/she must say*	кáза	*he/she said*
(трябва да)	кáжем	*we must say*	кáзахме	*we said*
(трябва да)	кáжете	*you must say*	кáзахте	*you said*
(трябва да)	кáжат	*they must say*	кáзаха	*they said*

Past tense of *can* мóга – можáх

Не можáхме да спим цяла нощ.	*We couldn't sleep all night.*
Тя не можá да ядé мнóго от кéкса.	*She wasn't able to eat much of the cake.*

Не можáх да се опрáвя цял мéсец. — *It took me a whole month to get over it.*

можáх	*I was able*	**можáхме**	*we were able*
можá	*you were able*	**можáхте**	*you were able*
можá	*he/she was able*	**можáха**	*they were able*

Past tense of *must/had to* тря́бва – тря́бваше

Тря́бва has only one past form – **тря́бваше** – for all persons singular and plural:

Тря́бваше да взи́мам антибиóтик. — *I had to take an antibiotic.*
Тря́бваше да стáне рáно. — *He/she had to get up early.*
Тря́бваше да чáкаме/чáкат дълго. — *We/they had to wait a long time.*

Depending on the context, тря́бваше can also mean *should have* or *ought to have* (but didn't), so тря́бваше да взи́мам антибиóтик could mean *I ought to have* (or *should have*) *taken an antibiotic* (but didn't).

5 Possessive and reflexive pronoun си

(**a**) This is another difficult little word, not to be confused with the **си** in ти си. It belongs to the group of short possessive pronouns you first came across in Unit 3 and is a short form of **свой** (**свóя**, **свóе**, **свóи**) *his/her/their own* (cf. Unit 9). In fact, it can be used to replace any possessive adjective (мой, твой, нéгов etc.) with any person, masculine or feminine, singular or plural. Unlike the possessive adjective, however, it is placed after the word it refers to.

Note also that the definite article moves from the possessive adjective to the noun:

Чáкам сво**я** при́тел = Чáкам при́теля **си**. — *I am waiting for my friend.*
Ви́наги се гри́жиш за свóе**то** здрáве = Ви́наги се гри́жиш за здрáве**то си**. — *You are always worrying about your health.*
Тя се гри́жи за свóи**те** килогрáми = тя се гри́жи за килогрáми**те си**. — *She is worrying about her weight* (lit. *kilograms*).

(**b**) **Си** can also be used as an equivalent of *myself, yourself, himself, herself, itself, ourselves, yourselves* and *themselves:*

Ку́пих **си** моде́рна блу́за.	*I bought **myself** a fashionable blouse.*
Неве́на **си** ку́пи дъ́лга ро́кля.	*Nevena bought **herself** a long dress.*
Никола́й **си** ку́пи но́во ви́део.	*Nikolai bought **himself** a new video.*

(**c**) Some verbs you always have to use with **си**:

Почи́вам **си**.	*I am taking a rest.*
Спо́мням **си**.	*I remember.*

To other verbs **си** adds a personalized, intimate sense of doing something for oneself. There is a difference, for example, between **оти́вам** *I am going* and **оти́вам си** *I am going home.* In the Dialogue, when Nadya suggests Milena goes home, she says: отиди́ **си** вкъщи.

(**d**) Like many other short grammatical words, **си** never appears as the first word in a sentence and is *always* stressed after **не**.

Exercises

1 Match the following questions and answers:

i	Какво́ ти се пи́е?	**a**	Яде́ ми се ки́село мля́ко.
ii	Гъ́рло (*throat*) ли те боли́?	**b**	Ло́шо ми е.
iii	Какво́ те боли́?	**c**	Пи́е ми се би́ра.
iv	И́маш ли хре́ма?	**d**	Студе́но ми е.
v	Какво́ ти се яде́?	**e**	Боли́ ме кракъ́т.
vi	Какво́ ти е?	**f**	Не, ня́мам хре́ма, но и́мам висо́ка температу́ра.
vii	Как се чу́встваш?	**g**	Не, боля́т ме уши́те.

2 You are interpreting for a Bulgarian doctor working with English-speaking tourists. Give a full negative answer to the doctor's questions using the model:

Боли́ ли го ухо́то? Не, не го́ боли́ ухо́то.

Watch the word order!

a **i** Боля́т ли го очи́те?
ii Боли́ ли я зъб?
iii Боля́т ли ги craка́та?
iv Боли́ ли го коля́ното?
v Боли́ ли я ръка́та?

Now give a full negative answer to the questions:

b i Хóди ли ти се на плаж?
ii Пúе ли Ви се чай?
iii Говóри ли ти се бъ́лгарски?
iv У́чи ли ти се?
v Рабóти ли ти се на компю́тър?

3 Now your friend is unwell. Complete your role in the dialogue:

– Не сé чу́вствам добрé.
• (*Ask your friend what is the matter with him.*)
– Болú ме кръ́стът (*small of the back*).
• (*Ask him what the doctor said to him.*)
– Лéкарят ми кáза да си почúвам.
• (*Ask whether he's feeling sleepy.*)
– Не, не мú се спи.
• (*Ask him whether he is bored.*)
– Да, мнóго ми е скý́чно.
• (*Tell him not to worry and reassure him that he'll soon be OK again.*)
– Да, и аз се надя́вам, че скóро ще ми мúне.

4 Now you've been to the doctor's and are answering your friend's questions. Using the model:

Каквó ти кáза лéкарят? Лéкарят ми кáза, че úмам алéргия (*allergy*).

and, at the risk of giving your friend a heart attack, say that:

a you have flu
b you have appendicitis
c you have a high temperature
d you have a cold in the head
e you have hepatitis (хепатúт)

5 Using the past of **мóга** fill in the answers. Follow the pattern:

Видя́хте ли фолклóрния концéрт? Не **можáхме** да го **вúдим,** защóто закъсня́хме.

a Джон **отúде** ли на гóсти?
______, защóто го болéше главáта. (cf. Unit 17)
b **Донéсе** ли чáнтата?
______, защóто ме болéше кръ́стът.
c Те **разглéдаха** ли курóрта?
______, защóто ги боля́ха кракáта.
d **Прáтихте** (*send*) ли писмóто?
______, защóто ня́махме мáрки.

e **Я́де** ли от бъ́лгарските специалите́ти?
______, защо́то и́мах бо́лки в стома́ха.

6 In this exercise you can practise saying *came* and *went*. Read out the sentences, filling in the answers according to the model:

Защо́ не дойдо́хте с нас на екску́рзия?
Тря́бваше да посре́щнем прия́телите си. Оти́дохме да посре́щнем прия́телите си.

a Защо́ не дойде́ с нас на екску́рзия?
Тря́бваше да си ку́пя марато́нки. ______.
b Защо́ не дойдо́хте с нас на плаж?
Тря́бваше да си почи́нем (*have a rest*). ______.
c Защо́ не дойде́ с нас на вече́ря (*dinner, supper*)?
Тря́бваше да си ку́пя лека́рства. ______.
d Защо́ не дойде́ с нас на го́сти?
Тря́бваше да посре́щна дъщеря́ си. ______.
e Защо́ не дойде́ с ме́не на Ви́тоша?
Тря́бваше да оти́да на ле́кар. ______.
f Защо́ не дойдо́хте с ме́не на ски?
Тря́бваше да пра́тим писмо́ на роди́телите си. ______.

Do you understand?

Dialogue 2: След пла́жа *After the beach*

Mr and Mrs Collins are at the doctor's in Varna. As usual, Mrs Collins prefers to do the talking.

г-жа́ Ко́линс До́бър ден, до́ктор Стоя́нов.
Ле́кар До́бър ден. Каже́те. Зле ли се чу́вствате?
г-жа́ Ко́линс Не, не а́з. Мъжъ́т ми не се́ чу́вства добре́.
Ле́кар Какво́ му е?
г-жа́ Ко́линс И́ма си́лно главобо́лие и все му е студе́но.
г-н Ко́линс Да, мно́го ми е студе́но, а навъ́н е то́лкова то́пло.
Ле́кар И́мате ли температу́ра?
г-жа́ Ко́линс Температу́рата му не е́ мно́го висо́ка – 37.1 [три́десет и се́дем и едно́.]
Ле́кар Боли́ ли го гъ́рло?
г-жа́ Ко́линс Ни́то го боли́ гъ́рло, ни́то и́ма хре́ма.
Ле́кар Ви́ждам, че ко́жата на ръце́те и крака́та му е до́ста черве́на.
г-жа́ Ко́линс О, да. Той мно́го оби́ча да стои́ на слъ́нце. Вче́ра цял ден бе́ше на пла́жа.
Ле́кар На ко́лко годи́ни сте г-н Ко́линс?

г-н Кóлинс	На шейсéт и две.
Лéкар	И́махте ли шáпка на главáта си, когáто бя́хте на плáжа?
г-н Кóлинс	Не.
г-жá Кóлинс	Кáзах му, че слъ́нцето е мнóго сúлно, но не можáх да го накáрам да слóжи шáпка.
Лéкар	Страхýвам се, че ще трябва да стойте на ся́нка ня́колко дни. От слъ́нцето Ви е лóшо.
г-жá Кóлинс	Чýваш ли, Джордж? Тря́бваше да ми вя́рваш катó ти кáзвах, че слъ́нцето тук е сúлно дорú през май!

дóктор	*doctor* (only when addressing)
стоя́, стойш	*to stay*
зле	*unwell*
главобóлие	*headache*
все	*all the time*
навъ́н	*outside*
нúто..., нúто...	*neither..., nor...*
кóжа	*skin*
шáпка	*hat*
главá	*head*
слъ́нце	*sun*
(да) накáрам, -раш	*to make* (somebody do something)
(да) слóжа, -жиш	*to put on*
ся́нка	*shade*
вя́рвам, -ваш	*to believe*
катó	*when*

a pharmacy sign in Sofia.

Questions

1 Кой не сé чýвства добрé?
2 Каквó му е на г-н Кóлинс?
3 Защó е червéна кóжата на г-н Кóлинс?
4 Каквó тря́бваше да слóжи на главáта си г-н Кóлинс?
5 Каквó тря́бва да напрáви той сегá?

16 ако́ бях на тво́е мя́сто ...

if I had been in your place ...

In this unit you will learn:

- **how to talk about things that might have happened but didn't (i.e. hypothetical situations)**
- **how to talk about giving presents**
- **how to form the past tense of some awkward verbs**

Dialogue 1

Following Michael Johnson's return to London, there is a short discussion over a cup of coffee back in the Sofia office.

Боя́н Анто́нов Никола́й, кажи́ как ми́на после́дният ден с Ма́йкъл Джо́нсън.

Никола́й Всѝчко ми́на норма́лно. Сутринта́ оти́дох да го взе́ма от хоте́ла. Плати́хме сме́тката. Моми́чето на реце́пцията поръ́ча такси́ за два без петна́йсет. Г-н Джо́нсън ка́за, че е мно́го дово́лен от хоте́ла. Осо́бено от това́ моми́че – ми́сля, че се ка́зва Неве́на. И́скаше да ѝ подари́ не́що за спо́мен. Стра́шни са те́зи англича́ни! Ако́ бях аз, щях да забра́вя дори́ да ка́жа дови́ждане. Но г-н Джо́нсън и́маше еди́н беле́жник и ѝ го подари́. Тя мно́го го харе́са.

На́дя Ако́ бях аз, и аз щях да го харе́сам!

Миле́на А ако́ бях аз, ня́маше да го прие́ма!

Боя́н Анто́нов Моми́чета, сти́га! Продължа́вай, Никола́й.

Никола́й По́сле оти́дохме в магази́на за пода́ръци. Избра́хме една́ сре́бърна гри́вна за жена́ му.

Боя́н Анто́нов Да́де ли му пода́ръка за жена́ му от мо́ята жена́?

Никола́й Разби́ра се, да́дох му го.

Боя́н Анто́нов Той пока́за ли ти програ́мата за тво́я престо́й в Че́лмсфорд?

Никола́й Не ми́ я пока́за. Ка́за, че ще ми я пра́ти с и́мейл.

Боя́н Анто́нов Ще те посре́щне ли в Ло́ндон?

Никола́й Да, ще до́йде на Хи́йтроу да ме посре́щне.

Боя́н Анто́нов И ни́е щя́хме да го посре́щнем, но той не и́скаше. Иде́ята му бе́ше да хо́ди нався́къде сам, за да гово́ри по́вече български.

Никола́й О, щях да забра́вя на́й-ва́жното – це́лия ден гово́рихме на англи́йски. Той ка́за, че напре́двам, но аз о́ще и́мам чу́вството, че ни́що не знам.

На́дя Сти́га, Никола́й! Ако́ бях на тво́е мя́сто, изо́бщо ня́маше да се безпокоя́.

Боя́н Анто́нов Мо́ля ви, по́сле ще гово́рите. И́скам да разбера́ – ти изпра́ти ли Ма́йкъл до лети́щето?

Никола́й	Да, да, изпра́тих го. Сла́ва Бо́гу, не закъсня́хме за самоле́та!
Боя́н Анто́нов	Е, на́й-по́сле разбра́х това́, кое́то и́сках да зна́я...
На́дя	И́скате ли о́ще кафе́, господи́н Анто́нов?
Боя́н Анто́нов	Не, благодаря́. Не и́скам по́вече.

Кажи́ как ми́на после́дният ден.	*Tell me how the final day went.*
нормáлно	*OK, normally*
да го взе́ма	*to take him*
осо́бено	*especially*
да ѝ подари́ не́що за спо́мен	*to give her something as a memento*
Стра́шни са те́зи англича́ни!	*Incredible, these English!*
Ако́ бях аз, щях да забра́вя дори́ да ка́жа довижда́не.	*If it had been me, I'd have forgotten even to say goodbye.*
Ако́ бях аз, и аз щях да го харе́сам!	*If it had been me, I'd have liked it too!*
А ако́ бях аз, ня́маше да го прие́ма!	*And if it had been me, I wouldn't have accepted it.*
Сти́га!	*Stop it! Enough!*
Продължа́вай!	*Go on!*
Избра́хме една́ сре́бърна гри́вна.	*We chose a silver bracelet.*
Да́де ли му пода́ръка?	*Did you give him the present?*
Той пока́за ли ти програ́мата?	*Did he show you the programme?*
Ка́за, че ще ми я пра́ти.	*He said he'd send it to me.*
Ще те посре́щне ли...?	*Will he be meeting you...?*
И ни́е щя́хме да го посре́щнем.	*And we too were intending to meet him.*
нався́къде	*everywhere*
по́вече	*more*
Щях да забра́вя на́й-ва́жното.	*I nearly forgot the most important thing.*
Той ка́за, че напре́двам.	*He said I was making progress.*
Ако́ бях на твое́ мя́сто...	*If I had been in your place...*
ня́маше да се безпокоя́	*I wouldn't have worried*
на́й-по́сле разбра́х	*at last I have found out*
о́ще кафе́	*some more coffee*
Не и́скам по́вече.	*I don't want any more.*

1 Questions

Nikolai has been asked these questions. What should he answer?

- **a** Какво́ пра́вихте после́дния ден с Ма́йкъл Джо́нсън в хоте́ла?
- **b** Какво́ подари́ Ма́йкъл Джо́нсън на Неве́на?
- **c** Какъ́в пода́рък избра́хте за г-жа́ Джо́нсън?
- **d** Да́де ли на Ма́йкъл Джо́нсън пода́ръка от г-жа́ Анто́нова?
- **e** Как ще ти пра́ти той програ́мата?
- **f** На какъ́в ези́к гово́рихте це́лия ден?

2 True or false?

- **a** Неве́на мно́го харе́са беле́жника, ко́йто Ма́йкъл Джо́нсън ѝ подари́.
- **b** На́дя на не́йно мя́сто също ще́ше да го харе́са.
- **c** Ма́йкъл Джо́нсън избра́ една́ сре́бърна гри́вна за дъщеря́ си.
- **d** Той пока́за на Никола́й програ́мата за не́говия престо́й в Че́лмсфорд.
- **e** Ако́ На́дя бе́ше на не́гово мя́сто, тя ще́ше да се безпокои́.
- **f** Боя́н Анто́нов не можа́ да разбере́ това́, ко́ето и́скаше да зна́е.

How do you say it?

- Saying *If I were you*

Ако́ бях на тво́е мя́сто.	*If I had been in your place.*
Ако́ бях аз.	*If it had been me.*

- Saying that you nearly forgot

Щях да забра́вя.	*I nearly forgot.* (*That reminds me.*)

- Telling someone to stop doing something

Сти́га!	*Stop it!*
Доста́тъчно!	*Enough!*

- Saying *At last* and *Thank heavens!*

На́й-по́сле!	*At last!*
Сла́ва Бо́гу!	*Thank heavens!* (lit. *Praise to God!*)

- Asking for and declining more

Йскам о́ще ма́лко.	*I would like a little more.*
Не йскам по́вече, благодаря́.	*I don't want any more, thank you.*

- Saying you would not have done something

Ня́маше да оти́да без те́бе.	*I would not have gone without you.*

Grammar

1 Past tense of (да) дам: да́дох

You will remember from Unit 7 that in all forms other than the *I* form of **(да) дам** there is a **-д-** before the present tense endings **(да) даде́ш, (да) даде́,** etc. As explained in Unit 14, the past endings are therefore added to **-о-**:

(аз)	да́до**х**	*I gave*	(ни́е)	да́до**хме**	*we gave*
(ти)	да́д**е**	*you gave*	(ви́е)	да́до**хте**	*you gave*
(той) (тя) (то)	да́д**е**	*he/she/it gave*	(те)	да́до**ха**	*they gave*

Remember: (**a**) in the *you* singular and *he*, *she*, *it* forms an **-е** replaces the **-о**; (**b**) in the *he*, *she*, *it* form it is only the position of the stress that distinguishes between the present (да) даде́ and the past да́де.

2 Past tense of (да) разбера́ and (да) избера́: разбра́х and избра́х

These verbs belong to a small group of **е**-pattern verbs which have **-ер-** in the present tense. So, too, does **(да) събера́** *to gather*. These verbs all drop the vowel **-е-** before **-р-** in the past tense:

(аз)	разбра́х	*I (have) understood*	(ни́е)	разбра́хме	*we (have) understood*
(ти)	разбра́	*you (have) understood*	(ви́е)	разбра́хте	*you (have) understood*
(той) (тя) (то)	разбра́	*he/she/it (has) understood*	(те)	разбра́ха	*they (have) understood*

3 Past tense of и́скам: и́сках

И́скам has the same past endings as **и́мам** and **съм**:

(аз)	иска**х**	*I wanted*	(ни́е)	иска**хме**	*we wanted*
(ти)	иска**ше**	*you wanted*	(ви́е)	иска**хте**	*you wanted*
(той) (тя) (то)	иска**ше**	*he/she/it wanted*	(те)	иска**ха**	*they wanted*

So far you have come across two patterns of past forms: with and without **-ше** in the *you* singular and *he*, *she*, *it* forms. We have been concentrating on the one without **-ше** which is used to describe a sequence of completed actions. Verbs like **и́скам**, **и́мам** and **съм**, however, stand for *states* rather than actions. That is why they are used in a past tense form with **-ше** which is used for describing incomplete actions. (You will find more on how to use the past forms with **-ше** with other verbs too in Unit 17.)

4 Pronoun word order with giving, sending and showing verbs

With verbs of giving, like **(да) дам** and **(да) подаря́**, sending, **(да) пра́тя**, and showing **(да) пока́жа**, you usually need to mention both the thing that is given (or shown or sent) – the direct object – and the 'beneficiary' – the indirect object – of whatever has been given, shown or sent. (Look back to Unit 7!) When you use the short pronouns as direct and indirect objects, pay attention to the word order. Look at the following sentences taken from the dialogue:

Г-н Джо́нсън и́маше еди́н беле́жник и **ѝ го** подари́. (i.e. на не́я, беле́жника)	*Mr Johnson had a diary and gave it to her.*
Тя не **ми́ я** пока́за. (i.e. на ме́не, програ́мата)	*She did not show it to me.*
Той ще **ми я** пра́ти. (i.e. на ме́не, програ́мата)	*He will send it to me.*
Да́дох **му го**. (i.e. на г-н Джо́нсън, пода́ръка)	*I gave it to him.*

What you need to remember here is:

(a) most importantly, that the indirect object pronouns always come before the direct object ones

(b) when the verb is not the first word in the sentence, then both short pronouns come immediately before the verb

(c) when the verb does come first in the sentence, they both come immediately after the verb (cf. the last example).

5 Щях да *I was going to (but I didn't)*

To express things you wanted or intended to do, but didn't, you need to use the past forms of **ще**, which, in fact, comes from **ща**, an old verb meaning *to want*:

щях	*I intended*	**щя́хме**	*we intended*
ще́ше	*you intended*	**щя́хте**	*you intended*
ще́ше	*he/she intended*	**щя́ха**	*they intended*

Аз щях да до́йда, но не можа́х.	*I was going to come, but I couldn't.*
Той ще́ше да до́йде, но не можа́.	*He was going to come, but couldn't.*

You also use this construction to refer to things that nearly happened (but didn't quite!):

Щях да закъсне́я, но взех такси́.	*I would have been late, but I took a taxi.*
Той ще́ше да оти́де без те́бе.	*He was about to go without you.*

In either case **щях** is followed by **да** and a verb in the present tense in the same person as the main verb.

6 Щях да забра́вя *I nearly forgot/That reminds me*

One of the most common occurrences of **щях** is in the phrase **щях да забра́вя** meaning *I nearly forgot* (but didn't quite!). Here are all the forms:

щях да забра́вя	*I nearly forgot*
ще́ше да забра́виш	*you nearly forgot*
ще́ше да забра́ви	*he/she nearly forgot*
щя́хме да забра́вим	*we nearly forgot*
щя́хте да забра́вите	*you nearly forgot*
щя́ха да забра́вят	*they nearly forgot*

When used with the *I* form **щях да забра́вя** is probably best translated as *that reminds me*.

7 Ня́маше да *I (you, he, she, it, we, etc) would not have*

You will remember from Unit 10 that the negative form of **ще** is **ня́ма да**, which stays the same for all persons. Its past form **ня́маше да**, which also stays the same for all persons, is used as the negative of **щях**:

Аз ня́маше да оти́да без тѐбе.	*I would not have gone without you.*
Ни́е ня́маше да оти́дем без тѐбе.	*We would not have gone without you.*

8 Ако́... щях *I would have done it, if...*

Щях is often used with **ако́** *if* to introduce conditions under which something would have taken place, had the conditions been fulfilled (which they weren't!) These are a type of so-called 'conditional' sentences and you will find out more about them in Unit 20. There are a number of examples in the dialogue:

Ако́ бях аз, щях да забра́вя да ка́жа дори́ довѝждане.	*If it had been me, I'd have forgotten even to say goodbye.*
Ако́ бях аз, и аз щях да го харѐсам.	*If it had been me, I'd have liked it too.*

Sometimes the *if* element, **ако́**, may only be implied:

И ни́е щя́хме да го посрѐщнем (**implied**: ако́ той и́скаше), но той не и́скаше.	*And we too were intending to meet him* (**implied**: *if he had wanted*), *but he didn't want us to.*

The negative form is again with **ня́маше да**:

Ако́ бях аз, ня́маше да го приѐма.	*If it had been me, I wouldn't have accepted it.*
Ако́ бях на тво́е мя́сто, ня́маше да се безпоко́я.	*If I had been in your place, I wouldn't have worried.*

9 По́вече and о́ще *more*

Bulgarian has two different words for *more*: **по́вече** and **о́ще**. It is not always easy to choose the right one, but if you remember the following simple rules, it will help.

(**a**) **По́вече** is to **мно́го** what *more* is to *much* or *many*. It is the irregular comparative of **мно́го**. It is used when you make comparisons and want to say that one person, for example, knows more words (or has more money!) than another:

Ма́йкъл зна́е **мно́го** български ду́ми.	*Michael knows a lot of Bulgarian words.*
Викто́рия зна́е **по́вече** (български ду́ми).	*Victoria knows more (Bulgarian words).*
Той и́ма **мно́го** пари́; аз и́мам **по́вече**.	*He has a lot of money; I have more.*

(**b**) **По́вече** is also used when you have had enough of something and don't want any more. It tends to be used with negatives and therefore has to do with not going beyond a limit that has already been reached:

И́скате ли о́ще би́ра?	*Would you like some more beer?*
Не, не и́скам **по́вече.**	*No, I don't want any more.*

(**c**) You use **о́ще** – and this is the difficult one! – when you are thinking of adding to what is (or **was**, if you are asking for **another** glass of beer!) already there:

И́скате ли о́ще би́ра?	*Would you like some more beer?*
Да, и́скам **о́ще** ма́лко.	*Yes, I'd like a bit more.* (i.e. in addition)

10 Indirect (reported) speech

When you repeat something someone else has said, a question asked or an answer given, you are creating what is called 'indirect' or 'reported speech', forming 'indirect' questions and answers. This usually occurs after an introduction such as *she asked* or *she said*. In English, the tense of the verbs used in indirect speech is changed. (You will see this in the examples given below, all of which are based on dialogues you have already studied.) In Bulgarian, in most instances, you can use the original verb tense of the question and answer. All you need to do is change the person of the speaker, from the *I* form to the *he* form, for example.

Ма́йкъл Джо́нсън

Мно́го съм дово́лен от хоте́ла.	*I am very pleased with the hotel.*

Никола́й

Ма́йкъл Джо́нсън ка́за, че **е** мно́го дово́лен от хоте́ла.	*Michael Johnson said (that) he **was** very pleased with the hotel.*

Мáйкъл Джóнсън
Ще ти прáтя прогрáмата. — *I'll send you the programme.*

Николáй
Мáйкъл Джóнсън кáза, че **ще ми прáти** прогрáмата. — *Michael Johnson said (that) he **would send me** the programme.*

Боя́н Антóнов (to Nadya)
Свобóден ли е Николáй? — *Is Nikolai free?*

Нáдя (to Nikolai)
Шéфът попи́та свобóден ли **си**. — *The boss asked if you **were** free.*

In questions like the last one, using **ли**, you can replace **ли** with **дали́** (*whether*). Note the change of word order:

Нáдя
Шéфът попи́та **дали́ си** свобóден. — *The boss asked **whether** you **were** free.*

Exercises

1 This, and the following two exercises, will help you to practise talking about things that might have happened – but didn't. Read out loud the two sentences in which Mark and Violeta explain what they would have done if they hadn't had more pressing things to attend to:

Марк и Виолéта И́скаме да оти́дем на екскýрзия. Акó ня́махме дрýга рáбота, щя́хме да оти́дем на екскýрзия.

Now read the following sentences out loud and following the model say what you would have done. Use **щя́хме да** or **щях да**.

- **a** И́скахме да оти́дем на плаж. Акó ня́махме вáжна срéща ______.
- **b** И́сках да оти́да на Ви́тоша. Акó ня́мах дрýга рáбота ______.
- **c** И́скахме да оти́дем на тéнис. Акó ня́махме дрýга рáбота ______.
- **d** И́сках да оти́да на гóсти. Акó ня́мах вáжна срéща ______.
- **e** И́сках да оти́да на ски. Акó ня́мах дрýга рáбота ______.

2 What would you buy from Bulgaria as a present? Using the words provided, write out sentences in answer to the question below:

Ако́ и́скахте да ку́пите пода́рък от Бълга́рия, какъ̀в пода́рък щя́хте да ку́пите?

кути́я бонбо́ни	**календа́р**
бути́лка (*bottle*) **ви́но**	**плака́т**
кути́я с луксо́зни (*deluxe*) **пли́кове**	**кни́га**

3 In the following sentences you are being asked what you would have done, had you been in the position of the speaker. Read the model out loud, then answer the questions first using **да**, then using **не**.

Model: Ако́ бе́ше на мо́е мя́сто, ще́ше ли да оти́деш на лети́щето?
Да, ако́ бях на тво́е мя́сто, щях да оти́да на лети́щето.
Не, ако́ бях на тво́е мя́сто, ня́маше да оти́да на лети́щето.

a Ако́ бе́ше на мо́е мя́сто, ще́ше ли да прие́меш пока́ната?
b Ако́ бе́ше на мо́е мя́сто, ще́ше ли да ку́пиш цветя́?
c Ако́ бе́ше на мо́е мя́сто, ще́ше ли да изпра́тиш моми́чето?

d Ако́ бя́хте на мо́е мя́сто, щя́хте ли да донесе́те пода́рък?

e Ако́ бя́хте на на́ше мя́сто, щя́хте ли да посре́щнете америка́неца?

4 The next two exercises will help you to practise and then to choose correctly between **о́ще** and **по́вече**. The first exercise will also help you practise using the past tense of **(да) дам**. So, following the model, complete the sentences altering or replacing the words in bold as necessary:

Model: **Да́дох** две ка́ртички от Ри́лския манасти́р на Джим. Той **и́скаше** о́ще, но аз **ня́мах** по́вече.

a Неве́на ______ на Марк и Виоле́та. Те ______.
b Ни́е ______ на тури́стите. Те ______.
c Г-н и г-жа́ Ко́линс ______ на свóя прия́тел. Той ______.

5 Choose **о́ще** or **по́вече** in the sentences below, remembering that **о́ще** has the sense of *in addition* or *another* while **по́вече** tends to be used with negatives and in comparisons.

a И́скаш ли ______ кекс?
b ______ две би́ри, мо́ля.
c Ня́маме ______ вре́ме да ча́каме.
d Миле́на и́ма ______ англи́йски кни́ги от Никола́й.
e Г-жа́ Ко́линс полу́чи две писма́ от А́нглия и ______ едно́ писмо́ от Аме́рика.
f Благодаря́, не и́скам ______ ви́но.
g И́маме ______ пет мину́ти до замина́ването (*the departure*) на самоле́та.

6 This exercise will help you practise the awkward irregular past forms of **(да) дам, (да) избера́** and **(да) разбера́**. First read the little story out loud.

Г-жа́ Анто́нова и́скаше да даде́ на Ма́йкъл Джо́нсън **ма́лък пода́рък.** Тя разбра́ от не́го, **че жена́ му мно́го оби́ча криста́лни** (*crystal*) **ва́зи**. Вче́ра сутринта́ тя оти́де **в магази́н за пода́рьци.** И́скаше да избере́ **на́й-краси́вата криста́лна ва́за**. Тя не ку́пи криста́лна ва́за, **защо́то криста́лните ва́зи бя́ха ужа́сно скъ́пи** (*expensive*). Г-жа́ Анто́нова избра́ **една́ краси́ва ико́на**. По́сле тя да́де пода́рька за г-жа́ Джо́нсън **на Никола́й.**

Now change the story into a dialogue between yourself and a friend. To do this, turn every sentence into a question. Your friend has the answers in the story. When asking questions, concentrate on the sections in heavy type and use **какво́**, **къде́**, **защо́** or **на кого́**.

7 Using the questions and statements in the first of these sentence pairs, complete the second, making the necessary alterations for indirect speech. Try to think of two possible versions for the **ли** question in (**b**).

- **a** Къде́ и́ма магази́н за плодове́ и зеленчу́ци?
  Г-н и г-жа́ Ко́линс пи́таха ______.
- **b** И́мате ли свобо́дно вре́ме?
  Неве́на попи́та г-н Джо́нсън ______.
- **c** Кога́ Ма́йкъл Джо́нсън ще изпра́ти програ́мата?
  Боя́н Анто́нов попи́та ______.
- **d** И́мам сре́ща в два часа́.
  Миле́на ка́за, че ______.
- **e** Ще зами́нем за Ва́рна на два́йсет и о́сми май.
  Джордж и Викто́рия ка́заха, че ______.
- **f** Благодаря́, не и́скам по́вече кафе́.
  Ше́фът ка́за, че ______.

Do you understand?

Dialogue 2: Чуде́сна възмо́жност
A wonderful opportunity

Nikolai and Milena accept an offer to exhibit in England.

Никола́й Миле́на, видя́ ли плака́та, ко́йто ни подари́ Ма́йкъл Джо́нсън?

Миле́на Да, На́дя ми го пока́за.

Никола́й Мно́го е интере́сен, нали́? На англи́йски се ка́зва 'по́стер'.

Миле́на И на бъ́лгарски мо́же да се ка́же 'по́стер'.

Никола́й Ма́йкъл ка́за, че ще ни изпра́ти о́ще рекла́ми.

Миле́на Мо́же да ги дадé на тébe да ги донесе́ш.

Никола́й Зна́еш ли какво́? Той ми предло́жи да напра́вим изло́жба с на́ши по́стери в А́нглия.

Миле́на Да, разбра́х от На́дя. Ти какво́ му отгово́ри?

Никола́й Ка́зах, че ще поми́слим. Ти на мо́е мя́сто щя́ше ли да се съгласи́ш веднáга?

Миле́на Разби́ра се, на тво́е мя́сто веднáга щях да прие́ма. Това́ е чуде́сна възмо́жност.

Никола́й О́ще не е́ къ́сно. Аз ве́че избра́х на́й-ху́бавите от на́шите плака́ти. Ако́ и́скаш, донеси́ от тво́ите и аз ще му ги дам, като́ зами́на.

Миле́на	Кога́ да ти ги донеса́?
Никола́й	Аз мо́га да до́йда у вас да ги взе́ма. А, щях да забра́вя – ще ми даде́ш ли и англи́йските списа́ния, който и́маш?
Миле́на	Ако́ зна́ех, че ги и́скаш, щях да ти ги донеса́.
Никола́й	Предпочи́там да те изпра́тя до вас. Мо́же ли?
Миле́на	Защо́ не? Ако́ ня́мах дру́га ра́бота, щях да те пока́ня на го́сти.
Никола́й	Ни́що. Ще ме пока́ниш, кога́то и́маш по́вече свобо́дно вре́ме.

(да) изпра́тя, -тиш	*to send; accompany*
рекла́ма	*advertisement*
(да) предло́жа, -жиш	*to offer*
по́стер	*poster*
(да) поми́сля, -лиш	*to think* (something) *over*
до вас	*to your home*
криста́лен, -лна	*crystal*
луксо́зен, -зна	*deluxe*
скъп	*expensive, dear*

Questions

1. Какво́ о́ще ще изпра́ти Ма́йкъл Джо́нсън?
2. На кого́ мо́же да даде́ рекла́мите Ма́йкъл Джо́нсън?
3. От кого́ разбра́ Миле́на за чуде́сната възмо́жност?
4. Какво́ ще́ше да напра́ви Миле́на, ако́ бе́ше на мя́стото на Никола́й?
5. Какво́ ще́ше да напра́ви Миле́на ако́ зна́еше, че той и́ска списа́нията?
6. Какво́ предпочи́та Никола́й?

какво правеше тя?

what was she doing?

In this unit you will learn:

- **how to talk about things breaking down/not working**
- **how to ask for help if something is wrong in your hotel room**
- **how to ask for help if you have trouble with your car**
- **how to refer to past events**

Dialogue 1

Boyan Antonov's secretary, Nadya, is late for work and nobody at the office knows why.

Боя̀н Анто̀нов Защо̀ я ня̀ма о̀ще На̀дя? Предѝ винаги ѝдваше наврѐме. Бо̀лна ли е?

Никола̀й Не, не ѐ бо̀лна. Мно̀го съм учу̀ден, че я ня̀ма, защо̀то та̀зи су̀трин я видя̀х от трамва̀я. Отѝваше на ра̀бота с кола̀та си.

Боя̀н Анто̀нов Милѐна, ти зна̀еш ли защо̀ я ня̀ма?

Милѐна Ня̀мам предста̀ва. Аз също я видя̀х на у̀лицата отдалѐче, но не бѐше с кола̀.

Боя̀н Анто̀нов Какво̀ пра̀веше?

Милѐна Гово̀реше с едѝн полица̀й пред бо̀лницата. Не мо̀жех да чу̀я какво̀ гово̀рят. Полица̀ят ѝ пока̀зваше зна̀ка СПЍРАНЕТО ЗАБРАНЀНО.

Никола̀й Я̀сно защо̀ я ня̀ма. Сѝгурно ѝма неприя̀тности с полѝцията.

Боя̀н Анто̀нов Ко̀лко пъ̀ти ѝ ка̀звах да не паркѝра пред бо̀лницата! Сега̀ ще тря̀бва да платѝ гло̀ба.

(*A little later Nadya comes in*.)

На̀дя Здравѐйте. Извиня̀вайте за закъснѐнието, но ѝмах неприя̀тности с кола̀та. Опѝтвах мно̀го пъ̀ти да се оба̀дя по телефо̀на в о̀фиса, но бѐше заѐто.

Милѐна Да, аз гово̀рех предѝ ма̀лко. Кажѝ какво̀ се слу̀чи.

На̀дя Отѝвах на ра̀бота с кола̀та, но пред бо̀лницата мото̀рът спря̀ и не мо̀жеше да запа̀ли. Ня̀мах предста̀ва какво̀ му е. От ня̀колко дни мото̀рът не рабо̀теше добрѐ, но аз продължа̀вах да ка̀рам кола̀та. Не мо̀жех да напра̀вя нѝщо дру̀го освѐн да оста̀вя кола̀та там.

Милѐна Аз те видя̀х. Гово̀реше с едѝн полица̀й.

На̀дя О, ужа̀сен бѐше, налѝ? Ка̀зах му, че кола̀та ѝма поврѐда, а той все ми пока̀зваше зна̀ка.

Боя̀н Анто̀нов Какво̀ ста̀на по̀сле?

На̀дя За ща̀стие, видя̀х едѝн позна̀т. Той стоѐше на ъ̀гъла до бо̀лницата. Купу̀ваше си вѐстник. Той намѐри поврѐдата веднàга.

Никола̀й Какво̀ ѝ бѐше на кола̀та?

На̀дя (*Evasively*.) Нѝщо осо̀бено. Поврѐдата не бѐше в мото̀ра.

Миле́на	Защо́ не ни ка́жеш каква́ по́-то́чно бе́ше повре́дата?
На́дя	Е, добре́. Ня́маше бензи́н... (*General mirth.*) За щастие, мо́ят позна́т и́маше бидо́нче с бензи́н в бага́жника.
Боя́н Анто́нов	Сле́дващия път ще бъ́де мото́рът. По́-добре́ иди́ веднага на серви́з!

Преди́ ви́наги и́дваше навре́ме.	*Before, she always used to come on time.*
Бо́лна ли е?	*Is she ill?*
Мно́го съм учу́ден.	*I'm very surprised.*
Оти́ваше на ра́бота.	*She was going to work.*
Ня́мам предста́ва.	*I have no idea.*
отдале́че	*from afar*
Какво́ пра́веше?	*What was she doing?*
Гово́реше с еди́н полица́й пред бо́лницата.	*She was talking to a policeman in front of the hospital.*
Не мо́жех да чу́я.	*I wasn't able to hear.*
Полица́ят ѝ пока́зваше зна́ка СПИ́РАНЕТО ЗАБРАНЕ́НО.	*The policeman was pointing out the NO STOPPING sign to her.*
я́сно защо́	*it's obvious why*
И́ма неприя́тности с...	*She is having trouble with...*
Ко́лко пъ́ти ѝ ка́звах...	*The times I've told her...*
гло́ба	*a fine*
опи́твах	*I tried/kept trying*
аз гово́рех	*I was speaking*
какво́ се слу́чи	*what happened*
мото́рът спря́	*the engine stopped*
не мо́жеше да запа́ли	*wouldn't start*
от ня́колко дни	*for the past few days*
не рабо́теше добре́	*hasn't been working properly*

не мо́жех да напра́вя ни́що дру́го осве́н...	*all I could do was...*
ужа́сен бе́ше	*he was awful*
кола́та и́ма повре́да	*the car has broken down*
все ми пока́зваше зна́ка	*he kept pointing to the sign*
Какво́ ста́на по́сле?	*What happened next?*
за ща́стие	*fortunately*
позна́т	*acquaintance*
той стое́ше на ъ́гъла	*he was standing on the corner*
Купу́ваше си ве́стник.	*He was buying (himself)* (cf. Unit 15) *a newspaper.*
повре́дата	*the fault*
ни́що осо́бено	*nothing special/nothing much*
бензи́н	*petrol/gas*
бидо́нче	*small can*
бага́жник	*boot/trunk*
сле́дващия път	*next time*
иди́ ведна́га на серви́з!	*go to a garage/service station immediately*

1 Questions

Answer pretending to be the person to whom the question is addressed.

a Миле́на, бо́лна ли е На́дя?
b Никола́й, защо́ си учу́ден, че На́дя о́ще не е́ на ра́бота?
c Никола́й, какво́ пра́веше На́дя, кога́то я видя́?
d Г-н Анто́нов, къде́ не тря́бваше да парки́ра На́дя?
e На́дя, какво́ се слу́чи с кола́та?
f На́дя, ти какво́ ка́за на полицая́?

2 True or false?

a Полица́ят пока́зваше на На́дя къде́ е серви́зът.
b На́дя зна́еше добре́ какво́ му е на мото́ра.
c Тря́бваше На́дя да оста́ви кола́та пред бо́лницата.
d На́дя видя́ еди́н позна́т, ко́йто си купу́ваше ве́стник.
e Не́йният позна́т не можа́ да наме́ри повре́дата.
f Кола́та и́маше серио́зна повре́да.

How do you say it?

- Saying that something has gone wrong

Ду́шът не рабо́ти.	*The shower is not working.*
Кола́та и́ма повре́да.	*The car has broken down.*
Повре́дата е в мото́ра.	*The fault is in the engine.*
Асансьо́рът е повре́ден.	*The lift is out of order.*
Ймам неприя́тности с кола́та.	*I'm having trouble with the car.*

- Asking *What happened* or *What is the matter?*

Какво́ ста́на?	*What happened?*
Какво́ се слу́чи?	*What happened?*
Какво́ и́ма?	*What's the matter?*
Какво́ ста́ва?	*What's up? What's going on?*

- Answering *Nothing special*

Ни́що осо́бено.	*Nothing special.*

- Expressing ignorance or surprise

Ня́мам предста́ва.	*I've no idea.*
Мно́го съм учу́ден.	*I'm very surprised.*

- Saying *Fortunately*

за ща́стие	*fortunately/luckily*

(cf. **за съжале́ние** *unfortunately* Unit 5)

Grammar

1 The past imperfect

You will find below examples of phrases describing not completed actions in the past but actions that are seen as going on at a given past moment. Usually, these are background actions accompanying the description of a past event. In all such cases you need to use a set of past forms known as the past imperfect.

Какво́ пра́веше тя? *What was she doing?*

Examples based on the dialogue:

На́дя оти́ваше на ра́бота.	*Nadya was going to work.*
Тя гово́реше с еди́н полица́й.	*She was talking to a policeman.*
Полица́ят ѝ пока́зваше зна́ка.	*The policeman was showing her the sign.*

Here the reference to another past event (which happened when this one was going on) is only implied, but it can also be mentioned either:

• in phrases like **в товá врéме** *just then*, **по същото врéме** *at the same time* and **през цялото врéме** *all that time*

• or in accompanying phrases introduced by **когáто** *when*, that describe another action with the 'ordinary' past tense:

През цялото врéме Милéна говóреше (past imperfect) по телефóна.	*All that time Milena was talking on the phone.*
В товá врéме мóят познáт си купýваше (past imperfect) вéстник.	*Just then my acquaintance was buying (himself) a newspaper.*
Нáдя отúваше (past imperfect) на рáбота, когáто я видях. ('ordinary' past')	*Nadya was going to work when I saw her.*

Аз продължáвах да кáрам колáта *I went on driving the car*

The verb **продължáвам** *to continue*, *to go on* is naturally used in the past imperfect because it describes the action as still going on. However, even without such a verb you can use the past imperfect forms to render English expressions such as *I went on* and *I kept (on)* (doing something):

Нáдя опúтваше да се обáди.	*Nadya kept (on) trying to get through (on the phone).*

Whenever you use time words like **все** *all the time* you also need the past imperfect:

Полицáят **все** ми покáзваше знáка.	*The policeman kept showing me the sign.*

Note too that a similar meaning of continuing for a period of time is present in the following examples:

От няколко дни мотóрът не рабóтеше добрé.	*(For) the past few days the engine has not been working properly.*
Предú дéсет годúни г-н Антóнов рабóтеше катó журналúст.	*Ten years ago Mr Antonov was working as a journalist.*

Тя вúнаги úдваше на врéме *She always used to come on time*

You also need to use past imperfect forms for actions that were habitual or were repeated in the past. Frequently, words like **мнóго пъти** *many times,* **кóлко пъти** *how many times* and **чéсто** are used to reinforce this meaning:

Ко́лко пъти ѝ ка́звах!	*The times I've told her!*
Ка́звах ѝ мно́го пъти.	*I've told her many times.*

Very often you can conveniently use the past imperfect forms to convey the meaning of the phrase '*used to*' (do something):

Преди́ На́дя ви́наги **и́дваше** навре́ме.	*Before, Nadya always **used to come** on time.*
Тя че́сто **пъту́ваше** с трамва́й.	*She often **used to go** by tram.*
Че́сто я **ви́ждах** от трамва́я.	*I often **used to see** her from the tram.*

2 How to form the past imperfect

As you can see from the list below, the endings for the past imperfect are almost identical with those for the simple past tense, except for the *you* singular and *he*, *she*, *it* forms. The main difference lies in the vowel preceding the endings.

(a) Verbs adding past imperfect endings to **-а-**: all **а**-pattern verbs:

(аз)	оти́в**ах**	*I used to go/ was going*	(ни́е)	оти́в**ахме**	*we used to go/ were going*
(ти)	оти́в**аше**	*you used to go/ were going*	(ви́е)	оти́в**ахте**	*you used to go/ were going*
(той) (тя) (то)	оти́в**аше**	*he/she/it used to go/was going*	(те)	оти́в**аха**	*they used to go/ were going*

(b) Verbs adding past imperfect endings to **-е-**: most verbs of **е-** and **и**-pattern except those in **(c)** below:

(аз)	гово́р**ех**	*I was speaking*	мо́ж**ех**	(ни́е)	гово́р**ехме**	мо́ж**ехме**
(ти)	гово́р**еше**	*you were speaking*	мо́ж**еше**	(ви́е)	гово́р**ехте**	мо́ж**ехте**
(той) (тя) (то)	гово́р**еше**	*he/she/it was speaking*	мо́ж**еше**	(те)	гово́р**еха**	мо́ж**еха**

(c) Verbs adding past imperfect endings to a stressed **-я́-** (**-а́-** after **ж, ч, ш**): these can be either verbs of **е-** or of **и**-pattern with the stress on the final syllable. But do note the change of **-я́-/-а́-** to **-е́-** in the *you* (singular) and *he, she, it* forms, as shown below in *to stand* **стоя́** and *to hold* **държа́**:

(аз)	сто**я́х**/ държ**а́х**	*I was standing/ holding*	(ни́е)	сто**я́хме**/ държ**а́хме**	*we were standing/ holding*
(ти)	сто**е́ше**/ държ**е́ше**	*you were standing/ holding*	(ви́е)	сто**я́хте**/ държ**а́хте**	*you were standing / holding*
(той) (тя) (то)	сто**е́ше**/ държ**е́ше**	*he/she/it was standing/holding*	(те)	сто**я́ха**/ държ**а́ха**	*they were standing/holding*

3 Compare 'ordinary' past with past imperfect

When you compare the two tenses you will see that the past imperfect goes most naturally with imperfective verbs since they, too, describe incomplete actions (Unit 12). That is why some verbs which make no distinction in the past form between perfective/imperfective like **съм, и́мам** (Unit 13) and **тря́бва** (Unit 15) normally appear in the past imperfect only.

Compare the following examples based on the dialogue (left-hand column), with similar sentences in the right-hand column using the corresponding perfective 'twin':

Past imperfect tense (used with imperfective verb)	**Past tense** (used with perfective verb)
и́двам Тя и́дваше навре́ме. *She used to come on time.*	**(да) до́йда** Вче́ра тя дойде́ навре́ме. *Yesterday she came on time.*
оти́вам На́дя оти́ваше на ра́бота. *Nadya was going to work.*	**(да) оти́да** На́дя оти́де на ра́бота в се́дем часа́. *Nadya went to work at seven o'clock.*
пока́звам Полица́ят ми пока́зваше зна́ка. *The policeman was showing me the sign.*	**(да) пока́жа** Полица́ят ми пока́за зна́ка. *The policeman showed me the sign.*

купу́вам
Мо́ят позна́т си купу́ваше ве́стник.
My acquaintance was buying (himself) a newspaper.

(да) ку́пя
Мо́ят позна́т си ку́пи ве́стник.
My acquaintance bought (himself) a newspaper.

ка́звам
Ка́звах ѝ мно́го пъ́ти.
I've told her many times.

(да) ка́жа
Ка́зах ѝ вче́ра.
I told her yesterday.

опи́твам
На́дя опи́тваше да се оба́ди.
Nadya kept trying to get through (on the phone).

(да) опи́там
На́дя опи́та да се оба́ди.
Nadya tried to get through. (on the phone)

4 Можа́х and мо́жех *I managed/I was able (to do something)*

Unlike the verbs used in the examples above, **мо́га** *can, be able,* has no proper perfective counterpart. It does, however, still have both a past tense form **можа́х** – as you saw in Unit 15 – and a past imperfect form **мо́жех**. It is not easy to make a clear distinction between the usage of the two forms in English, but the following examples will show in practice the difference in meaning in Bulgarian:

Past tense

можа́х

Можа́х да обясня́.	*I managed to explain.*
Не можа́х да чу́я какво́ ка́за.	*I did not manage to hear what you/he/she said.*

Here there is a sense of having a go and then bringing the action to an end, either, as in the first example, because you managed to achieve what you wanted, or, as in the second, because you did not.

Past imperfect

мо́жех

Ми́налата годи́на **не мо́жех** да говоря́ бъ́лгарски.	*Last year I couldn't/wasn't able to speak Bulgarian.*
Мо́жех да обясня́, но не обясни́х.	*I could have explained, but didn't.*

Here it is more a case of having – or not having! – the ability or potential to do something over a period of time. It is a state rather than an action.

5 Мóга *Being allowed*

Finally, you should note that when *can* really means *being allowed* – or *not allowed*! – to do something, in the past you should always use the past imperfect form of **мóга**. Compare these present and past usages:

Present	**Past**
Там (не) мóже да се паркѝра. *One can/cannot park there.* (i.e. is/isn't allowed)	Там (не) мóжеше да се паркѝра. *One could/n't park there.* (i.e. was/wasn't allowed)
Мóга да паркѝрам там. *I can park there.* (i.e. am allowed)	Мóжех да паркѝрам там. *I could park there.* (i.e. was allowed)

Exercises

1 In this story you will learn about Nadya's misfortunes with the car in a slightly different way. Can you choose the missing words from the list?

От ня́колко дни колáта на Нáдя не ______ добрé. Ѝмаше ня́какъв шум (*noise*) ______. Нáдя не отѝде на ______. Тя продължáваше да ______ колáта, защóто не обѝча да хóди на рáбота ______ трамвáй.

Вчéра Нáдя ______ неприя́тности. Когáто отѝваше на рáбота, колáта спря́ ______ бóлницата. Тя мѝслеше, че колáта ѝма поврéда, но не знáеше каквá е ______. Тя ______ да остáви колáта там. Пред бóлницата ______ е забранéно. Едѝн полицáй ѝскаше Нáдя да платѝ ______. Нáдя ѝскаше да му обяснѝ, че колáта ______ поврéда, но той все ѝ покáзваше знáка СПЍРАНЕТО ______. Едѝн ______ на Нáдя ѝ помóгна. Той разбрá веднáга, че ______ не é поврéдена. Прóсто (*simply*) ня́маше ______!

бензѝн	ѝмаше	сервѝз	рабóтеше
глóба	кáра	поврéдата	с
ЗАБРАНÉНО	колáта	познáт	спѝрането
ѝма	в мотóра	пред	тря́бваше

2 Complete the short dialogues below, inserting **Какво́ пра́веше?** or **Какво́ пра́веха?** and the right personal pronoun. Read the sentences out loud and then try to repeat them without looking.

a Вче́ра видя́х Никола́й и Миле́на. ______? Ни́що осо́бено. Оти́ваха на о́пера.

b Вче́ра видя́х твоя́ прия́тел. ______? Ни́що осо́бено. Ча́каше трамва́я.

c Вче́ра видя́х Неве́на. ______? Ни́що осо́бено. Гово́реше с еди́н англича́нин.

d Вче́ра видя́хме Са́шко. ______? Ни́що осо́бено Игра́еше фу́тбол.

e Вче́ра видя́х Викто́рия и Джордж Ко́линс. ______? Ни́що осо́бено. Купу́ваха плодове́.

f Видя́хме гру́па америка́нци. ______? Ни́що осо́бено. Стоя́ха на пла́жа.

3 Somebody has stolen your suitcase and a policeman is taking evidence from you. Answer his questions.

Полица́й Кога́ ста́на това́?
Ви́е (Say that it happened 15 minutes ago.)
Полица́й Къде́ бя́хте Ви́е, кога́то това́ се слу́чи?
Ви́е (Say you were in the hotel.)
Полица́й Какво́ пра́вехте?
Ви́е (Say you were waiting for a taxi.)
Полица́й И́маше ли мно́го хо́ра във фоайе́то на хоте́ла?
Ви́е (Say there was only one man.)
Полица́й Какво́ пра́веше той?
Ви́е (Say that he was speaking on the phone.)
Полица́й Къде́ бе́ше портие́рът (*the doorman*)?
Ви́е (Say that he was standing in front of the hotel.)
Полица́й Благодаря́. Ще оти́да да гово́ря с портие́ра.

4 Practise saying what you used to do for a job by changing the sentences to the *I* form:

a Преди́ те рабо́теха в еди́н магази́н.
b Преди́ две годи́ни На́дя рабо́теше в музе́я.
c Преди́ той рабо́теше като́ сервитьо́р. (Сервитьо́рка is *waitress*, remember!)
d Викто́рия и Джордж Ко́линс рабо́теха като́ учи́тели преди́ мно́го годи́ни.
e Преди́ ни́е рабо́техме в ба́нката.

5 In this exercise you can check how good you are at distinguishing between repeated and single actions in the past. Don't forget that repeated actions usually go with an imperfective verb and single actions with a perfective one. Choose from the pair given with each set of sentences.

a **йдваше/дойдé**?
 i На́дя ви́наги ______ ра́но на ра́бота.
 ii Вчéра На́дя ______ къ̀сно на ра́бота.

b **ка́зваше/ка́за**?
 i Г-н Антóнов чéсто ______ на На́дя да не парки́ра пред бóлницата.
 ii Милéна ______, че не зна́е къдé е На́дя.

c **купу́вах/ку́пих**?
 i Вчéра ______ пода́рък за бра́т ми.
 ii Преди́ аз чéсто ______ вéстници.

Do you understand?

Dialogue 2: Прия́тна изнена́да *A pleasant surprise*

In the Odessa Hotel outside the Collins' room, there is a bouquet of birthday surprises for Victoria.

г-жа́ Кóлинс (*Rather flustered.*) Мóля Ви, кажéте на рецéпцията, че не мóга да спра ду́ша. Кра́нът е повредéн. Освéн това́, не зна́я къдé е мъжъ́т ми. Тря́бва да го намéря.

Камериéрка Аз видя́х г-н Кóлинс преди́ ма́лко. Оти́ваше към Мóрската гради́на.

г-жа́ Кóлинс Така́ ли? Мнóго съм учу́дена. Той ни́къде не хóди без мéне. Ще пи́там портиéра дали́ зна́е къдé е мъжъ́т ми.

Гост на хотéла (*Overhearing and joining in.*) Аз съ́що видя́х г-н Кóлинс. Той говóреше с една́ жена́ пред вхóда на Мóрската гради́на.

г-жа́ Кóлинс Но той не позна́ва ни́кого тук. Чу́хте ли за каквó говóрят?

Гост на хотéла Ни́що осóбено... Г-н Кóлинс пи́таше за посóката, но не разбра́х къдé и́скаше да оти́де.

г-жа́ Кóлинс Но той не зна́е добрé бъ́лгарски. Кóлко пъ́ти му ка́звах да не изли́за сам! Той е тóлкова

	разсе́ян. Ще пресече́ у́лицата не ка́кто тря́бва и ще и́ма неприя́тности.
Портие́р	(*Seeing Mrs Collins in a state of agitation.*) Добро́ у́тро, г-жа́ Ко́линс. Неприя́тности ли и́мате?
г-жа́ Ко́линс	За съжале́ние, да. Първо кра́нът на ду́ша се развали́. От ня́колко дни ду́шът не рабо́теше добре́, а сега́ не мо́га да го спра. По́сле мъжъ̀т ми изче́зна.
Портие́р	Не се́ безпоко́йте, аз също видя́х г-н Ко́линс. Изгле́ждаше съвсе́м добре́. Купу́ваше не́що, но не можа́х да ви́дя какво́.

(*Mr Collins appears at the end of the corridor.*)

г-жа́ Ко́линс	Джордж, какво́ ста́на? Защо́ изли́заш сам, без ме́не? Страху́вах се, че ще загу́биш пътя.
г-н Ко́линс	Е, ми́сля, че мо́га сам да ку́пя буке́т цветя́! (*Produces a bunch of flowers from behind his back.*) Чести́т рожде́н ден, ми́ла Ви́ки!
Всѝчки	Чести́т рожде́н ден, госпо́жо Ко́линс!
г-жа́ Ко́линс	Благодаря́. Каква́ приятна изнена́да!
Портие́р	Ни́е всички зна́ехме къде́ е г-н Ко́линс.
Камерие́рка	О́леле, забра́вихме за кра́на! Тря́бва бързо да се оба́дя на ма́йстора.

изнена́да	*surprise*
кран	*tap*
освѐн	*apart from, besides*
дали́	*whether*
изли́зам, -заш	*to go out*
разсе́ян	*absent-minded*
кра́нът се развали́	*the tap is not working*
(да) изче́зна, -неш	*to disappear*
е!	*well, really!*
мил	*dear*
камерие́рка	*chambermaid*
о́леле!	*oh dear me!*
ма́йстор	*workman* (here: *plumber*)

Questions

1 Защó г-жá Кóлинс не мóже да спре дýша?
2 Каквó прáвеше г-н Кóлинс, когáто го видя́ еди́н гост на хотéла?
3 Какви́ неприя́тности и́ма г-жá Кóлинс?
4 Каквó прáвеше г-н Кóлинс, когáто го видя́ портиéрът?
5 Каквó знáеха всѝчки?

18 ве́че съм реши́ла

I've already made up my mind

In this unit you will learn:

- **how to talk about results: things that did or did not happen in the past and have affected the present**
- **how to say you have forgotten something**
- **how to talk about your leisure**

Dialogue 1

Nikolai has come to collect Milena for the opera but finds she is not yet dressed for going out.

Николáй	Милéна, óще не сú готóва. Не сú забрáвила, че тáзи вéчер сме на óпера, налú?
Милéна	Не, не съм, но óще не съм се облякла.
Николáй	Какво́ прáви досегá?
Милéна	Една́ приятелка дойде́ на гóсти. Бях я покáнила предú да кýпиш билéти за óпера.
Николáй	Óще ли не сú е отúшла?
Милéна	Отúде си предú петнáйсет минýти.
Николáй	Хáйде, ще закъснéем, акó не сé облечéш пó-бързо. Представлéнието запóчва в сéдем часá.
Милéна	Ня́ма да закъснéем. Ще бъдем там в сéдем.
Николáй	Мнóго се съмнявам.
Милéна	Вéче съм решúла каквó да облекá. Вечéрял ли си?
Николáй	Не, не съм. Мúсля да вечéряме зáедно след представлéнието.

Outside the opera house. They've made it for 7 o'clock but the place looks suspiciously empty. They go to the ticket office.

Милéна	Запóчнало ли е представлéнието?
Касиéрка	Óще не, госпóжице. Представлéнието е от сéдем и половúна.
Николáй	Милéна, съжалявам! Винáта е мóя. Ня́мам предстáва как съм напрáвил такáва грéшка.
Милéна	Ня́ма значéние, слу́чва се. Врéмето е ху́баво. Хáйде да се разхóдим.
Николáй	Съглáсен съм. Такá ще бъдем зáедно половúн час пóвече. Мóже да си кýпим сладолéд.
Милéна	Разбúра се. Ня́ма да ни бъде скýчно.
Николáй	О, не..! (*After a pause, groaning and throwing up his arms.*) Амú сегá?
Милéна	Каквó се е слýчило?
Николáй	Не съм взел парú! Забрáвил съм ги в джóба на дънките си.
Милéна	Мнóго си смéшен! Налú мóжеш да платúш с крéдитна кáрта?
Николáй	Чáкай! ... (*with relief*) О, тук е, нéя не съм забрáвил.
Милéна	Стáнал си мнóго разсéян. Сúгурно си се уморúл от мнóго ýчене.
Николáй	Да, нúкога не съм бил тóлкова разсéян. Но далú е сáмо от ýчене е друг въпрóс...

не си́ забра́вила	*you haven't forgotten*
О́ще не съм се обля́кла.	*I haven't dressed yet.*
досега́	*until now*
една́ приятелка дойде́	*a friend came*
Бях я пока́нила.	*I had invited her.*
О́ще ли не си́ е оти́шла?	*Hasn't she gone yet?*
ако́ не се́ облече́ш	*if you don't get dressed*
представле́ние	*performance*
Мно́го се съмня́вам.	*I very much doubt it.*
Ве́че съм реши́ла.	*I've already made up my mind.*
Вече́рял ли си?	*Have you had supper?*
Не, не съм.	*No, I haven't.*
Запо́чнало ли е представле́нието?	*Has the performance started?*
Вина́та е мо́я.	*It's my fault.*
как съм напра́вил така́ва гре́шка	*how I made such a mistake*
Ха́йде да се разхо́дим.	*Let's go for a walk.*
Ня́ма да ни бъ́де ску́чно.	*We won't be bored.*
Ами́ сега́?	*And now what?!*
Какво́ се е слу́чило?	*What's happened?/ What's the matter?*
Не съм взел пари́!	*I haven't taken any money!*
Забра́вил съм ги в джо́ба на дъ́нките си.	*I must have left it in the pocket of my jeans.*
сме́шен	*funny*
не́я не съм забра́вил	*that I haven't forgotten*
Ста́нал си мно́го разсе́ян.	*You have become very absent-minded.*
Си́гурно си се умори́л от мно́го у́чене...	*You must have got tired with all that studying...*
ни́кога не съм бил то́лкова разсе́ян	*I have never been so absent-minded*
друг въпро́с	*a different matter*

1 Questions

- **a** Какво́ не е́ напра́вила Миле́на?
- **b** Оти́шла ли си е приятелката на Миле́на?
- **c** Кога́ предла́га Никола́й да вече́рят?
- **d** Защо́ не е́ запо́чнало представле́нието?
- **e** Какъ́в е ста́нал Никола́й?
- **f** От какво́ се е умори́л Никола́й споре́д Миле́на?

2 True or false?

- **a** Милéна бéше покáнила еднá приятелка предú Николáй да кýпи билéти.
- **b** Ще закъснéят, защóто Милéна óще не é решúла каквó да облечé.
- **c** Николáй вéче е вечéрял.
- **d** Представлéнието óще не é запóчнало.
- **e** Николáй нýма предстáва как е напрáвил такáва грéшка.
- **f** Николáй мóже да пpатú с крéдитна кáрта.
- **g** На Николáй ще му е скýчно с Милéна.

How do you say it?

- Acknowledging guilt

Винáта е мóя.	*It's my fault.*
Мóя е винáта.	*The fault is mine.*

- Asking someone if they have eaten

Вечéрял(а) ли си?	*Have you had supper?*
Вечéряли ли сте?	*Have you had supper?*

- Expressing disbelief

Съмнявам се.	*I doubt it.*
Мнóго се съмнявам.	*I very much doubt it.*
Не é вярно.	*It's not true.*
Товá е друг въпрóс.	*That's a different matter.*

- Making little of something

Нýма значéние.	*It doesn't matter./Never mind.*

- Expressing panic and confusion

Амú сегá?	*Now what?!*
Óлеле!	*Oh dear me!*

- Saying *I've made up my mind*

Вéче съм решúл(а).	*I've already made up my mind.*

Grammar

1 Вѐче съм решѝл(а) *I've already made up my mind*

In Bulgarian, as in English, you need a special tense to talk about actions that happened in the past, but the results of which are still evident in the present. We can call this the **present perfect tense**. You usually use it when you are focusing on the effect a past action has on the here and now. You are not interested or not sure when it happened. Very often the meaning of result is reinforced by words like **вѐче** *already* or **ǒще не** *not yet.*

Here are some examples based on the dialogue – all, notice, corresponding to an English form using *have* or *has*:

Не съм забра́вила.	*I haven't forgotten.*
О́ще ли не си́ е оти́шла?	*Hasn't she gone yet?*
Запо́чнало ли е представле́нието?	*Has the performance started?*
О́ще не е́ запо́чнало.	*It hasn't started yet.*

2 How to form the present perfect tense

As in English, the **present perfect** is made up of two parts. However, instead of *have* or *has*, Bulgarian uses the present forms of **съм** together with a distinct form of the main verb, called the **past participle**. (In English these are the words *forgotten*, *gone* and *started* in the translations of the sentences you have just read. The form often ends in *-ed* or *-en*.) The past participle in Bulgarian ends in **-л** in the masculine, but you can think of it as an adjective, for it changes its ending to **-ла** in the feminine, **-ло** in the neuter and **-ли** in the plural. You will find a list of past participles in the Appendix.

Here is a list of forms in all persons for **вечѐрям**. Notice the word order!

вечѐрял(а) съм/ не съм вечѐрял(а)	*I have/have not had supper (i.e. dined!)*
вечѐрял(а) си/ не си́ вечѐрял(а)	*you have/ have not had supper*
вечѐрял(а) е/ не е́ вечѐрял(а)	*he/she has/ has not had supper*
вечѐряли сме/ не сме́ вечѐряли	*we have/ have not had supper*

вечéряли сте/ не сте́ вечéряли	*you have/ have not had supper*
вечéряли са/ не са́ вечéряли	*they have/ have not had supper*

Word order with this tense is awkward. Normally **съм** (or **си**, **е**, etc.) comes immediately before the past participle, as in the **не** (negative) forms above, and in the following examples:

Николáй е напрáвил грéшка.	*Nikolai has made a mistake.*
Милéна не é забрáвила.	*Milena hasn't forgotten.*

You will remember, however, that **съм** (or **си**, **е**, etc.) can never come first in a sentence. When the past participle comes first, **съм** (or **си**, **е**, etc.) comes immediately after it, as in the positive forms on the previous page.

Word order is particularly awkward when you have to use a verb with **се** like Óще не съ́м **се** облякла *I haven't got dressed yet.* In the Appendix you will find a table setting out the relative positions of **съм** and **се**.

3 How to form past participles

Regular past participles

To form regular past participles you start from the past *I* form of the verb and replace the ending **-х** by **-л**, **-ла**, **-ло-**, **-ли**. Again a look at the Appendix will help!

Past tense	Past participle
забрáвих	забрáви**л**, забрáви**ла**, забрáви**ло**, забрáви**ли** (*forgotten*)
реши́х	реши́**л**, реши́**ла**, реши́**ло**, реши́**ли** (*decided*)
хóдих	хóди**л**, хóди**ла**, хóди**ло**, хóди**ли** (*gone, walked*)
вечéрях	вечéря**л**, вечéря**ла**, вечéря**ло**, вечéря**ли** (*dined*)
видя́х	видя́**л**, видя́**ла**, видя́**ло**, видé**ли*** (*seen*)
започнах	запóчна**л**, запóчна**ла**, запóчна**ло**, запóчна**ли** (*begun*)

Irregular past participles

Now for some *irregular* past participles:

(a) With verbs ending in **-сох**, **-зох**, **-кох** (Unit 14), replace **-ох** by **-ъл** and drop the **-ъ-** in the feminine, neuter and plural:

обля́к**ох**	обля́к**ъл**, обля́к**ла**, обля́к**ло**, облéк**ли*** (*dressed*)
донéс**ох**	донéс**ъл**, донéс**ла**, донéс**ло**, донéс**ли** (*brought*)

(*See Unit 8 for the change from **я** to **е**.)

(b) **(да) оти́да** has **оти́шъл (-шла, -шло, -шли)** *gone* for its past participle, and **(да) до́йда** has **дошъ́л (-шла́, -шло́, -шли́)** *come, arrived.* You will recognize **дошъ́л** from the expression **Добре́ дошъ́л!** (Unit 6). Here too, notice, you drop the **-ъ-** in the feminine, neuter and plural:

Прия́телката ми о́ще не си́ е оти́шла.	*My friend has not yet gone.*
Никола́й о́ще не е́ дошъ́л.	*Nikolai has not yet come.*

(c) The past participle of **съм** is бил, била́, било́, били́

Ни́кога не съ́м бил по́-щастли́в.	*I've never been happier.*
Ни́кога не съ́м била́ в Москва́.	*I've never been to Moscow.*

4 *Ever* and *never* with the present perfect

The present perfect is frequently used in statements and questions including or implying the adverbs *ever* and *never*:

Хо́дили ли сте в Пари́ж?	*Have you (ever) been to Paris?*
Не, ни́кога не съ́м хо́дил в Пари́ж./ Не, не съ́м.	*No, I've never been to Paris./ No, I haven't.*
Да, хо́дил съм.	*Yes, I have.*

Note that in Bulgarian the negative answer is, like the English, without the participle **хо́дил**. (See Unit 11.5 for a special use of the Bulgarian present where English has present perfect *has/have been* – after **от**.)

5 The past perfect

Бях я **пока́нила** (преди́ да ку́пиш биле́ти).	*I had invited her (before you bought tickets).*

You need this form – the past perfect tense – to refer to events that took place before other past events. It differs from the present perfect tense only in that you use the past forms of *to be* instead of the present. Here is a list of all forms of the verb *to go*:

аз **бях оти́шъл/-шла**	*I had gone*	ни́е **бя́хме оти́шли**	*we had gone*
ти **бе́ше оти́шъл/-шла**	*you had gone*	ви́е **бя́хте оти́шли**	*you had gone*
той **бе́ше оти́шъл**	*he had gone*	те **бя́ха оти́шли**	*they had gone*
тя **бе́ше оти́шла**	*she had gone*		
то **бе́ше оти́шло**	*it had gone*		

6 (Да) Взéма *To take*

This verb loses the **-м-** in its past forms, and also in its past participle:

Past tense

аз взех	*I took*	**нѝе взéхме**	*we took*
ти взе	*you took*	**вѝе взéхте**	*you took*
той / тя / то взе	*he/she/it took*	**те взéха**	*they took*

Past participle

взел, взéла, взéло, взéли (*taken*)

The verbs **(да) наéма** *to rent, hire* (Unit 11) and **(да) приéма** *to accept* and some other verbs related to **(да) взéма** (Unit 16) also lose the **-м-** in the same way:

Мáйкъл Джóнсън наé колá и отѝде в Бóровец.	*Michael Johnson rented a car and went to Borovets.*
Те приéха покáната.	*They accepted the invitation.*

7 (Да) се облекá *To get dressed;* (да) се съблекá *to get undressed*

A number of sound changes occur in these verbs and also in **(да) пресекá** *to cross* (the street). First, you replace **-к-** by **-ч-** before all endings containing **-е-**. Second, in the past, the shift of stress means that you have to change the first **-е-** to **-я́-** (Unit 8):

Present

Тря́бва да	се облекá	*I must get dressed*
	се облечéш	*you must get dressed*
	се облечé	*he/she/it must get dressed*
	се облечéм	*we must get dressed*
	се облечéте	*you must get dressed*
	се облекáт	*they must get dressed*

Past

Аз се обля́кох/обля́кох се	*I got dressed*
Ти се облéче	*You got dressed*
Той/тя/то се облéче	*He/she/it got dressed*
Нѝе се обля́кохме	*We got dressed*
Вѝе се обля́кохте	*You got dressed*
Те се обля́коха	*They got dressed*

What with the rules for positioning **се**, these sound changes may seriously undermine your desire to talk about getting dressed, or undressed, in Bulgarian. But it is still worth trying!

Exercises

1 Practise using the present perfect by rearranging the words so as to reproduce sentences from the dialogue.

a е, представлéнието, ли, запóчнало ...?
b се, не, óще, съм, облякла
c грéшка, как, нямам, съм, предстáва, напрáвил, такáва ...!
d слýчило, каквó, е, се ...?
e решúла, вéче, каквó, съм, да облекá

2 Read the sentences below in which a friend is inviting you to see what Nikolai has done:

a Виж, Николáй е дошъл!
b Виж, Николáй е донéсъл цветя!
c Виж, Николáй е кýпил бонбóни!
d Виж, Николáй е напрáвил кафé!

Now you say it is not true **(Не é вярно)**, it is Nadya who has done all these things. Don't forget to make the participle feminine!

3 The receptionist at the Odessa hotel asks Mr and Mrs Collins whether they have been to Borovets: Хóдили ли сте в Бóровец?

Ask the following people the same question:

a a young girl
b the couple sharing your table
c an elderly gentleman
d a small boy

4 A friend, who has taken you out, suddenly says: Забрáвил съм да взéма парú. Стáнал съм мнóго разсéян! Now imagine:

a You are a woman and you have forgotten to take an umbrella.
b You are a man and you have forgotten to take a camera.
c You and your partner have forgotten to take any money.

What would you say? Don't forget the second half of the answer!

5 Read the sentences on the next page and then, using the model: Нямаше мляко. Милéна бéше забрáвила да кýпи мляко, complete the other sentences in the same way:

a Ня́маше би́ра. Г-н Антóнов ______.
b Ня́маше хляб. Г-жá Антóнова ______.
c Ня́маше домáти. Г-н и г-жá Кóлинс ______.
d Ня́маше гази́рана водá. Аз ______.

6 Continuing with our absent-minded, forgetful heroes, what would you say if you thought you'd taken, but now can't find:

(*a*) ФÓТОАПАРÁТ (*d*) БЕЛÉЖНИК
(*b*) ШÁПКА (*e*) КНИ́ГА
(*c*) СНИ́МКИ (*f*) ВÉСТНИК

Base your answers on the model:
Взех чадъ́ра, но сегá го ня́ма. Си́гурно съм го загу́бил/а.

Do you understand?

Dialogue 2: Ску́чно ми е! *I am bored!*

Victoria Collins comes back from the beach. George, who still has not got over the mild sunstroke he suffered in Unit 15, has stayed back at the hotel. They increasingly speak Bulgarian to one another.

Виктóрия Как се чýвстваш, Джордж?
Джордж Гóре-дóлу. Но главáта óще ме болú.
Виктóрия Óще не сú се облякъл. Каквó си прáвил цяла сýтрин?
Джордж Чéтох учéбника по бъ́лгарски – *Teach Yourself Bulgarian*.
Виктóрия Каквó нóво наýчи?
Джордж В Бългáрия úма хýбаво морé. В Бългáрия úма хýбаво вúно. И вéче úма хýбава бúра.
Виктóрия Мнóго добрé, мнóго си наýчил.
Джордж Но няма игрúще за голф наблúзо! Виктóрия, ти не мóжеш да разберéш! Скýчно ми е! I AM BORED!
Виктóрия Съжалявам, Джордж. Винáта е твоя! Акó не бéше стоял на слъ́нце тóлкова, сегá щéше да мóжеш да хóдиш на плаж. И разбúра се че úма игрúще за голф.
Джордж Такá ли? Защó не сú ми кáзала?
Виктóрия Не сú ме пúтал.
Джордж Къдé úма игрúще?
Виктóрия Úма еднó блúзо до Балчúк. Товá не é далéче от Вáрна. Нúкога не смé хóдили там.
Джордж Хáйде да отúдем!
Виктóрия Добрé, ще отúдем. Но óще не смé обядвали.
Джордж А с каквó ще игрáя? Не съм взел стúковете си.
Виктóрия Предполáгам, че там ще мóжеш да взéмеш стúкове под нáем. Пúтай францýзина от съсéдната стáя. Той вéче е бил там. Ще взéмеш и шáпка за слъ́нцето!

гóре-дóлу	*so-so* (lit. *up and down*)
четá, -тéш	*to read*
(да) наýча, -чиш	*to learn*
игрúще за голф	*golf course*
стик	*golf club*
съсéден, -дна	*next (door), neighbouring*

Questions

1 Каквó го болú Джордж óще?
2 Каквó му е на нéго?
3 Каквó не é кáзала досегá Виктóрия на Джордж?
4 Каквó не é взел Джордж?
5 С каквú стúкове ще игрáе Джордж?
6 Кой вéче е игрáл голф на игрúщето?

Имате ли оплаквания?

do you have any complaints?

In this unit you will learn:

- **how to complain if things go wrong**
- **how to distinguish between reporting what you know first hand and what you know from other sources**

Dialogue 1

Nevena is listening to the complaints of a businessman who has not been lucky with his room.

Бизнесме́н Добро́ у́тро, госпо́жице! И́скам да сменя́ ста́ята си. Не съм householdдово́лен от ста́ята, коя́то сте ми да́ли.

Неве́на Какви́ опла́квания и́мате?

Бизнесме́н Конта́ктът за самобръсна́чка не рабо́ти. Прозо́рецът е счу́пен, вентила́торът в ба́нята е развале́н. Сно́щи и климати́кът се развали́! Осве́н това́, и́ма мно́го шум. Ста́ята е то́чно над дискоте́ката и му́зиката не спи́ра ця́ла нощ!

Неве́на Съжаля́вам да чу́я това́, господи́не. Ще опи́там да Ви наме́ря по́-добра́ стáя. Мо́ля, поча́кайте във фоайе́то.

Бизнесме́н Сега́ не мо́га да ча́кам, защо́то и́мам ва́жна сре́ща. Ще се въ́рна в хоте́ла към шест часа́.

Неве́на Добре́, не се́ безпоко́йте. Аз ще гово́ря с упра́вителя.

(*Later, in the manager's office*.)

Неве́на Господи́нът от ста́я сто и двана́йсета и́ска да смени́ ста́ята си.

Упра́вител От какво́ се опла́ква?

Неве́на Ка́зва, че конта́ктът за самобръсна́чка не рабо́тел, прозо́рецът бил счу́пен. Вентила́торът и климати́кът били́ развале́ни.

Упра́вител Е, не е́ то́лкова стра́шно. Кажи́ му, че всѝчко ще попра́вим.

Неве́на Не́го го ня́ма. Ка́за, че и́мал ва́жна сре́ща. Щял да се въ́рне към шест часа́.

Упра́вител Мно́го добре́. Като́ се въ́рне, всѝчко в ста́ята му ще бъ́де наре́д.

Неве́на Страху́вам се, че пак ня́ма да бъ́де дово́лен. И́ска дру́га ста́я, защо́то и́мало мно́го шум от дискоте́ката.

Секрета́рка И дру́ги го́сти се опла́кват от шум. Ка́зват, че не мо́жели да спят от шума́ на трамва́ите.

Упра́вител Да, зна́я. Тога́ва ще го сло́жим в ста́я на двана́йсетия ета́ж. Там е по́-ти́хо.

Неве́на Добра́ иде́я. Да се надя́ваме, че асансьо́рите рабо́тят!

И́скам да сменя́ стáята си.	*I want to change my room.*
стáята, коя́то сте ми дáли	*the room you have given me*
Какви́ оплáквания и́мате?	*What complaints do you have?*
контáктът за самобръснáчка	*shaver socket*
счу́пен	*broken*
вентилáтор	*extractor fan*
е развалéн	*is broken/has gone wrong*
Снóщи и кмиматѝкът се развали́.	*Last night the air conditioner, too, went wrong.*
освéн товá	*apart from that*
шум	*noise*
Му́зиката не спи́ра ця́ла нощ.	*The music doesn't stop all night.*
Съжаля́вам да чу́я товá.	*I am sorry to hear that.*
ще опи́там	*I'll try*
упрáвител	*manager, director*
От каквó се оплáква?	*What is he complaining about?*
контáктът за самобръснáчка не рабóтел	(he says) *the shaver socket doesn't work*
прозóрецът бил счу́пен	(he says) *the window is broken*
вентилáторът и климати́кът били́ развалéни	(he says) *the extractor fan and the air conditioner isn't working*
Не é тóлкова стрáшно.	*That's not so terrible.*
Вси́чко ще попрáвим.	*We'll put everything right.*
и́мал вáжна срéща	(he said) *he had an important meeting*
щял да се върне	(he said) *he'd be back*
и́мало мнóго шум	(he said) *there was a lot of noise*
И дру́ги гóсти се оплáкват от шум.	*Other hotel residents too complain of noise.*
не мóжели да спят от шумá на трамвáите	(they say) *they couldn't sleep because of the noise from the trams*
Тогáва ще го слóжим в стáя на дванáйсетия етáж.	*Then we'll put him in a room on the twelfth floor.*

1 Questions

a Каквó и́ска бизнесмéнът?
b Какви́ оплáквания и́ма той?
c Защó е шу́мна стáята му?
d Защó бизнесмéнът не мóже да чáка?
e От какъв шум се оплáкват и дру́ги гóсти на хотéла?
f Къдé предлáга упрáвителят да слóжат бизнесмéна?

2 True or false?

- **a** Бизнесмéнът кáза, че бил довóлен от стáята, коя́то са му дáли.
- **b** Огледáлото (*the mirror*) билó счýпено.
- **c** Бизнесмéнът кáза, че в стáята му и́мало мнóго шум от дискотéката.
- **d** Той щял да се вéрне след мáлко.
- **e** Дрýги гóсти също се оплáквали от шумá на трамвáите.

How do you say it?

- Asking to have something changed

Искам да сменя́ стáята си.	*I'd like to change my room.*

- Saying something *isn't working*

Асансьóрът не рабóти.	*The lift isn't working.*
Дýшът е развалéн.	*The shower has gone wrong.*
Прозóрецът е счýпен.	*The window is broken.*

- Recognizing requests for possible complaints

Имате ли оплáквания?	*Do you have any complaints?/ Is there anything wrong?*
Каквú оплáквания úмате?	*What complaints do you have?*
От каквó се оплáквате?	*What is your complaint?* (The doctor may ask you this too!)

- Expressing dissatisfaction

Не съм довóлен/довóлна от хотéла.	*I'm not happy with the hotel.*
Искам да се оплáча.	*I want to make a complaint.*

- Apologizing

Искам да се извиня́.	*I want to apologize.*

- Reassuring someone

Не сé безпокóйте!	*Don't worry.*

Grammar

1 Renarrated forms

(Ка́за, че) и́мало мно́го шум	*(He said) there was a lot of noise.*

You will have noticed in the dialogue that when Nevena repeats the businessman's complaints she puts them in a slightly different form:

Бизнесме́н	Конта́ктът... **не рабо́ти.**
Неве́на	Конта́ктът... **не рабо́тел.**
Бизнесме́н	Прозо́рецът **е счу́пен.**
Неве́на	Прозо́рецът **бил счу́пен.**
Бизнесме́н	Сега́... **и́мам** ва́жна сре́ща.
Неве́на	Ка́за, че **и́мал** ва́жна сре́ща.

In Bulgarian, you have to observe a clear distinction between what you know from first-hand experience and what you know from other sources. The form which Nevena uses shows that she is conveying second-hand information and that she has not herself been a witness to any of the events or facts she is presenting. She is only passing the information on, retelling the events. That is why the verb forms she is using are called 'renarrated' forms.

Every so often in the book so far we have actually found it quite difficult to avoid these renarrated forms, especially in the exercises. Go back briefly to the questions after the dialogue in Unit 13, for example. You were asked there to imagine you were Mrs Collins and, as it were, to answer from 'first-hand experience':

Към ко́лко часа́ присти́гнахте?	*What time did you arrive?*
Как бе́ше пъту́ването ви?	*How was your journey?*

It was not possible for us to ask you to talk about the journey yourself, because you were not a participant. You only read about it in the dialogue! Let's now compare Mrs Collins' answers with what you would need to say if you were 'renarrating' what she answered:

Г-жа́ Ко́линс	**Присти́гнахме** към се́дем часа́.
Ви́е	Те (г-н и г-жа́ Ко́линс) **присти́гнали** към се́дем часа́.
Г-жа́ Ко́линс	Пъту́ването **бе́ше** прия́тно.
Ви́е	Пъту́ването **било́** прия́тно.

Fairy tales are written using the renarrated forms. So are history books, unless, of course, the writer was an eye-witness to the events described.

2 How to construct the renarrated forms

Getting to grips with all the Bulgarian renarrated forms would be a pretty formidable task, as each tense has its equivalent renarrated version. For practical purposes, however, you will only need to use one or two of them, usually in the *he*, *she*, *it* and *they* forms, so it is on these that we will concentrate, both here and in the Appendix. In the Appendix, incidentally, you will find a slightly fuller set of tables enabling you to recognize some additional forms.

To start with, the renarrated forms are all based on the past participles ending in **-л**, **-ла**, **-ло**, **-ли**. This makes them look like the present perfect tense which you came across in Unit 18. The difference is that the renarrated form drops the **е** and **са**. Compare:

Present perfect tense

Той е присти́гнал.	*He has arrived.*
Те са присти́гнали.	*They have arrived.*

Renarrated

Той присти́гнал.	(I hear/they said) *he has arrived.*
Те присти́гнали.	(I hear) *they have arrived.*

3 Renarrating present and past events

Go back to the dialogue earlier in the unit. You will see that the secretary repeats a complaint made by other hotel residents: Не **мо́жели** да спят от шума́ на трамва́ите. The form **мо́жели** tells us that the original complaint was made in the present tense: Не **мо́жем** да спим от шума́ на трамва́ите.

If the hotel residents had complained in the past tense (Не **можа́хме** да спим от шума́), the secretary would have said: Не **можа́ли** да спя́т от шума́ на трамва́ите. To be technical for a moment, and if you've got this far, you'll surely manage to cope, the difference between **мо́жели** and **можа́ли** is in the *type* of past participle being used. **Мо́жел (-а, -о, -и)** comes from the past imperfect form **мо́жех** (Unit 17). As an imperfective form it is suitable for reproducing the present or past imperfect tense. **Можа́л (-а, -о, -и)** comes from the past form for ***completed*** actions **можа́х** (Unit 15). It is therefore suitable for reproducing things said in the past tense. Luckily, for many verbs the two participles are identical.

4 Щял да се върне към шест *He will be back about six (he said)*

When you want to renarrate things said in the future tense, you merely replace **ще** with **щял (щя́ла, щя́ло** or **щя́ли/ще́ли) да...** You may remember Nevena saying the businessman would be back about six:

Бизнесме́н	**Ще** се върна към шест часа́.
Неве́на	**Щял** да се върне към шест часа́.

5 The present perfect of (да) дам

Дал, да́ла, да́ло, да́ли are the past participle forms of the verb **(да) дам** *to give.* It is an irregular form, because it is not directly derived from the past tense form **да́дох** (Unit 16). Instead of just replacing **-х** by **-л**, the past participle loses the last **three** letters: **-дох** and then adds **-л, -ла, -ло, -ли**:

ста́ята, коя́то сте ми да́ли	*the room you've given me*

This happens with all verbs which end in **-дох** or **-тох** in the past, as with **чета́** *to read* (past: **че́тох**) and **(да) преведа́** *to translate* (past: **преве́дох**):

Аз съм чел та́зи кни́га.	*I have read this book.*
Г-жа́ Ко́линс е преве́ла ня́колко кни́ги.	*Mrs Collins has translated a number of books.*

6 Ста́ята, коя́то сте ми да́ли: where to put the short indirect object pronoun

In present perfect sentences such as **ста́ята, коя́то сте ми да́ли,** you put the short pronoun for the person who is given something between the appropriate form of **съм** and the past participle:

Аз **съм ти дал** една́ кни́га.	*I've given **you** a book.*
Ти **си ми дал** една́ кни́га.	*You've given **me** a book.*
Ни́е **сме му да́ли** една́ кни́га.	*We've given **him** a book.*
Ви́е **сте им да́ли** една́ кни́га.	*You've given **them** a book.*
Те **са ѝ да́ли** една́ кни́га.	*They've given **her** a book.*

With **той, тя** and **то,** however, the short pronoun comes *before* the verb *to be*:

Той ми е дал едно́ писмо́.	*He's given **me** a letter.*
Тя му е да́ла едно́ писмо́.	*She's given **him** a letter.*

When the past participle is the first word in the sentence, these sequences are preserved. The verb *to be* is followed by the pronoun in the *I*, *you*, *we* and *they* forms, but in the *he*, *she*, *it* form the pronoun comes *before* the verb *to be*. Compare:

Да́ла съм му ло́ша стя́я.	*I've given **him** a bad room.*

and

Да́ла му е ло́ша стя́я.	*She's given **him** a bad room.*

7 Introducing a reason or cause: от *because of*

The preposition **от** corresponds to a number of expressions in English. You have already come across **от** meaning *from* referring to time and space as in:

Магази́нът е отво́рен от 9 до 12.	*The shop is open from 9 to 12.*
Самоле́тът от Ло́ндон присти́га в о́сем часа́.	*The plane from London gets in at eight o'clock.*
И́ма шум от дискоте́ката.	*There is noise from the disco.*

От is also frequently used to express reason or cause. Note the possible English equivalents in these expressions taken from the dialogue:

Не съм **дово́лен от стя́ята** си.	*I'm not happy with my room.*
И дру́ги го́сти се опла́кват **от шум**.	*Other hotel residents too complain of noise.*
Не мо́гат да спя́т **от шума́** на трамва́ите.	*They can't sleep because of the noise from the trams.*

Exercises

1 If you were asked: **И́мате ли опла́квания?**, how would you answer if you were not happy with:

a	the price	**e**	the food (use **храна́**)
b	the shop assistant	**f**	the quality of the photos (use **ка́чество**)
c	the waiter		
d	the service station	**g**	the service (use **обслу́жване**)?

Model: Не съм дово́лен/дово́лна от камерие́рката.

2 Nothing is right in the restaurant. Complete the sentences using the model provided by the dissatisfied businessman in the dialogue:

Стáята, коя́то сте ми дáли, не ми харéсва.

Don't forget to change to **кóйто, коя́то, коéто, кои́то** where necessary (cf. Unit 5).

a Кюфтéто, ______, не ми́ харéсва.
b Сýпата, ______, не ми́ харéсва.
c Ви́ното, ______, не ми́ харéсва.
d Салáтите, ______, не ми́ харéсват.
e Сладолéдът, ______, не ми́ харéсва.

3 In this exercise you can practise using two different tenses of **(да) дам** and also putting the pronouns in the right order. First read out loud the short dialogue:

г-н и г-жá Кóлинс	Не сте́ ни дáли клю́човете.
Портиéр	Дáдох ви ги. Éто ги.

Now, still reading out loud, complete the dialogues below, making sure you have chosen the correct short pronouns. If necessary, look them up in the Appendix.

a – Не сте́ ми дáли паспóрта.
• ______.

b – Не сте́ ни дáли билéтите.
• ______.

c – Не сте́ ни дáли смéтката.
• ______.

d – Не сте́ ни дáли ключ.
• ______.

e – Не сте́ ми дáли визи́тна кáртичка (*business card*).
• ______.

4 Read the following sentences in which you give several reasons why you cannot get off to sleep:

a Не мóга да спя от кафéто.
b Не мóга да спя от главобóлие.
c Не мóга да спя от горещинá (*heat*).
d Не мóга да спя от комáрите (*mosquitoes*).
e Не мóга да спя от мýзиката в ресторáнта.

Now, giving the same reasons, say why you couldn't get off to sleep last night:

Снóщи не можáх да спя от шумá на трамвáите.

5 The story below tells of Michael Johnson's trip to Plovdiv which you first learnt about at the end of Unit 13. It consists of two parts – one told by Nikolai, who was there with Mr Johnson, and one told by Nadya, who was not. Read the story and try to work out who is talking first and where the first part finishes.

В Пло́вдив било́ мно́го интере́сно. Ма́йкъл хо́дил в на́й-интере́сните къщи, разгле́дал Ри́мската стена́ и цъ́рквата „Свети́ Константи́н и Еле́на". Вре́мето било́ мно́го прия́тно. И́мало мно́го хо́ра на панаи́ра. Ма́йкъл и́маше възмо́жност да бъ́де преводa̍ч на една́ гру́па англича́ни. Той им помо́гна да наме́рят свo̍я преводa̍ч. Той ку́пи мно́го ка́ртички от Пло́вдив, защо́то ми́слеше, че е загу́бил фо́тоапара́та си.

6 Read aloud the following conversation at the reception desk. Eli and the young American Jim surprise Nevena with news of their marriage.

Е́ли	Неве́на, аз съм Е́ли. Ни́е с Джим се оже́нихме. (*got married*).
Неве́на	Каква́ изнена́да! Чести́то!
Е́ли и Джим	Благодари́м.
Неве́на	Кога́ бе́ше сва́тбата?
Е́ли	Вче́ра. Празну́вахме (*celebrated*) в ресторa̍нт „Москва́".
Неве́на	Отда́вна ли се позна́вате?
Е́ли	Запозна́хме се ми́налата зи́ма в Ба́нско. Джим бе́ше там като́ тури́ст. След това́ той дойде́ в Со́фия, за да се запозна́е с роди́телите (*parents*) ми.
Неве́на	Жела́я ви мно́го ща́стие. Сега́ какво́ ще пра́вите?
Е́ли	Пъ́рво ще оти́дем на море́. След това́ ще оти́дем на фолкло́рния фестива́л в Копри́вщица.

The questions we are now going to ask are all in the special renarrated form, because we weren't in on the conversation. Answer using the same forms – you weren't there either!

- **a** Кога́ била́ сва́тбата?
- **b** В кой ресторa̍нт празну́вали?
- **c** Къде́ се запозна́ли Джим и Е́ли?
- **d** Защо́ дошъ́л Джим в Со́фия?
- **e** Къде́ ще́ли да оти́дат сега́ Джим и Е́ли?

Do you understand?

Dialogue 2: Гре́шката е мо́я *My mistake*

Nadya receives a misdirected phone complaint from an agitated customer.

Клие́нт А́ло? До́бър ден. И́скам да гово́ря с дире́ктора на фи́рма „Търго́вска рекла́ма", мо́ля.

На́дя Г-н Анто́нов разгова́ря с клие́нти в моме́нта. Да му преда́м ли не́що?

Клие́нт Да, ако́ оби́чате. Оба́ждам се от фи́рма „Тра́нс-Прое́кт". И́скам да се опла́ча. Преда́йте му, че не сме́ дово́лни от ва́шата ра́бота.

На́дя От какво́ по́-то́чно се опла́квате?

Клие́нт Поръ́чахме 1 200 (хиля́да и две́ста) рекла́мни брошу́ри, а полу́чихме са́мо 600 (ше́стстотин). Па́пките, които поръ́чахме, и́мат дефе́кти, а визи́тните ка́ртички са на ло́ша харти́я.

На́дя Ще преда́м на дире́ктора опла́кванията Ви. Ще Ви се оба́дя у́тре. Дочу́ване!

На́дя (*Later, to the director.*) Г-н Анто́нов, оба́ди се еди́н не́рвен клие́нт от фи́рма „Тра́нсПрое́кт". И́маше цял куп опла́квания.

г-н Анто́нов Какво́ е ста́нало?

На́дя Поръ́чали 1 200 брошу́ри, а полу́чили са́мо 600. Па́пките и́мали дефе́кти, а визи́тните ка́ртички били́ на ло́ша харти́я.

г-н Анто́нов Ча́кай, ча́кай! Тук и́ма ня́каква гре́шка. Фи́рма „Тра́нсПрое́кт" е поръ́чала 1 200 брошу́ри и ни́е сме изпра́тили 1 200 – в два кашо́на по 600. Си́гурно о́ще не са́ полу́чили вто́рия кашо́н. Поръ́чка за па́пки и визи́тни ка́ртички от тях не сме́ и́мали.

(*Telephone rings.*)

Клие́нт А́ло? Оба́ждам се пак от фи́рма „Тра́нс-Прое́кт". И́скам да се извиня́. Ока́за се, че вси́чко е наре́д.

На́дя Г-н Анто́нов е тук. И́скате ли да гово́рите с не́го?

Клие́нт Ня́ма ну́жда да го безпокои́те. Полу́чихме вси́чки брошу́ри. Ка́кто разбра́х от секрета́рката, па́пките и визи́тните ка́ртички били́ поръ́чани на дру́го мя́сто, в дру́га фи́рма.

	Гре́шката е мо́я. Извиня́вайте о́ще веднъ́ж. Дочу́ване!
г-н Анто́нов	Не́рвният клие́нт ли бе́ше?
На́дя	Да, извини́ се. Бил напра́вил гре́шка.
г-н Анто́нов	Ни́що чу́дно. Ка́зват, че в та́зи фи́рма ста́вали мно́го гре́шки...

Търго́вска рекла́ма	*Trade Publicity*
(да) преда́м, -даде́ш	*to pass on/leave a message*
(да) се опла́ча, -чеш	*to make a complaint*
рекла́мен, -мна	*publicity* (adj.)
и́ма дефе́кт	*has something wrong with it*
не́рвен, -вна	*agitated, stressed out*
цял куп	*a whole lot* (of)
харти́я	*paper*
кашо́н	*cardboard box*
(да) се извиня́, -ни́ш	*to apologize*
ока́за се (*it* form)	*it turned out*
на дру́го мя́сто	*elsewhere*
о́ще веднъ́ж	*once again*

Questions

Try to use the renarrated forms in your answers!

1 Какво́ тря́бва да предаде́ На́дя на дире́ктора?
2 От какво́ се опла́ква клие́нтът?
3 Защо́ се оба́жда клие́нтът вто́ри път?
4 Какво́ е разбра́л клие́нтът от секрета́рката?
5 Какво́ ка́зват за фи́рма „Тра́нсПрое́кт“?

20 би́хме и́скали да до́йдем пак!

we would like to come again!

In this unit you will learn:

- **how to take your leave of someone**
- **how to use some sentences with *if***
- **how to express wishes and requests being especially polite**
- **how to agree to stay in touch**

Dialogue 1

At Sofia airport Mrs Collins sees a young couple with a trolley.

г-жа́ Ко́линс Извине́те, би́хте ли ми ка́зали откъде́ взе́хте коли́чка за бага́ж?

Миле́на О, но ни́е се позна́ваме. Здраве́йте! Видя́хме се в едно́ кафе́. По́мните ли?

г-жа́ Ко́линс Да, вя́рно – Ви́е сте моми́чето, кое́то ни пока́за Центра́лна по́ща, нали́?

Миле́на То́чно така́! Запозна́йте се – това́ е мо́ят коле́га Никола́й. Той замина́ва за А́нглия.

г-жа́ Ко́линс Зна́чи ще пъту́ваме за́едно. (*Shaking hands*.) Прия́тно ми е.

Миле́на Никола́й, би ли взел коли́чка за г-н и г-жа́ Ко́линс?

Никола́й Да, разби́ра се. Еди́н моме́нт.

Миле́на Дово́лни ли сте от престо́я във Ва́рна?

г-жа́ Ко́линс Да, изка́рахме чуде́сно. Ми́сля, че видя́хме по́вечето забележи́телности о́коло града́.

Миле́на Ще до́йдете ли пак в Бълга́рия сле́дващата годи́на?

г-жа́ Ко́линс Мно́го би́хме и́скали да до́йдем пак. Ако́ и́маме възмо́жност да до́йдем през зи́мата, би́хме оти́шли в Бо́ровец то́зи път.

Миле́на Ако́ и́двате пак, обаде́те ми се непреме́нно! Е́то, Никола́й и́два с коли́чката.

г-н Ко́линс Благодаря́, Никола́й. Викто́рия, тря́бва да бъ́рзаме. Дови́ждане, Миле́на! Ще Ви пи́шем от А́нглия.

Миле́на Всичко ху́баво, г-н Ко́линс! Г-жа́ Ко́линс, и́мам една́ молба́ към Вас. Би́хте ли помо́гнали на Никола́й на Хи́йтроу? Той се безпоко́й, че не разби́ра англи́йски мно́го добре́.

г-жа́ Ко́линс Ще му помо́гна с удово́лствие. Дови́ждане, Миле́на!

Миле́на Прия́тен път! (*To Nikolai*.) Никола́й, ще ми пра́тиш ли и́мейл от Че́лмсфорд?

Никола́й Зна́еш, че ще ти пра́тя... (*With a sigh*.) Ко́лко бих и́скал ти да пъту́ваш с ме́не!

Миле́на Ха́йде, ха́йде, тръ́гвай! Ще закъсне́еш за самоле́та. Прия́тно изка́рване!

Никола́й Благодаря́! До ско́ро!

Бихте ли ми ка́зали?	*Could you please tell me?*
По́мните ли?	*Do you remember?*
Би ли взел коли́чка?	*Could you please take a trolley?*
Еди́н моме́нт.	*Just a moment.*
Изка́рахме чуде́сно.	*We had a marvellous time.*
Видя́хме по́вечето забележи́телности о́коло градá.	*We saw most of the sights around the town.*
Би́хме и́скали да до́йдем пак.	*We'd like to come again.*
би́хме оти́шли	*we would go*
обаде́те ми се непреме́нно	*don't fail to/do let me know*
Ще Ви пи́шем.	*We'll write to you.*
Вси́чко ху́баво.	*All the best.*
Би́хте ли помо́гнали?	*Could you please help?*
Ще ми пра́тиш ли и́мейл?	*Will you send me an email?*
Ко́лко бих и́скал ти да пъту́ваш с ме́не!	*How I wish you were going with me!*
Ха́йде, ха́йде, тръ́гвай.	*Come on/now, now, off you go.*
До ско́ро!	*See you soon/later.*

1 Questions

- **a** Какво́ пока́за Миле́на на г-н и г-жа́ Ко́линс?
- **b** Кога́ би́ха и́скали да до́йдат г-н и г-жа́ Ко́линс пак в Бълга́рия?
- **c** Къде́ би́ха оти́шли те, ако́ и́маха възмо́жност?
- **d** Каква́ молба́ и́ма Миле́на към г-жа́ Ко́линс?
- **e** Какво́ би и́скал Никола́й?

2 True or false?

- **a** Никола́й ня́ма да пъту́ва за́едно с г-н и г-жа́ Ко́линс.
- **b** Г-н и г-жа́ Ко́линс са виде́ли вси́чки забележи́телности о́коло Ва́рна.
- **c** Г-н и г-жа́ Ко́линс би́ха и́скали да до́йдат пак в Бълга́рия.
- **d** Г-н и г-жа́ Ко́линс ня́ма да пи́шат на Миле́на от А́нглия.
- **e** Никола́й ще пра́ти ка́ртичка на Миле́на от Че́лмсфорд.

How do you say it?

- Taking your leave

До скоро (виждане)!	*See you soon/later.*
Приятен път!	*Have a pleasant journey.*

- Expressing a wish politely

Бих йскал/а...	*I would like...*
(Много) бихме йскали...	*We would (very much) like...*

- Intensifying a statement or a wish

Елате непременно!	*Do come!*
Непременно ще дойда.	*I certainly will come.*

- Making a polite request for assistance

Бихте ли ми казали...?	*Would you be so kind as to tell me...?*
Би ли взел количка?	*Would you be so kind as to take a trolley?*
Бихте ли ми помогнали?	*Could you please help me?*

- Asking someone to wait a moment

Един момент!	*Just a moment/hold on!*

- Saying you have enjoyed yourself very much

Изкарахме чудесно.	*We had a marvellous time.*

- Expressing eager expectation

Очаквам Николай с нетърпение.	*I'm looking forward to seeing Nikolai.*
С нетърпение очаквам да се обадите.	*I'm looking forward to hearing from you.*

Grammar

1 Expressing wishes and requests more formally

Бих йскал да... *I would like to...*

In Unit 6 you learned that the Bulgarian equivalent of *I want to* is **Йскам да**, and you may have felt this way of expressing a wish rather rude. Although **йскам** in Bulgarian is socially more acceptable than *I want* in English – ('I want never gets', remember!) – Bulgarian does also have more formal polite alternatives. These are based on a special form of **съм** and come close to English polite expressions with *would* and *could*. Compare:

Йскам да сменя стаята си.	*I want to change my room.*
and	
Бих йскал(а) да сменя стаята си.	*I would like to change my room.*
Йскам да говоря с директора.	*I want to speak to the director.*
and	
Бих йскал(а) да говоря с директора.	*I would like to speak to the director.*

These ultra-polite forms, *would like to…,* and also the conditionals about which you will discover more below, consist of the special form of **съм** plus a past participle, usually from a verb of *wanting* or *wishing*.

(аз) бих йскал(а) да...	(ние) бихме йскали да...
(ти) би йскал(а) да...	(вие) бихте йскали да...
(той) би йскал да...	(те) биха йскали да...
(тя) би йскала да...	
(то) би йскало да...	

Бихте ли...? *Would you be so kind as to...? (Could you...?)*

You can use the same form of **съм** to make polite requests:

Би ли ми казал(а) колко е часът?	*Could you tell me what the time is?*
Бихте ли ми показали пътя за Варна?	*Would you be so kind as to show me the way to Varna?*

These requests are a degree more formal than questions using **Може ли...?** (see Unit 6).

2 Бих отишъл (ако...) *I would go (if...)*

The same forms are used to express willingness to do something if the circumstances permit or if certain conditions are fulfilled. (Unlike constructions with **щях** in Unit 16, these are things that still can happen, they are 'open' conditions):

Бихме отишли в Боровец, ако дойдем през зимата.	*We'd go to Borovets if we were to come in winter.*
Бих отишла в Англия (ако имам пари)	*I'd go to England (if I were to have the money).*
Бихме дошли с вас, ако не сме заети.	*We will come with you if we aren't busy.*

In the last example the statement is more tentative and the Bulgarian expresses willingness and politeness as much as condition. In all three examples the Bulgarian polite form could be replaced by the normal future: **ще оти́дем, ще оти́да** and **ще до́йдем**, all of which are more assertive and definite – *I will* rather than *I would*.

3 Catching up with new verbs with 'ce'

In Unit 6 you learned that some Bulgarian verbs, called reflexive verbs, are accompanied by the 'satellite' word **ce**. Since then you have come across more reflexive verbs and they can be now summed up in three groups:

(**a**) when the object of the verb in English is *myself*, *yourself*, etc. (or such an object is implied) as in:

Момче́то се обле́че.	*The boy got (himself) dressed.*
Той се чу́вства по́-добре́ сега́.	*He feels better now.*
Той се безпоко́и.	*He is worried.*

These verbs can usually also appear without **ce** and with an object. Compare:

Неве́на обле́че момче́то.	*Nevena got the boy dressed.*
Чу́вствам бо́лка в кръ́ста.	*I feel a pain in the back.*
Извиня́вай, че те безпокоя́.	*Forgive me for troubling you.*

Other similar verbs include:

(да) въ́рна	*to return, give back*
(да) оже́ня	*to marry someone off*
(да) разваля́	*to break something*
(да) се въ́рна	*to return, go back*
(да) се оже́ня	*to get married*
(да) се разваля́	*to break down, go wrong*

(**b**) when the object of the verb in English is *each other* or *one another*. These verbs can also be used without **ce**:

Аз позна́вам Никола́й.	*I know Nikolai.*
but	
Ни́е се позна́ваме.	*We know each other.*
Миле́на видя́ г-жа́ Ко́линс.	*Milena saw Mrs Collins.*
but	
Те се видя́ха в едно́ кафе́.	*They saw one another in a café.*

Ще запознáя Николáй с тéзи англичáни.	*I'll introduce Nikolai to these Englishmen.*
but	
Те ще се запознáят на летúщето.	*They'll get to know one another at the airport.*

(c) when the verb denotes feelings or emotions. These verbs never appear without **се**:

грúжа се	*to look after*	страхýвам се	*to be afraid*
надя́вам се	*to hope*	съмня́вам се	*to be in doubt*
рáдвам се	*to be pleased*	шегýвам се	*to joke*
смéя се	*to laugh*		

4 To be doing something and to begin doing something

The difference in meaning of 'twin' verbs like **рáдвам се** *to be glad* and **(да) се зарáдвам** *to rejoice* or **смéя се** *to be laughing* and **да се засмéя** *to begin to laugh* is often difficult to render succinctly in English. One is imperfective, the other perfective (see Unit 12). When the prefix **за-** is added to a verb it often denotes the beginning of an action. Compare the beginning perceived as a moment in time A, with B, an action that is going on:

A	Тя го видя́ и се засмя́.	*She saw him and began to laugh.*
	Той я видя́ и веднáга го заболя́ главáта.	*He saw her and immediately got a headache.*
B	Тя пак се смéе.	*She's laughing again.*
	Пак го болú главáта.	*He's having a headache again.*

Also compare the verb **пóмня** *to remember* with the verb **(да) запóмня**. The first verb can be paraphrased as '*to be keeping something in one's memory*' (that is why it is imperfective) and the second one as '*to get something fixed in one's memory*' (that is why it is perfective).

5 Keeping in touch

(Да) се обáдя *to get in touch*, *to phone* does not fit into any of the three groups and literally means '*to let oneself be heard*' (see Unit 11). When you use it in the phrase **обадú ми се!** you have to remember where to put the two little unstressed words. The indirect object pronoun **(ми)** always comes before **се**, no matter whether they both follow or precede the verb (see Appendix):

Тря́бва да **ми се** оба́диш.	*You must get in touch/give me a ring/ call.*
Обаде́те **ми се**!	*Give me a ring/call.*

Exercises

1 Following the model, respond to the requests below. Watch the word order!

Request: Обади́ се на г-н Анто́нов, мо́ля те.
Responses: **a** Ще му се оба́дя.
b Оба́дих му се ве́че.
c Ве́че му се оба́дих.

i Обаде́те се на секрета́рката, мо́ля Ви.
ii Обади́ се на Никола́й, мо́ля те.
iii Обади́ се на Джим и Е́ли, мо́ля те.
iv Обаде́те се на Неве́на Петко́ва, мо́ля Ви.

2 Make these requests, already quite decently civil, even more polite. The model may help:

Model: Покаже́те ми, мо́ля Ви, та́зи ва́за.
Би́хте ли ми пока́зали та́зи ва́за?

a Мо́ля Ви, каже́те ми Ва́шия адре́с.
b Обаде́те ми се по́-къснo, мо́ля Ви.
c Мо́ля Ви, помогне́те ни да наме́рим пътя за Ва́рна.
d Да́йте ми дру́га ста́я, ако́ оби́чате.
e Мо́ля Ви, поръ́чайте ми такси́ за де́сет часа́.

Here are the past participles to choose from. You won't need them all!

ка́зал дал доне́съл поръ́чал помо́гнал се оба́дил спрял

3 Answer these questions using the future form and, demonstrating your willingness to do what you are asked (provided certain conditions are met!), by using бих and the past participle.

Model: Ще оти́деш ли на мач (*match*)? Ще оти́да/бих оти́шъл, ако́ не вали́ дъжд.

a Ще ку́пите ли пода́ръци за жена́ Ви? (ако́ наме́ря не́що ху́баво)
b Ще се оба́диш ли от лети́щето? (ако́ и́мам вре́ме)
c Ще до́йдеш ли на те́нис? (ако́ се чу́вствам по́-добре́)
d Ще уча́ствате ли в конфере́нцията? (ако́ и́мам пари́)

Past participles to choose from (again, you won't need them all):

дошъ́л ку́пил уча́ствал се оба́дил разбра́л

4 If you have ever attended a conference in Bulgaria, you might find parts of the following brief address familiar. It contains several polite expressions which you yourself might have occasion to try out. Read the address out loud, then answer the questions in English.

Да́ми и господа́, скъ́пи прия́тели!
Бих и́скал(а) да ви поздравя́ с „Добре́ дошли́" в на́шата краси́ва сто́лица и да ви пожела́я успе́х в ра́ботата ви на та́зи конфере́нция. Мно́го се ра́дваме, че ви́ждаме тук то́лкова мно́го прия́тели на Бълга́рия от цял свят. Би́хме се ра́двали, ако́ та́зи конфере́нция е поле́зна за все́ки от вас.

О́ще веднъ́ж добре́ дошли́ в Бълга́рия! От все сърце́ (*all my heart*) ви пожела́вам прия́тна и плодотво́рна (*fruitful*) ра́бота и до но́ви тво́рчески (*creative*) и прия́телски сре́щи.

a On what occasion is this address given?
b At what point in the proceedings is the speech made?
c How does the speaker address his audience?
d Where do the conference participants come from?
e What else do they have in common?
f In what city is this particular conference taking place?
g What benefit does the speaker hope the participants will derive from the conference?

5 Back in Britain, Michael Johnson is attending another conference. In the coffee break he dashes off a postcard to his friends in Bulgaria. Read aloud what he says:

Скъ́пи прия́тели!

Пи́ша ви от Ло́ндон, къде́то съм на конфере́нция. На конфере́нцията и́ма два́ма бизнесме́ни от Пло́вдив, който добре́ позна́ват г-жа́ Ко́линс. Ка́зват, че говоря ве́че не по́-ло́шо от не́я... Бих и́скал да ви благодаря́ о́ще веднъ́ж за помощта́ ви и за прия́тните дни в Бълга́рия. Оча́квам Никола́й с нетърпе́ние. Надя́вам се да се ви́дим ско́ро пак. Всичко ху́баво и до ско́ро ви́ждане!

С по́здрав (*kind regards*),
Ма́йкъл Джо́нсън

Ло́ндон, 6.VI. 2008

Now you write a postcard, also in Bulgarian, to Nikolai and Nadya.

Do you understand?

Dialogue 2: На лети́щето *At the airport*

Sofia airport is not large, and shortly before taking off for Heathrow Mr and Mrs Collins bump into some more acquaintances.

г-н Ко́линс Викто́рия, виж! О́ще една́ позна́та.

г-жа́ Ко́линс А, да – моми́чето от реце́пцията в хоте́ла в Со́фия.

Неве́на Каква́ изнена́да! Здраве́йте, г-н Ко́линс! Здраве́йте, г-жа́ Ко́линс!

г-жа́ Ко́линс Здраве́йте, Неве́на. И Ви́е ли ще пъту́вате за А́нглия?

Неве́на Не, аз изпра́щам едни́ прия́тели – Марк Де́йвис и жена́ му. По́мните ли, аз Ви ка́зах за не́го.

г-жа́ Ко́линс Да, по́мня. Америка́нският журнали́ст, нали́?

Неве́на То́чно така́. Ела́те да Ви запозна́я с тях, те мно́го ще се заза́двaт.

Марк Прия́тно ми е. Неве́на мно́го ми е разка́звала за Вас. Щях да Ви изпра́тя съобще́ние чрез не́я от О́лбани, за да Ви пока́ня на една́ конфере́нция за Бълга́рия. Би́хте ли и́скали да уча́ствате?

г-жа́ Ко́линс Бих уча́ствала с удово́лствие, ако́ не съм зае́та по съ́щото вре́ме.

Марк Чуде́сно, ще Ви пра́тя пока́на и програ́мата. Би́хте ли ми да́ли и́мейла си, мо́ля.

г-жа́ Ко́линс Заповя́дайте, това́ е визи́тната ми ка́ртичка. Ви́е в Аме́рика ли живе́ете?

Марк Да, по́вечето вре́ме живе́ем в Аме́рика, но мно́го че́сто и́дваме в Бълга́рия.

г-жа́ Ко́линс Надя́вам се да се ви́дим пак! Обаде́те се!

(*The public address system crackles into life.*) Моля за внимание! Всички пътници, заминаващи за Лондон, да се явят на изход номер четири!

г-жа Колинс	Сега трябва да бързаме. Довиждане на всички!
Невена	Довиждане и всичко хубаво! Елате пак непременно!
Всички	НЕПРЕМЕННО!

(да) се зарадвам, -ваш	*to be pleased*
разказвам, -ваш	*to tell, relate*
през	*through, by means of*
(да) участвам, -ваш	*to take part*
пътник, (pl) -ици	*passenger, traveller*
заминаващ за	*travelling to*
(да) се явя, явиш	*to present oneself*
изход	*gate; exit*
толкова много	*so many/much*
плодотворен, -рна	*fruitful*

Questions

1 Коя позната виждат г-н и г-жа Колинс на летището?
2 Защо е на летището Невена?
3 За кого е разказвала много Невена на Марк?
4 За какво щял Марк да изпрати съобщение на г-жа Колинс?
5 В какъв случай би участвала г-жа Колинс в конференцията?
6 Какво дава г-жа Колинс на Марк?

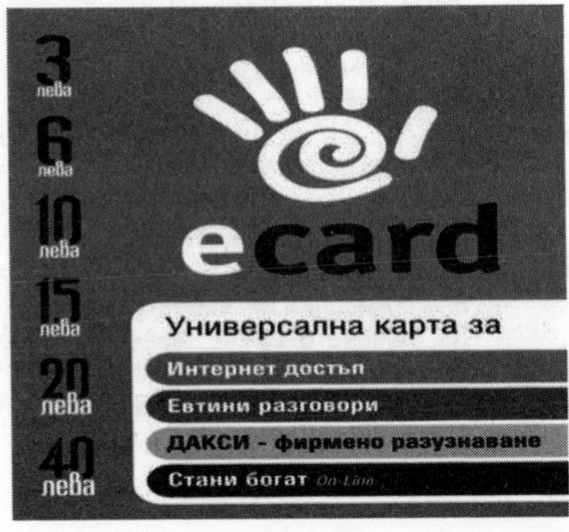

taking it further

We hope you have found it fun working your way through *Teach Yourself Bulgarian*. We also hope you will wish to develop further your knowledge of the language, the country and its people. At present there is a sad lack of dedicated printed English language materials for intermediate learners of Bulgarian. We cannot direct you to any single book or course that takes you logically on from where you left off at the end of Unit 20. The only self-study course book we can confidently recommend to take you further is *Bulgarian: Beyond the First Steps*, also by Mira Kovatcheva, published in 2005 by Prosveta, Sofia. Other courses published in Sofia are primarily aimed at complete beginners. What you will have to do, therefore, is pick and mix from a variety of sources, combining limited printed materials with the expanding and ever changing offerings of the internet. To help you on your way, we have listed below a few books and other sources you might find useful.

Dictionaries and phrasebooks

Many of the bilingual dictionaries that have long been in service have recently been revised and reissued. You will also find an increasing number of new dictionaries, large and small, mostly targeted at Bulgarian learners of English, but nevertheless of value to English-language learners of Bulgarian. Few of them will be on the shelves of bookshops, so you need to ask for them by name, giving the author and publisher. Try the two-way pocket dictionary by Levkova and Pishtalova: *English-Bulgarian, Bulgarian-English Dictionary*, Colibri, Sofia (2001). Daniela Shurbanova and Krasimira Rangelova have compiled a number of useful new dictionaries all in the 21st Century Reference series published by Prozorets i Trud in Sofia. Ask for their *English-Bulgarian Dictionary* (2000 and 2008) and their *Bulgarian-English*

Dictionary (2004). Or get the two in one in their single volume *English-Bulgarian, Bulgarian-English Dictionary*, Sofia (2005), which is excellent. The greatest variety of reference works has been produced by the German publisher Ernst Klett Verlag, operating in Bulgaria as 'PONS Bulgaria'. Look for the firm's distinctive light green bindings. We can particularly recommend the *Нов училищен речник* (*New Learner's Dictionary*), an up-to-date Bulgarian learner's dictionary, with maps, pictures, model letters, cultural explanations and a concise grammar of both English and Bulgarian. If you are looking for something really substantial, then go for the two big PONS dictionaries: the *Нов универсален българско-английски речник* and the *Нов универсален английско-български речник*. With 121,000 and 97,000 words respectively, they should have all you need. For further PONS publications, go to the website: **pons.bg**.

It is difficult to choose between the numerous phrasebooks currently on offer, but you won't go far wrong with either of the following: firstly, and top of the price range, the handsome, illustrated *Pons Bulgarian Travellers' Language Guide* (2004) by Edward Richards; secondly, the handy, very practical *Bulgarian Phrasebook*, published by Chambers (2007). This contains thematic vocabulary lists, related sentences, a mini grammar section and a 4,000-word two-way dictionary. Phrasebooks are generally more available than dictionaries on the shelves of bookshops – especially in Bulgaria – so take a look and choose what best suits your needs.

Grammars, primers

For the intermediate learner the most appropriate primer is *Intensive Bulgarian: a textbook and reference grammar* by Ronelle Alexander assisted by Olga Mladenova. Published by the University of Wisconsin Press (2000), it comes in two hefty volumes, combines grammar and exercises and will both help you revise and take you further. Grammars of Bulgarian produced in Bulgaria are traditionally on the turgid side and are intended for a largely academic readership. They are also, of course, mostly in Bulgarian and written in an appropriate style! For a relatively modern grammar of Bulgarian in English, try *A Short Grammar of Contemporary Bulgarian* by Kjetil Ra Hauge, published by Slavica in Bloomington, Indiana (1999).

Courses

A number of Bulgarian universities organize short courses in Bulgarian language and culture, usually in the summer, for keen and interested foreigners. Try the Sofia University Faculty of Slavic

Studies website: **slav.uni-sofia.bg** (e-mail: **summercourse@ slav.uni-sofia.bg**), or the International Centre for Bulgarian Studies at the University of Veliko Turnovo: **uni-vt.bg** and follow the link: Летен семинар по български език. For short courses run at intervals throughout the year, go to **deo.uni-sofia.bg.**

Book buying

Most large internet booksellers can supply Bulgarian books if they are in print. In the UK, the specialist booksellers Grant and Cutler Ltd (55–57 Great Marlborough Street, London W1F 7AY) supply a variety of learning materials published in and outside Bulgaria. They have dictionaries, including technical dictionaries, phrasebooks, literature in Bulgarian and even Bulgarian scrabble. Try **grantandcutler.com** or e-mail to **mail@grantandcutler.com** or phone 00 44 (0)207 734 2012 and ask for the Slavonic Section.

Ура! (*Hurrah!*) for the .bg internet address!

By far the most exciting source of authentic Bulgarian language material today is the internet. The .bg sites, and the information they provide, multiply by the minute. Here are just a few promising addresses for you to get started on.

An excellent site, in Bulgarian and English, with a multitude of links, is **online.bg.** Here you will find newspapers, literary journals, theatre and cinema programmes and much else besides. Also try the lively **dir.bg**, which even has a section titled 'FUN'. Most Bulgarian newspapers also have their own websites, so try **capital.bg**, **standartnews.bg** or **duma.bg** for a start. The **sofiaecho.com** site – all in English – is an excellent source of up-to-date information about Sofia and beyond. If you are looking for authentic Bulgarian literature, try **liternet.bg**. A good general site, with useful links and lots of information on Bulgaria, is **kirildouhalov.net**. There are lots of online courses, almost exclusively for beginners, but they are still worth investigating. Google 'Bulgarian language online' or simply 'Bulgarian grammar', and you'll be on your way!

For a thoroughly absorbing time, and more substantial sustenance for Bulgarian learners than on any other single site, click into the Bulgarian language and literature offering at the University of Oslo either on **hf.uio.no/east/bulg/mat/index.html** or **hf.uio.no/ilos/studier/studenttjenester/Nettressurser/bulg/mat.** Although Bulgarian is no longer on offer at Oslo, the hugely rewarding Bulgarian Links on the site are still very useful. You can find Bulgarian newspapers, radio and TV programmes, the Sofia telephone directory, Bulgarian literary texts glossed in English and much else besides. It may be a long address, but it's well worth the journey!

Finally, if you want to discover more about Bulgarian life and culture, the most honest, entertaining and informative book we can recommend is *The Insider's Guide to Sofia and Beyond*, written by Christine Milner and Paromita Sanatani and published in Sofia by Inside and Out Ltd (2005). Order via the website: **insidesofia.com.**

Congratulations on completing *Teach Yourself Bulgarian*!

We hope you have enjoyed working your way through the course. We are always keen to receive feedback from people who have used our course, so why not contact us and let us know your reactions? We'll be particularly pleased to receive your praise, but we should also like to know if you think things could be improved. We always welcome comments and suggestions and we do our best to incorporate constructive suggestions into later editions.

You can contact us through the publishers at:

Teach Yourself Books, Hodder Headline Ltd, 338 Euston Road, London NW1 3BH.

So **приятен път! приятно изкáрване!** and **на добър час!** (*farewell!*). And happy hunting!

Michael Holman and Mira Kovatcheva,
Tunbridge Wells and Sofia, 2008

key to the exercises

Introduction

1 Alaska, address, Estonia, espresso, Canada, credit, Milan, minute, Ottawa, omelette, Texas, telephone. **2** Berlin, bar, Glasgow, garage, Dakota, vodka, Geneva, jury, Zambezi, Arizona, Istanbul, India, York, Mallorca, London, Balkan, Panama, police, Frankfurt, Sofia, Zurich, Donetsk, Chad, Churchill, Sheffield, show business, Stuttgart, Budapest, Updike, Bulgaria, chauffeur, signora, Yukon, Leeds United, Yalta, Yankee. **3** Vienna, Vivian, Namibia, Varna, Richard, Yorkshire, Sinatra, Amsterdam, Hungary, Liverpool, Hyde Park, Sahara. **4** Address, espresso, telephone, credit, Ottawa, garage, minute, Donetsk, show business, Budapest, Vivian, Amsterdam.

Exercises

1 (*a*) iv, (*b*) xii, (*c*) v, (*d*) x, (*e*) xi, (*f*) iii, (*g*) i, (*h*) vi, (*i*) vii, (*j*) ii, (*k*) ix, (*l*) viii. **2** (*a*) v, (*b*) iii, (*c*) vii, (*d*) viii, (*e*) vi, (*f*) ix, (*g*) i, (*h*) x, (*i*) iv, (*j*) ii. **3** (*a*) viii, (*b*) xiv, (*c*) iii, (*d*) v, (*e*) vi, (*f*) xvi, (*g*) ix, (*h*) iv, (*i*) ii, (*j*) i, (*k*) xiii, (*l*) xv, (*m*) xi, (*n*) vii, (*o*) xii, (*p*) x. **4** 201 Business Club, 202 Restaurant, 203 Reception, 204 Fitness centre, 205 Bar, 206 Taxi, 207 Information, 166 Police. **5** (*a*) Milano (*b*) Moskva (*c*) Sheraton (*d*) Orient. **6** (*a*) 17.25, (*b*) 17.05, (*c*) 16.35, (*d*) 18.05, (*e*) 18.30, (*f*) 15.40, (*g*) 16.10.

Unit 1

1 Questions (*a*) Да, и́ма (*b*) Не, ня́ма (*c*) Ка́звам се… **2** (*a*) T (*b*) F: Бизнесме́н съм (*c*) T.
Exercises 1 (*a*) *agency* (f), (*b*) *address* (m), (*c*) *aspirin* (m) (*d*) *bank* (f), (*e*) *business* (m), (*f*) *beer* (f) (*g*) *vodka* (f) (*h*) *computer* (m), (*i*) *show* (n), (*j*) *music* (f), (*k*) *calendar* (m), (*l*) *problem* (m), (*m*) *soda water* (f), (*n*) *sport* (m), (*o*) *tonic* (m),

(*p*) *tourist* (m), (*q*) *firm* (f), (*r*) *football* (m), (*s*) *chauffeur* (m), (*t*) *printer* (m), (*u*) *office* (m), (*v*) *fax* (m), (*w*) *video* (n), (*x*) *xerox* (m). **2** (*a*) здраве́й, (*b*) здраве́йте, (*c*) здраве́йте, (*d*) здраве́йте, (*e*) здраве́й, (*f*) здраве́й, (*g*) здраве́йте. **3** (*a*) Добро́ у́тро, (*b*) До́бър ден, (*c*) До́бър ден, (*d*) До́бър ве́чер. **4** i (*f*), ii (*e*), iii (*a*), iv (*c*), v (*d*), vi (*b*). **5** (*a*) Да, и́ма. (*b*) Да, и́ма. (*c*) Не, ня́ма. (*d*) Не, ня́ма. (*e*) Да, и́ма. (*f*) Не, ня́ма. **6** (*a*) И́ма ли уи́ски? (*b*) И́ма ли би́ра? (*c*) И́ма ли лимона́да? (*d*) И́ма ли чай? **7** (*a*) Уи́ски, мо́ля. Джин, мо́ля. (*b*) Би́ра, мо́ля. Ко́ка-Ко́ла, мо́ля. (*c*) Капучи́но, мо́ля. Еспре́со, мо́ля. (*d*) Кафе́, мо́ля. Чай, мо́ля. **8** (*a*) a lovely hotel. (*b*) a good-looking man. (*c*) a beautiful sea. (*d*) lovely beer. (*e*) a beautiful name. (*f*) a beautiful Bulgarian (female!). (*g*) Ху́бава ста́я! (*h*) Ху́бав апартаме́нт! (*i*) Ху́баво българско ви́но!

9

(*a*)	(*b*)
Майкъл Джонсън	България
4, Маунт Драйв	1000 София
Челмсфорд	хотел „Родина"
Есекс	апартамент 8
Англия	Майкъл Джонсън

Do you understand? (*a*) Evening. (*b*) Yes. (*c*) There's no music. (*d*) No. (*e*) Whisky and mineral water.

Unit 2

1 Questions (*a*) Благодаря́, добре́ съм. (*b*) Не, ни́що. (*c*) Това́ е но́ва брошу́ра от господи́н Джо́нсън. (*d*) Самоле́т от Ло́ндон и́ма в се́дем часа́. (*e*) Да, той присти́га днес.
2 (*a*) F: На́дя е добре́. (*b*) T. (*c*) T. (*d*) F: Господи́н Анто́нов ня́ма вре́ме за кафе́, (*e*) F: Господи́н Анто́нов и́ма мно́го ра́бота.
Exercises 1 (*a*) Къде́ е тя? (*b*) Той е добре́. (*c*) Как е той? (*d*) Къде́ са те? (*e*) Тя е в хоте́л „Роди́на". (*f*) Той и́ма ра́бота. (*g*) Тук ли са те? **2** (*a*) Ка́звам се Джу́ли Дже́ймсън; (*b*) Ка́звам се То́ни; (*c*) Ка́звам се Боя́н Анто́нов; (*d*) Ка́зваме се Ко́линс. **3** (*a*) Как се ка́зваш? (*b*) Как се ка́звате? (*c*) Как се ка́звате? **4** Не, аз съм г-жа́/г-н _____ (Try writing out your name!) Не, аз съм в ста́я но́мер се́дем. **5** Трамва́й но́мер две, пет, шест, о́сем. Троле́й но́мер едно́, че́тири, се́дем, де́вет.

6 (*a*) Какво́ е това́? (*b*) Как е тя? (*c*) Как са те? (*d*) Какво́ е това́? (*e*) Как си? (*f*) Какво́ е това́ (*g*) Как сте? (*h*) Какво́ е това́? **7** i (*b*), ii (*d*), iii (*a*), iv (*e*), v (*c*). **8** (*a*) Това́ ли е рестора́нт „Криста́л"? Не, рестора́нт „Криста́л" е там. (*b*) Това́ ли е булева́рд Ле́вски? Не, булева́рд Ле́вски е там. (*c*) Това́ ли е Центра́лна по́ща? Не, Центра́лна по́ща е там. (*d*) Това́ ли е хоте́л „Хе́мус"? Не, хоте́л „Хе́мус" е там. (*e*) Това́ ли е у́лица Рако́вски? Не, у́лица Рако́вски е там. **9** (*a*) Не, ня́мам; (*b*) Да, и́мам; (*c*) Не, ня́мам; (*d*) Да, и́мам; (*e*) Да, и́мам. **10** (*a*) Мо́ля, къде́ и́ма рестора́нт? (*b*) Мо́ля, къде́ и́ма ба́нка? (*c*) Мо́ля, къде́ и́ма телефо́н? (*d*) Мо́ля, къде́ и́ма тоале́тна? (*e*) Мо́ля, къде́ и́ма по́ща? (*f*) Мо́ля, къде́ и́ма фи́тнес це́нтър? **11** (*a*) съм, е; (*b*) съм, е; (*c*) съм, е; (*d*) сме, са; (*e*) съм, е.

Do you understand? 1 F: Булева́рд Ви́тоша не е́ бли́зо. **2** F: Г-н Джо́нсън ня́ма ка́рта на Со́фия. **3** T. **4** F: И́ма трамва́й до булева́рд Ви́тоша. **5** T. **6** T. **7** F: Той присти́га в Бо́ровец в де́сет часа́.

Unit 3

1 Questions (*a*) Тя е от Ма́нчестър. (*b*) Тя е преводáчка. (*c*) Да, омъ́жена е. (*d*) Да, и́ма едно́ дете́. (*e*) Той е учи́тел. (*f*) Да, тя позна́ва Бълга́рия добре́. **2** (*a*) F: Г-жа́ Ко́линс е от Ма́нчестър. (*b*) F: Г-жа́ Ко́линс и́ма едно́ дете́. (*c*) T. (*d*) T. (*e*) F: Г-жа́ Ко́линс не е́ за пъ́рви път в Бълга́рия. (*f*) T.

Exercises 1 (*a*) И́мам едно́ дете́. (*b*) Омъ́жена ли сте? (*c*) Г-жа́ Ко́линс е преводáчка. (*d*) Каква́ е профе́сията Ви, госпо́жо? (*e*) За пъ́рви път ли е г-жа́ Ко́линс в Бълга́рия? (*f*) Откъде́ са г-жа́ Ко́линс и г-н Ко́линс? (*g*) Позна́вам страна́та ви добре́. **2** i (*d*), ii (*f*), iii (*a*), iv (*b*), v (*c*), vi (*g*), vii (*h*), viii (*e*). **3** (*a*) Не, не съ́м ле́карка. Каква́ сте? Секрета́рка/учи́телка съм. (*b*) Не, не съ́м бъ́лгарка. Каква́ сте? Ирла́ндка/англича́нка/ шотла́ндка съм. (*c*) Не, не съ́м сервитьо́р. Какъ́в сте? Преводáч/ле́кар/студе́нт съм. (*d*) Не, не съ́м англича́нин. Какъ́в сте? Ирла́ндец / шотла́ндец /америка́нец съм. **4** (*a*) Марк Де́йвис е журнали́ст. Той е от Са́нта Ба́рбара. Той е же́нен. (*b*) Миле́на е фотогра́фка. Тя е от Со́фия. Тя не е́ омъ́жена. (*c*) А́ндрю е студе́нт. Той е от Гла́згоу. Той не е́ же́нен. (*d*) Г-жа́ Ко́линс е преводáчка. Тя е от Ма́нчестър. Тя е омъ́жена. (*e*) На́дя е секрета́рка. Тя е от Пло́вдив. Тя не е́ омъ́жена. (*f*) Ма́йкъл Джо́нсън е бизнесме́н. Той е от Че́лмсфорд. Той е же́нен. (*g*) Г-н Анто́нов е дире́ктор. Той е от Бурга́с. Той е же́нен. (*h*) Никола́й е програми́ст. Той е от Ва́рна. Той не е́

же́нен. **5** (*a*) ът, (*b*) та, (*c*) ът, (*d*) та, (*e*) та, (*f*) ът, (*g*) ът, (*h*) ът. **6** (*a*) Ле́карят е шотла́ндец. (*b*) Учи́телят е англича́нин. (*c*) Ча́ят е ху́бав. Той е от А́нглия. **7** (*a*) Запозна́йте се - мъжъ́т ми! (*b*) Запозна́йте се - синъ́т ми! (*c*) Запозна́йте се - дъщеря́ ми! (*d*) Запозна́йте се - брат ми! (*e*) Запозна́йте се - сестра́ ми! **8** (*a*) Синъ́т ми се ка́зва А́ндрю. (*b*) Дете́то ми се ка́зва Ви́ктор. (*c*) Ма́йка ми се ка́зва Ири́на. (*d*) Жена́ ми се ка́зва Мари́я. (*e*) Дъщеря́ ми се ка́зва Си́лвия. (*f*) Баща́ ми се ка́зва Пол. **9** (*a*) Но тя е студе́на! (*b*) Но той е студе́н! (*c*) Но тя е то́пла! (*d*) Но то е то́пло! (*e*) Но тя е то́пла! (*f*) Но той е то́пъл. **10** Заповя́дайте, това́ е ви́зата ми. Заповя́дайте, това́ е резерва́цията ми. Заповя́дайте, това́ е биле́тът ми. **11** (*a*) ка́рта(та), (*b*) Че́рно море́, (*c*) Ду́нав, (*d*) Гъ́рция и Ту́рция. (*e*) Со́фия.
Do you understand? 1 T. **2** F: Миле́на е фотогра́фката на фи́рмата. **3** T. **4** T. **5** F: Никола́й и Миле́на и́мат вре́ме за кафе́.

Unit 4

1 Questions (*a*) Три писма́. (*b*) Не, той не разби́ра бъ́лгарски добре́. (*a*) Той и́ма сре́ща то́чно в двана́йсет часа́. (*d*) Сре́щата на г-н Джо́нсън е в це́нтъра. (*e*) Той и́ма пет мину́ти вре́ме. (*f*) Той е в Бълга́рия за две се́дмици. **2** (*a*) T. (*b*) T. (*c*) F: В хоте́ла и́ма англи́йски ве́стници и списа́ния. (*d*) F: Неве́на и́ма са́мо еди́н въпро́с. (*e*) F: Той е в Бълга́рия за две се́дмици. (*d*) F: Часъ́т е двана́йсет без два́йсет и пет.
Exercises 1 Автобу́сът за Мальо́вица замина́ва в шест (часа́) и три́йсет и пет (мину́ти) и присти́га в де́вет (часа́) и петна́йсет (мину́ти)./Автобу́сът за Ба́нкя замина́ва в де́сет (часа́) и де́сет (мину́ти) и присти́га в де́сет (часа́) и чети́рисет и пет (мину́ти)./Автобу́сът за Са́моков замина́ва в едина́йсет (часа́) и два́йсет (мину́ти) и присти́га в трина́йсет (часа́) и три́йсет (мину́ти)./Автобу́сът за Бо́ровец замина́ва в трина́йсет (часа́) и петдесе́т (мину́ти) и присти́га в седемна́йсет (часа́) и два́йсет и пет (мину́ти). **2** (*a*) Автобу́сът за Са́моков замина́ва след пет мину́ти. (*b*) Автобу́сът за Бо́ровец замина́ва след два́йсет мину́ти. (*c*) Автобу́сът за Мальо́вица замина́ва след де́сет мину́ти. **3** (*a*) Автобу́сът за Пло́вдив замина́ва в едина́йсет часа́ и два́йсет мину́ти. (*b*) Самоле́тът от Ло́ндон присти́га в деветна́йсет часа́ и чети́рисет мину́ти. (*c*) И́ма самоле́т за Ва́рна в де́сет часа́

и петна́йсет мину́ти. (*d*) Замина́вам за Со́фия в петна́йсет часа́ и три́йсет мину́ти (три и полови́на). (*e*) Сре́щата на г-н Джо́нсън е то́чно в двана́йсет часа́. **4** (*a*) Аз съм в Бълга́рия за двана́йсет/петна́йсет/два́йсет дни. (*b*) Аз съм в хоте́ла за три/трина́йсет но́щи. (*c*) Аз съм във Ва́рна за една́ се́дмица/две се́дмици. **5** от се́дем часа́ до два́йсет часа́ и три́йсет мину́ти; от де́вет до два́йсет и еди́н часа́; от осемна́йсет до два́йсет и три часа́; от о́сем до двана́йсет и от шестна́йсет до два́йсет часа́; от де́сет до трина́йсет и от четирина́йсет до деветна́йсет часа́. (*a*) По́щата рабо́ти от се́дем часа́ сутринта́ до о́сем и полови́на вечерта́. (*b*) Апте́ката рабо́ти от де́вет часа́ сутринта́ до де́вет часа́ вечерта́. (*c*) Рестора́нтът рабо́ти от шест до едина́йсет часа́ вечерта́. (*d*) Сладка́рницата рабо́ти от де́сет часа́ сутринта́ до еди́н часа́ на о́бед и от два часа́ следо́бед до се́дем часа́ вечерта́. **6** (*a*) Ко́лко америка́нки и́ма в хоте́ла? (*b*) За ко́лко се́дмици е г-н Джо́нсън в Бълга́рия? (*c*) След ко́лко дни присти́га брат ти? (*d*) От ко́лко дни са г-н и г-жа́ Ко́линс в Со́фия? (*e*) В ко́лко часа́ замина́ва автобу́сът? (*f*) Ко́лко писма́ и ка́ртички и́мам днес? (*g*) Ко́лко деца́ и́ма г-н Джо́нсън? **7** (*a*) На́дя пи́е кафе́ с Никола́й и Миле́на. (*b*) На́дя пи́е кафе́то с ма́лко за́хар. (*c*) Никола́й пи́е кафе́то с мно́го за́хар. (*d*) Миле́на и́ска кафе́ без за́хар. (*e*) Те оби́чат кафе́то с ма́лко мля́ко. (*f*) Аз оби́чам кафе́то ______ **8** (*a*) В кафе́то и́ма за́хар, нали́? Да, и́ма ма́лко за́хар. (*b*) В кафе́то и́ма мля́ко, нали́? Да, и́ма ма́лко мля́ко. (*c*) В ча́я и́ма мля́ко, нали́? Да, и́ма ма́лко мля́ко. **9** (*a*) В кафе́то ня́ма мля́ко, нали́? Не, ня́ма/Да, ня́ма. (*b*) В кафе́то ня́ма за́хар, нали́? Не, ня́ма/Да, ня́ма. (*c*) В ча́я ня́ма за́хар, нали́? Не, ня́ма/Да, ня́ма. **10** (*a*) две легла́; (*b*) чужденци́; (*c*) америка́нци; (*d*) бъ́лгарски ве́стници; (*e*) мно́го въпро́си; (*f*) мно́го ези́ци; (*g*) мно́го продава́чки; (*h*) трамва́и; (*i*) мно́го чужденки́. **11** (*a*) о́фисът е до рестора́нта. (*b*) Рестора́нтът е до о́фиса. (*c*) Магази́нът е до теа́търа. (*d*) Теа́търът е до магази́на. (*e*) Музе́ят е до па́рка. (*f*) Па́ркът е до музе́я.

Do you understand? 1 F: Никола́й замина́ва за А́нглия. **2** F: Той не разби́ра англи́йски. **3** F: Еди́н англича́нин от фи́рмата разби́ра ма́лко бъ́лгарски. **4** F: Фи́рмата е в Че́лмсфорд. **5** T. **6** T. **7** F: Прое́ктът с фи́рмата в А́нглия е нов. **8** F: Той замина́ва след три се́дмици.

Unit 5

1 Questions (*a*) Англича́ни и́ма в мно́го страни́ по света́. (*b*) Тя гово́ри мно́го добре́ бъ́лгарски ези́к (*c*) Г-жа́ Ко́линс е англича́нката в стя́я но́мер де́сет. (*d*) Неве́на гово́ри три ези́ка. (*e*) Тя зна́е фре́нски, ру́ски и испа́нски. (*f*) Той живе́е в Че́лмсфорд. **2** (*a*) F: Не мно́го англича́ни гово́рят бъ́лгарски. (*b*) F: Г-жа́ Ко́линс е англича́нката, коя́то живе́е в стя́я но́мер де́сет. (*c*) T. (*d*) T. (*e*) F: Тя гово́ри фре́нски на́й-добре́. (*f*) F: Мно́го бъ́лгари гово́рят чу́жди ези́ци. **Exercises 1** (*a*) Мно́го англича́ни ли и́ма в хоте́ла? (*b*) Мно́го бъ́лгари ли гово́рят англи́йски? (*c*) Бъ́лгари ли са г-н Анто́нов и Никола́й? (*d*) Бъ́лгари и англича́ни ли рабо́тят във фи́рмата? (*e*) Англича́ни ли са г-н и г-жа́ Ко́линс? **2** (*a*) дру́ги; (*b*) дру́го; (*c*) дру́га; (*d*) дру́ги; (*e*) друг; (*f*) дру́ги; (*g*) друг; (*h*) дру́го; (*i*) дру́га; (*j*) дру́ги. **3** (i) (*a*) Тук на ка́ртата и́ма два ресторáнта. Кой (рестора́нт) е по́-бли́зо? (*b*) Тук на ка́ртата и́ма два гра́да. Кой (град) е по́-бли́зо? (*c*) Тук на ка́ртата и́ма два куро́рта. Кой (куро́рт) е по́-бли́зо? (*d*) Тук на ка́ртата и́ма два къ́мпинга. Кой (къ́мпинг) е по́-бли́зо? (*e*) Тук на ка́ртата и́ма два моте́ла. Кой (моте́л) е по́-бли́зо? (ii) (*a*) На ка́ртата и́ма две апте́ки. Коя́ (апте́ка) е по́-бли́зо? (*b*) На ка́ртата и́ма две бензиноста́нции. Коя́ (бензиноста́нция) е по́-бли́зо? (*c*) На ка́ртата и́ма две спи́рки. Коя́ (спи́рка) е по́-бли́зо? **4** (*a*) Кой, (*b*) Кой, (*c*) Коя́, (*d*) Кой, (*e*) Коя́, (*f*) Кой. **5** (*a*) Ко́лко чу́жди ези́ка гово́ри Неве́на? (*b*) Ко́лко биле́та и́скат те? (*c*) Ко́лко джи́на серви́ра сервитьо́рът? (*d*) Ко́лко чу́жди ези́ка зна́е Ма́йкъл Джо́нсън? **6** (*a*) **Тури́ст:** Извине́те, и́ма ли хоте́ли до га́рата? **Гра́жданин:** Да, до га́рата и́ма ня́колко хоте́ла. (*b*) **Тури́ст:** Извине́те, и́ма ли рестора́нти до га́рата? **Гра́жданин:** Да, до га́рата и́ма ня́колко рестора́нта. (*c*) **Тури́ст:** Извине́те, и́ма ли музе́и до га́рата? **Гра́жданин:** Да, до га́рата и́ма ня́колко музе́я. (*d*) **Тури́ст** Извине́те, и́ма ли о́фиси до га́рата? **Гра́жданин** Да, до га́рата и́ма ня́колко о́фиса. **7** (*a*) мъжа́, ко́йто присти́га от Ло́ндон; жена́та, коя́то гово́ри ху́баво бъ́лгарски; англича́ни, ко́йто живе́ят в Бълга́рия; семе́йството, кое́то живе́е в стя́я но́мер де́сет. (*b*) бъ́лгарина, ко́йто замина́ва за А́нглия? англича́ни, ко́йто са же́нени за бъ́лгарки?/ ко́йто не пи́ят уи́ски? шотла́ндци, ко́йто не пи́ят уи́ски?/ко́йто са же́нени за бъ́лгарки? бъ́лгарката, коя́то е омъ́жена за англича́нин? **8** (*a*) Е́то трамва́я. Е́то два трамва́я. (*b*) Е́то троле́я. Е́то два троле́я. (*c*) Е́то автобу́са.

Éто два автобу́са. (*d*) Éто къ́мпинга. Éто два къ́мпинга. (*e*) Éто компю́търа. Éто два компю́търа. (*f*) Éто банкома́та. Éто два банкома́та. **9** (*a*) Éто биле́та ми. (*b*) Éто паспо́рта ми. (*c*) Éто мъжа́ ми. (*d*) Éто сина́ ми. (*e*) Éто бага́жа ми. **10** Извине́те, ну́ла, о́сем, о́сем, о́сем, три, две, едно́, о́сем, де́вет, едно́ ли е? Извине́те, ну́ла, о́сем, де́вет, о́сем, едно́, пет, шест, се́дем, три, две ли е? Извине́те, се́дем, о́сем, де́вет, ну́ла, две, шест, шест ли е?
Do you understand? 1 F: Никола́й у́чи англи́йски, **2** T. **3** F: Миле́на позна́ва ня́колко учи́тели по англи́йски, **4** F: Миле́на и́ма два уче́бника по англи́йски. **5** F: Никола́й и́ма ну́жда от уче́бници. **6** T. **7** F: Никола́й е на два́йсет и шест годи́ни.

Unit 6

1 Questions (*a*) Ма́йкъл Джо́нсън и́ма сре́ща с г-н Анто́нов. (*b*) Г-н Анто́нов ча́ка г-н Джо́нсън. (*c*) Не, той ня́ма пробле́ми в Со́фия. (*d*) Той и́ска да оти́де пъ́рво в ба́нката. (*e*) Ма́йкъл Джо́нсън тря́бва да обмени́ пари́. (*f*) Той тря́бва да гово́ри по́-ба́вно. **2** (*a*) F: Г-н Джо́нсън е дово́лен от хоте́ла. (*b*) T. (*c*) F: Ба́нката и рестора́нтът не са́ дале́че от о́фиса. (*d*) T. (*e*) F: Г-н Анто́нов и г-н Джо́нсън ня́мат ну́жда от преводa̋ч. (*f*) T.
Exercises 1 И́мате ли пи́нкод/паро́ла/кре́дитна ка́рта? Не. Тря́бва ли да и́мам пи́нкод/паро́ла/кре́дитна ка́рта? Да, тря́бва. **2** И́скате ли да оти́дем: (*a*) на о́пера? (*b*) на конце́рт? (*c*) на сладка́рница? (*d*) на дискоте́ка? (*e*) на теа́тър? (*f*) на екску́рзия? (*g*) на ски? (*h*) на плаж? **3** Никола́й тря́бва да оти́де в Че́лмсфорд след три се́дмици. **4** i (*g*), ii (*d*), iii (*a*), iv (*f*), v (*c*), vi (*b*), vii (*e*), viii (*a*), ix (*a*). **5** (*a*) не́я; (*b*) не́го; (*c*) тях. **6** (*a*) не́го; (*b*) не́го; (*c*) не́я; (*d*) не́го; (*e*) не́я; (*f*) не́го. **7** Ка́звам се (*your name*) И́мате ли биле́ти/писма́/пока́на/ма́са за ме́не? **8 Никола́й:** И́скам да/мо́же ли да гово́ря с Вас? **Г-н А** Съжаля́вам, но сега́ ня́мам вре́ме за те́бе. И́мам сре́ща с г-н Джо́нсън. **На́дя:** Г-н Анто́нов, и́мате ли ну́жда от ме́не? **Г-н А:** Ми́сля, че ня́маме ну́жда от преводa̋ч. Мо́же ли да напра́виш кафе́ за нас? **На́дя:** Ня́мам ни́що проти́в. **9** (*a*) юти́я, (*b*) чадъ́р, (*c*) коли́чка, (*d*) такси́, (*e*) носа́ч, (*f*) пари́. **10** (*a*) се надя́вам; (*b*) се ра́двам; (*c*) се чу́вствам добре́.
Do you understand? 1 Еди́н клие́нт и́ска да гово́ри с дире́ктора. **2** Не, не е́ свобо́ден. **3** Той тря́бва да се оба́ди по́-къ́сно следо́бед. **4** Той и́ска да оти́де на те́нис. **5** Да, На́дя и́ска да оти́де с тях.

Unit 7

1 Questions (*a*) Нáй-добрé е да отúдат на пазáра. (*b*) Плодовéте и зеленчýците на пазáра не сá éвтини, но са нáй-прéсни. (*c*) Г-жá Кóлинс не обúча тúквички. (*d*) Той úска едúн килогрáм домáти. (*e*) Тя продáва ябълки, прáскови и грóзде. (*f*) Всúчко стрýва дванáйсет лéва и осемдесéт стотúнки. **2** (*a*) F: Г-н и г-жá Кóлинс úскат Невéна да им покáже магазúн за плодовé и зеленчýци. (*b*) F: Г-н Кóлинс не úска да кýпи тúквички. (*c*) T. (*d*) T. (*e*) F: Г-жá Кóлинс не úска прáскови. (*f*) T.

Exercises 1 (*a*) плúкове, (*b*) два плúка, (*c*) два банáна, (*d*) банáни, (*e*) два пъпеша. (*f*) пъпеши, (*g*) ножóве. (*h*) няколко нóжа, (*i*) няколко български грáда (*j*) градовé **2** (*a*) Платéте на кáсата! Не пúпай! (*b*) Пазéте чистотá! Не газéте тревáта! (*c*) Бутнú! Дръпнú (*d*) Не пúпай! **3** Мóже ли да ми кáжете: (*a*) къдé úма пóща? (*b*) къдé úма бáнка? (*c*) къдé úма аптéка? (*d*) къдé úма павилиóн? **4** Мóже ли да ми покáжете: (*a*) тóзи чадър/крем? (*b*) тáзи кáрта/чáша? (*c*) товá списáние/ лекáрство? (*d*) тéзи ножóве/списáния/ крéмове/чáши? **5** (*a*) Кóлко стрýват крáставиците? Дáйте ми еднó килó крáставици. (*b*) Кóлко стрýват тúквичките? Дáйте ми еднó килó тúквички. (*c*) Кóлко стрýват ябълките? Дáйте ми еднó килó ябълки. (*d*) Кóлко стрýват прáсковите? Дáйте ми еднó килó прáскови. **6** (*a*) Да, да отúдем! (*b*) Да, да отúдем! (*c*) Да, да платúм! (*d*) Да, да се обáдим! **7** (*a*) Да, мнóго обúчам да пътýвам. (*b*) Не, не обúчам да игрáя на компютър. (*c*) Не, не обúчам да пазарýвам. (*d*) Да, мнóго обúчам да кáрам ски. (*e*) Да, мнóго обúчам да четá. **8** (*a*) Купú мляко, мóля! (*b*) Елá, мóля! (*c*) Седнú, мóля! (*d*) Вúж, мóля! (*e*) Кажú, мóля! (*f*) Дáй, мóля! **9** (*a*) Да Ви дам ли солтá? (*b*) Мóже ли да ни покáжете стáята? (*c*) Дáйте ни ключа, мóля! (*d*) Мóля, покажéте ми товá списáние! (*e*) Мóже ли да ми дадéте тóзи пъпеш? **10** (*a*) Ябълките са пó-éвтини от прáсковите, (*b*) Домáтите са пó-прéсни от тúквичките, (*c*) Пъпешът е пó-слáдък от грóздето, (*d*) Нáдя е пó-заéта от Невéна, (*e*) Крáставиците са пó-голéми от тúквичките.

Do you understand? 1 Голéмият букéт рóзи стрýва осемнáйсет лéва. **2** Лалéтата са пó-éвтини. **3** Тя úска да кýпи и нéщо за подáрък. **4** Мáлки плúкчета от осемдесéт стотúнки и пó-голéми плúкове от лев и петдесéт. **5** Тя трябва да платú осемнáйсет и петдесéт.

Unit 8

1 Questions (*a*) Г-н Джо́нсън и́ска да ви́ди меню́то. (*b*) Той предла́га шо́пската сала́та. (*c*) Тарато́р е студе́на су́па от ки́село мля́ко и кра́ставици. (*d*) Той предпочи́та то́пла су́па. (*e*) За пи́ене г-н Джо́нсън и́ска пло́дов сок. (*f*) Г-н Анто́нов и́ска да поръ́ча ча́ша ви́но. **2** (*a*) F: Шо́пската сала́та е с дома́ти, кра́ставици и си́рене. (*b*) T. (*c*) T. (*d*) F: Г-н Анто́нов и г-н Джо́нсън и́скат че́тири бе́ли хле́бчета. (*e*) T. (*f*) F: На о́бед г-н Анто́нов пи́е бя́ло ви́но.
Exercises 1 (*a*) Сервитьо́рката предла́га пи́лзенска би́ра, но аз предпочи́там бъ́лгарска. Да поръ́чаме бъ́лгарска би́ра! (*b*) Сервитьо́рката предла́га гро́здова раки́я, но аз предпочи́там сли́вова. Да поръ́чаме сли́вова раки́я! (*c*) Сервитьо́рката предла́га пи́лешка су́па, но аз предпочи́там зеленчу́кова. Да поръ́чаме зеленчу́кова су́па! **2** (*a*) предла́гате or предпочи́тате; (*b*) поръ́ча; (*c*) предпочи́тате; (*d*) предла́га/предпочи́та; (*e*) поръ́чаме; (*f*) предпочи́та; (*g*) поръ́чате. **3** В тарато́ра и́ма ки́село мля́ко, кра́ставица, че́сън, сол, о́лио и о́рехи. **4** (*a*) И́ма не́скафе и еспре́со; (*b*) И́ма че́рен чай, ме́нтов чай и би́лков чай; (*c*) И́ма пло́дова то́рта, шокола́дова то́рта и о́рехова то́рта; (*d*) И́ма портока́лов сок, гро́здов сок, я́бълков сок и сок от я́годи. **5** (*a*) две, две; (*b*) два, две; (*c*) две; (*d*) две; (*e*) два, две; (*f*) два; (*g*) два́ма; (*h*) два; (*i*) две; (*j*) два́ма; (*k*) две; (*l*) два. **6** Try the following menus – other combinations will also do: (*a*) Една́ зеленчу́кова су́па и еди́н омле́т със си́рене; (*b*) Две вегетариа́нски су́пи и два пъ́ти омле́т с шу́нка/кюфте́та; (*c*) Че́тири зеленчу́кови су́пи и че́тири пъ́ти кюфте́та/пи́ца с кашкава́л. **7** Какви́ са́ндвичи и́мате?/Два са́ндвича с шу́нка и еди́н с кашкава́л, мо́ля./Еди́н портока́лов сок, две ко́ли и три кафе́та, мо́ля. **8** (i) (*a*) две кеба́пчета; (*b*) кеба́пчетата; (ii) (*a*) две хле́бчета; (*b*) хле́бчетата; (iii) (*a*) две кюфте́та; (*b*) кюфте́тата. **9** (*a*) бя́лото ви́но; (*b*) сли́вовата раки́я; (*c*) вегетариа́нската су́па; (*d*) шокола́довата то́рта; (*e*) бъ́лгарските специалите́ти; (*f*) пи́лзенската би́ра.
10 (*a*) вегетериа́нската су́па; (*b*) пъ́лнените чу́шки; (*c*) бя́лото гро́зде; (*d*) пи́лешката су́па; (*e*) черве́ните я́бълки; (*f*) пло́довата то́рта; (*g*) бе́лите хле́бчета; (*h*) бъ́лгарското ки́село мля́ко.
Do you understand? 1 Часъ́т е о́сем и полови́на. **2** Да, о́ще е ра́но за ра́бота. **3** Не, кафе́то е отво́рено. **4** За заку́ска и́ма са́ндвичи, ки́фли и ба́нички. **5** За я́дене те и́скат два са́ндвича и две парче́та то́рта. **6** За пи́ене те и́скат две кафе́та еспре́со и два я́бълкови со́ка.

Unit 9

1 Questions (*a*) Виолéта и́ска да поръ́ча такси́ за лети́щето. (*b*) Пи́колото ще помóгне с багáжа. (*c*) Във фоайéто и́ма кýфари и чáнти на дрýги гóсти на хотéла. (*d*) Виолéта не мóже да намéри чáнтата на Марк. (*e*) Марк нóси свóята чáнта. (*f*) Чáнтата на Марк е голя́ма и чéрна. **2** (*a*) F: Виолéта и́ска да поръ́ча такси́ за дéсет и петнáйсет. (*b*) T. (*c*) T. (*d*) F: Чéрният кýфар и си́нята рáница са на Марк и Виолéта. (*e*) T.
Exercises 1 (*a*) С каквó мóга да Ви помóгна? (*b*) Гóстите от Амéрика и́мат нýжда от такси́. (*c*) Виолéта не мóже да намéри чáнтата на свóя мъж. (*d*) Товá не é мóят багáж. (*e*) Мáлката си́ня чáнта е на Марк/Мáлката чáнта на Марк е си́ня. **2** Да, мóга да/Не, не мóга да: (*a*) игрáя тéнис; (*b*) кáрам ски; (*c*) плýвам; (*d*) кáрам колá; (*e*) игрáя на кáрти. **3** Извинéте, мóжете ли да ми покáжете: (*a*) къдé е аптéката? (*b*) къдé е метрóто? (*c*) къдé е хотéл „Шéратон“? (no definite article needed with names of hotels!) (*d*) къдé е спи́рката на тролéй нóмер две? (*e*) къдé е Централна гáра? (no definite article here either.) **4** i (*e*); ii (*d*); iii (*a*); iv (*b*); v (*c*). **5** (**a**) Твóят кýфар ли е товá? Не, тóзи кýфар не é мой. Мóят кýфар е пó-голя́м. (**b**) Твóето портмонé ли е товá? Не, товá портмонé не é мóе. Мóето портмонé е пó-голя́мо. (**c**) Твóят чадъ́р ли е товá? Не, тóзи чадъ́р не é мой. Мóят чадъ́р е пó-голя́м. (**d**) Твóята пáпка ли е товá? Не, тáзи пáпка не é мóя. Мóята пáпка е пó-голя́ма. (**e**) Твóят моди́лен телефóн ли е товá? Не, тóзи моби́лен телефóн не éя́ мой. Мóят моби́лен телефóн е пó-голя́м. (**f**) Твóят моли́в ли е товá? Не, тóзи моли́в не é мой. Мóят моли́в е пó-голя́м. (**g**) Твóят белéжник ли е товá? Не, тóзи белéжник не é мой. Мóят белéжник е пó-голя́м. (**h**) Твóята химикáлка ли е товá? Не, тáзи химикáлка не é мóя. Мóята химикáлка е пó-голя́ма. **6** Портмонéто ми го ня́ма! or Чáнтата ми я ня́ма! Багáжът ми го ня́ма! Чадъ́рът ми го ня́ма! Белéжникът ми го ня́ма! Пáпката ми я ня́ма! Пари́те ми ги ня́ма! **7** (*a*) Тури́стът не мóже да намéри свóя хотéл. (*b*) Не, тури́стът не знáе и́мето му/и́мето на хотéла. (*c*) Хотéлът е бли́зо до спи́рката на тролéй нóмер еднó и тролéй нóмер пет. (*d*) До Университéта и́ма два хотéла. (*e*) Нéговият хотéл се кáзва „Сóфия Рáдисън“.
Тури́ст Извинéте, мóжете ли да ми помóгнете? Не мóга да намéря свóя хотéл. **Полицáй** Как се кáзва хотéлът Ви? **Тури́ст** За съжалéние, не знáя. Знáя сáмо, че е бли́зо до спи́рката на тролéй нóмер еднó и тролéй нóмер пет. **Полицáй** На кóя ýлица е хотéлът? **Тури́ст** Не знáя на кóя

у́лица е, но е бли́зо до Университе́та. **Полица́й** И́ма два хоте́ла бли́зо до Университе́та. Еди́ният се ка́зва „Со́фия Ра́дисън", дру́гият се ка́зва хоте́л „Бълга́рия". **Тури́ст** Ве́че зна́я и́мето на хоте́ла ми. Мо́ят хоте́л се ка́зва „Со́фия Ра́дисон". **8** (*a*) Ня́ма я; (*b*) Ня́ма го; (*c*) Ня́ма го; (*d*) Ня́ма ги; (*e*) Ня́ма я. (*f*) Ня́ма го.
Do you understand? 1 F: До г-н и г-жа́ Ко́линс и́ма свобо́дни места́. **2** T. **3** T. **4** F: Г-н и г-жа́ Ко́линс и́мат ма́лко ра́бота в Со́фия. **5** T. **6** F: Еди́н не́ин коле́га замина́ва ско́ро за А́нглия. **7** F: Те не зна́ят къде́ е Центра́лна по́ща.

Unit 10

1 Questions (*a*) Никола́й бъ́рза, защо́то тря́бва да поръ́ча такси́ и да запа́зи ма́са в рестора́нта за Ма́йкъл Джо́нсън и Боя́н Анто́нов. (*b*) Те мо́гат да чу́ят прогно́зата по ра́диото. (*c*) У́тре по висо́ките планини́ вре́мето ще бъ́де о́блачно. Възмо́жно е да вали́. (*d*) На́дя предла́га да оти́дат в Ме́лник. (*e*) В кра́я на се́дмицата вре́мето ще бъ́де ху́баво. (*f*) На́дя ще гово́ри с ше́фа. **2** (*a*) T. (*b*) F: Никола́й тря́бва да поръ́ча такси́ и да запа́зи ма́са в рестора́нта.
(*c*) T. (*d*) F: У́тре вре́мето на Ви́тоша ня́ма да бъ́де мно́го ху́баво. (*e*) F: Г-н Джо́нсън си́гурно не но́си марато́нки. (*f*) F: Ше́фът ще се съгласи́ да оти́де в Ме́лник.
Exercises 1 (*a*) У́тре ще бъ́де ли о́блачно и мра́чно? Не, у́тре ня́ма да бъ́де о́блачно и мра́чно. (*b*) У́тре ще бъ́де ли мъгли́во? Не, у́тре ня́ма да бъ́де мъгли́во. (*c*) У́тре ще бъ́де ли то́пло и слъ́нчево? Не, у́тре ня́ма да бъ́де то́пло и слъ́нчево. (*d*) У́тре ще бъ́де ли студе́но и вла́жно? Не, у́тре ня́ма да бъ́де студе́но и вла́жно. (*e*) У́тре ще бъ́де ли дъждо́вно? Не, у́тре ня́ма да бъ́де дъждо́вно. **2** (*a*) Наи́стина, мно́го е горе́що. Не съм съгла́сен/съгла́сна. Изо́бщо не е́ горе́що. (*b*) Наи́стина, мно́го е къ́сно. Не съм съгла́сен/съгла́сна. Изо́бщо не е́ къ́сно. (*c*) Наи́стина, мно́го е заба́вно. Не съм съгла́сен/съгла́сна. Изо́бщо не е́ заба́вно. (*d*) Наи́стина, мно́го е удо́бно. Не съм съгла́сен/съгла́сна. Изо́бщо не е́ удо́бно. (*e*) Наи́стина, мно́го е възмо́жно. Не съм съгла́сен/съгла́сна. Изо́бщо не е́ възмо́жно. **3** i (*d*); ii (*e*); iii (*a*); iv (*c*); v (*b*). **4** (*a*) Не, у́тре ще бъ́де я́сно и горе́що. (*b*) Не, вя́търът по Черномо́рието ще бъ́де слаб до уме́рен. (*c*) Ще бъ́де между́ два́йсет и о́сем и три́йсет и два гра́дуса. (*d*) Температу́рата на море́то ще бъ́де о́коло два́йсет и три гра́дуса. **5** Ня́ма да до́йда, защо́то ня́мам вре́ме./У́тре./Предла́гам да оти́дем

на екску́рзия. Съгла́сна ли си?/Вре́мето ще бъ́де слъ́нчево и то́пло. Добре́. И аз ще взе́ма мо́ето я́ке. **6** (*a*) Г-н Анто́нов ще се съгласи́ бъ́рзо/тру́дно. (*b*) Тру́дно/ бъ́рзо ще наме́рим га́рата. (*c*) Ш-ш-ш! Говори́ по́-ти́хо! (*d*) Тру́дно/бъ́рзо ще наме́рим бага́жа.
Do you understand? 1 T. **2** F: На Ви́тоша ви́наги е по́-студе́но. **3** F: Ме́лник е на юг. **4** T. **5** F: Миле́на не оби́ча да ста́ва ра́но. **6** T.

Unit 11

1 Questions (*a*) Г-н Анто́нов и г-н Джо́нсън трябва да напра́вят план за сле́дващата се́дмица. (*b*) Г-н Джо́нсън и́ска да оти́де в Бо́ровец, за да разгле́да хоте́лите. (*c*) Г-н Джо́нсън и г-н Анто́нов са пока́нени на изло́жба във вто́рник преди́ о́бед. (*d*) Те ще оти́дат на панаи́ра на пъ́рвия ден, за да и́мат вре́ме да разгле́дат вси́чко. (*e*) Г-н Анто́нов тря́бва да се въ́рне в Со́фия на два́йсет и вто́ри май. **2** (*a*) F: Г-н Джо́нсън и́ска да оти́де сам. (*b*) T. (*c*) F: Пре́говорите ще бъ́дат на вто́рия и тре́тия ден. (*d*) F: Г-н Анто́нов ще посре́щне делега́ция, коя́то присти́га от Япо́ния. (*e*) T.
Exercises 1 (*a*) На па́ртера и́ма пода́ръци и козме́тика. (*b*) На пъ́рвия ета́ж и́ма вси́чко за дете́то. (*c*) На вто́рия ета́ж и́ма обу́вки. (*d*) На тре́тия ета́ж и́ма тепеви́зори, компю́три, моби́лни телефо́ни. (*e*) На четвъ́ртия ета́ж и́ма кили́ми. (*f*) На пе́тия ета́ж и́ма ресторант и тоале́тна. **2** (*a*) Прода́ват марато́нки на вто́рия ета́ж. (*b*) Прода́ват парфю́ми на па́ртера. (*c*) Прода́ват компю́три на тре́тия ета́ж. (*d*) Прода́ват шампоа́ни на па́ртера. **3** (*a*) на не́го, го; (*b*) на не́я, я; (*c*) на не́го, го; (*d*) на тях, ги. **4** (*a*) съ́бота, за съ́бота; (*b*) пе́тък, в пе́тък; (*c*) сря́да, за у́тре. **5** (*a*) Еди́н прия́тен уи́кенд. (*b*) Луксо́зен автобу́с. (*c*) В хоте́л в це́нтъра на Бе́лград. (*d*) Два́йсет и о́сми апри́л; вто́ри ю́ни; четвъ́рти а́вгуст; о́сми септе́мври; трина́йсети окто́мври. (*e*) Екску́рзия до Но́ви Сад. (*f*) Бъ́лгарски ези́к. (*g*) Не. Цена́та не вклю́чва биле́ти за музе́и. **6** (*a*) В понеде́лник На́дя ще помо́гне на Никола́й с докуме́нтите. (*b*) Във вто́рник На́дя ще ка́же на ше́фа за да́тата на изло́жбата. (*c*) В сря́да На́дя ще отгово́ри на писмо́то на диза́йнера. (*d*) В четвъ́ртък На́дя ще изпра́ти пока́ни на вси́чки, които рабо́тят във фи́рмата. (*e*) В пе́тък На́дя ще се оба́ди на коле́гата в Пло́вдив. (*f*) В съ́бота На́дя ще ку́пи пода́рък на сина́ на Анто́нови. (*g*) В неде́ля На́дя ще пока́же на Миле́на но́вите плака́ти./**Dates**: Какво́ ще пра́виш на осемна́йсети, деветна́йсети, два́йсети, два́йсет и пъ́рви, два́йсет и вто́ри, два́йсет и тре́ти и два́йсет и четвъ́рти май?

Do you understand? **1** T. **2** F: Г-н и г-жá Кóлинс ще бъ̀дат във Вáрна до четвъ̀рти ю́ни. **3** T. **4** F: Джим не мóже да пътýва на двáйсет и втóри ю́ли. **5** T. **6** F: Джим тря́бва да оти́де в агéнцията в понедéлник.

Unit 12

1 Questions (*a*) Нáдя не оби́ча да чáка. (*b*) Милéна кáзва на Нáдя да не поръ̀чва óще, защóто Николáй ще дóйде след мáлко. (*c*) Спорéд Нáдя Николáй ще дóйде, защóто харéсва Милéна. (*d*) Милéна и́ска да се обáди на Николáй, за да го попи́та защó не и́два. (*e*) Да, тя и́ма моби́лен телефóн (GSM). (*f*) Николáй оби́ча да ся́да до хýбави моми́чета. **2** (*a*) F: Николáй тря́бва да дóйде след мáлко. (*b*) F: Нáдя кáзва, че Николáй ви́наги закъсня́ва. (*c*) T. (*d*) F: Милéна не оби́ча да чáка. (*e*) T.

Exercises **1** (*a*) Остави́; (*b*) остáвя; (*c*) остáвяш. **2** (*a*) ii; (*b*) i; (*c*) v; (*d*) vi; (*e*) iii; (*f*) iv. **3** (*a*) помáга; (*b*) стáваме; (*c*) и́два; (*d*) поръ̀чва. **4** И́скам да ви́дя; Ще дóйдеш; Хáйде да влéзем; Искам да сéднем; да изберéм; Мóжеш ли да ги ви́диш; поръ̀чаме; и́ска да се обáди; Ще напрáви; Искам да оти́да; за да чýя; ще запóчна. **5** Éто, тя и́два, ви́жда, вли́за. Éто ви́жда, ся́да. Éто изби́ра, поръ̀чва. Éто нóси. Éто, не чáка. Éто, плáща, стáва и оти́ва. **6** (*a*) оби́ча; (*b*) харéсва/оби́ча; (*c*) оби́ча; (*d*) харéсва; (*e*) оби́ча; (*f*) харéсате; (*g*) харéсват/оби́чат; (*h*) оби́чам; (*i*) оби́ча; (*j*) харéса; (*k*) харéсва.

Do you understand? **1** Г-н Джóнсън не тря́бва да парки́ра до табéлката, защóто хотéлът е в ремóнт и поня́кога пáдат тéжки предмéти. **2** Пáркингът е зад хотéла. **3** Полицáят предлáга мáлкия ресторáнт, защóто г-н Джóнсън ня́ма да чáка дъ̀лго там. **4** Г-н Джóнсън не мóже да сéдне на мáсата в ъ̀гъла, защóто тя е запáзена. **5** Г-н Джóнсън кáзва „Мóля, недéйте да бъ̀рзате". **6** Сервитьóрката ще помóгне на г-н Джóнсън, защóто той не разби́ра всѝчко в меню́то.

Unit 13

1 Questions (*a*) Прести́гнахме към сéдем часá. (*b*) Пътýването ни бéше прия́тно. (*c*) И́махме проблéми, защóто ня́махме кáрта на градá. (*d*) Проблéмите ни запóчнаха, когáто присти́гнахме в градá. (*e*) Не, когáто присти́гнахме, бéше óще свéтло. (*f*) Не сти́гнахме до площáда с цъ̀рквата, защóто ýлицата бéше в ремóнт. **2** (*a*) F: Г-н и г-жá Кóлинс ще кáрат напрáво и ще сти́гнат еди́н площáд, на кóйто и́ма цъ̀рква. (*b*) F: Хотéл „Одéса" е вдя́сно, срещу́ Мо́рската гради́на. (*c*) F: Г-н и г-жа́ Ко́линс присти́гнаха във Ва́рна към се́дем часа́. (*d*) T. (*e*) F: Рестора́нтът е на па́ртера вля́во.

Exercises 1 i (*e*); ii (*f*); iii (*a*); iv (*c*); v (*d*); vi (*b*). **2** (*a*) Кога́ запо́чна да вали́? (*b*) Защо́ загу́бихте пъ́тя? (*c*) Къде́ е ба́нката? (*d*) Кого́ пи́тахте къде́ е магистра́лата? (*e*) Кой ви помо́гна да наме́рите пъ́тя? (*f*) Къде́ зави́хте надя́сно? **3** (*a*) обя́двах; (*b*) ку́пи; (*c*) зами́наха; (*d*) напра́ви; (*e*) запо́чна; (*f*) попи́тахме; (*g*) пор́ъчах; (*h*) изпра́ти. **4** Вѐрнах се по съ́щата у́лица. Сти́гнах до еди́н булева́рд. Зави́х надя́сно и ка́рах напра́во. Като́ сти́гнах до площа́да, парки́рах на па́ркинга и попи́тах пак. Музе́ят не бе́ше дале́че от площа́да. **5** Вървéте напра́во по та́зи у́лица. На вто́рата у́лица зави́йте наля́во и по́сле ведна́га зави́йте надя́сно. Вървéте напра́во и ще сти́гнете до еди́н площа́д. На тре́тата у́лица вля́во зави́йте наля́во. Апте́ката е на о́коло два́йсет ме́тра вля́во. **6** Ка́рахме напра́во по та́зи у́лица. На вто́рата у́лица зави́хме наля́во и по́сле ведна́га зави́хме надя́сно. Ка́рахме напра́во и сти́гнахме до еди́н площа́д. На тре́тата у́лица вля́во зави́хме наля́во. Апте́ката бе́ше на о́коло два́йсет ме́тра вля́во.

Do you understand? (*a*) Ня́мах предста́ва от бъ́лгарската исто́рия. (*b*) В ста́рия град разгле́дах Ри́мската стена́, ста́рия теа́тър и цъ́рквата „Свети́ Константи́н и Еле́на“. (*c*) Вре́мето бе́ше прия́тно, защо́то не бе́ше мно́го горе́що. (*d*) Кога́то присти́гна гру́па англича́ни, и́мах възмо́жност да бъ́да преводa̍ч. (*e*) Англича́ните тъ́рсиха превода́ча във фоайе́то вля́во от реце́пцията. (*f*) Ще пока́жа на На́дя ка́ртички, а не сни́мки, защо́то загу́бих фо́тоапара́та си.

Unit 14

1 Questions (*a*) Кога́то се хо́ди на го́сти в Бълга́рия на домаки́нята се но́сят цветя́ или́ бонбо́ни. (*b*) Днес се празну́ва деня́т на бъ́лгарската култу́ра. (*c*) Ма́йкъл Джо́нсън не мо́же да ка́же на Са́шко „Чести́т рожде́н ден“, защо́то днес не е́ рожде́ният ден да Са́шко. (*d*) Са́шко благодари́ на Ма́йкъл Джо́нсън за шокола́да и моли́вите. (*e*) Пода́ръци се получа́ват на рожде́н ден. (*f*) Боя́н Анто́нов ще донесе́ ви́ното от ку́хнята. **2** (*a*) F: Мно́го хо́ра купу́ват цветя́ днес. (*b*) T. (*c*) T. (*d*) F: Зла́тка ще пока́ни го́стите в хо́ла. (*e*) F: Са́шко оби́ча да пома́га. (*f*) T.

Exercises 1 Поздравя́вам Ви с но́вата ра́бота. Чести́то! Поздравя́вам Ви с но́вия апартаме́нт. Чести́то! Поздравя́вам Ви със сва́тбата. Чести́то! Поздравя́вам Ви с успе́ха.

Честúто! Поздравя́вам Ви с прáзника. Честúто! Поздравя́вам ви с добрúя úзбор. Честúто! **2** (*a*) Милéна е покáнена на óпера. (*b*) Покáнен(а) съм на свáтба. (*c*) Мáйкъл Джóнсън е покáнен на излóжба. (*d*) Те са покáнени на пáрти. (*e*) Покáнени ли сте на коктéйла? **3** (*a*) Къдé се обмéня валýта? (*b*) Каквó не сé продáва на малолéтни? (*c*) Когá се прáвят резервáции? (*d*) Къдé се отúва с тóзи трамвáй? (*e*) Каквó се вúжда оттýк? (*f*) Каквó се вúжда оттýк? (Singular verb after **каквó**, remember?). **4** Видя́ ли катедрáлата „Светú Алексáндър Нéвски"? • Да, видя́х я. — Харéса ли ти? • Мнóго ми харéса. — Разглéда ли крúптата? • Да, разглéдах и нéя. Пред крúптата се продáваха икóни. Кýпих еднá мáлка икóна. — Мóже ли да я вúдя? • Разбúра се. Éто я. Харéсва ли ти? — Аз не разбúрам от икóни, но тáзи ми харéсва. **5** (*a*) Да, компáктдискът с бъ́лгарска мýзика мнóго ми харéсва. (*b*) Да, таратóрът мнóго ми харéсва. (*c*) Да, бáницата мнóго ми харéсва. (*d*) Да, тéзи цветя́ мнóго ми харéсват. (*e*) Да, бъ́лгарското вúно мнóго ми харéсва. (*f*) Да, пъ́лнените чýшки мнóго ми харéсват. (*g*) Да, бонбóните мнóго ми харéсват. (*h*) Да, шóпската салáта мнóго ми харéсва. **6** (*a*) Вчéра Мáйкъл Джóнсън и Николáй донéсоха рóзи за Злáтка Антóнова. (*b*) Вчéра Милéна донéсе едúн учéбник за Николáй. (*c*) Вчéра донéсохме брошýри от панаира в Плóвдив. (*d*) Вчéра донéсохте ли подáрък за свóите прия́тели? (*e*) Вчéра Мáйкъл Джóнсън донéсе шоколáд за Сáшко. (*f*) Вчéра г-н Антóнов и синъ́т му донéсоха две бутúлки вúно от кýхнята.

Do you understand? 1 Г-н Джóнсън úска да знáе как се купýва къ́ща в Бългáрия. 2 Съвéтът на брóкерката е Мáйкъл да отúде да вúди къ́щата с адвокáт. 3 Къ́щата, коя́то г-н Джóнсън харéсва, е блúзо до Бáнско. 4 Цветя́ се нóсят в цъ́рквата на прáзника на Светú Кúрил и Метóдий. 5 Боя́н Антóнов пожелáва на г-н Джóнсън щáстливи дни и мнóго прáзници в Бългáрия.

Unit 15

1 Questions (*a*) Милéна не úска пóвече кекс, защóто не ѝ се ядé. (*b*) Тя не сé чýвства добрé. От вчéра я болú стомáхът. (*c*) Пúе ѝ се водá./На Нáдя ѝ се пúе водá. (*d*) Мúналата годúна по товá врéме тя úмаше грип с висóка температýра. (*e*) Човéк тря́бва да се грúжи за здрáвето си. **2** (*a*) F: Милéна не úска кекс, защóто я болú стомáхът/ úма бóлки в стомáха. (*b*) F: Кéксът мнóго ѝ харéса. (*c*) T. (*d*) F: Тя ня́ма хрéма и кáшлица. (*e*) T.

Exercises **1** i (*c*); ii (*g*); iii (*e*); iv (*f*); v (*a*); vi (*b*), (*d*), (*e*); vii (*b*), (*d*), (*e*). **2** (*a*) (i) Не, не гó болят очите. (ii) Не, не я́ боли́ зъб. (iii) Не, не ги́ боля́т крака́та. (iv) Не, не гó боли́ коля́ното. (v) Не, не я́ боли́ ръка́та. (*b*) (i) Не ми́ се хóди на плаж. (ii) Не ми́ се пи́е чай. (iii) Не ми́ се говóри български. (iv) Не ми́ се у́чи. (v) Не ми́ се рабóти на компю́тър. **3** Каквó ти е?/Каквó ти ка́за ле́карят?/Спи ли ти се?/Ску́чно ли ти е?/Не сé безпокóй! Скóро ще ти ми́не. **4** Ле́карят ми ка́за, че и́мам (*a*) грип; (*b*) апендиси́т; (*c*) висóка температу́ра; (*d*) хре́ма, (*e*) хепати́т. **5** (*a*) Не можа́ да оти́де, защóто го боле́ше глава́та. (*b*) Не можа́х да я донеса́, защóто ме боле́ше кръ́стът. (*c*) Не можа́ха да го разгле́дат, защóто ги боля́ха крака́та. (*d*) Не можа́хме да го пра́тим, защóто ня́махме ма́рки. (*e*) Не можа́х да ям от тях, защóто и́мах бóлки в стома́ха. **6** (*a*) Оти́дох да си ку́пя маратóнки. (*b*) Оти́дохме да си почи́нем. (*c*) Оти́дох да си ку́пя лека́рства. (*d*) Оти́дох да посре́щна дъщеря́ си. (*e*) Оти́дох на ле́кар. (*f*) Оти́дохме да пра́тим писмó на роди́телите си.

Do you understand? **1** Мъжъ́т на г-жа́ Кóлинс не сé чу́вства добре́. **2** Той и́ма си́лно главобóлие и все му е студе́но. **3** Кóжата на г-н Кóлинс е черве́на, защóто вче́ра цял ден бе́ше на пла́жа. **4** Г-н Кóлинс тря́бваше да слóжи ша́пка. **5** Сега́ той тря́бва да стои́ на ся́нка ня́колко дни.

Unit 16

1 Questions (*a*) После́дния ден в хоте́ла плати́хме сме́тката. (*b*) Той ѝ подари́ еди́н беле́жник. (*c*) За г-жа́ Джóнсън избра́хме една́ сре́бърна гри́вна. (*d*) Да, да́дох го. (*e*) Той ще ми я пра́ти с и́мейл или́ с факс. (*f*) Це́лия ден говóрих на български. **2** (*a*) T. (*b*) T. (*c*) F: Ма́йкъл Джóнсън избра́ една́ сре́бърна гри́вна за жена́ си. (*d*) F: Той не му́ пока́за програ́мата. (*e*) F: Акó На́дя бе́ше на не́гово мя́сто, тя ня́маше да се безпокои́. (*f*) F: Боя́н Антóнов разбра́ това́, коéто и́скаше да зна́е.

Exercises **1** (*a*) Акó ня́махме ва́жна сре́ща, щя́хме да оти́дем на плаж. (*b*) Акó ня́мах дру́га ра́бота, щях да оти́да на Ви́тоша. (*c*) Акó ня́махме дру́га ра́бота, щя́хме да оти́дем на те́нис. (*d*) Акó ня́мах ва́жна сре́ща, щях да оти́да на гóсти. (*e*) Акó ня́мах дру́га ра́бота, щях да оти́да на ски. **2** Акó и́сках да ку́пя пода́рък от Бълга́рия, щя́х да ку́пя кути́я бонбóни/календа́р/плака́т/бути́лка ви́но/кни́га/кути́я с луксóзни пли́кове. **3** (*a*) Да, акó бях на твóе мя́сто, щях да прие́ма покáната. Не, акó бях на твóе мя́сто, ня́маше да прие́ма пока́ната. (*b*) Да, ако́ бях на тво́е мя́сто, щях да ку́пя цветя́. Не, ако́ бях на тво́е мя́сто, ня́маше да ку́пя цветя́. (*c*) Да, ако́ бях на тво́е мя́сто, щях да изпра́тя моми́чето. Не, ако́ бях на тво́е мя́сто, ня́маше да изпра́тя моми́чето. (*d*) Да, ако́ бях на тво́е мя́сто, щях да донеса́ пода́рък. Не, ако́ бях на тво́е мя́сто, ня́маше да донеса́ пода́рък. (*e*) Да, ако́ бях на тво́е мя́сто, щях да посре́щна америка́неца. Не, ако́ бях на тво́е мя́сто, ня́маше да посре́щна америка́неца. **4** (*a*) Неве́на да́де две ка́ртички от Ри́лския манасти́р на Марк и Виоле́та. Те и́скаха о́ще, но тя ня́маше по́вече. (*b*) Ни́е да́дохме две ка́ртички от Ри́лския манасти́р на тури́стите. Те и́скаха о́ще, но ни́е ня́махме по́вече. (*c*) Г-н и г-жа́ Ко́линс да́доха две ка́ртички от Ри́лския манасти́р на сво́я прия́тел. Той и́скаше о́ще, но те ня́маха по́вече. **5** (*a*) о́ще; (*b*) о́ще; (*c*) по́вече; (*d*) по́вече; (*e*) о́ще; (*f*) по́вече; (*g*) о́ще. **6** *You* Какво́ и́скаше да даде́ г-жа́ Анто́нова на Ма́йкъл Джо́нсън? *Your friend* Г-жа́ Анто́нова и́скаше да даде́ на Ма́йкъл Джо́нсън ма́лък пода́рък. *You* Какво́ разбра́ тя от не́го? *Your friend* Тя разбра́ от не́го, че жена́ му мно́го оби́ча криста́лни ва́зи. *You* Къде́ оти́де тя вче́ра сутринта́? *Your friend* Вче́ра сутринта́ тя оти́де в магази́н за пода́ръци. *You* Какво́ и́скаше да избере́? *Your friend* И́скаше да избере́ на́й-краси́вата криста́лна ва́за. *You* Защо́ тя не ку́пи криста́лна ва́за? *Your friend* Тя не ку́пи криста́лна ва́за, защо́то криста́лните ва́зи бя́ха ужа́сно скъ́пи. *You* Какво́ избра́ г-жа́ Анто́нова? *Your friend* Г-жа́ Анто́нова избра́ една́ краси́ва ико́на. *You* На кого́ да́де тя по́сле пода́ръка за г-жа́ Джо́нсън? *Your friend* По́сле тя да́де пода́ръка за г-жа́ Джо́нсън на Никола́й. **7** (*a*) Г-н и г-жа́ Ко́линс пи́таха къде́ и́ма магази́н за плодове́ и зеленчу́ци. (*b*) Неве́на попи́та г-н Джо́нсън дали́ и́ма/и́ма ли/свобо́дно вре́ме. (*c*) Боя́н Анто́нов попи́та кога́ Ма́йкъл Джо́нсън ще изпра́ти програ́мата. (*d*) Миле́на ка́за, че и́ма сре́ща в два часа́. (*e*) Джордж и Викто́рия ка́заха, че ще зами́нат за Ва́рна на два́йсет и о́сми май. (*f*) Ше́фът ка́за, че не и́ска по́вече кафе́.

Do you understand? **1** Ма́йкъл Джо́нсън ще изпра́ти о́ще рекла́ми. **2** Той мо́же да даде́ рекла́мите на Никола́й. **3** Миле́на разбра́ за чуде́сната възмо́жност от На́дя. **4** Ако́ бе́ше на мя́стото на Никола́й, Миле́на ведна́га ще́ше да прие́ме. **5** Тя ще́ше да му ги донесе́. **6** Никола́й предпочи́та да изпра́ти Миле́на.

Unit 17

1 Questions (*a*) Не, не е́ бо́лна. (*b*) Учу́ден съм, защо́то та́зи су́трин я видя́х от трамва́я. (*c*) Кога́то я видя́х, На́дя оти́ваше на ра́бота. (*d*) На́дя не тря́бваше да парки́ра пред бо́лницата. (*e*) Мото́рът спря́ пред бо́лницата. (*f*) Ка́зах му, че кола́та и́ма повре́да. **2** (*a*) F: Полица́ят пока́зваше на На́дя зна́ка „Спи́рането забране́но". (*b*) F: На́дя ня́маше предста́ва какво́ му е на мото́ра. (*c*) Т. (*d*) Т. (*e*) F: Не́йният позна́т наме́ри повре́дата ведна́га. (*f*) F: Кола́та ня́маше бензи́н.

Exercises 1 не **рабо́теше** добре́, в **мото́ра,** на **серви́з,** да **ка́ра** кола́та, **с** трамва́й, **и́маше** неприя́тности, **пред** бо́лницата, **повре́дата, тря́бваше, спи́рането** е забране́но, **гло́ба, и́ма** повре́да, „Спи́рането **забране́но**", **позна́т, кола́та**, ня́маше **бензи́н**. **2** (*a*) Какво́ пра́веха те? (*b*) Какво́ пра́веше той? (*c*) Какво́ пра́веше тя? (*d*) Какво́ пра́веше той? (*e*) Какво́ пра́веха те? (*f*) Какво́ пра́веха те? **3** Това́ ста́на преди́ петна́йсет мину́ти. Аз бях в хоте́ла. Ча́ках такси́. И́маше са́мо еди́н мъж. Той гово́реше по телефо́на. Той стое́ше пред хоте́ла. **4** (*a*) Преди́ аз рабо́тех в еди́н магази́н. (*b*) Преди́ две годи́ни аз рабо́тех в музе́я. (*c*) Преди́ аз рабо́тех като́ сервитьо́р. (сервитьо́рка if you are a woman!) (*d*) Аз рабо́тех като́ учи́тел(ка) преди́ мно́го годи́ни. (*e*) Преди́ рабо́тех в ба́нката. **5** (*a*) (i) и́дваше, (ii) дойде́; (*b*) (i) ка́зваше, (ii) ка́за; (*c*) (i) ку́пих. (ii) купу́вах.

Do you understand? 1 Г-жа́ Ко́линс не мо́же да спре ду́ша, защо́то кра́нът е повре́ден. **2** Той гово́реше с една́ жена́ пред вхо́да на Мо́рската гради́на. **3** Пъ́рво кра́нът на ду́ша се развали́. По́сле мъжъ́т ѝ изче́зна. **4** Кога́то го видя́ портие́рът, г-н Ко́линс купу́ваше не́що. **5** Вси́чки зна́еха къде́ е г-н Ко́линс.

Unit 18

1 Questions (*a*) Миле́на о́ще не се́ е обля́кла. (*b*) Да, приятелката на Миле́на си е оти́шла. (*c*) Никола́й предла́га да вечеря́т след представле́нието. (*d*) Представле́нието не е́ запо́чнало, защо́то е о́ще ра́но. (*e*) Никола́й е ста́нал мно́го разсе́ян. (*f*) Споре́д Миле́на Никола́й се е умори́л от мно́го у́чене. **2** (*a*) Т. (*b*) F: Ня́ма да закъсне́ят, защо́то Миле́на ве́че е реши́ла какво́ да облече́. (*c*) F: Никола́й о́ще не е́ вече́рял. (*d*) Т. (*e*) Т. (*f*) Т. (*g*) F: На Никола́й ня́ма да му еску́чно с Миле́на.

Exercises 1 (*a*) Запо́чнало ли е представле́нието? (*b*) О́ще не съм се облякла. (*c*) Ня́мам предста́ва как съм напра́вил така́ва гре́шка! (*d*) Какво́ се е слу́чило? (*e*) Ве́че съм реши́ла какво́ да облека́. **2** (*a*) Не é вя́рно, На́дя е дошла́! (*b*) Не é вя́рно, На́дя е доне́сла цветя́! (*c*) Не é вя́рно, На́дя е ку́пила бонбо́ни! (*d*) Не é вя́рно, На́дя е напра́вила кафе́! **3** (*a*) Хо́дила ли си в Бо́ровец? (*b*) Хо́дили ли сте в Бо́ровец? (*c*) Хо́дили ли сте в Бо́ровец? (*d*) Хо́дил ли си в Бо́ровец? **4** (*a*) Забра́вила съм да взе́ма чадъ̀р. Ста́нала съм мно́го разсе́яна! (*b*) Забра́вил съм да взе́ма фо́тоапара́т. Ста́нал съм мно́го разсе́ян! (*c*) Забра́вили сме да взе́мем пари́. Ста́нали сме мно́го разсе́яни! **5** (*a*) Ня́маше би́ра. Г-н Анто́нов бе́ше забра́вил да ку́пи би́ра. (*b*) Ня́маше хляб. Г-жа́ Анто́нова бе́ше забра́вила да ку́пи хляб. (*c*) Ня́маше дома́ти. Г-н и г-жа́ Ко́линс бя́ха забра́вили да ку́пят дома́ти. (*d*) Ня́маше гази́рана вода́. Аз бях забра́вил/а да ку́пя гази́рана вода́. **6** (*a*) Взех фо́тоапара́та, но сега́ го ня́ма. Си́гурно съм го загу́бил/а. (*b*) Взех ша́пката, но сега́ я ня́ма. Си́гурно съм я загу́бил/а. (*c*) Взех сни́мките, но сега́ ги ня́ма. Си́гурно съм ги загу́бил/а. (*d*) Взех беле́жника, но сега́ го ня́ма. Си́гурно съм го загу́бил/а. (*e*) Взех кни́гата, но сега́ я ня́ма. Си́гурно съм я загу́бил/а. (*f*) Взех ве́стника, но сега́ го ня́ма. Си́гурно съм го загу́бил/а.

Do you understand? **1** Джордж о́ще го боли́ глава́та. **2** На не́го му е ску́чно. **3** Тя не му́ е ка́зала досега́, че бли́зо до Балчи́к и́ма игри́ще за голф. **4** Джордж не é взел сти́ковете си. **5** Джордж ще взе́ме сти́кове под на́ем. **6** Францу́зинът от съсе́дната ста́я ве́че е игра́л голф на игри́щето.

Unit 19

1 Questions (*a*) Бизнесме́нът и́ска да смени́ ста́ята си. (*b*) Конта́ктът за самобръсна́чка не рабо́ти, прозо́рецът е счу́пен и вентила́торът в ба́нята е развале́н. (*c*) Ста́ята му е шу́мна, защо́то е то́чно над дискоте́ката. (*d*) Бизнесме́нът не мо́же да ча́ка, защо́то и́ма ва́жна сре́ща. (*e*) Дру́гите го́сти на хоте́ла се опла́кват от шума́ на трамва́ите. (*f*) Той предла́га да го сло́жат в ста́я на двана́йсетия ета́ж. **2** (*a*) F: Бизнесме́нът ка́за, че не би́л дово́лен от ста́ята, коя́то са му да́ли. (*b*) F: Прозо́рецът бил счу́пен. (*c*) T. (*d*) F: Той щял да се въ́рне към шест часа́. (*e*) T.

Exercises **1** Не съ́м дово́лен/дово́лна от: (*a*) цена́та, (*b*) продава́чката, (*c*) сервитьо́ра, (*d*) серви́за, (*e*) храна́та, (*f*) ка́чеството на сни́мките, (*g*) обслу́жването. **2** (*a*) Кюфте́то, коéто сте ми дáли, не мú харéсва. (*b*) Сýпата, коя́то сте ми дáли, не мú харéсва. (*c*) Вúното, коéто сте ми дáли, не мú харéсва. (*d*) Салáтите, който сте ми дáли, не мú харéсват. (*e*) Сладолéдът, кóйто сте ми дáли, не мú харéсва. **3** (*a*) Дáдох Ви го. Éто го. (*b*) Дáдох ви ги. Éто ги. (*c*) Дáдох ви я. Éто я. (*d*) Дáдох ви го. Éто го. (*e*) Дáдох Ви я. Éто я. **4** (*a*) Снóщи не можáх да спя от кафéто. (*b*) Снóщи не можáх да спя от главобóлие. (*c*) Снóщи не можáх да спя от горещинá. (*d*) Снóщи не можáх да спя от комáрите. (*e*) Снóщи не можáх да спя от мýзиката в ресторáнта. **5** Nadya is talking as far as „Ймало мнóго хóра на панаúра“. Then Nikolai takes over. **6** (*a*) Свáтбата билá вчéра. (*b*) Те празнýвали в ресторáнт „Москва“. (*c*) Те се запознáли в Бáнско. (*d*) Той дошъл в Сóфия на гóсти на родúтелите на Éли. (*e*) Сегá щéли да отúдат на морé.

Do you understand? 1 Нáдя тря́бва да предадé на дирéктора, че клиéнтите не билú довóлни от тя́хната рáбота. **2** Поръчали 1 200 брошýри, а полýчили сáмо 600. Пáпките úмали дефéкти, а визúтните кáртички билú на лóша хартúя. **3** Клиéнтът се обáжда за втóри път, за да се извинú. **4** Пáпките и визúтните кáртички билú порчани на дрýго мя́сто в дрýга фúрма. **5** Кáзват, че в тáзи фúрма стáвали мнóго грéшки.

Unit 20

1 Questions (*a*) Милéна покáза Централна пóща на г-н и г-жá Кóлинс. (*b*) Г-н и г-жá Кóлинс бúха úскали да дóйдат в България през зúмата. (*c*) Акó úмаха възмóжност, те бúха отúшли в Бóровец. (*d*) Милéна би úскала г-жá Кóлинс да помóгне на Николáй на Хúйтроу. (*e*) Николáй би úскал Милéна да пътýва с нéго. **2** (*a*) F: Николáй ще пътýва зáедно с г-н и г-жá Кóлинс. (*b*) F: Г-н и г-жá Кóлинс са видя́ли пóвечето забележúтелности óколо Вáрна. (*c*) T. (*d*) F: Г-н и г-жá Кóлинс ще пúшат на Милéна от Áнглия. (*e*) F: Николáй ще прáти úмейл на Милéна от Чéлмсфорд.

Exercises 1 (i) (*a*) Ще ѝ се обáдя, (*b*) Обáдих ѝ се вéче, (*c*) Вéче ѝ се обáдих; (ii) (*a*) Ще му се обáдя, (*b*) Обáдих му се вéче, (*c*) Вéче му се обáдих; (iii) (*a*) Ще им се обáдя, (*b*) Обáдих им се вéче, (*c*) Вéче им се обáдих; (iv) (*a*) Ще ѝ се обáдя, (*b*) Обáдих ѝ се вéче, (*c*) Вéче ѝ се обáдих. **2** (*a*) Бúхте ли ми кáзали Вáшия адрéс? (*b*) Бúхте ли ми се обáдили пó-късно? (*c*) Бúхте ли ни помóгнали да намéрим пътя за Вáрна? (*d*) Бúхте ли ми дáли дрýга стáя? (*e*) Бúхте ли ми поръ́чали такси́ за де́сет часа́? **3** (*a*) Ще ку́пя/Бих ку́пил, ако́ наме́ря не́що ху́баво. (*b*) Ще се оба́дя/Бих се оба́дил(а), ако́ и́мам вре́ме. (*c*) Ще до́йда/Бих дошъ́л (дошла́), ако́ се чу́вствам по́-добре́. (*d*) Ще уча́ствам/Бих уча́ствал(а), ако́ и́мам пари́. **4** (*a*) At a conference in Bulgaria. (*b*) At the beginning of the conference. (*c*) Ladies and Gentlemen, Dear Friends. (*d*) From all over the world. (*e*) They are all friends of Bulgaria. (*f*) Sofia. (*g*) He hopes their deliberations will be enjoyable and fruitful.

Do you understand? **1** На лети́щето г-н и г-жа́ Ко́линс ви́ждат Неве́на. **2** Неве́на е на лети́щето, защо́то тя изпра́ща Марк Де́йвис и жена́ му. **3** Неве́на мно́го е разка́звала на Марк за г-жа́ Ко́линс. **4** Марк щял да изпра́ти съобще́ние на г-жа́ Ко́линс за една́ конфере́нция за Бълга́рия. **5** Г-жа́ Ко́линс би уча́ствала в конфере́нцията, ако́ не е́ зае́та по съ́щото вре́ме. **6** Г-жа́ Ко́линс да́ва на Марк визи́тната си ка́ртичка.

Pronunciation and spelling

Bulgarian letters are, for the most part, constant and reliable. English letters are fickle. In English, one letter can have many sounds and the right sound depends on the letters that come before and after it. This makes English spelling and pronunciation very difficult. Compare, for example, *laughter* and *slaughter* or *bough*, *cough* and *enough*. Bulgarian letters are altogether more trustworthy and their pronunciation only rarely depends on the company they keep. One letter has basically one sound. So you can usually pronounce Bulgarian correctly by moving logically through the words and combining the sounds of the individual letters as you go. This also makes spelling relatively straightforward.

A few Bulgarian letters do, however, alter their pronunciation depending on the company they keep and also on their position in the word. This particularly affects certain consonants which we can conveniently group in pairs. In each pair one of the letters is 'voiced' (i.e. pronounced with your vocal chords vibrating) and the other is 'voiceless' (i.e. pronounced without using your vocal chords, almost as if whispering). Read these letters out loud, holding your Adam's apple between your thumb and forefinger and you'll see the difference!

Voiced	Voiceless
б	**п**
в	**ф**
г	**к**
д	**т**
ж	**ш**
з	**с**

(Additional pairs are **дж/ч** and **дз/ц**. The consonant **х**, which has no partner, is also voiceless.)

Remember particularly that:

(**a**) When a voiced consonant is the last letter in a word, you usually pronounce it as if it were its voiceless partner:

Written		**Pronounced**
хля**б**	*bread*	хля**п**
ху́ба**в**	*beautiful*	ху́ба**ф**
Бо**г**	*God*	Бо**к**
мла**д**	*young*	мла**т**
мъ**ж**	*man*	мъ**ш**
вле**з**!	*come in*	вле**с**!

(Did you notice ху́ба**в** (ху́ба**ф**) and мла**д** (мла**т**) when you listened to the alphabet on the recording? And you will remember how Victoria Collins has to spell her name in Bulgarian: **Ко́линс**.) (See p. xvii.)

(**b**) When **б**, **в**, **г**, **д**, **ж** or **з** come before a voiceless consonant, they too become voiceless: а**вт**обу́с (а**фт**обу́с) *bus*, **вкъщи** (**фкъщи**) *at home*, командиро́**вк**а (командиро́**фк**а) *business trip*, ирла́н**дк**а (ирла́н**тк**а) *Irishwoman*, дъ**жд** (дъ**шт**) *rain*, и́**зх**о**д** (и́**сх**о**т**) *exit*.

(**c**) Bulgarian vowels are all single syllables and pure sounds, unlike the English vowels which begin on one sound and end on another (diphthongs). In Bulgarian, such sounds are formed by placing the vowels **а**, **е**, **и**, **о** or **у** before or after the letter **й**, which is itself not a vowel and fulfils the function of the English '*y*' (as in *yes*, *soya* or *York*): ха́**й**де! *come on!*; здраве́**й**! *hello!*; **й**о́га *yoga*.

(**d**) Bulgarians do tend to speak fast and the faster they speak the further they depart from 'standard' pronunciation. Listen, for example, how the letter '**о**', when unstressed, particularly when coming after a stressed syllable, is pronounced more like the letter '**у**', as in Ви́т**о**ша and бли́з**о** (pronounced Ви́т**у**ша and бли́з**у**). Similarly, the letter '**а**', especially when coming after or before a stressed syllable, gets 'reduced' to '**ъ**', as in ма́с**а**, ч**а**со́вник and р**а**зби́р**а** се (pronounced ч**ъ**со́вник and р**ъ**зби́р**ъ** се).

(**e**) The letter **ь** is only found after consonants and in combination with the letter **о**: шофьо́р *driver*.

(**f**) The diphthong **йо/йе** is only found after a vowel: фоа**й**е́ *foyer* or at the beginning of a word: **Й**орк *York*.

Numerals

Cardinals

0 ну́ла
1 едно́ (еди́н, една́)
2 две (два)
3 три
4 че́тири
5 пет
6 шест
7 се́дем
8 о́сем
9 де́вет
10 де́сет
11 едина́йсет
12 двана́йсет
13 трина́йсет
14 четирина́йсет
15 петна́йсет
16 шестна́йсет
17 седемна́йсет
18 осемна́йсет
19 деветна́йсет
20 два́йсет (два́десет)
21 два́йсет и едно́
22 два́йсет и две
23 два́йсет и три
24 два́йсет и че́тири
25 два́йсет и пет
26 два́йсет и шест
27 два́йсет и се́дем
28 два́йсет и о́сем
29 два́йсет и де́вет
30 три́йсет (три́десет)
40 чети́рисет (чети́ридесет)
50 петдесе́т
60 шейсе́т (шестдесе́т)
70 седемдесе́т
80 осемдесе́т
90 деветдесе́т
100 сто
101 сто и едно́ (еди́н, една́)
110 сто и де́сет
123 сто два́йсет и три
200 две́ста
300 три́ста
400 че́тиристотин
500 пе́тстотин

Numbers of four digits and more are separated by a space where English uses a comma.

1 000 хиля́да
2 000 две хи́ляди
3 000 три хи́ляди
1 000 000 еди́н милио́н
2 000 000 два милио́на

Ordinals

1st пъ́рви
2nd вто́ри
3rd тре́ти
4th четвъ́рти
5th пе́ти
6th ше́сти
7th се́дми
8th о́сми
9th деве́ти
10th десе́ти
11th едина́йсети
21st два́йсет и пъ́рви
22nd два́йсет и вто́ри

Grammatical terms

1 Prepositions

Spatial prepositions

Location (*Where?*)

в	*in*
върху́	*on top of*
до	*next to*
зад	*behind*
между́	*between*
на	*on, at*
над	*above*
под	*under*
пред	*in front of*
срещу́	*opposite*
у	*at, with*

Movement (*Where to/from?*, etc.)

към	*to(wards)*
о́коло	*(a)round*
от	*from; out of*
по	*on; along*
през	*through*
след	*after*

Bulgarian prepositions and their English equivalents

без	*without*	без прево́да́ч
	to	часъ́т е три без пет
в (във)	*in*	в Пло́вдив
	to	(оти́вам) в ба́нката, в Ме́лник
	at	(рабо́тя) във фи́рма Тра́нсПрое́кт, в двана́йсет часа́, в моме́нта
	on	в сря́да
до	*next to*	хоте́лът е до ба́нката
	to	(сти́гам) до площа́да, екску́рзия до Ви́тоша
	until	до четвъ́рти ю́ни
	till	до къ́сно
за	*for*	писмо́ за Вас, магази́н за плодове́, за две се́дмици, (замина́вам) за А́нглия
	about	(гово́ря) за англича́нката
	to	пъ́тят за Ва́рна
	—	(пи́там) за пътя
към	*towards*	(оти́вам) към Мо́рската гради́на
	around	към шест часа́
	—	молба́ към Вас

на	*on*	на ка́ртата, на па́ртера, на почи́вка, на у́лица Рако́вски, на Ви́тоша, на петна́йсети май
	at	на ма́сата, на лети́щето, на светофа́ра
	of	ка́рта на Со́фия, ча́нтата на Марк
	in	на юг; на англи́йски ези́к
	to	(оти́вам) на море́, на о́пера
	for	(да ку́пя) пода́рък на сина́ на Анто́нови
о́коло	*around*	о́коло града́
	about	о́коло пет часа́
от	*from*	писмо́ от Ло́ндон
	(made) of	су́па от зеленчу́ци
	with	дово́лен съм от хоте́ла
	since	в Со́фия съм от четвъ́рти май
	—	и́мам ну́жда от преводáч
по	*on*	по ра́диото, по телефо́на
	over	по висо́ките планини́
	along	по пъ́тя, по Черномо́рието
под	*under*	под ма́сата
	—	(да взе́ма) кола́ под на́ем
преди́	*before*	преди́ о́бед
	ago	преди́ две се́дмици
през	*through*	през града́
	in/during	през зи́мата, през ме́сец май
	at	през нощта́
проти́в	*against*	проти́в не́го
с (със)	*with*	сре́ща с не́го, с удово́лствие
	on	(поздравя́вам) с пра́зника
	—	(да запозна́я) с г-н Анто́нов

след	*after*	след тéбе, след рáбота
	in	след две сéдмици
у	*at*	у нас
	with	кни́гата е у нéя
чрез	*through*	
	by means of	чрез нéя
	via	

Gender	Indefinite singular	Indefinite plural	Definite singular	Definite plural
Masculine				
consonant	хотéл	хотéли	хотéлът	хотéлите
	вéстник	вéстници	вéстникът	вéстниците
	лéкар	лéкари	лéкарят	лéкарите
	учи́тел	учи́тели	учи́телят	учи́телите
-й	музéй	музéи	музéят	музéите
one syllable	ключ	клю́чове	клю́чът	клю́човете
	NB Plural after numbers: хотéла вéстника музéя клю́ча		NB Non-subject definite: хотéла вéстника лéкаря учи́теля музéя клю́ча	
Feminine				
-а	женá	жени́	женáта	жени́те
-я	стáя	стáи	стáята	стáите
consonant	вéчер	вéчери	вечертá	вéчерите
	нарóдност	нарóдности	народносттá	нарóдностите
	нощ	нóщи	нощтá	нóщите
	прóлет	прóлети	пролеттá	прóлетите
	сýтрин	сýтрини	сутринтá	сýтрините
Neuter				
-о	писмó	писмá	писмóто	писмáта
-е	кафé	кафéта	кафéто	кафéтата
-ие	списáние	списáния	списáнието	списáнията
-и	такси́	такси́та	такси́то	такси́тата
-ю	меню́	меню́та	меню́то	меню́тата

2 Nouns

Some irregular plurals

Masculine	**Feminine**	**Neuter**
брат-брáтя		
бъ̀лгарин-бъ̀лгари	ръкá-ръцé	детé-децá
господи́н-господá		и́ме-именá
гост-гóсти		окó-очи́
ден-дни		ухó-уши́
крак-краká		
мъж-мъжé		

3 Adjectives and adverbs

	Masculine	Feminine	Neuter	Plural
without loss of vowel				
Indefinite	висо́к	висо́ка	висо́ко	висо́ки
	син	си́ня	си́ньо	си́ни
Definite	висо́кият	висо́ката	висо́кото	висо́ките
	си́ният	си́нята	си́ньото	си́ните
with loss of vowel				
Indefinite	добъ́р	добра́	добро́	добри́
	прия́тен	прия́тна	прия́тно	прия́тни
Definite	добри́ят	добра́та	добро́то	добри́те
	прия́тният	прия́тната	прия́тното	прия́тните
ending in -ски				
Indefinite	български	българска	българско	български
Definite	българският	българската	българското	българските

Comparison of adjectives

добъ́р	*good*	по́-добъ́р	*better*	на́й-добъ́р	*best*

Comparison of adverbs

бъ́рзо	*quickly*	по́-бъ́рзо	*quicker*	на́й-бъ́рзо	*quickest*
добре́	*well*	по́-добре́	*better*	на́й-добре́	*best*
ма́лко	*little*	по́-ма́лко	*less*	на́й-ма́лко	*least*
мно́го	*much*	по́вече	*more*	на́й-мно́го	*most*

4 Pronouns

Subject form	Object form Full	Object form Short	Indirect object form Full	Indirect object form Short
аз	ме́не	ме	на ме́не	ми
ти	те́бе	те	на те́бе	ти
той	не́го	го	на не́го	му
тя	не́я	я	на не́я	ѝ
то	не́го	го	на не́го	му
ни́е	нас	ни	на нас	ни
*ви́е	*вас	*ви	на *вас	*ви
те	тях	ги	на тях	им

(*When the polite form for *you* is used referring to a single person, then you must use a capital letter in writing. This also applies to the possessives.)

Subject form		Possessive adjectival forms Masculine	Feminine	Neuter	Plural
аз	indefinite	мой	мо́я	мо́е	мо́и
	definite	мо́ят	мо́ята	мо́ето	мо́ите
ти	indefinite	твой	тво́я	тво́е	тво́и
	definite	тво́ят	тво́ята	тво́ето	тво́ите
той	indefinite	не́гов	не́гова	не́гово	не́гови
	definite	не́говият	не́говата	не́говото	не́говите
тя	indefinite	не́ин	не́йна	не́йно	не́йни
	definite	не́йният	не́йната	не́йното	не́йните
то	indefinite	не́гов	не́гова	не́гово	не́гови
	definite	не́говият	не́говата	не́говото	не́говите
ни́е	indefinite	наш	на́ша	на́ше	на́ши
	definite	на́шият	на́шата	на́шето	на́шите
ви́е	indefinite	ваш	ва́ша	ва́ше	ва́ши
	definite	ва́шият	ва́шата	ва́шето	ва́шите
те	indefinite	те́хен	тя́хна	тя́хно	те́хни
	definite	те́хният	тя́хната	тя́хното	те́хните
		own			
той тя то те	indefinite definite	свой сво́ят	сво́я сво́ята	сво́е сво́ето	сво́и сво́ите

Definiteness and possession

(*a*) Short forms (noun + definite article + short indirect object pronoun)
(*b*) Full forms (possessive adjective + definite article + noun)

Singular Short		Full	Plural Short		full
ле́карят ми	=	мо́ят ле́кар	ку́фарите ми	=	мо́ите ку́фари
ста́ята ми	=	мо́ята ста́я	ча́нтите ми	=	мо́ите ча́нти
дете́то ми	=	мо́ето дете́	деца́та ми	=	мо́ите деца́

Other pronouns

	Persons					Things
	Subject form				Object form	
	Masc.	Fem.	Neuter	Plural		
Demonstrative pronouns	то́зи	та́зи	това́	те́зи		това́
Questions (interrogative pronouns)	кой какъв	коя́ каква́	кое́ какво́	кой какви́	кого́	какво́
Relative pronouns	ко́йто какъ́вто	коя́то каква́то	кое́то какво́то	ко́йто какви́то	кого́то	какво́то
Indefinite pronouns	ня́кой	ня́коя	ня́кое	ня́кои	ня́кого	не́що
Negative pronouns	ни́кой	ни́коя	ни́кое	ни́кои	ни́кого	ни́що
Generalizing pronouns	все́ки	вся́ка	вся́ко	вси́чки	все́киго	вси́чко

Other question words and their relative equivalents

защо́?	*why?*	защо́то	*because*
как?	*how?*	ка́кто	*as*
кога́?	*when?*	кога́то	(the time) *when*
къде́?	*where?*	къде́то	(the place) *where*

5 Verbs

съм *to be*

Present		**Future** **Positive**	**Negative**
аз	съм	ще съм/бъ́да	ня́ма да съм/бъ́да
ти	си	ще си/бъ́деш	ня́ма да си/бъ́деш
той тя то	е	ще е/бъ́де	ня́ма да е/бъ́де
ни́е	сме	ще сме/бъ́дем	ня́ма да сме/бъ́дем
ви́е	сте	ще сте/бъ́дете	ня́ма да сте/бъ́дете
те	са	ще са/бъ́дат	ня́ма да са/бъ́дат

Past		**Present perfect**
аз	бях	бил съм/била́ съм/било́ съм
ти	бе́ше	бил си/била́ си/било́ си

той / тя / то	бéше	бил е / билá е / билó е
нúе	бя́хме	билú сме
вúе	бя́хте	билú сте
те	бя́ха	билú са

Future in the past

	Positive	Negative
аз	щях да съм/бъ́да	ня́маше да съм/бъ́да
ти	щéше да си/бъ́деш	ня́маше да си/бъ́деш
той / тя / то	щéше да е/бъ́де	ня́маше да е/бъ́де
нúе	щя́хме да сме/бъ́дем	ня́маше да сме/бъ́дем
вúе	шя́хте да сте/бъ́дете	ня́маше да сте/бъ́дете
те	щя́ха да са/бъ́дат	ня́маше да са/бъ́дат

Present tense

	e-pattern (1st Conjugation)	и-pattern (2nd Conjugation)	a-pattern (3rd Conjugation)
аз	пúша	рабóтя	úмам
ти	пúшеш	рабóтиш	úмаш
той / тя / то	пúше	рабóти	úма
нúе	пúшем	рабóтим	úмаме
вúе	пúшете	рабóтите	úмате
те	пúшат	рабóтят	úмат

Imperative (commands)

	Positive (Perfective and imperfective) Singular	Plural	Negative (Imperfective) Singular	Plural
e-pattern			**a-pattern**	
(да) сéдна	седнú! *sit down*	седнéте!	не ся́дай! недéй да ся́даш	не ся́дайте! недéйте да ся́дате
и-pattern				
платя́	платú! *pay*	платéте!	не плáщай! недéй да плáщаш	не плáщайте! недéйте да плáщате

a-pattern				
ча́кам	ча́кай! *wait*	ча́кайте!	не ча́кай! неде́й да ча́каш	не ча́кайте! неде́йте да ча́кате
Verbs with two vowels				
пи́я	пий! *drink*	пи́йте!	не пий! неде́й да пи́еш	не пи́йте! неде́йте да пи́ете
Irregular				
(да) ви́дя	виж! *look*	ви́жте!	не гле́дай! неде́й да гле́даш	не гле́дайте! неде́йте да гле́дате
(да) вля́за	влез! *go/come in*	вле́зте!	не вли́зай! неде́й да вли́заш	не вли́зайте! неде́йте да вли́зате
(да) до́йда	ела́! *come*	ела́те!	не и́два! неде́й да и́дваш	не и́двайте! неде́йте да и́двате
(да) държа́	дръж! *hold*	дръ́жте!	не дръж! неде́й да държи́ш	не дръ́жте! неде́йте да държи́те
(да) изля́за	изле́з! *go out*	изле́зте!	не изли́зай! неде́й да изли́заш	не изли́зайте! неде́йте да изли́зате
(да) (от)и́да	(от) иди́! *go*	(от) иде́те!	не оти́вай! неде́й да оти́ваш	не оти́вайте! неде́йте да оти́вате
(да) ям	яж! *eat*	я́жте!	не яж! неде́й да яде́ш	не я́жте! неде́йте да яде́те

Past tense (personal endings*)

	Past				**Past imperfect**			
аз	-ах	-ях**	-их	-ох	-ех	-ах	-ях	-я́х
ти	-а	-я	-и	-е	-еше	-аше	-яше	-е́ше
той / тя / то	-а	-я	-и	-е	-еше	-аше	-яше	-е́ше
ни́е	-ахме	-яхме	-ихме	-охме	-ехме	-ахме	-яхме	-я́хме
ви́е	-ахте	-яхте	-ихте	-охте	-ехте	-ахте	-яхте	-я́хте
те	-аха	-яха	-иха	-оха	-еха	-аха	-яха	-я́ха

(*For the main conjugation patterns in the past see Verb Tables 1 and 2.)
(**With and without stress.)

Table 1 Ordinary past tense

Here are the main verb patterns of the ordinary past tense (+ past participles derived from them), arranged according to features 1–8 below. The verbs are mostly perfective. Imperfective verbs in the table are indicated with *.

1 Verbs ending in two vowels.
2 Verbs with **д/т**, **з/с** and **к** before the ending.
3 Verbs with **-на** before the ending.
4 Verbs with **ш** or **ж** before the ending change them to **с** and **з** in the past.
5 Verbs with **-бер-/-пер-** lose the **е** in the past.
6 Irregular verbs.
7 Verbs *without* stress on the final syllable in the past.
8 Verbs *with* stress on the final syllable in the past.

Present	Past	Past participle			
		Masculine	Feminine	Neuter	Plural
e-pattern					
1 *живéя *live*	живя́х	живя́л	живя́ла	живя́ло	живéли
*пи́я *drink*	пих	пил	пи́ла	пи́ло	пи́ли
2 вля́за *go in*	вля́зох	вля́зъл	вля́зла	вля́зло	влéзли
дам *give*	дáдох	дал	дáла	дáло	дáли
донесá *bring*	донéсох	донéсъл	донéсла	донéсло	донéсли
оти́да *go*	оти́дох	оти́шъл	оти́шла	оти́шло	оти́шли
облекá *get dressed*	облякох	обля́къл	обля́кла	обля́кло	облéкли
3 запóчна *begin*	запóчнах	запóчнал	запóчнала	запóчнало	запóчнали
4 *пи́ша *write*	пи́сах	пи́сал	пи́сала	пи́сало	пи́сали
кáжа *say*	кáзах	кáзал	кáзала	кáзало	кáзали
5 разберá *understand*	разбрáх	разбрáл	разбрáла	разбрáло	разбрáли
6 взéма *take*	взех	взел	взéла	взéло	взéли
*мóга *can*	можáх	могъ́л	моглá	моглó	могли́
спра *stop*	спрях	спрял	спря́ла	спря́ло	спрéли
и-pattern					
7 *рабóтя *work*	рабóтих	рабóтил	рабóтила	рабóтило	рабóтили
*у́ча *study*	у́чих	у́чил	у́чила	у́чило	у́чили
8 ви́дя *see*	видя́х	видя́л	видя́ла	видя́ло	видéли
*стоя́ *stand*	стоя́х	стоя́л	стоя́ла	стоя́ло	стоéли
a-pattern					
*вечéрям *have supper*	вечéрях	вечéрял	вечéряла	вечéряло	вечéряли
*кáзвам *say*	кáзвах	кáзвал	кáзвала	кáзвало	кáзвали

Table 2 Past imperfect

Main patterns of past imperfect + past participles derived from them.

The past imperfect endings depend on stress and not on the conjugation pattern (see Past endings above). Table 2 contains all the imperfective (starred) verbs from Table 1 together with the imperfective twins of the perfective verbs found there. Here the verbs are organized differently, for the conjugation patterns of the perfective and imperfective twins are often not the same. Most imperfectives, you will see, are 3rd Conjugation.

Present	**Past imperfect**	**Past participle**			
		Masculine	**Feminine**	**Neuter**	**Plural**
е-pattern					
живе́я *live*	живе́ех	живе́ел	живе́ела	живе́ело	живе́ели
пи́ша *write*	пи́шех	пи́шел	пи́шела	пи́шело	пи́шели
пи́я *drink*	пи́ех	пи́ел	пи́ела	пи́ело	пи́ели
мо́га *can*	мо́жех	мо́жел	мо́жела	мо́жело	мо́жели
и-pattern					
но́ся *carry*	но́сех	но́сел	но́села	но́село	но́сели
рабо́тя *work*	рабо́тех	рабо́тел	рабо́тела	рабо́тело	рабо́тели
у́ча *study*	у́чех	у́чел	у́чела	у́чело	у́чели
стоя́ *stand*	стоя́х	стоя́л	стоя́ла	стоя́ло	стое́ли
а-pattern					
взи́мам *take*	взи́мах	взи́мал	взи́мала	взи́мало	взи́мали
ви́ждам *see*	ви́ждах	ви́ждал	ви́ждала	ви́ждало	ви́ждали
вли́зам *go in*	вли́зах	вли́зал	вли́зала	вли́зало	вли́зали
да́вам *give*	да́вах	да́вал	да́вала	да́вало	да́вали
запо́чвам *begin*	запо́чвах	запо́чвал	запо́чвала	запо́чвало	запо́чвали
и́мам *have*	и́мах	и́мал	и́мала	и́мало	и́мали
ка́звам *say*	ка́звах	ка́звал	ка́звала	ка́звало	ка́звали
обли́чам *get dressed*	обли́чах	обли́чал	обли́чала	обли́чало	обли́чали
оти́вам *go*	оти́вах	оти́вал	оти́вала	оти́вало	оти́вали
разби́рам *understand*	разби́рах	разби́рал	разби́рала	разби́рало	разби́рали
спи́рам *stop*	спи́рах	спи́рал	спи́рала	спи́рало	спи́рали
вече́рям *have supper*	вече́рях	вече́рял	вече́ряла	вече́ряло	вече́ряли

Table 3 Tense forms with the past participle

Present perfect *(I have had supper)*	**Past perfect** *(I had had supper)*	**Conditional** *(I would have had supper, if...)*
аз съм вечéрял(а)	бях вечéрял(а)	бих вечéрял(а), акó...
ти си вечéрял(а)	бéше вечéрял(а)	би вечéрял(а), акó...
той е вечéрял	бéше вечéрял	би вечéрял, акó...
тя е вечéряла	бéше вечéряла	би вечéряла, акó...
то е вечéряло	бéше вечéряло	би вечéряло, акó...
нíе сме вечéряли	бя́хме вечéряли	бúхме вечéряли, акó...
вúе сте вечéряли	бя́хте вечéряли	бúхте вечéряли, акó...
те са вечéряли	бя́ха вечéряли	бúха вечéряли, акó...

Table 4 Renarrated forms (3rd person only)

Tenses	**Statements**	**Renarrated forms** Кáзват, че... *(They say that...)*
Present	той пúше тя пúше то пúше те пúшат	той пúшел* тя пúшела то пúшело те пúшели
Past Imperfect	той пúшеше тя пúшеше то пúшеше те пúшеха	
Past	той пúса тя пúса то пúса те пúсаха	той пúсал** тя пúсала то пúсало те пúсали
Future	той ще пúше тя ще пúше то ще пúше те ще пúшат	той щял да пúше (ня́мало да пúше) тя щя́ла да пúше (ня́мало да пúше) то щя́ло да пúше (ня́мало да пúше) те щéли да пúшат) (ня́мало да пúшат)

(* See Table 2 for past participles (mainly imperfective).)
(**See Table 1 for past participles (mainly perfective).)

Table 5 Passive participles

Endings and verb group (Present)	Past form	Passive participle			
		Masculine	Feminine	Neuter	Plural
-ен **и**-pattern **е**-pattern verbs with:					
т/д	да́дох	да́ден (*given*)	да́дена	да́дено	да́дени
с/з	доне́сох	доне́сен (*brought*)	доне́сена	доне́сено	доне́сени
к	обля́кох*	обле́чен (*dressed*)	обле́чена	обле́чено	обле́чени
-ан **а**-pattern **е**-pattern verbs with:	заплану́вах	заплану́ван (*planned*)	заплану́вана	заплану́вано	заплану́вани
-ая	игра́х	игра́н (*played*)	игра́на	игра́но	игра́ни
ш/ж	пи́сах	пи́сан (*written*)	пи́сана	пи́сано	пи́сани
	ка́зах	ка́зан (*said*)	ка́зана	ка́зано	ка́зани
-бер/пер	разбра́х	разбра́н (*understood*)	разбра́на	разбра́но	разбра́ни
-ян **е**-pattern verbs with: **-ея**	живя́х	живя́н (*lived*)	живя́на	живя́но	живе́ни
и-pattern verbs with: stressed ending	видя́х	видя́н (*seen*)	видя́на	видя́но	виде́ни
-т **е**-pattern verbs in: **-ия, -ея**	изпи́х	изпи́т (*drunk*)	изпи́та	изпи́то	изпи́ти
	изпя́х	изпя́т (*sung*)	изпя́та	изпя́то	изпя́ти
-на-	запо́чнах	запо́чнат (*begun*)	запо́чната	запо́чнато	запо́чнати
-ема	взех	взет (*taken*)	взе́та	взе́то	взе́ти

(*2nd person **ти обле́че**).

Passive forms

Reflexive

Вентила́торът се развали́.	*The fan broke down.*
Тарато́рът се серви́ра студе́н.	*Tarator is served cold.*
Биле́тите се прода́доха бъ́рзо.	*The tickets sold out quickly.*

Resultative

Вентила́торът е развале́н.	*The fan is broken.*
Тарато́рът е серви́ран.	*The tarator has been served.*
Биле́тите са прода́дени.	*The tickets have been sold.*

6 Word order

With subject noun or pronoun

Subject	Negative	Unstressed† (pronoun, *to be*, reflexive)	Main part of verb phrase	Object(s)
Аз	(не)		позна́вам	Ива́н
Аз	(не)	го	позна́вам	
Ни́е	(не)	се	позна́ваме	
Ива́н	(не)	е	добре́	
Ни́е	(не)	сме	англича́ни	
Кафе́то	(не)	ми	харе́сва	
На́дя	(не)		да́де	ча́нтата на Ива́н
Тя	(не)	я	да́де	на Ива́н
Тя	(не)	му	да́де	ча́нтата
Тя	(не)	му я	да́де	
На́дя	(не)	се	оба́ди	на Никола́й
Тя	(не)	му се	оба́ди	
Аз	(не)	съм	напра́вил(а)	кафе́
Аз	(не)	съм го	напра́вил(а)	
Ти	(не)	си го	напра́вил(а)	
Той	(не)	*го е	напра́вил	
Тя	(не)	*го е	напра́вила	
Ни́е	(не)	сме го	напра́вили	
Ви́е	(не)	сте го	напра́вили	
Те	(не)	са го	напра́вили	
Аз	(не)	съм се	обля́къл(-кла)	
Ти	(не)	си се	обля́къл(-кла)	
Той	(не)	*се е	обля́къл	
Тя	(не)	*се е	обля́кла	
Ни́е	(не)	сме се	обле́кли	
Ви́е	(не)	сте се	обле́кли	
Те	(не)	са се	обле́кли	

(†Stressed if after **не**.)

(*Note that *to be* changes places in the 3rd person singular.)

Without subject noun or pronoun

Other	Negative	Unstressed† (pronouns, *to be*, reflexive)	Main part of verb phrase	Unstressed (pronouns, *to be*, reflexive)	Object
	(Не)		Познáвам		Ивáн
			Познáвам	го	
	Не	го	познáвам		
			Познáваме	се	
	Не	се	познáваме		
			Добрé	е	
	Не	е	добрé		
Мнóго		е	добрé		
			Англичáни	сме	
	Не	сме	англичáни		
			Харéсва	ми	
	Не	ми	харéсва		
Мнóго		ми	харéсва		
			Прия́тно	ми е	
	Не	ми е	прия́тно		
Мнóго		ми е	прия́тно		
На мéне	(не)	ми е	прия́тно		
			Дáде		чáнтата на Ивáн
			Дáде	му	чáнтата
			Дáде	му я	
	Не	му я	дáде		
			Обáдих	се	на Ивáн
	Не	се	обáдих		на Нáдя
	Не	й се	обáдих		
Вчéра		се	обáдих		на Ивáн
Вчéра	(не)	му се	обáдих		
			Напрáвил(а)	съм	кафé
	Не	съм	напрáвил(а)		кафé
Вéче		съм го	напрáвил(а)		
			Облякъл(-кла)	съм	се
	Не	съм се	облякъл(-кла)		
Вéче		съм се	облякъл(-кла)		

(†Stressed if after **не**.)

Bulgarian–English vocabulary

In this Vocabulary you should be able to find all the words used in this book with the meanings they have in the book. Occasionally, when a word has another very common meaning not used in the book, you will find the additional meaning.

The words are listed in a way that will be useful to you. The verbs, for example, show the *I* form followed by the final three letters of the *you* singular form. (Occasionally, with very short verbs, we have given the full *you* singular form.) All perfective verbs are preceded by (да). Where nouns have awkward plurals, the abbreviation (pl) is used and you will find either the last few letters — usually the last three — or the full plural form. The adjectives are listed in the masculine singular, but where the feminine, neuter and plural forms lose the letter **e**, we give you the last three letters of the feminine form too. Where a word has an odd gender, feminine nouns ending in consonants, for example, we give you the gender. The letter (f) means the word is feminine; the letter (n) that it is neuter.

Phrases are shown either under the most important word or according to the first word in the phrase.

Some words you will find in the Appendix rather than in the Vocabulary. You should look for most of the numerals, for example, and the different verb and pronoun forms, in the Appendix. The Appendix is really an addition to the Vocabulary, so use the two together.

а *but*
áвгуст *August*
áвиокомпáния *airline*
автобýс *bus*
агéнция *agency*
адвокáт *lawyer, attorney*
администрáтор(ка) *receptionist*
адрéс *address*
аз *I*
акó *if*
алéргия *allergy*
алкохóл *alcohol*
áло(?) *hello* (on the phone)
Амéрика *America*
американéц (pl) **-нци** *an American*
америкáнка *American woman*
америкáнски *American*
ами́ сегá *and now what*
амфитеáтър *amphitheatre*
англи́йски *English*
англичáнин (pl) **-áни** *Englishman*
англичáнка *English woman*
Áнглия *England*

антибио́тик *an antibiotic*
апартаме́нт *flat, apartment*
апендиси́т *apendicitis*
апри́л *April*
апте́ка *chemist's, pharmacy*
асансьо́р *lift, elevator*
аспири́н *aspirin*
а-ха́ *a-ha*

ба́ба *grandmother*
ба́вно *slowly*
бага́ж *luggage, baggage*
бага́жник (pl) **-ици** *boot/trunk*
балка́нски *Balkan* (adj)
бана́н *banana*
ба́ница *cheese pasty*
ба́ничка *cheese roll*
ба́нка *bank*
банкно́та *banknote*
банкома́т *cashpoint, ATM*
ба́ня *bathroom*
бар *bar*
бащá *father*
без *without; less; to* (telling time)
безпокоя́, -ои́ш *to worry, trouble*
безпокоя́, -ои́ш се *be anxious, to worry*
беле́жник (pl) **-ици** *diary, notebook*
бензи́н *petrol, gas*
бензиноста́нция *petrol/gas station*
бидо́нче *small (petrol, gas) can*
би́знес *business*
бизнесме́н *businessman*
биле́т *ticket*
би́лка *herb*
би́лков (made with) *herb*(*s*)
би́ра *beer*
благодаря́ *thank you*
благодаря́, -ри́ш *to thank*
бли́зо *near*
блок *block*
блу́за *blouse*
Бог *God*
(сла́ва) Бо́гу *thank heavens*
бо́лен, -лна *ill, sick*
боли́ (*it* form) *it hurts*
бо́лка *pain*
бо́лница *hospital*
бонбо́н (chocolate) *sweet, candy*
брат (pl) **бра́тя** *brother*
братовче́д(ка) *cousin*
брой (pl) **бро́еве** *number; copy*
бро́кер(ка) *(real) estate agent*
брошу́ра *brochure*
буке́т *bunch*
булева́рд *boulevard*
бути́лка *bottle*
бутни́ *push*
бъдеще *future*
българин (pl) **българи** *a Bulgarian*
Бълга́рия *Bulgaria*
българка *Bulgarian woman*
български *Bulgarian*
бързам, -заш *to be in a hurry*
бързо *quickly, fast*
бюро́ *agency, office*
бял (pl) **бе́ли** *white*

в/във *in; at; to; on*
в ремо́нт *under repair, reconstruction*
в такъв слу́чай *in that case*
ва́жен, -жна *important*
ва́жно (е) *(it's) important*
ва́за *vase*
вали́ *it's raining*
валу́та *(hard) currency*
ва́рненски *Varna* (adj)
ваш, Ваш *your*(*s*)
вдя́сно *on the right*
вегетариа́нски *vegetarian*
една́га *immediately*
ведн́ъж *once*
Вели́кден *Easter*
вентила́тор *extractor fan*
ве́сел *merry, happy*
ве́стник (pl) **-ици** *newspaper*
ветрови́то *windy*
ве́че *already*
ве́чер (f) *evening*
вечертá *in the evening*
вече́ря *dinner, supper*
вече́рям, -ряш *to have supper/ dinner*
(да) взе́ма, -меш *to take*
взимам, -маш *to take*
ви́део *video*
(да) ви́дя, -диш *to see*
ви́е or **Ви́е** *you*
ви́ждам, -даш *to see*
ви́за *visa*
визи́тна ка́ртичка *business card*
ви́лица *fork*
вина́ *fault*
ви́наги *always*
ви́но *wine*
висо́к *high, tall*

включвам, -ваш *to include*
вку́сен, -сна *nice* (to eat), *delicious*
вкъ́щи *at home/*(go) *home*
вла́жен, -жна *damp*
вли́зам, -заш *to go in*
вля́во *on the left*
(да) вля́за, вле́зеш *to go in*
вме́сто *instead of*
внима́вам, -ваш *to watch out*
внима́ние! *danger! watch out!; attention!*
вода́ *water*
во́дка *vodka*
врата́ *door*
вре́ме (pl) **времена́** *time*
вре́ме *weather*
все *all the time*
все едно́/пак *all the same*
все́ки, вся́ка *each*
вси́чки *everybody*
вси́чко *all*
вто́рник *Tuesday*
вход *entrance*
вче́ра *yesterday*
въ́здух *air*
възмо́жно (е) *(it's) possible, likely*
възмо́жност (f) *possibility, opportunity*
въпро́с *question*
вървя́, -ви́ш *to walk*
(да) въ́рна, -неш *to return, give back*
(да) се въ́рна, -неш *to return, go back*
върху́ *on top of*
вя́рвам, -ваш *to believe*
вя́рно (е) *(it's) true*
вя́тър (pl) **ветрове́** *wind*

гази́ран *fizzy, sparkling*
гази́рана вода́ *soda water*
гале́рия *gallery*
га́ра *railway station*
гара́ж *garage*
гардеро́б *cloakroom; wardrobe*
г-жа́ = госпожа́ *Mrs*
глава́ *head*
главобо́лие *headache*
гла́ден, -дна *hungry*
гле́дам, -даш *to look*
гло́ба *fine*
г-н = господи́н *Mr*
говоря́, -ри́ш *to speak, talk*
годи́на *year*
големина́ *size*
голф *golf*
голя́м (pl) **голе́ми** *big*
го́ре-до́лу *so-so (*lit. *up and down)*
горещина́ *heat*
горе́що (е) *(it's) hot*
господи́н (pl) **-да́** *Mr*
госпожа́ *Mrs*
госпо́жица *Miss*
гост (pl) **го́сти** *guest, resident*
гото́в *ready*
гото́во (е) *(it's) ready, done, there you go!*
град (pl) **градове́** *town, city*
гради́на *garden, park*
гра́дус *degree*
градче́ *little town*
гра́жданин (pl) **-ани** *citizen*
грам *gram*
гра́ница *border*
гре́шка *mistake*
гри́вна *bracelet*
гри́жа, -жиш се *to look after, worry about*
грип *flu*
гро́зде *grapes*
гро́здов (made with) *grapes*
гру́па *group*
гъ́рло *throat*
Гъ́рция *Greece*

да *yes; to*
да́вам, -ваш *to give*
да́же *even*
дале́че *far*
дали́ *whether, if*
(да) дам, даде́ш *to give*
да́ми и господа́ *ladies and gentlemen*
да́мски *women's*
да́та *date*
два́ма (ду́ши) *two (people)*
двое́н, двойна *double*
дворе́ц (pl) **дворци́** *palace*
деке́мври *December*
делега́ция *delegation*
ден, деня́т (pl) **дни** *day*
дете́ (pl) **деца́** *child*
дефе́кт *defect, flaw*
джиесе́м *mobile phone*
джин *gin*
джоб *pocket*
ди́види *DVD*
дие́та *diet*

дизáйнер *designer*
дирéктор *director*
дискотéка *disco*
днес *today*
до *next to; until, till; to*
добрé *well; OK, fine*
добрé дошъ́л, -шлá, -шли́! *welcome!*
добрé завáрил! lit. *well met!* (response to добрé дошъ́л!)
добъ́р, -брá *good*
дóбър ден! *good morning/afternoon!*
добъ́р път! *have a good/safe journey!*
дови́ждане! *goodbye!*
довóлен, -лна (от) *happy* (with)
(да) дóйда, -деш *to come*
докатó *while*
дóктор *doctor*
докумéнт *document; paper*
дóлар *dollar*
домаки́н *host*
домаки́ня *hostess, lady of the house*
домáт *tomato*
(да) донесá, -сéш *to bring*
дори́ *even*
досегá *until now*
дóста *quite, pretty (very)*
дочу́ване *goodbye* (on the phone)
дошъ́л: добрé дошъ́л! *welcome!*
друг *another; other*
дру́го? *anything else?*
дръпни́ *pull*
ду́ма *word*
Ду́нав *Danube*
(двáма) ду́ши *two people*
душ *shower*
дъжд (pl) **дъждовé** *rain*
дъждóвно (е) (*it's*) *rainy*
дъ́лъг, дъ́лга *long*
дъ́нки *jeans*
държá, -жи́ш *to hold*
дъщеря́ *daughter*
дя́до *grandfather*

е! *well!; really!*
éвро *euro*
Еврóпа *Europe*
éвтин *cheap*
ези́к (pl) **ези́ци** *language, tongue*
екску́рзия *outing, excursion*
екскурзовóд *guide*
éсен (f) *autumn, fall*
еспрéсо *espresso*
етáж *floor*
éто *here is*

Ж *ladies (toilet)*
жáлко *it's a pity*
женá *woman; wife*
жéнен *married*
живéя, -éеш *to live*
живóт *life*
жу́ри *jury*
журнали́ст *journalist*

за *for; to; at; about*
за да *(in order) to*
забáвен, -вна *amusing*
забáвно (е) (it's) *fun, amusing*
забележи́телност (f) *sight, tourist attraction*
(да) заболи́ (*it* form) *begins to hurt*
(да) забрáвя, -виш *to forget*
забранéно *prohibited*
(да) зави́я, -и́еш *to turn*
загу́бен *lost*
(да) загу́бя, -биш *to lose*
зад *behind*
зáедно *together*
заéт *busy, engaged*
заку́ска *breakfast, snack*
закъснéние *delay*
(да) закъснéя, -éеш *to be late*
закъсня́вам, -ваш *to be late*
зáла *hall*
(да) зами́на, -неш *to leave*
заминáвам, -ваш *to leave*
заминáване *departure*
заминáващ за *leaving for, travelling to*
(на) зáпад *(to the) west*
запáзен *reserved; preserved*
(да) запáзя, -зиш *to reserve, book*
(да) запáли (*it* form) *to start* (car)
(да) заплану́вам, -ваш *to plan*
заплану́ван *planned*
заповя́дай(те)! *here you are, there you go; welcome*
запознáвам, -ваш се *to get to know one another*
запознáйте се! *meet ...*
(да) запознáя, -áеш *to introduce*
(да) се запознáя, -áеш *to get to know one another*

(да) запо́мня, -ниш *to remember*
запо́чвам, -ваш *to begin*
(да) запо́чна, -неш *to begin*
(да) се зара́двам, -ваш *to be pleased*
засега́ *for now*
(да) се засме́я, -е́еш *to begin to laugh*
затва́рям, -ряш *to close*
затво́рен *closed*
(да) затво́ря, -риш *to close*
затова́ *that's why*
за́хар (f) *sugar*
защо́ *why*
защо́то *because*
здра́ве *health*
здраве́й(те)! *hello! hi!*
зеленчу́к (pl) **-у́ци** *vegetable*
зеленчу́ков (made with) *vegetable(s)*
зи́ма *winter*
Зла́тни пя́съци *Golden Sands*
зле *poorly*
знак (pl) **зна́ци** *sign*
значе́ние *significance, meaning*
зна́чи *so, that means, that is to say*
зна́я, -а́еш *to know*
зъб (pl) **зъ́би** *tooth*
зъболе́кар(ка) *dentist*

и *and, too, as well*
игра́я, -а́еш *to play*
игри́ще за голф *golf course*
(да) и́да see **(да) оти́да**
и́двам, -ваш *to come*
иде́я *idea*
(да) избера́, -ре́ш *to choose*
изби́рам, -раш *to choose*
извине́те! *excuse/pardon me!*
(да) се извиня́, -ни́ш *to apologize*
извиня́вай(те)! *excuse/forgive me!*
извъ́н *outside*
и́зглед *view*
изгле́ждам, -даш *to look*
изго́ден, -дна *favourable*
(да) изка́рам, -раш *to spend (time)*
изка́рвам, -ваш *to spend (time)*
изка́рване, прия́тно *~ have a pleasant stay*
изключи́телен, -лна *exceptional*
изли́зам, -заш *to go out, leave*
изло́жба *exhibition*
(да) изля́за, -ле́зеш *to go out, leave*
изнена́да *surprise*
изо́бщо *at all*
изо́бщо не е́... *it's not at all...*
(да) изпе́я, -е́еш *to sing*
(да) изпи́я, -и́еш *to drink*
(да) изпра́тя, -тиш *to accompany, to see off; to send*
изпра́щам, -щаш *to accompany, to see off; to send*
(на) и́зток *(to the) east*
и́зточен, -чна *(from/to the) east*
и́зход *exit; gate*
(да) изче́зна, -неш *to disappear*
ико́на *icon*
или́ *or*
и́ма (*it* form) *there is, are*
и́мам, -маш *to have*
и́ме (pl) **имена́** *name*
и́мейл *email*
интервю́ *interview*
интере́сен, -сна *interesting*
и́нтернет *internet*
информа́ция *information (desk)*
ирла́ндец (pl) **-дци** *Irishman*
Ирла́ндия *Ireland*
ирла́ндка *Irishwoman*
и́скам, -каш *to want*
испа́нец (pl) **-нци** *Spaniard*
испа́нка *Spanish woman*
испа́нски *Spanish*
исто́рия *history*
италиа́нец (pl) **-нци** *an Italian*
италиа́нка *Italian woman*
италиа́нски *Italian*

(да) ка́жа, -жеш *to say*
ка́звам, -ваш *to say*
ка́звам, -ваш се *my (your) name is*
каже́те? *can I help you?* (lit. *say!*)
как *how*
какво́ *what*
ка́кто *as*
какъ́в, каква́ *what (kind of)*
календа́р *calendar, diary*
камерие́рка *chambermaid*
капучи́но *capuccino*
ка́рам, -раш *to drive*
ка́рам, -раш ски *to ski*
ка́рта *map; card*
(кре́дитна) ка́рта *credit card*
(бо́рдна) ка́рта *boarding card/pass*
ка́ртичка (*post*) *card*
ка́са *checkout; ticket office; till*

касиéрка *cashier, checkout operator*
катедрáла *cathedral*
катó *as; when; like*
кафé *coffee; café*
кáчество *quality*
кашкавáл (*yellow*) *cheese*
кáшлица *cough*
кашóн *cardboard box*
кебáпче *'kebapche' sausage*
кекс (*sponge*) *cake*
килúм *carpet, rug*
килогрáм *kilogram*
кúсело мляко *yoghurt*
китáйски (adj) *Chinese*
кúфла *bun*
класúчески *classical*
клиéнт(ка) *customer*
климатúк *air conditioner*
клуб *club*
ключ *key*
кнúга *book*
когá(то) *when*
кóжа *skin*
козмéтика *cosmetics*
кой, коя̀, коé, кои́ *who*
кóйто, коя̀то, коéто, коúто (the one) *who*
коктéйл *cocktail party*
(кóка-)кóла *coke*
колá *car*
колéга *colleague*
Кóледа *Christmas*
колúчка *trolley, shopping cart*
кóлко *how many, how much*
коля̀но (pl) **коленá** *knee*
командирóвка *business trip*
комáр *mosquito*
комбинáция *combination*
компáктдиск (pl) **-кове** *CD*
компю́тър (pl) **-три** *computer*
контáкт *contact; socket*
конфéкция *ready-made clothes*
конферéнция *conference*
концéрт *concert*
коня̀к *brandy*
кóраб(че) *(small) boat*
коридóр *corridor*
край (pl) **крáища** *end*
крак (pl) **крака́** *foot; leg*
кран *tap*
красúв *beautiful*
крáставица *cucumber*
крéдит *loan, credit*
крéдитна кáрта *credit card*
крем *cream*
крéпостен, -тна *fortification* (adj)
крúпта *crypt*
кристáлен, -лна *crystal*
кроасáн *croissant*
кръст *(small of the) back; cross*
ксéрокс *photocopier, xerox*
култýра *culture*
купýвам, -ваш *to buy*
(да) кýпя, -пиш *to buy*
курóрт *resort, spa*
кутúя *box*
кýфар *suitcase*
кýхня *kitchen*
къдé(то) *where*
към *about; around; towards; to*
къмпинг *campsite*
късно *late*
къща *house*
кюфтé *meatball*

лалé *tulip*
лéв(че) *lev*
леглó *bed*
лек *light* (adj)
лéка нощ! *good night!*
лéкар(ка) *doctor*
лекáрство *medicine*
летúще *airport*
ли (question word)
лимóн *lemon*
лимонáда *lemonade*
лимóнов (made with) *lemon*
(англúйска) лúра *pound sterling*
литератýра *literature*
лúтър (pl) **лúтри** *litre*
лифт *(ski/chair) lift*
лóндонски *London* (adj)
лондончáнин (pl) **-áни** *Londoner*
лош *bad*
луксóзен, -зна *deluxe*
ля̀то *summer*

М *gents (toilet, washroom)*
магазúн *shop, store*
магистрáла *motorway, freeway*
май *May*
мáйка *mother*
мáйстор *workman; master*
Македóния *Macedonia*
мáлко *a little*
малолéтен, -тна *juvenile, young*
мáлък, мáлка *small*
мáма *mum, mother*

манастѝр *monastery*
маратóнки *trainers, athletic shoes*
мáрка *(postage) stamp*
март *March*
маршрýтка *minibus (taxi)*
мáса *table*
материáли *materials*
мач *match*
машѝна *machine*
междý *between*
междунарóден, -дна *international*
мéнта *(pepper)mint*
мéнтов (made with) *mint*
меню́ *menu*
мерсѝ *thank you*
мéсец *month*
метрó *metro, underground, subway*
мéтър (pl) **мéтри** *metre*
механá *tavern*
мил *dear, sweet, kind*
(да) мѝна, -неш *to go, pass* (of time)
(ще ми) мѝне *I'll be OK*
мѝнал *past*
минерáлна водá *mineral water*
минýта *minute*
мѝсля, -лиш *to think*
млад *young*
мля́ко *milk*
мнóго *a lot, much, many*
мóга, мóжеш *I can, am able*
модéрен, -рна *modern, fashionable, up-to-date*
мóже *it is possible*
мóже би *maybe*
мóже ли? *may I?, could you?*
мой *my, mine*
молбá *request*
молѝв *pencil*
мóля *please; I beg your pardon; don't mention it*
момéнт *moment*
монéта *coin*
момѝче (n) *girl*
момчé (n) *boy*
морé *sea*
мóрски (of the) *sea, marine*
мотéл *motel*
мотóр *engine*
мрáчен, -чна *dull*
музéй *museum*
мýзика *music*
музикáнт *musician*
мъглѝво *foggy*
мъж (pl) **мъжé** *man; husband*
мъ̀жки *man's*
мя́сто (pl) **местá** *place*

на *on; of; at; in; to; for*
наблѝзо *nearby*
наврéме *in/on time*
нався́къде *everywhere*
навъ̀н *outside*
над *above*
надя́вам, -ваш се *to hope*
надя́сно *to the right*
наздрáве! *cheers!*
(под) нáем *hired*
(да) наéма, -меш *to rent, hire*
наистина *really, indeed*
нáй-пóсле *at last*
(да) накáрам, -раш *to make* (someone do something)
налѝ? *isn't that so?*
наля́во *to the left*
(да) намéря, -риш *to find*
наóколо *nearby*
напѝтка *drink*
напрáво *straight ahead*
(да) напрáвя, -виш *to make; to do*
напрéдвам, -ваш *to make progress*
нарéд *in order*
наредéн *arranged*
(да) наредя́, -дѝш *to arrange*
нарóден, -дна *national*
нарóдност (f) *nationality*
натурáлен, -лна *natural, pure*
(да) наýча, -чиш *to learn*
национáлен, -лна *national*
нáция *nation*
начáло *beginning*
наш *our(s)*
не *no, not*
невя́рно *false*
нéгов *his*
недéй! *don't!*
недéля *Sunday*
нéин *her(s)*
нéмец (pl) **нéмци** *a German*
немкѝня *German woman*
нéмски *German*
непрекъ̀снато *all the time*
непремéнно *certainly; don't fail to*
неприя́тно *unpleasant*
неприя́тност (f) *unpleasantness, trouble*
непушáч *non-smoker*

не́рвен, не́рвна *agitated, stressed out*
не́с(кафе) *instant* (*coffee*)
с нетърпе́ние *eagerly*
не́що *something*
не́що дру́го *some/anything else*
не́що за пи́ене *something to drink*
не́що за я́дене *something to eat*
ни́е *we*
ни́кой *nobody*
ни́сък, -ска *short* (stature)
ни́то..., ни́то... *neither, nor...*
ни́що *nothing; no matter; never mind*
ни́що чу́дно *(that's) hardly surprising*
но *but*
нов *new*
Но́ва годи́на *New Year*
новина́ *news* (item)
нож (pl) **ножо́ве** *knife*
ное́мври *November*
но́мер *number*
норма́лно *normally; OK*
korса́ч *porter*
но́ся, -сиш *to carry, have with one, bring, take*
нощ (f) *night*
(ле́ка) нощ! *good night!*
ну́жда *need*
ну́ла *zero, nought*
ня́как *somehow*
ня́какъв, ня́каква *some kind of*
ня́кога *sometime*
ня́кой *somebody, some*
ня́колко *some, a few*
ня́къде *somewhere*
ня́ма *there isn't*
ня́ма защо́ *you're welcome, don't mention it*
ня́мам, -маш *not to have*

(да) се оба́дя, -диш *to ring, phone, call*
оба́ждам, -даш се *to ring, phone, call*
о́бед and **обя́д** *lunch (time), noon*
обикнове́но *usually*
оби́чам, -чаш *to love, like*
о́блачно *cloudy*
(да) се облека́, -че́ш *to get dressed*
обме́нно бюро́ *bureau de change, currency exchange office*
(да) обменя́, -ни́ш *to change*
обмя́на на валу́та *currency exchange*
обра́тен, -тна *opposite; reverse*
обслу́жване *service* (e.g. in a restaurant)
обу́вки *shoes, footwear*
обя́д see **о́бед**
обя́двам, -ваш *to have lunch*
(да) обясня́, -ни́ш *to explain*
огледа́ло *mirror*
(да) оже́ня, -ниш *to marry off*
(да) се оже́ня, -ниш *to get married*
ока́за се *it turned out*
око́ (pl) **очи́** *eye*
о́коло *about, around*
окто́мври *October*
о́леле! *oh dear me!*
о́лио *vegetable oil*
омле́т *omelette*
омъ́жена *married* (for a woman)
о́нзи *that*
опа́сен, -сна *dangerous*
о́пера *opera*
о́пит *practice, experience*
(да) опи́там, -таш *to try*
опи́твам, -ваш *to try*
о́питен, -тна *experienced*
опла́квам, -ваш се *to complain*
опла́кване (pl) **-ния** *complaint*
(да) се опла́ча, -чеш *to complain*
(да) се опра́вя, -виш *to get better*
организи́ра се (*it* form) *is organized*
организи́рам, -раш *to organize*
о́рех(ов) (made with) *walnut(s)*
ориента́лски *oriental*
осве́н *apart from, besides*
осо́бено *especially*
(ни́що) осо́бено *nothing special*
оста́ва(т) *is/are left*
(да) оста́вя, -виш *to leave*
оста́вям, -вяш *to leave*
от *from; (because) of; than; made of; with; since; out of*
от ня́колко дни *(for) the past few days*
отво́рен *open*
отгова́рям, -ряш *to answer*
(да) отгово́ря, -риш *to answer*
отда́вна *long since, long ago*
отдале́че *from afar*
оти́вам, -ваш *to go*

(да) оти́да, -деш *to go (there)*
отклоне́ние *diversion*
отко́лкото *than*
откъде́ *where from*
отли́чно! *excellent!*
отпа́дък (pl) **отпа́дъци** *litter, rubbish*
отту́к *from here*
о́фис *office*
о́ще *more; still; even; yet*
о́ще веднъ́ж *once again*
о́ще не *not yet*

павилио́н *kiosk*
па́дам, -даш *to fall*
па́дащи предме́ти *falling objects*
(да) па́дна, -неш *to fall*
паза́р *market*
пазару́вам, -ваш *to do the shopping*
па́зя, -зиш *to keep, preserve*
пак *again*
панаи́р *fair*
па́пка *folder, file*
пари́ (pl) *money*
парк *park; garden*
па́ркинг *car park, parking lot*
парки́рам, -раш *to park*
Парламе́нт *Parliament*
паро́ла *password*
па́ртер *ground floor*
па́рти *party*
парфю́м *perfume*
парче́ *piece*
паспо́рт *passport*
(брита́нски) па́унд *pound sterling*
пе́тък *Friday*
(не́що за) пи́ене *something to drink*
пи́во *beer, ale*
пи́коло *bellboy*
пи́лзенска би́ра *Pilsner (beer)*
пи́лешки (made with) *chicken*
пи́нкод *PIN (code)*
пи́пам, -паш *to touch*
писа́лка *pen*
писмо́ *letter*
пи́там, -таш *to ask*
пи́ца *pizza*
пицари́я *pizzeria*
пи́ша, -шеш *to write*
пи́я, пи́еш *to drink*
плаж *beach*
плака́т *poster, placard*
план *plan*
планина́ *mountain(s)*
(да) платя́, -ти́ш *to pay*
пла́щам, -щаш *to pay*
плик *envelope; (plastic) bag*
пли́кче *small (plastic) bag, envelope*
плод (pl) **плодове́** *fruit*
пло́дов (made of) *fruit*
плодотво́рен, -рна *fruitful*
площа́д *square*
плу́вам, -ваш *to swim*
по *along; over; on*
по́вече *more*
по́вечето *most of*
повре́да *fault*
повре́ден *out of order*
под *under*
пода́рък (pl) **-ъци** *present*
(да) подаря́, -ри́ш *to give*
подходя́щ *suitable*
пожела́вам, -ваш *to wish*
(да) пожела́я, -а́еш *to wish*
(с) по́здрав *kind regards*
поздравле́ния! *congratulations!*
(да) поздравя́, -ви́ш *to welcome, greet; congratulate*
поздравя́вам, -ваш *to welcome, greet; congratulate*
позна́вам, -ваш *to know* (someone, one another)
позна́т(а) *acquaintance*
(да) пока́жа, -жеш *to show, point*
пока́звам, -ваш *to show, point*
пока́на *invitation*
пока́нен *invited*
(да) пока́ня, -ниш *to invite*
поле́зен, -зна *useful*
по́лет *flight*
полица́й *policeman*
поли́ция *police*
полови́н *half*
полови́на *a half*
(да) полу́ча, -чиш *to receive*
получа́вам, -ваш *to receive*
пома́гам, -гаш *to help*
(да) поми́сля, -лиш *to think over*
(да) помо́гна, -неш *to help*
по́мня, -ниш *to remember*
по́мощ (f) *help, assistance*
понеде́лник *Monday*
поня́когa *sometimes*
(да) попи́там, -таш *to ask*
(да) попра́вя, -виш *to mend*

портиéр *doorman*
портмонé *purse, (hand)bag*
портокáл(ов) (made with) *orange(s)*
(да) порѣчам, -чаш *to order*
порѣчвам, -ваш *to order*
порѣчка *order*
пóсле *after that, then*
послéден, -дна *final, last*
посóка *direction*
(да) посрéщна, -неш *to meet*
пóстер *poster*
(да) почáкам, -каш *to wait a little*
почи́вам, -ваш си *to be resting*
почи́вка *rest, break, holiday, vacation*
(да) си почи́на, -неш *to have a rest*
почти́ *almost*
пóща *post office*
прав *right*
прáвя, -виш *to do; to make*
прáзник (pl) **-ици** *festival, holiday*
празну́вам, -ваш *to celebrate*
прáскова *peach*
(да) прáтя, -тиш *to send*
(да) преведá, -дéш *to translate*
прéвод *translation*
преводáч(ка) *translator; interpreter*
прéговори (pl) *negotiations; talks*
пред *in front of*
(да) предáм, -дадéш *to leave/pass on/a message*
преди́ *before; ago*
предлáгам, -гаш *to suggest, make an offer, propose*
(да) предлóжа, -жиш *to suggest; make an offer*
предполáгам, -гаш *to suppose*
предпочи́там, -таш *to prefer*
предстáва *idea*
представлéние *performance*
през *during; through; in; at*
(да) пренесá, -сéш *to take* (somewhere)
препорѣчвам, -ваш *to recommend*
(да) пресекá, -ечéш *to cross*
прéсен, прясна, прéсни *fresh*
престóй (duration of) *stay*
(да) придружá, -жи́ш *to accompany*
(да) приéма, -меш *to accept*
при́нтер *printer*
прести́гам, -гаш *to arrive*
прести́гащ *arriving*
(да) прести́гна, -неш *to arrive*
прия́тел(ка) *friend*
прия́телски *friendly*
прия́тен, -тна *pleasant*
прия́тен път! *have a pleasant journey!*
прия́тно изкáрване! *have a nice time!/pleasant stay*
проблéм *problem*
прови́нция *the country outside the capital*
прогнóза *forecast*
прогрáма *program(me)*
програми́ст *(computer) programmer*
прогрéс *progress*
продáвам, -ваш *to sell*
продавáч(ка) *shop assistant, sales person*
продáден *sold*
проду́кт *product*
продължáвам, -ваш *to continue*
прозóрец (pl) **-рци** *window*
проéкт *project*
прóлет (f) *spring*
прóсто *simply*
проти́в *against*
профéсия *occupation*
прови́нция *the country (outside) the capital*
пу́ша, -шиш *to smoke*
пушáч *smoker*
пу́шене *smoking*
пѣлен, -лна с *full of*
пѣлнени чу́шки *stuffed peppers*
пѣпеш *melon*
пѣрво *firstly*
път (pl) **пѣти** *time*
път (pl) **пѣтища** *road, way*
пѣтник (pl) **-ици** *passenger, traveller*
пъту́вам, -ваш *to travel*
пъту́ване *journey*

рáбота *work*
рабóтник (pl) **-ици** *worker*
рабóтно врéме *opening hours*
рабóтя, -тиш *to work*
рáдвам, -ваш се *to enjoy, be glad*
рáдио *radio*
рáдостен, -тна *joyous, glad*
(да) разберá, -рéш *to understand*

разбúра се *of course*
разбúрам, -раш *to understand*
развалéн *broken, not working*
(да) разваля́, -ли́ш *to break* (something)
(да) се разваля́, -ли́ш *to go wrong; to break down*
развéден *divorced*
(да) разглéдам, -даш *to look at/around*
разглéждам, -даш *to look at/round*
рáзговор *conversation*
разкáзвам, -ваш *to tell*
разписáние *timetable*
разсéян *absent-minded*
разхóдка *trip, walk*
(да) се разхóдя, -диш *to have a walk*
ракúя *rakiya, brandy*
рáница *rucksack, backpack*
рáно *early*
резервáция *reservation*
рекá *river*
реклáма *publicity* (adj)
реклáмен, -мна *publicity, advertisement*
релúгия *religion*
(в) ремóнт *(under) repair*
ресторáнт *restaurant*
рецéпция *reception*
рéчник (pl) **-ици** *vocabulary, dictionary*
(да) решá, -ши́ш *to decide*
Рúла планинá *the Rila Mountains*
рúмски *Roman* (adj)
родéн(а) съм *I was born*
родúна *fatherland, motherland*
родúтел *parent*
рождéн ден *birthday*
рóза *rose*
рóкля *dress*
романтúчен, -чна *romantic*
Румъ́ния *Romania*
рýски *Russian* (adj)
ръкá (pl) **ръцé** *hand; arm*
ря́дко *rarely*

с/със *with; on*
сайт *(internet) site*
салáта *salad*
салфéтка *serviette, napkin*
сам *alone*
сáмо *only, just*
самобръснáчка *razor, shaver*
самолéт *airplane*
сáндвич *sandwich*
свáтба *wedding*
(по) светá *around the world*
светú, светá *Saint, holy*
свéтло *light*
свéтло пúво *lager*
светофáр *traffic light*
свобóден, -дна *free*
свой *one's own*
свят *world*
(на) сéвер *(to the) north*
се (reflexive particle) *-self*
сегá *now*
сéдмица *week*
(да) сéдна, -неш *to sit*
секретáр(ка) *secretary*
сéло *village*
семéйство *family*
септéмври *September*
сервúз *garage, service station*
сервитьóр(ка) *waiter, waitress*
сервúрам, -раш *to serve*
сериóзно *seriously*
сестрá *sister*
сигнáл *beep, signal*
сúгурен, -рна, ~ съм *I am sure; surely*
сúгурно *most probably; certainly*
сúлен, -лна *strong*
симпатúчен, -чна *nice*
син, (pl) **синовé** *son*
син, сúня, сúньо, сúни *blue*
сúрене *white cheese, feta*
ски (pl) *skis*
на ски *skiing*
скóро *soon*
скýчно *boring*
скъп *dear; expensive*
слáб *light; weak*
слáва Бóгу! *thank heavens!*
славя́нски *Slavonic*
сладкáрница *café, cakeshop, patisserie*
сладолéд *ice-cream*
слáдък, слáдка *sweet*
след (катó) *after; in*
слéдващ *(up)coming, following*
слéдващия(т) път *next time*
следóбед *(in the) afternoon*
слúва *plum*
слúвов (made of) *plum*
(да) слóжа, -жиш *to put*

служе́бен, -бна *official; for staff only*
служи́тел(ка) *counter assistant, clerk*
(по) слу́чай *(on the) occasion (of)*
слу́чва се *it happens*
(да) се слу́чи (*it* form) *happen*
слъ́нце *sun*
Слъ́нчев бряг *Sunny Beach*
слъ́нчево *sunny*
(да) сменя́, -ни́ш *to change*
смета́на *cream*
сме́тка *bill*
сме́я, -е́еш се *to laugh*
сме́шен, -шна *funny*
сни́мане *taking pictures*
сни́мка *photo, picture*
сно́щи *last night*
сняг *snow*
со́да *soda water*
сок *juice*
сол (f) *salt*
софи́йски *Sofia* (adj)
спа́лня *bedroom*
специали́ст *specialist*
специалите́т *speciality*
специа́лно *specially*
спи́рам, -раш *to stop*
спи́ране *stopping*
спи́рка *(bus) stop*
списа́ние *magazine*
споко́йно *calmly*
спо́мен *memento*
спо́мням, -няш си *to remember*
споре́д *according to*
спорт *sport*
(да) спра, спреш *to stop*
спя, спиш *to sleep*
сре́бърен, -рна (made of) *silver*
сре́ща *appointment, meeting, get-together*
срещу́ *opposite*
сря́да *Wednesday*
ста́вам, -ваш *to stand/get up; to happen; become*
(да) ста́на, -неш *to stand/get up; to happen; become*
стар *old*
старт *start*
ста́я *room*
стена́ *wall*
сти́га! *stop it! enough!*
(да) сти́гна, -неш *to reach*
стик *golf club*
сто *hundred*
сто́лица *capital*
стома́х (pl) **стома́си** *stomach*
стоти́нка *stotinka*
стоя́, стои́ш *to stand; stay*
страна́ *country*
страху́вам, -ваш се *to be afraid*
стра́шен, -шна *incredible; terrible*
(ко́лко) стру́ва? *how much does it cost?*
студе́н *cold*
студе́нт(ка) *student*
стъкло́ *glass*
су́па *soup*
су́пер *super, ace*
су́пермаркет *supermarket*
су́трин (f) *morning*
сутринта́ *in the morning*
счу́пен *broken, not working*
(да) счу́пя, -пиш *to break*
(да) събера́, -ре́ш *to gather*
съ́бота *Saturday*
съве́т *advice*
съгла́сен, -сна съм *I agree*
(да) се съглася́, -си́ш *to agree*
(за) съжале́ние *unfortunately*
съжаля́вам, -ваш *to be sorry, regret*
(да) създа́м, -даде́ш *to create*
съм *I am* (to be)
съмня́вам, -ваш се *to doubt*
съобще́ние *message*
Съ́рбия *Serbia*
(от все) сърце́ *with all my heart*
съсе́ден, -дна *next door, neighbouring*
същ, съ́ща *same*
съ́що *also*
ся́дам, -даш *to sit down*
ся́нка *shade, shadow*

табе́лка *notice*
та́зи (f) *this*
така́ *right, so, likewise*
така́ ли? *really?, is that so?*
та́кса *fee*
така́ е *that is so*
такси́ (n) *taxi*
такъ́в, така́ва *such*
тало́ни *tickets in a booklet*
там *there*
танц *dance*
тарато́р *tarator* (Bulgarian cold summer soup)

твой *your(s)*
твóрчески *creative*
те *they*
теáтър (pl) **-три** *theatre*
тéжък, -жка *heavy*
тéзи (pl) *these*
телевѝзор *television*
телефóн *telephone*
телефóнен секретáр *answerphone*
температýра *temperature*
тéнис *tennis*
тéхен, тя́хна *their(s)*
тéхника *equipment, technology*
ти *you*
тѝквичка *courgette, zucchini*
типѝчно *typically*
тѝхо *quietly*
то *it*
тоалéтна *toilet, bathroom, restroom*
товá (n) *this*
тогáва *then*
тóзи (m) *this*
той *he*
тóлкова *so*
тóник *tonic water*
тóпъл, -пла *warm, hot*
тóрта *gateau, cake*
тóчен, -чна *punctual*
тóчно *exact(ly), precise(ly)*
трамвáй *tram*
транспóрт *transport(ation)*
тревá *grass*
трѝма (дýши) *three people*
тролéй *trolleybus*
трýден, -дна *difficult*
тръ́гвам, -ваш *to set off*
тря́бва *have to; must*
тря́бва да ѝма *there should be*
тук *here*
турѝст(ка) *tourist*
тýрски *Turkish*
Тýрция *Turkey*
тъ́мно *dark*
търгóвски *trade* (adj)
търгóвски цéнтър *shopping mall*
тъ́рся, -сиш *to look (ask) for*
тя *she*

у *at, with*
удóбен, -бна *convenient, comfortable*
удовóлствие *pleasure*
ужáсен, -сна *terrible, awful*
ужáсно *terribly*
ýикенд *weekend*
ýиски (n) *whisky*
ýлица *street*
умéрен *moderate*
умѝрам *to die,* **-раш за** *to be dying for*
уморéн *tired*
(да) се уморя́, -рѝш *to get tired*
университéт *university*
упрáвител *manager, director*
урóк (pl) **урóци** *lesson*
успéх *success*
ýтре *tomorrow*
ýтро *morning*
ухó (pl) **ушѝ** *ear*
ýча, -чиш *to study, learn*
учáствам, -ваш *to take part*
учéбник (pl) **-ници** *textbook*
ýчене *studying*
ученѝк (pl) **ѝци** *pupil, student*
учѝтел(ка) *teacher*
учýден *surprised*

факс *fax*
(не é) фатáлно *(it's not) fatal*
февруáри *February*
финáл *finish*
фѝрма *firm*
фѝтнес цéнтър/клуб *fitness centre*
фоайé *foyer; lounge*
фолклóр *folklore*
фолклóрен фестивáл *folklore festival*
фонокáрта *(pay) phone-card*
фóрма *shape*
фóтоапарáт *camera*
фотогрáф *photographer*
францýзин (pl) **-зи** *Frenchman*
французóйка *Frenchwoman*
фрéнски *French*
фýтбол *football*

хáйде! *come on!*
хáйде, хáйде! *now, now!*
(да) харéсам, -саш *to like*
харéсвам, -ваш *to like*
хартѝя *paper*
ха-ха! *ha-ha!*
хвъ́рлям, -ляш *to throw*
хепатѝт *hepatitis*
хиля́да (pl) **хѝляди** *thousand*
Хѝйтроу *Heathrow*
химикáлка *(ball-point) pen, biro*

хле́бче *bread roll*
хляб *bread*
хо́дя, -диш *to go, walk*
хол *sitting/living room*
хо́ра (pl) *people*
хоте́л *hotel*
храна́ *food*
хре́ма (head) *cold*
християнски *Christian*
ху́бав *nice, beautiful, handsome*
худо́жник (pl) **-ици** *artist*
худо́жничка *artist* (woman)
ху́мор *humour*
хълм *hill*

цве́те (pl) **цветя́** *flower*
цел (f) *aim, purpose*
целодне́вен, -вна *whole day*
цена́ *price*
це́нност (f) (something) *valuable*
це́нтър (pl) **це́нтрове** *centre, downtown*
цига́ра *cigarette*
це́рква *church*
цял (pl) **це́ли** *all; whole*
цял куп *a whole lot of*

чадъ́р *umbrella*
чай *tea*
ча́кам, -каш *to wait, expect*
ча́нта *bag, purse*
час *hour*
часа́ *o'clock*
часо́вник (pl) **-ици** *watch; clock*
част (f) *part*
ча́ша *cup; glass*
че *that*
черве́н *red*
че́рен, -рна *black*
Черномо́рието *the Black Sea coast*
че́сън *garlic*
честит рожде́н ден! *happy birthday!*
честито! *congratulations!*
че́сто *often*
чета́, -те́ш *to read*
че́твърт (f) *quarter*
четвъ́ртък *Thursday*
чистота́ *cleanliness*
чове́к (pl) **хо́ра** *person, human being*
чрез *through, by means of, via*
чу́вам, -ваш *to hear*
чу́вствам, -ваш (се) *to feel*
чу́вство *feeling, sense*
чуде́сен, -сна *wonderful, marvellous*
чужд *foreign*
чужденец (pl) **-нци́** *foreigner*
чужденка́ *foreigner* (woman)
чу́шка *bell pepper, capsicum*
(да) чу́я, чу́еш *to hear*

шампа́нско *champagne*
шампоа́н *shampoo*
ша́пка *hat*
шегу́вам, -ваш се *to joke*
шеф *boss*
шокола́д *bar of chocolate*
шокола́дов (made of) *chocolate*
шо́пска сала́та *'shopska' salad*
шотла́ндец *Scot*
Шотла́ндия *Scotland*
шотла́ндка *Scotswoman*
шотла́ндски *Scottish*
шо́у *show*
шофьо́р *driver*
шум *noise*
шу́мен, -мна *noisy*
шу́нка *ham*
шшш! *sh-sh-sh!*

ща́стие *happiness*
(за) ща́стие *fortunately, luckily*
щастли́в *happy*
щом *since, seeing that*

ъ́гъл (pl) **ъ́гли** *corner*

(на) юг *(to the) south*
ю́ли *July*
ю́ни *June*
юти́я *iron*

я́бълка *apple*
я́бълков (made with*) apple*
(да) се явя́, -ви́ш *to present oneself*
я́года *strawberry*
я́годов (made with) *strawberry*
(не́що за) я́дене *something to eat*
я́ке *jacket*
ям, яде́ш *to eat*
януа́ри *January*
Япо́ния *Japan*
я́сен, я́сна *clear, obvious*
я́сно защо́ *it's obvious why; now I see why*

English–Bulgarian vocabulary

This is a 'survival' vocabulary and you should use it in conjunction with the Appendix and the Bulgarian–English Vocabulary. It includes most of the Bulgarian words you come across in the course – and a good few more besides. You'll be pleased to see that we have given most verbs in both imperfective and perfective forms. All other words we have listed in their basic form only, so for irregularities of form in nouns and adjectives, for example, or, indeed, for verb patterns, you'll have to turn to the Bulgarian–English vocabulary. If an English word has more than one equivalent in Bulgarian, we have attempted to list the more common word first. Where you might confuse forms, we have listed nouns before adjectives and verbs.

Although we trust that the Bulgarian equivalents of the 900 or so English words listed here will ensure your linguistic survival in a Bulgarian environment, do not expect it to replace a good English–Bulgarian dictionary.

Some words you will find in the Appendix rather than in the Vocabulary. You should look for most of the numerals, for example, and the different verb and pronoun forms, in the Appendix. The Appendix is really an addition to the Vocabulary, so use the two together.

able, be ~ *мóга*
about *óколо, към*
above *над*
accept *приéмам, (да) приéма*
accompany *изпрáщам, (да) изпрáтя; придружáвам, (да) придружá*
according to *спорéд*
acquaintance *познáт*
address *адрéс*
advertisement *реклáма*
advice *съвéт*
afraid, be ~ *страхýвам се*
after *след*
afternoon *следóбед;* **in the ~** *следóбед*
again *пак*
against *срещý*
agency *агéнция*
agitated *нéрвен*
ago *преди́*
agree, I ~ *съглáсен съм*
air *въздух*
airline *áвиокомпáния*
airplane *самолéт*
airport *лети́ще, аерогáра*
alcohol *алкохóл*
all *всúчко;* **~ of us** *всúчки*
allergy *алéргия*
almost *почтú*
alone *сам*
along *по, покрáй*
already *вéче*
also *същó*

always *ви́наги*
America *Аме́рика*
American *америка́нец; америка́нски*
amusing *заба́вен*
and *и, а*
another *друг*
answer *о́тговор; отгова́рям, (да) отгово́ря*
anxious, be ~ *безпокоя́ се*
anybody *ня́кой*
anything *не́що*
apart from *осве́н*
apartment *апартаме́нт*
apologize *извиня́вам се, (да) се извиня́*
apple *я́бълка*
appointment *сре́ща*
arm *ръка́*
around *о́коло, към*
arrival *присти́гане*
arrive *присти́гам, (да) присти́гна*
artist *худо́жник*
as *ка́кто, като́*
ask *пи́там, (да) попи́там*
assistance *по́мощ*
at *на, у, в, през*
attention *внима́ние*
attorney *адвока́т*
attraction (tourist) *забележи́телност*
Australia *Австра́лия*
Australian *австрали́ец; австрали́йски*
autumn *е́сен*
awful *ужа́сен*

back *гръб;* **small of the ~** *кръст;* **go ~** *върне́те се обра́тно!*
bad *лош*
bag *ча́нта*
(plastic) bag *пли́к(че)*
baggage *бага́ж*
banana *бана́н*
bank *ба́нка*
bar *бар;* **~ of chocolate** *шокола́д*
bathroom *ба́ня, тоале́тна*
be *съм*
beach *плаж*
beard *брада́*
beautiful *краси́в, ху́бав*
because *защо́то*
become *ста́вам, (да) ста́на*
bed *легло́*
bedroom *спа́лня*
beer *би́ра, пи́во*
before *преди́*
begin *запо́чвам, (да) запо́чна*
beginning *нача́ло*
behind *зад*
beside *до*
besides *осве́н*
between *между́*
big *голя́м*
bill *сме́тка*
birth *ра́ждане*
birthday *рожде́н ден;* **happy ~!** *чести́т ~!*
black *че́рен*
block *блок*
blond *рус*
blue *син*
book *кни́га; запа́звам, (да) запа́зя*
boot, car-~ *бага́жник*
border *гра́ница*
boring *ску́чен*
born, I was ~ *роде́н съм*
boss *шеф*
bottle *бути́лка*
boulevard *булева́рд*
box *кути́я*
boy *момче́*
brandy *коня́к;* **Bulgarian ~** *раки́я*
bread *хляб;* **~ roll** *хле́бче*
break (something) *чу́пя (да) счу́пя; почи́вка, вака́нция*
break down *разва́лям се, (да) се разваля́*
breakfast *заку́ска*
bring *но́ся, (да) донеса́*
Britain *Великобрита́ния*
British *брита́нски;* **the ~** *брита́нците*
broken *счу́пен, развале́н*
brother *брат*
Bulgaria *Бълга́рия*
Bulgarian *бъ́лгарин; бъ́лгарски*
bun *ки́фла*
bunch *буке́т*
bus *автобу́с*
business *би́знес;* **~ card** *визи́тна ка́ртичка;* **~man** *бизнесме́н*
busy *зае́т*
but *но, а, оба́че*
butter *ма́сло*
buy *купу́вам, (да) ку́пя*

café *кафé, кафенé, сладкáрница*
cake *тóрта, кекс*
calendar *календáр*
call *обáждам се, (да) се обáдя*
calmly *спокóйно*
camera *фóтоапарáт*
campsite *кѐмпинг*
can *мóга; мóже;* **(petrol, gas) ~** *бидóнче*
Canada *Канáда*
Canadian *канáдец; канáдски*
candy *бонбóн*
capsicum *чýшка*
car *колá, автомобѝл;* **~ park** *пáркинг*
card *кáрта;* **credit ~** *крéдитна ~,* **post~** *кáртичка*
carry *нóся, (да) донесá*
case *слýчай; кýфар*
CD *компáктдиск*
celebrate *празнýвам, (да) отпразнýвам*
central *центрáлен*
centre *цéнтър*
certainly *сѝгурно; разбѝра се; непремéнно*
chambermaid *камериéрка*
champagne *шампáнско*
change *обмéням, (да) обменя́; промéням, (да) променя́*
cheap *éвтин*
checkout *кáса*
cheers! *наздрáве!*
cheese (white, feta) *сѝрене,* **(yellow)** *кашкавáл*
chemist's *аптéка*
chicken *пѝле;* **grilled ~** *пѝле на грил*
child *детé*
China *Китáй*
Chinese *китáец; китáйски*
chocolate *бонбóн;* **bar of ~** *шоколáд*
choose *избѝрам, (да) изберá*
Christmas *Кóледа;* **merry ~ !** *честѝта ~!*
church *цѐрква*
cinema *кѝно*
cigarette *цигáра*
citizen *грáжданин*
city *град*
clean *чист*
clear *я́сен*
cloakroom *гардерóб*
clock *часóвник*
close *затвáрям, (да) затвóря;* **~d** *затвóрен*
clothes *дрéхи*
cloud *óблак;* **it's ~y** *óблачно е*
coffee *кафé;* **instant ~** *нéс(кафе)*
coke *кóла*
cold *студéн;* **head ~** *хрéма*
colleague *колéга*
come *ѝдвам, (да) дóйда;* **~ on!** *хáйде!*
come in *влѝзам, (да) вля́за*
come out *излѝзам, (да) изля́за*
comfortable *удóбен*
complain *оплáквам се, (да) се оплáча*
computer *компю́тър*
concert *концéрт*
conference *конферéнция*
congratulate *поздравя́вам, (да) поздравя́*
congratulations! *поздравлéния! честѝто!*
continue *продължáвам, (да) продължá*
continuously *непрекѐснато*
convenient *удóбен*
conversation *рáзговор*
corner *ѐгъл*
cost, how much does it ~? *кóлко стрýва?*
cough *кáшлица*
cousin *братовчéд*
country *странá*
cream *крем; сметáна*
create *създáвам, (да) създáм*
creative *твóрчески*
credit card *крéдитна кáрта*
cross *кръст; пресѝчам, (да) пресекá*
cucumber *крáставица*
culture *култýра*
cup *чáша*
currency *валýта;* **~ exchange office** *обмéнно бюрó*
customer *клиéнт*

damp *влáжен*
dance *танцýвам*
danger *опáсност; внимáние!*
dangerous *опáсен*
dark *тѐмен*
date *дáта*
daughter *дъщеря́*
day *ден*

dear *скъп*
decide *решáвам, (да) решá*
degree *грáдус*
delay *закъснéние*
delegation *делегáция*
delicious *вкýсен*
dentist *зъболéкар*
departure *заминáване*
dialogue *рáзговор, диалóг*
diary *днéвник, белéжник*
dictionary *рéчник*
die *умúрам, (да) умрá*
diet *диéта, режúм*
different *разлúчен*
difficult *трýден*
dinner *вечéря*
direction *посóка*
director *дирéктор*
disappear *изчéзвам, (да) изчéзна*
disco *дискотéка*
distance *разстоя́ние*
diversion *отклонéние*
do *прáвя, (да) напрáвя*
doctor *лéкар*
document *докумéнт*
don't! *недéй!*
door *вратá;* **~man** *портиéр*
doubt *съмня́вам се*
downtown *цéнтър*
dress (oneself) *облúчам се, (да) се облекá*
drink *напúтка, нéщо за пúене; пúя, (да) изпúя*
drive *кáрам;* **~r** *шофьóр*
dull *мрáчен*
during *през*
DVD *дúвидú*

each *всéки*
ear *ухó*
early *рáно*
east *úзток;* **in/to the ~** *на úзток*
eat *ям, (да) изя́м;* **something to ~** *нéщо за я́дене*
elevator *асансьóр*
email *úмейл, електрóнна пóща*
end *край*
engaged *заéт*
engine *мотóр*
England *Áнглия*
English *англúйски*
Englishman *англичáнин*
enough *достáтъчно; стúга!*
entrance *вход*
envelope *плик*
especially *специáлно, осóбено*
estate agent *брóкер*
even *дорú, дáже; рáвен*
evening *вéчер;* **in the ~** *вечертá*
every *всéки;* **~body** *всéки;* **~thing** *всúчко;* **~where** *нався́къде*
exact *тóчен;* **~ly!** *тóчно такá!*
excellent *отлúчен*
except *освéн*
exceptional *изключúтелен*
excursion *екскýрзия*
excuse *извинéние;* **~ me!** *извинéте! извиня́вайте!*
exhibition *излóжба*
exit *úзход*
expensive *скъп*
explain *обясня́вам, (да) обясня́*
eye *окó*

fall *пáдам, (да) пáдна; éсен*
false *невя́рно*
far *далéче*
family *семéйство*
fast *бърз*
fat *сланúна;* (adj) *дебéл*
father *бащá*
fault *дефéкт, поврéда; винá*
favour *услýга*
fax *факс*
feel *чýвствам;* **~ing** *чýвство*
festival *прáзник, фестивáл*
few *мáлко* **a ~** *ня́колко*
file *пáпка, файл*
final *послéден;* **~ly** *нáй-накрáя*
find *намúрам, (да) намéря*
fine *глóба;* **~!** *добрé!*
finish *свъ́ршвам, (да) свъ́рша*
firm *фúрма*
fish *рúба*
fizzy *газúран*
flat *апартамéнт;* (adj) *рáвен*
floor *етáж*
flower *цвéте*
flu *грип*
fly *мухá;* (vb) *летя́*
fog *мъглá*
folklore *фолклóр* (adj); *фолклóрен*
food *хранá*
foot *крак*
for *за*
forbidden *забранéн*
forecast *прогнóза*

foreign *чужд;* **~er** *чужденéц*
forget *забрáвям, (да) забрáвя*
forgive *прощáвам, (да) простя́;* **~ me** *извинéте! извиня́вайте!*
fork *ви́лица*
fortunately *за щáстие*
free *свобóден; безплáтен*
freeway *магистрáла*
France *Фрáнция*
French *фрéнски*
Frenchman *францу́зин*
frequent *чест*
fresh *свеж, прéсен*
friend *прия́тел;* **~ly** *прия́телски*
from *от*
front: in ~ of *пред*
fruit *плод;* **~ful** *плодотвóрен*
full of *пъ́лен с*
fun, it's ~ *забáвно е*
funny *смéшен*
future *бъ́деще*

game *игрá*
garage *гарáж; серви́з*
garden *гради́на*
garlic *чéсън*
gas *бензи́н; газ*
German *гермáнец, нéмец; гермáнски, нéмски*
Germany *Гермáния*
get *получáвам, (да) полу́ча*
get to know one another *запознáвам се, (да) се запознáя*
get up *стáвам, (да) стáна*
girl *моми́че*
give *дáвам, (да) дам*
give back *връ́щам, (да) вѐрна*
glad *довóлен;* **be ~** *рáдвам се*
gladly *с удовóлствие*
glass *чáша*
go *хóдя;* (somewhere) *оти́вам, (да) оти́да*
go back *връ́щам се, (да) се вѐрна*
go in *вли́зам, (да) вля́за*
go out *изли́зам, (да) изля́за*
God *Бог*
good *добъ́р*
goodbye *дови́ждане;* (on the phone) *дочу́ване*
gram *грам*
grandmother *бáба*
grapes *грóзде*
grass *тревá*
great *голя́м;* **~!** *чудéсно!*
green *зелéн*
Greece *Гъ́рция*
Greek *грък; гръ́цки*
greet *поздравя́вам, (да) поздравя́;* **~ing** *пóздрав*
grey *сив*
grill *скáра; грил*
ground floor *пáртер*
group *гру́па*
guest *гост*
guide *екскурзовóд*

hair *косá; кóсъм*
half *полови́н;* **a ~** *полови́на*
hall *зáла*
ham *шу́нка*
hand *ръкá*
handsome *ху́бав, краси́в*
happen, it ~s *стáва, (да) стáне*
happiness *щáстие*
happy *щастли́в, вéсел;* **~ with** *довóлен от;* **~ ...!** *чести́т...!*
hard *твърд, тру́ден*
hat *шáпка*
have *и́мам;* **not to ~** *ня́мам;* **~ to** *тря́бва*
he *той*
head *главá*
headache *главобóлие*
health *здрáве*
hear *чу́вам, (да), чу́я*
heart *сърцé;* **with all my ~** *от все сърцé*
heat *топлинá; горещинá*
heavy *тéжък*
hello! *здравéй(те)!;* (on the phone) *áло(?]*
help *пóмощ; помáгам, (да) помóгна*
her(s) *нéин*
here *тук;* **~ is** *éто;* **~ you are** *заповя́дай(те)*
high *висóк;* **~way** *магистрáла*
hill *хълм*
his *нéгов*
history *истóрия*
hold *държá (се), (да) се хвáна*
holiday *прáзник, почи́вка*
home *дом;* **(go) ~/at ~** *вкъ́щи*
hope *надéжда; надя́вам се*
hospital *бóлница*
host *домаки́н*

hot *горéщо*
hotel *хотéл*
hour *час*
house *къща*
how *как;* **~ many/much** *кóлко*
however *обáче*
hungry *глáден*
hurry, be in a ~ *бързам*
hurt, it ~s *болú*
husband *мъж, съпрýг*

I *аз*
ice-cream *сладолéд*
icon *икóна*
idea *идéя, представа*
if *акó*
ill *бóлен*
immediately *веднáга*
important *вáжен;* **it's ~** *вáжно е*
impossible *невъзмóжен;* **it's ~** *невъзмóжно е*
in *в/във, на, през, след;* **~ front of** *пред*
indeed *наистина*
information *информáция*
instead of *вмéсто*
interesting *интерéсен*
international *междунарóден*
interpreter *преводáч*
introduce *see* **get to know…**
invitation *покáна*
invite *кáня, (да) покáня* **~d** *покáнен*
Ireland *Ирлáндия*
Irish *ирлáндски* **~ man** *ирлáндец*
iron *ютия*
it *то*
Italian *италиáнец; италиáнски*
Italy *Итáлия*
its *нéгов*

jacket *сакó, яке*
jeans *дънки*
job *рáбота*
joke *шегýвам се*
journalist *журналист*
journey *пътýване*
juice *сок*
just *сáмо*
juvenile *малолéтен*

keep *пáзя, (да) запáзя*
key *ключ*
kilogram *килогрáм*
kind *добър, любéзен, мил; вид, род*
kitchen *кýхня*
knee *колянó*
knife *нож*
know *знáя, познáвам;* **get to ~ one another** *(да) се запознáя*

lady *дáма;* **~ of the house** *домакúня*
land *земя*
language *език*
last *послéден;* **at ~** *нáй-пóсле*
late *късно;* **to be ~** *закъснявам, (да) закъснéя*
laugh *смéя се*
lawyer *адвокáт*
learn *ýча, (да) наýча*
leave (go out) *излúзам, (да) изляза; тръгвам, (да) тръгна; заминáвам, (да) замúна*
leave (behind) *остáвям, (да) остáвя*
left *ляв;* **on/to the ~** *налявo*
leg *крак*
lemon *лимóн;* **~ade** *лимонáда*
lesson *урóк*
let's! *(хáйде) да!*
letter *писмó, бýква*
lie (nn) *лъжá;* (vb) *лъжа, (да) излъжа*
lie (vb) *лежá*
lie down *лягам, (да) лéгна*
life *живóт*
lift *асансьóр;* **ski/chair ~** *лифт*
light *светлинá;* (adj) *свéтъл, лек, слаб*
like *катó*
like *харéсвам, (да) харéсам, обúчам*
likewise *такá*
line *лúния*
lion *лъв*
listen *слýшам*
litre *лúтър*
little *мáлък;* **a ~** *мáлко*
live *живéя*
long *дълъг;* **~ ago** *отдáвна*
look *глéдам; разглéждам, (да) разглéдам*
look after *грúжа се (за)*
look at/round *разглéждам, (да) разглéдам*
look for *търся*

lose *гу́бя, (да) загу́бя*
lot, a ~ of *мно́го*
love *любо́в; оби́чам*
luckily *за ща́стие*
luggage *бага́ж*
lunch *обя́д, о́бед;* **have ~** *обя́двам*

machine *маши́на*
make *пра́вя, (да) напра́вя; ка́рам, (да) нака́рам*
man *мъж; чове́к*
manager *дире́ктор, ме́ниджър, упра́вител*
many *мно́го*
map *ка́рта*
market *паза́р*
married *же́нен/омъ́жена*
marry *(да) се оже́ня/омъ́жа*
may I? *мо́же ли?*
maybe *мо́же би*
meaning *значе́ние*
mean, I ~ *и́скам да ка́жа*
meat *месо́*
medicine *лека́рство*
meet *сре́щам, (да) сре́щна; посре́щам, (да) посре́щна*
meeting *сре́ща*
melon *пъ́пеш*
memory *па́мет*
mend *попра́вям, (да) попра́вя*
mention *споменa̋вам, (да) спомена́*
menu *меню́*
merry *ве́сел*
message *съобще́ние*
metre *ме́тър*
mile *ми́ля*
milk *мля́ко*
mine *мой*
minute *мину́та*
mirror *огледа́ло*
Miss *госпо́жица*
mistake *гре́шка*
mobile (phone) *моби́лен телефо́н,* **GSM** *(джи́есе́м)*
modern *моде́рен*
monastery *манасти́р*
money *пари́*
month *ме́сец*
more *по́вече, о́ще*
morning *су́трин, у́тро;* **in the ~** *сутринта́*
mosquito *кома́р*
most *на́й-мно́го;* **~ of** *по́вечето*
mother *ма́йка*
motorway *магистра́ла*
mountain(s) *планина́*
mouth *уста́*
Mr *господи́н*
Mrs *госпожа́*
much *мно́го*
museum *музе́й*
music *му́зика*
must *тря́бва*
my *мой*

name *и́ме*
napkin *салфе́тка*
nation *на́ция*
national *национа́лен, наро́ден;* **~ity** *наро́дност*
natural *натура́лен, есте́ствен;* **~ly** *есте́ствено*
near *бли́зо;* **~by** *набли́зо*
need *ну́жда*
neither... nor... *ни́то ... ни́то*
nervous *не́рвен, притесне́н*
never *ни́кога*
new *нов*
news (item) *новина́;* **~paper** *ве́стник*
next *сле́дващ;* **~ to** *до*
nice *ху́бав; симпати́чен*
night *нощ;* **last ~** *сно́щи*
no *не*
nobody *ни́кой*
noise *шум*
noisy *шу́мен*
none *ни́какъв*
non-smoker *непуша́ч*
nose *нос*
normally *норма́лно, обикнове́но*
north *се́вер;* **in/to the ~** *на се́вер*
not *не;* **~ yet** *о́ще не*
note *беле́жка;* **~book** *беле́жник*
notice *табе́лка*
nothing *ни́що*
nought *ну́ла*
now *сега́*
number *но́мер, брой*
nurse *сестра́*

object *предме́т*
obvious *я́вен, я́сен*
occasion *слу́чай*
occupation *профе́сия*
of *на;* **~ course** *разби́ра се*

offer *предложе́ние; предла́гам, (да) предло́жа*
office *о́фис, бюро́*
official *служе́бен*
often *че́сто*
OK *добре́, мо́же*
old *стар*
on *на, върху́, по, в*
once *веднъ́ж;* **~ again** *о́ще веднъ́ж*
only *са́мо*
open *отво́рен; отва́рям, (да) отво́ря;* **~ing hours** *рабо́тно вре́ме*
opposite *срещу́*
or *или́*
orange (nn) *портока́л*
order *ред;* **out of ~** *повре́ден; поръ́чка; поръ́чвам, (да) поръ́чам*
ordinary *обикнове́н*
organize *организи́рам;* **~d** *организи́ран*
other (pl) *дру́ги*
our(s) *наш*
outside *навъ́н*
over *над*
own *свой*

pain *бо́лка*
paper *харти́я, докуме́нт*
pardon? *мо́ля?*
parent *роди́тел*
park *парк; парки́рам*
Parliament *Парламе́нт*
parking lot *па́ркинг*
part *част*
party *па́рти*
pass *мина́вам, (да) ми́на*
passenger *пъ́тник*
passport *паспо́рт*
password *паро́ла*
pay *пла́щам, (да) платя́*
peach *пра́скова*
pen *писа́лка, химика́лка*
pencil *моли́в*
people *хо́ра*
pepper *чу́шка; че́рен пипе́р*
performance *представле́ние*
petrol *бензи́н;* **~ station** *бензиноста́нция;* **~ can** *бидо́нче*
pharmacy *апте́ка*
phone *оба́ждам се, (да) се оба́дя*
photo *сни́мка;* **~grapher** *фотогра́ф*
picture *сни́мка*
PIN (code) *пи́нкод*
piece *парче́*
pity, it's a ~ *жа́лко*
pizzeria *пицари́я*
place *мя́сто*
plate *чини́я*
pleasant *прия́тен*
please *мо́ля*
pleased *дово́лен;* **be ~** *ра́двам се*
pleasure *удово́лствие*
plum *сли́ва*
pocket *джоб*
point *пока́звам, (да) пока́жа*
police *поли́ция;* **~man** *полица́й*
possible *възмо́жен;* **it's ~** *възмо́жно е, мо́же*
post (office) *по́ща;* **~card** *ка́ртичка*
prefer *предпочи́там, (да) предпочета́*
present *пода́рък*
price *цена́*
private *ча́стен*
probably *вероя́тно*
problem *пробле́м*
program(me) *програ́ма*
punctual *то́чен*
pupil *учени́к*
purpose *цел*
purse *портмоне́, ча́нта*
put *сла́гам, (да) сло́жа*

quality *ка́чество*
quarter *че́твърт*
question *въпро́с*
quick *бърз*
quiet *тих*
quite *до́ста*

railway station *га́ра*
rain *дъжд;* **it's ~ing** *вали́*
rarely *ря́дко*
reach *сти́гам, (да) сти́гна*
read *чета́, (да) прочета́*
ready *гото́в*
real estate agent *бро́кер*
really *наистина;* **~?** *така́ ли?*
receive *получа́вам, (да) полу́ча*
reception *реце́пция, при́ем*
receptionist *администра́тор*
recommend *препоръ́чвам, (да) препоръ́чам*

red *черве́н*
regret *съжаля́вам, (да) съжаля́*
religion *рели́гия*
remember *по́мня, (да) запо́мня; спо́мням си, (да) си спо́мня*
rent *на́ем; нае́мам, (да) нае́ма;* **~ed** *под на́ем*
repeat *повта́рям, (да) повто́ря*
repair *ремо́нт*
request *молба́*
reserve *запа́звам, (да) запа́зя;* **~d** *запа́зен, резерви́ран*
rest *почи́вам си, (да) си почи́на;* **~ room** *тоале́тна*
restaurant *рестора́нт*
return *вра́щам (се), (да) (се) въ́рна*
right *прав, де́сен;* **on/to the ~** *надя́сно*
river *река́*
road *път*
room *ста́я*
rose *ро́за*
route *маршру́т, път*
Russia *Руси́я*
Russian *русна́к,* (f) *руски́ня; ру́ски*

salad *сала́та*
sales person *продава́ч*
salt *сол*
same, the ~ *съ́щият*
sandwich *са́ндвич*
say *ка́звам, (да) ка́жа*
school *учи́лище*
Scot *шотла́ндец*
Scotland *Шотла́ндия*
Scottish *шотла́ндски*
sea *море́*
see *ви́ждам, (да) ви́дя*
sell *прода́вам, (да) прода́м*
send *пра́щам, (да) пра́тя; изпра́щам, (да) изпра́тя*
serious *серио́зен*
service (in a restaurant) *обслу́жване*
service station *серви́з*
serviette *салфе́тка*
several *ня́колко*
shape *фо́рма*
shaver *самобръсна́чка*
she *тя*
shoe *обу́вка*
shop *магази́н*
shop assistant *продава́ч*
shopping, do the ~ *пазару́вам*
short (stature) *ни́сък,* (time) *кра́тък*
show *пока́звам, (да) пока́жа*
shower *душ*
sick *бо́лен*
side *страна́*
sight, tourist ~ *забележи́телност*
sign *знак, табе́лка*
simply *про́сто*
since *тъй като́, щом,* (time) *от*
sing *пе́я, (да) изпе́я*
single *едини́чен; неже́нен/ неомъ́жена*
sister *сестра́*
sit *седя́*
sit down *ся́дам, (да) се́дна*
size *големина́, разме́р*
ski *ка́рам ски;* **~ run** *пи́ста*
skin *ко́жа*
sleep *спя*
slow *ба́вен*
small *ма́лък*
smoke (vb) *пу́ша*
smoker *пуша́ч*
smoking *пу́шене*
snack *заку́ска*
snow *сняг*
so *така́; то́лкова*
sock *чора́п*
soda water *гази́рана вода́, со́да*
soft *мек;* **~ drink** *безалкохо́лна напи́тка*
some *ня́кои, ня́колко; ня́какъв;* **~body** *ня́кой;* **~how** *ня́как;* **~thing** *не́що;* **~ time** *ня́кога,* **~times** *поня́кога* **~where** *ня́къде*
son *син*
soon *ско́ро*
sorry, to be ~ *съжаля́вам, (да) съжаля́*
soup *су́па*
south *юг;* **in/to the ~** *на юг*
Spain *Испа́ния*
Spaniard *испа́нец*
Spanish *испа́нски*
speak *говоря́*
special *специа́лен, осо́бен*
spend (time) *изка́рвам, (да) изка́рам;* **(money)** *ха́рча, (да) поха́рча*
spoon *лъжи́ца*
spring *про́лет*

square *площа́д*
stamp, (postage) ~ *ма́рка*
stand *стоя́*
stand up *ста́вам, (да) ста́на*
stomach *стома́х, коре́м*
stop *спи́рам, (да) спра;* **bus ~** *спи́рка*
straight *прав*
strawberry *я́года*
street *у́лица*
strong *си́лен*
student *студе́нт, учени́к*
study (vb) *у́ча*
subway *метро́*
success *успе́х*
such *такъ́в*
sugar *за́хар*
suggest *предла́гам, (да) предло́жа*
suit *костю́м*
suitcase *ку́фар*
summer *ля́то*
sun *слъ́нце*
supper *вече́ря;* **have ~** *вече́рям*
suppose *предпола́гам, (да) предполо́жа*
sure *си́гурен*
surprise *изнена́да*
sweet *бонбо́н;* (adj) *сла́дък, мил*
swim *плу́вам*

table *ма́са*
take *взи́мам, (да) взе́ма;* **~ part** *уча́ствам;* **~ pictures** *пра́вя сни́мки*
take away (nn) *(храна́) за вкъ́щи*
talk *гово́ря*
tall *висо́к*
taxi *такси́*
tea *чай*
teacher *учи́тел*
telephone *телефо́н;* **mobile ~** *моби́лен телефо́н, джи́есе́м*
television *телеви́зор*
tell *ка́звам, (да) ка́жа*
temperature *температу́ра*
terrible *ужа́сен, стра́шен*
than *от, отко́лкото*
thank *благодаря́;* **~ you** *благодаря́, мерси́*
that *това́; онова́; че*
theatre *теа́тър*
their(s) *те́хен*
then *тога́ва*
there *там;* **~ is/are** *и́ма;* **~ isn't/aren't** *ня́ма*
these *те́зи*
they *те*
thin *тъ́нък, слаб*
think *ми́сля*
this *това́*
throat *гъ́рло*
through *през*
ticket *биле́т;* **~-office** *ка́са*
till *ка́са*
time *вре́ме;* **in ~** *навре́ме;* **two ~s** *два пъ́ти*
timetable *разписа́ние*
tired *уморе́н*
to *до, към;* **in order ~** *за да*
today *днес*
together *за́едно*
toilet *тоале́тна*
tomato *дома́т*
tomorrow *у́тре*
tongue *ези́к*
too *съ́що, и; прекале́но*
tooth *зъб*
touch *пи́пам, (да) пи́пна*
tourist *тури́ст*
toward(s) *към*
town *град*
tram *трамва́й*
translate *преве́ждам, (да) преведа́*
translator *преводáч*
travel *пъту́вам*
tree *дърво́*
trip *екску́рзия*
trolleybus *троле́й*
trouble *неприя́тност*
trousers *панталó̗н*
true, it's ~ *вя́рно (е)*
trunk (car) *бага́жник*
try *опи́твам, (да) опи́там*
tulip *лале́*
Turk *ту́рчин*
Turkey *Ту́рция*
Turkish *ту́рски*
turn *зави́вам, (да) зави́я*

umbrella *чадъ́р*
under *под;* **~ground** *метро́*
understand *разби́рам, (да) разбера́*
unfortunately *за съжале́ние*
university *университе́т*
unpleasant *неприя́тен*

until *до, докато́;* **~ now** *досега́*
up-to-date *моде́рен*
useful *поле́зен*
usually *обикнове́но*

vacation *почи́вка*
vase *ва́за*
vegetable *зеленчу́к*
vegetarian *вегетариа́нец; вегетариа́нски*
very *мно́го, тве́рде, до́ста*
village *се́ло*
visit (stay) *престо́й*

wait *ча́кам*
waiter *сервитьо́р*
Wales *Уе́лс*
walk *разхо́дка; вървя́, хо́дя*
wall *стена́*
want *и́скам*
war *война́*
warm *то́пъл*
wash *ми́я (се), (да) (се) изми́я*
washroom *тоале́тна*
watch *часо́вник*
watch out! *внима́ние!*
water *вода́;* **mineral ~** *минера́лна вода́*
way *път*
we *ни́е*
weak *слаб, лек*
wear *но́ся*
weather *вре́ме*
wedding *сва́тба*
week *се́дмица*
welcome! *добре́ дошъ́л! заповя́дай(те)!*
well *добре́*
Welsh *уе́лсец; уе́лски*
west *за́пад;* **in/to the ~** *на за́пад*

what *какво́, какво́то;* **~ kind of** *какъ̀в*
when *кога́; кога́то*
where *къде́; къде́то;* **~ from** *откъде́*
whether *дали́*
which *кой; ко́йто*
while *докато́*
white *бял*
who *кой; ко́йто*
whole *цял*
why *защо́*
wife *жена́, съпру́га*
wind *вя́тър*
window *прозо́рец*
wine *ви́но*
winter *зи́ма*
wish *жела́ние; жела́я; пожела́вам, (да) пожела́я*
with *с/със*
without *без*
woman *жена́*
wonderful *чуде́сен*
word *ду́ма*
work *ра́бота; рабо́тя*
world *свят*
worry *гри́жа; безпокоя́ се*
write *пи́ша, (да) напи́ша*

year *годи́на*
yellow *жълт*
yes *да*
yesterday *вче́ра*
yet *о́ще; все пак*
yoghurt *ки́село мля́ко*
you *ти; ви́е*
young *млад*
your(s) *твой; ваш*

zero *ну́ла*

index to grammar and usage

Although the grammatical explanations in this course are based on a pragmatic, need-to-know basis and we try to avoid grammatical jargon, grammatical categories are a very useful aid to learning. We hope, therefore, that this index, arranged according to grammatical features, will be a handy additional aid to finding your way around the book and the Bulgarian language.

The numbers refer you to the units. An asterisk indicates that you will find further material in the Appendix.

teach yourself

bulgarian conversation

mira kovatcheva & michael holman

- Do you want to talk with confidence?
- Are you looking for basic conversation skills?
- Do you want to understand what people say to you?

Bulgarian Conversation is a three-hour, all-audio course which you can use at any time, whether you want a quick refresher before a trip or whether you are a complete beginner. The 20 dialogues on CDs 1 and 2 will teach you the Bulgarian you will need to speak and understand, without getting bogged down with grammar. CD 3, uniquely, teaches skills for listening and understanding. This is the perfect accompaniment to **Bulgarian** in the **teach yourself** range: www.teachyourself.co.uk.

Dr Mira Kovatcheva is Associate Professor in the Department of English and American Studies at the University of Sofia. **Professor Michael Holman** is Emeritus Professor of Russian and Slavonic Studies, University of Leeds.

teach yourself

croatian

david norris

- Do you want to cover the basics then progress fast?
- Do you want to communicate in a range of situations?
- Do you want to reach a high standard?

Croatian starts with the basics but moves at a lively pace to give you a good level of understanding, speaking and writing. You will have lots of opportunity to practise the kind of language you will need to be able to communicate with confidence and understand Croatian culture.

David Norris has taught Serbian and Croatian Studies since 1980. He is currently Senior Lecturer at the University of Nottingham.

teach yourself

romanian

dennis deletant & yvonne alexandrescu

- Do you want to cover the basics then progress fast?
- Do you want to communicate in a range of situations?
- Do you want to learn Romanian in depth?

Romanian starts with the basics but moves at an energetic pace to give you a good level of understanding, speaking and writing. You will have lots of opportunity to practise the kind of language you will need to be able to communicate with confidence and understand Romanian culture.

Dennis Deletant is Professor of Romanian Studies, School of Slavonic and East European Studies, University College, London. **Yvonne Alexandrescu** taught in Romania for 20 years. She now teaches Romanian to corporate and government sectors.

teach yourself

hungarian

zsuzsa pontifex

- Do you want to cover the basics then progress fast?
- Do you want to communicate in a range of situations?
- Do you want to learn Hungarian in depth?

Hungarian starts with the basics but moves at an energetic pace to give you a good level of understanding, speaking and writing. You will have lots of opportunity to practise the kind of language you will need to be able to communicate with confidence and understand Hungarian culture.

Zsuzsa Pontifex, a professional teacher of Hungarian, runs a language school Budapest.

teach yourself®

From Advanced Sudoku to Zulu, you'll find everything you need in the **teach yourself** range, in books, on CD and on DVD.

Visit **www.teachyourself.co.uk** for more details.

Advanced Sudoku and Kakuro
Afrikaans
Alexander Technique
Algebra
Ancient Greek
Applied Psychology
Arabic
Arabic Conversation
Aromatherapy
Art History
Astrology
Astronomy
AutoCAD 2004
AutoCAD 2007
Ayurveda
Baby Massage and Yoga
Baby Signing
Baby Sleep
Bach Flower Remedies
Backgammon
Ballroom Dancing
Basic Accounting
Basic Computer Skills
Basic Mathematics
Beauty
Beekeeping
Beginner's Arabic Script
Beginner's Chinese Script
Beginner's Dutch
Beginner's French
Beginner's German
Beginner's Greek
Beginner's Greek Script
Beginner's Hindi
Beginner's Hindi Script
Beginner's Italian
Beginner's Japanese
Beginner's Japanese Script
Beginner's Latin
Beginner's Mandarin Chinese
Beginner's Portuguese
Beginner's Russian
Beginner's Russian Script
Beginner's Spanish
Beginner's Turkish
Beginner's Urdu Script
Bengali
Better Bridge
Better Chess
Better Driving
Better Handwriting
Biblical Hebrew
Biology
Birdwatching
Blogging
Body Language

Book Keeping
Brazilian Portuguese
Bridge
British Citizenship Test, The
British Empire, The
British Monarchy from Henry VIII, The
Buddhism
Bulgarian
Bulgarian Conversation
Business French
Business Plans
Business Spanish
Business Studies
C++
Calculus
Calligraphy
Cantonese
Caravanning
Car Buying and Maintenance
Card Games
Catalan
Chess
Chi Kung
Chinese Medicine
Christianity
Classical Music
Coaching
Cold War, The
Collecting
Computing for the Over 50s
Consulting
Copywriting
Correct English
Counselling
Creative Writing
Cricket
Croatian
Crystal Healing
CVs
Czech
Danish
Decluttering
Desktop Publishing
Detox
Digital Home Movie Making
Digital Photography
Dog Training
Drawing
Dream Interpretation
Dutch
Dutch Conversation
Dutch Dictionary
Dutch Grammar
Eastern Philosophy
Electronics
English as a Foreign Language
English Grammar
English Grammar as a Foreign Language
Entrepreneurship
Estonian
Ethics
Excel 2003
Feng Shui
Film Making
Film Studies
Finance for Non-Financial Managers
Finnish
First World War, The
Fitness
Flash 8
Flash MX
Flexible Working
Flirting
Flower Arranging
Franchising
French
French Conversation
French Dictionary
French for Homebuyers
French Grammar
French Phrasebook
French Starter Kit
French Verbs
French Vocabulary
Freud
Gaelic
Gaelic Conversation
Gaelic Dictionary
Gardening

Genetics
Geology
German
German Conversation
German Grammar
German Phrasebook
German Starter Kit
German Vocabulary
Globalization
Go
Golf
Good Study Skills
Great Sex
Green Parenting
Greek
Greek Conversation
Greek Phrasebook
Growing Your Business
Guitar
Gulf Arabic
Hand Reflexology
Hausa
Herbal Medicine
Hieroglyphics
Hindi
Hindi Conversation
Hinduism
History of Ireland, The
Home PC Maintenance and Networking
How to DJ
How to Run a Marathon
How to Win at Casino Games
How to Win at Horse Racing
How to Win at Online Gambling
How to Win at Poker
How to Write a Blockbuster
Human Anatomy & Physiology
Hungarian
Icelandic
Improve Your French
Improve Your German
Improve Your Italian
Improve Your Spanish
Improving Your Employability
Indian Head Massage
Indonesian
Instant French
Instant German
Instant Greek
Instant Italian
Instant Japanese
Instant Portuguese
Instant Russian
Instant Spanish
Internet, The
Irish
Irish Conversation
Irish Grammar
Islam
Israeli-Palestinian Conflict, The
Italian
Italian Conversation
Italian for Homebuyers
Italian Grammar
Italian Phrasebook
Italian Starter Kit
Italian Verbs
Italian Vocabulary
Japanese
Japanese Conversation
Java
JavaScript
Jazz
Jewellery Making
Judaism
Jung
Kama Sutra, The
Keeping Aquarium Fish
Keeping Pigs
Keeping Poultry
Keeping a Rabbit
Knitting
Korean
Latin
Latin American Spanish
Latin Dictionary
Latin Grammar
Letter Writing Skills
Life at 50: For Men
Life at 50: For Women
Life Coaching
Linguistics
LINUX

Lithuanian
Magic
Mahjong
Malay
Managing Stress
Managing Your Own Career
Mandarin Chinese
Mandarin Chinese Conversation
Marketing
Marx
Massage
Mathematics
Meditation
Middle East Since 1945, The
Modern China
Modern Hebrew
Modern Persian
Mosaics
Music Theory
Mussolini's Italy
Nazi Germany
Negotiating
Nepali
New Testament Greek
NLP
Norwegian
Norwegian Conversation
Old English
One-Day French
One-Day French – the DVD
One-Day German
One-Day Greek
One-Day Italian
One-Day Polish
One-Day Portuguese
One-Day Spanish
One-Day Spanish – the DVD
One-Day Turkish
Origami
Owning a Cat
Owning a Horse
Panjabi
PC Networking for Small Businesses
Personal Safety and Self Defence
Philosophy
Philosophy of Mind
Philosophy of Religion
Phone French
Phone German
Phone Italian
Phone Japanese
Phone Mandarin Chinese
Phone Spanish
Photography
Photoshop
PHP with MySQL
Physics
Piano
Pilates
Planning Your Wedding
Polish
Polish Conversation
Politics
Portuguese
Portuguese Conversation
Portuguese for Homebuyers
Portuguese Grammar
Portuguese Phrasebook
Postmodernism
Pottery
PowerPoint 2003
PR
Project Management
Psychology
Quick Fix French Grammar
Quick Fix German Grammar
Quick Fix Italian Grammar
Quick Fix Spanish Grammar
Quick Fix: Access 2002
Quick Fix: Excel 2000
Quick Fix: Excel 2002
Quick Fix: HTML
Quick Fix: Windows XP
Quick Fix: Word
Quilting
Recruitment
Reflexology
Reiki
Relaxation
Retaining Staff
Romanian
Running Your Own Business

Russian
Russian Conversation
Russian Grammar
Sage Line 50
Sanskrit
Screenwriting
Second World War, The
Serbian
Setting Up a Small Business
Shorthand Pitman 2000
Sikhism
Singing
Slovene
Small Business Accounting
Small Business Health Check
Songwriting
Spanish
Spanish Conversation
Spanish Dictionary
Spanish for Homebuyers
Spanish Grammar
Spanish Phrasebook
Spanish Starter Kit
Spanish Verbs
Spanish Vocabulary
Speaking On Special Occasions
Speed Reading
Stalin's Russia
Stand Up Comedy
Statistics
Stop Smoking
Sudoku
Swahili
Swahili Dictionary
Swedish
Swedish Conversation
Tagalog
Tai Chi
Tantric Sex
Tap Dancing
Teaching English as a Foreign Language
Teams & Team Working
Thai
Thai Conversation
Theatre
Time Management
Tracing Your Family History
Training
Travel Writing
Trigonometry
Turkish
Turkish Conversation
Twentieth Century USA
Typing
Ukrainian
Understanding Tax for Small Businesses
Understanding Terrorism
Urdu
Vietnamese
Visual Basic
Volcanoes, Earthquakes and Tsunamis
Watercolour Painting
Weight Control through Diet & Exercise
Welsh
Welsh Conversation
Welsh Dictionary
Welsh Grammar
Wills & Probate
Windows XP
Wine Tasting
Winning at Job Interviews
Word 2003
World Faiths
Writing Crime Fiction
Writing for Children
Writing for Magazines
Writing a Novel
Writing a Play
Writing Poetry
Xhosa
Yiddish
Yoga
Your Wedding
Zen
Zulu